CITY cuisine

S U S A N F E N I G E R

M A R Y S U E M I L L I K E N

written with

Helene Siegel

. . . .

designed and photographed

by Mike Fink

WILLIAM MORROW AND COMPANY, INC.

NEW YORK

Library of Congress Cataloging-in-Publication Data

Milliken, Mary Sue Feniger
    City cuisine/Mary Sue Milliken and Susan Feniger; written with
Helene Siegel.
        p.   cm.
    Includes index.
    ISBN 0-688-06983-5
    1. Cookery.   I. Feniger, Susan.   II. Siegel, Helene.
III. Title.
TX714.F46 1989
641.5—dc 19   88-21551
CIP

Printed in the United States of America

First Edition

1 2 3 4 5 6 7 8 9 10

M.S.M. dedicates her efforts in these pages to R.M., J.M., and C.D.

Acknowledgments

City Cuisine and our restaurants are the product of a strong partnership, tempered by the constant input of new and creative experiences. We wish to acknowledge directly some of the people who strongly influence us, past, present and future. Jovan Treboyevic, Gus Reidi, Wolfgang Puck, Gregory Duda, Patrick Terrail, and Alan Wagner have provided the wisdom and talent of great mentors. Our enthusiastic staff inspires us daily with a burning energy that feeds our creative fires. We thank our mothers, Ruth and Ruthie, who taught us to appreciate fine food from the very start. We depend endlessly, on the creativity, strength, and love of Gai Gherardi, Barbara McReynolds, and Josh Schweitzer. But how to thank those who awoke in us a love for cooking in its most essential and cultural forms—from the Indian women who cooked naan for five hundred to the many international vendors whose "street foods" are the basis of many of our recipes?

Contents

City Cuisine is food that speaks to you with assertive flavors, textures, and colors. It is the result of a partnership, not only between two dedicated chefs, but between two worlds of cuisine. After ten years of rigorous training in French kitchens, our sensibilities were shocked by visits to India, Mexico, Thailand, and Japan. We saw food being transformed from its most essential and primitive forms into country dishes with spirit and heart. The science and technicality of food preparation that we had been trained to follow was augmented with a cultural cooking tradition that demanded attention for its uniqueness and quality.

In reading *City Cuisine*, you will notice the counterbalance of these varied styles of cooking. We've taken the best of ethnic foods, brought some to a more refined level, and left others in their original form. The discipline rules of haute cuisine are bent in our kitchen, and without losing quality, we've added flexibility and richness to our recipes. We follow five main points when cooking, and list them here to help guide you into our culinary perspective.

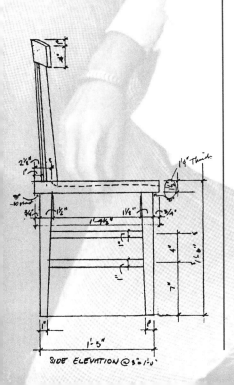

The Flavor We are drawn to strong, bold flavors and exotic seasonings. Remember, this food is direct and forceful, not subtle.

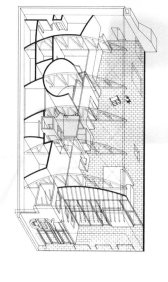

The Taste During the process of cooking these recipes, your best tool is your tongue. Taste, adjust, taste again, readjust, and most important, trust what you like. If there is a single key to our success with food, it is this.

The Look A combination of textures, shapes, heights, and colors makes a plate appealing. Focus on the main ingredient, keeping it simple, yet sophisticated. Make the food precise, not overly handled.

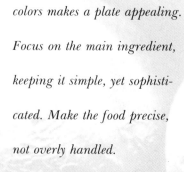

The Ingredients *Inspir-*

ational moments begin for us

during visits to various markets.

Try Oriental fish markets, eth-

nic groceries, simple roadside

stands, or your own organic

gardens.

Health *Through the use of*

powerful seasonings we have

been able to reduce our depen-

dency on creams, butters, and

oils. We also incorporate many

basic, healthful ethnic ingredi-

ents into our everyday cooking.

1   Starters

Spicy Starters

Small portions are just the right place to begin experimenting with spicy flavors and exotic combinations. Our goal in these personal favorites from India and Thailand is to balance spicy flavors with sweet and salty.

Blending spices is truly an interpretive art. Please adjust the amounts of chiles, Tabasco, and cayenne in these recipes to suit you and your guests' tastes. Simply start with less than the amount called for, then taste, and adjust, if necessary.

We prefer the smaller and hotter serranos to jalapeño chile peppers. Once again, this is purely personal. If you want less heat, just use a larger chile or remove the seeds. Always wash your hands after handling chile peppers to remove the hot oils.

Fried Fish Fingers with Honey-Mustard Dipping Sauce

Beer is the secret to this exceptionally light batter-fried fish. The yeast from the beer causes the batter to rise and expand.

1	CUP ALL-PURPOSE FLOUR
2	TEASPOONS CAYENNE
2	TEASPOONS SALT
½	TEASPOON BAKING POWDER
1	TEASPOON GRANULATED SUGAR
1	(8-OUNCE) BOTTLE OF BEER, ROOM TEMPERATURE
1½	POUNDS SKINLESS HALIBUT, SOLE, OR FLOUNDER FILLETS
4	CUPS PEANUT OIL FOR FRYING
	LEMON WEDGES FOR GARNISH
	HONEY-MUSTARD DIPPING SAUCE, RECIPE FOLLOWS

Combine flour, cayenne, salt, baking powder, and sugar in a medium bowl. Add beer, all at once, and whisk until smooth. Set aside, uncovered, at least an hour.

Slice fish into ¼ x 2-inch strips.

Heat oil to deep-fry temperature (350°F) in a large saucepan. Test oil by sprinkling in a few drops of batter. If they immediately rise to the surface, the oil is ready. Thoroughly coat strips by dipping one at a time in batter. Fry 4 or 5 pieces at a time until crisp and golden, about 2 minutes. Remove with a slotted spoon and drain on paper towels. Serve immediately with lemon wedges and Honey-Mustard Dipping Sauce.

6 Servings

Honey-Mustard Dipping Sauce

6	TABLESPOONS HONEY
¼	CUP DIJON MUSTARD
15–30	DASHES OF TABASCO

Mix ingredients together in a small bowl.

Makes ⅔ Cup

Vegetable Fritters with Chick-Pea Batter and Two Sauces

These spicy fritters are a popular late afternoon snack at the restaurant with a cool glass of Lemon Ginger Tea (page 243). Almost any vegetable can be substituted for those listed—cabbage and onion are popular in India, where Susan learned this recipe.

1	CUP FINE CHICK-PEA FLOUR (PAGE 247)
1	TABLESPOON GROUND CUMIN
1	TABLESPOON BLACK MUSTARD SEEDS (PAGE 245)
1	TEASPOON SALT
1	TEASPOON DRIED RED PEPPER FLAKES
½	TEASPOON TURMERIC
½	TEASPOON CAYENNE
½	TEASPOON CORNSTARCH
¼	TEASPOON GROUND CORIANDER
¼	TEASPOON BAKING POWDER
¾–1	CUP WATER
1	TEASPOON PEANUT OR VEGETABLE OIL
6	CUPS VEGETABLE OIL FOR FRYING
1	BELL PEPPER, CORED, SEEDED, AND SLICED IN ½-INCH STRIPS
6	MEDIUM MUSHROOMS, WHOLE OR SLICED IN HALF
1	CUP BROCCOLI FLORETS
2	CUPS CAULIFLOWERETS
	MINT AND CILANTRO CHUTNEY, RECIPE FOLLOWS
	YOGURT SAUCE, RECIPE FOLLOWS

Mix flour and dry ingredients together in a large bowl. Add ¾ cup water and stir to combine. Gradually add more water until mixture is thick enough to coat a finger. Stir in peanut oil. The batter may be made up to 2 hours in advance.

To make fritters, heat oil in a large saucepan to deep-fry temperature (350°F). Dip vegetables, one at a time, in batter to evenly coat. Fry, a few at a time, until deep brown, about 2 minutes. Remove with a slotted spoon and drain on paper towels. Serve immediately with Mint and Cilantro Chutney, Yogurt Sauce, and soy sauce for dipping.

6 Servings

Mint and Cilantro Chutney

3 BUNCHES CILANTRO, STEMS TRIMMED AND FINELY CHOPPED
1 SMALL BUNCH FRESH MINT, LEAVES ONLY, FINELY CHOPPED
2 GARLIC CLOVES, MINCED
1½ TABLESPOONS FRESHLY GRATED GINGER (PAGE 249)
1–2 SERRANO CHILES, FINELY CHOPPED WITH SEEDS
½ TEASPOON SALT
JUICE OF 1 SMALL LEMON
½ TABLESPOON PEANUT OIL

Mix ingredients in a bowl. Turn out onto a board and chop until a paste is formed.

Makes 1¾ Cups

Yogurt Sauce

3 TABLESPOONS PEANUT OIL
2 TEASPOONS BLACK (PAGE 246) OR YELLOW MUSTARD SEEDS
2 TEASPOONS CUMIN SEEDS
2 TEASPOONS PUREED GARLIC (PAGE 250)
1 TEASPOON FRESHLY GRATED GINGER (PAGE 249)
½ TEASPOON TURMERIC
½ TEASPOON PAPRIKA
⅛ TEASPOON DRIED RED PEPPER FLAKES
½ TEASPOON SALT
1 PINT PLAIN YOGURT

Have ingredients measured and nearby before beginning. Heat oil in a small skillet over high heat. Add mustard seeds. (They will begin popping immediately so have a cover close at hand for escaping seeds). Cook until popping stops.

Lower heat, add cumin seeds, and cook until they turn golden, about 1 minute. Stir in garlic for 10 seconds, then ginger for 10 seconds more, and remove from heat. Stir in turmeric, paprika, pepper flakes, and salt. Mix spices and yogurt in a bowl. Chill before serving.

Makes 2 Cups

Fried Clams with Homemade Tartar and Spicy Cocktail Sauces

Great fried clams are surprisingly easy to prepare at home. In this dish, the spice is in the sauce, so your guests can indulge their hot tooth accordingly. We have found Ipswich clams to be extraordinary for this dish, though littlenecks can be good also.

4   DOZEN CLAMS, FRESHLY SHUCKED, OR 1 POUND
     SHUCKED
4   EGGS
1½   CUPS ALL-PURPOSE FLOUR
1½   CUPS FINE DRY BREAD CRUMBS
6   CUPS VEGETABLE OIL FOR FRYING
     LIME WEDGES FOR GARNISH
     HOMEMADE TARTAR SAUCE, RECIPE FOLLOWS
     SPICY COCKTAIL SAUCE, RECIPE FOLLOWS

Pat clams dry and reserve. Beat eggs in a medium bowl and place flour and bread crumbs in individual bowls. Dip clams, 3 to 4 at a time, in flour, patting off any excess. Then dip in eggs and bread crumbs. Set aside on a platter.

Heat oil to deep-fry temperature (350° F) in a large saucepan. Add clams, a handful at a time, being careful of spattering oil. Do not overcrowd pan or oil will become too cool. Fry until golden brown all over, about 1 minute, taking care not to overcook. Remove with a slotted spoon and drain on paper towels. Serve immediately with Homemade Tartar Sauce and Spicy Cocktail Sauce.

6 Servings

Homemade Tartar Sauce

¾   CUP MAYONNAISE (PAGE 194)
1   TABLESPOON FRESH LEMON JUICE
2   TABLESPOONS DILL PICKLE FINELY CHOPPED
2   TABLESPOONS FINELY CHOPPED RED ONION
2   TABLESPOONS FINELY CHOPPED CAPERS
2   TABLESPOONS FINELY CHOPPED CELERY
2   TABLESPOONS FINELY CHOPPED PARSLEY LEAVES
½   TEASPOON SALT
½   TEASPOON FRESHLY GROUND PEPPER
1   TABLESPOON STONEGROUND MUSTARD

Mix ingredients together in a bowl.

Makes 1 Cup

Spicy Cocktail Sauce

¾	CUP KETCHUP
1—2	SERRANO CHILES, FINELY CHOPPED WITH SEEDS
3	TABLESPOONS CHOPPED FRESH CILANTRO LEAVES
3	TABLESPOONS FINELY CHOPPED RED ONION
1½	TABLESPOONS FRESH LIME JUICE
½	TEASPOON SALT
½	TEASPOON WHITE PEPPER
	TABASCO TO TASTE

Mix ingredients together in a bowl.

Makes 1 Cup

Thai Melon Salad

This authentic Thai dressing, packed with savory ingredients like garlic, chiles, peanuts, and dried shrimp, accentuates the coolness of summer melons. This dish looks lovely prepared with alternating rows of brightly colored melons: Cantaloupe, watermelon, crenshaw, and honeydew are some we use at the restaurant.

3	GARLIC CLOVES, PUREED (PAGE 250)
2	TABLESPOONS PALM SUGAR (PAGE 248) OR BROWN SUGAR
¼	CUP THAI FISH SAUCE (PAGE 248)
¼	CUP FRESH LIME JUICE
3	OR MORE SERRANO CHILES TO TASTE, STEMS REMOVED AND THINLY SLICED WITH SEEDS
1	TABLESPOON CHOPPED KAFFIR LIME LEAVES (PAGE 247) OR 1 TEASPOON GRATED LIME ZEST
½	CUP DRIED SHRIMP (PAGE 247)
½	CUP ROASTED, UNSALTED PEANUTS
6	CUPS ASSORTED MELON CUBES, IN ½-INCH CUBES, EACH VARIETY SEPARATED
¼	CUP FRESH CILANTRO LEAVES FOR GARNISH

Mix garlic, palm or brown sugar, Thai Fish Sauce, lime juice, chiles, and lime leaves in a medium bowl. Roughly chop shrimp and peanuts by hand or in a food processor and add to garlic mixture. (The dressing can be made in advance and stored up to 3 days in the refrigerator.)

To serve, arrange each variety of melon cubes in alternating rows on a platter or in individual bowls. Spoon dressing over melon in a stripe and garnish with cilantro. Serve chilled.

6 Servings

Pâtés and Purees

Pâtés are wonderful to have on hand when you are planning to entertain. They can be served with cocktails, as elegant appetizers, as quick suppers, or even on sandwiches, as we do at the restaurant. Once unmolded, they can sit wrapped in the refrigerator an additional week with no loss of flavor. Our favorite accompaniments are: Kalamata olives, cornichons, little radishes, pickled onions, sauerkraut, Dijon mustard, and plenty of French bread, toasted or plain.

There are no shortcuts for making really fine pâtés and terrines. All our recipes are of the traditional French variety—many calling for marination before baking and then a refrigeration period afterward, to allow the flavors to ripen.

The warm purees—Liver Flan with Tomato Coulis (page 28) and Brandade of Salmon with Warm Mustard Sauce (page 26)—are comforting wintertime starters before a dinner of Confit of Duck (page 125) or Braised Lamb Shanks with Oregano and Feta (page 102).

Pork Rillettes

This is an excellent choice for the beginning pâté maker. Unlike the smooth pâtés, this rustic rillettes does not require long marination or any special equipment. With its rough texture and full flavor, it's always right for casual occasions.

2	POUNDS BONELESS PORK BUTT
1½	POUNDS FATBACK
12	GARLIC CLOVES, PEELED
4–6	TABLESPOONS GREEN PEPPERCORNS, CRUSHED
¼	CUP DIJON MUSTARD
6	DASHES OF TABASCO
	SALT TO TASTE
	MUSTARD FOR DIPPING
	CORNICHONS FOR GARNISH

Trim pork of all fat and tendons and cut into ½-inch cubes. Skin fatback and cut into 1-inch cubes. Blanch pork in a large stockpot of rapidly boiling salted water until water returns to a boil. Remove with a slotted spoon, rinse with cold water, and reserve. Blanch fatback in the same pot of boiling water until water returns to a boil again. Drain in a colander and rinse with warm water to remove impurities. Puree fat in a food processor until smooth.

Cook pureed fat in a medium-heavy saucepan over low heat, uncovered, until solids sink to bottom and oil just stops bubbling. Take care not to brown the bubbling fat.

Place reserved pork cubes in another medium saucepan and strain clarified fat into the pan. Add garlic and cook over low heat, uncovered, until pork is tender, about 1½ hours. Be careful not to cook it too quickly. You want to avoid browning the pork, which would give the pâté a crisp texture.

Transfer to a bowl, cover, and refrigerate a minimum of a day or as long as a week.

Remove from refrigerator and skim off and discard the hard, white layer of fat that has risen to the top. The fat between the pork cubes should remain.

In a heavy-duty electric mixer fitted with a chilled bowl and paddle, beat at the lowest speed until it just starts to break up. Then turn speed to medium and beat an additional minute. Do not overmix or the heat of the beaters will begin melting fat, making pâté watery. Add green peppercorns, mustard, Tabasco, and salt, mixing to combine between additions.

Spoon onto lettuce leaves and serve with cornichons, toasted French bread, and mustard for dipping. For canapés, spread mustard, then *rillettes* on toast points and garnish with sliced cornichons.

Makes 3 Cups, 6 Appetizers or 48 Canapés   ✕

Chinese Sausage Salad

This sweet and spicy dish was part of an elaborate midday buffet Mary Sue prepared during her first trip to Thailand. The festive salad is served in hollow red onion cups—a typical Thai presentation.

1	(12-OUNCE) PACKAGE SWEET CHINESE SAUSAGE (PAGE 247)
2	MEDIUM RED ONIONS, WIDE AROUND THE MIDDLE
5	PICKLING CUCUMBERS OR KIRBIES (PAGE 247), WITH SKINS
	INNER LEAVES FROM 1 BUNCH CELERY, WASHED AND ROUGHLY CHOPPED
1	BUNCH CILANTRO, LEAVES ONLY
4–6	SERRANO CHILES, STEMS REMOVED AND THINLY SLICED, DIAGONALLY
1	TABLESPOON CHOPPED KAFFIR LIME LEAVES (PAGE 247) OR 1 TEASPOON GRATED LIME ZEST
2	TEASPOONS PUREED GARLIC (PAGE 250)
¼	CUP PALM SUGAR (PAGE 248) OR BROWN SUGAR
½	CUP FRESH LIME JUICE
½	CUP THAI FISH SAUCE (PAGE 248)

Preheat broiler. Place sausages in one layer on a large baking sheet and broil until charred on all sides, about 5 minutes per side. Set aside to cool.

To make onion cups, slice off root ends and tops, then peel. Cut each in half horizontally, and separate layers by pressing with your thumbs against root end to release rings. Reserve 12 largest as serving cups. Slice remaining onion into thin strips for use in salad.

Slice cucumbers in half lengthwise. Then thinly slice cucumbers and charred sausages, diagonally.

Combine sausage, cucumbers, onion strips, celery leaves, and cilantro in a medium bowl. In another bowl, whisk together serrano chiles, lime leaves, garlic, palm or brown sugar, lime juice, and Thai Fish Sauce. Pour over salad and toss to combine.

To serve, place onion cups open-side up on each serving plate. Spoon salad into cups and serve.

6 Servings

Poona Pancakes

These crisp and savory pan-cakes, named for the city in India where Susan first tasted them, are a pleasant surprise to American tastebuds. In India they are served topped with a fried egg for breakfast, quite a contrast to our sweet breakfast cakes.

1	CUP BASMATI RICE (PAGE 246)
1	CUP BLACK BEAN DAL (PAGE 247) OR LENTILS
3	CUPS WATER
5	TABLESPOONS PLAIN YOGURT
1½	TEASPOONS SALT
2	TOMATOES, PEELED, SEEDED, AND DICED
2	SERRANO CHILES, STEMS AND SEEDS REMOVED, DICED
1	SMALL RED ONION, DICED
½	BUNCH CILANTRO, STEMS TRIMMED, ROUGHLY CHOPPED
⅓	CUP VEGETABLE OIL
	YOGURT, CHOPPED TOMATOES, AND CHOPPED CILANTRO FOR GARNISH

Pick over rice and dal to remove any pebbles or dirt. Process in a food processor or blender until a coarse flour, about 5 minutes.

Mix ground mixture with water, yogurt, and salt in a bowl. Cover with plastic wrap and set aside in a warm place at least 12 hours or as long as 24. When ready, batter should be smooth and foamy, a bit thinner than pancake batter.

Just before cooking, add tomatoes, serrano chiles, red onion, and cilantro. Stir to combine.

Heat 1 tablespoon oil in a small, well-seasoned cast-iron skillet over high heat until very hot. Pour in ⅓ cup batter, reduce heat to low, and spread batter evenly with a ladle or spatula. Fry until well browned, about 2 to 3 minutes per side. Repeat this procedure, heating an additional tablespoon oil each time, until all batter is fried.

Stack pancakes between layers of aluminum foil in a roasting pan and keep warm in a 200°F oven. To serve, arrange 2 pancakes on each plate and top with yogurt, tomatoes, and cilantro. For smaller servings, slice each pancake into quarters and serve with garnishes for dipping.

8 Servings or 64 Canapés

Duck Terrine

We favor this delicate terrine for elegant dinner parties and champagne occasions. Its subtle flavor is unhindered by strong competing flavors.

2	(5-POUND) DUCKS
1	POUND 5 OUNCES FATBACK
1	CUP MADEIRA
1	TABLESPOON SALT
1	TABLESPOON WHITE PEPPER
½	CUP BRANDY
2	TABLESPOONS VEGETABLE OIL
10	OUNCES CHICKEN LIVERS, TRIMMED
1	BUNCH FRESH THYME, LEAVES ONLY
1	TEASPOON GROUND CLOVES
½	TEASPOON FRESHLY GRATED NUTMEG
3	EGGS
2	SLICES DAY-OLD WHITE BREAD, CRUSTS REMOVED
1	CUP PISTACHIOS, BLANCHED AND SKINNED
6	BAY LEAVES
5	GARLIC CLOVES, PEELED

Have a butcher skin and bone ducks or do it yourself. Reserve any breast meat in excess of 1 pound 12 ounces of meat, for garnish. Skin fatback and cut into 1-inch cubes. Cut the 1 pound 12 ounces of duck meat into 1-inch cubes. Pass fatback and cubed duck meat through medium hole of a meat grinder. Transfer to a large bowl.

Add Madeira, salt, and pepper and stir well to combine. Transfer to a large plastic or ceramic container. Place reserved duck breast on top and add brandy. Cover with plastic wrap touching top and refrigerator 1 to 3 days.

After marinating, remove duck breasts and slice into ½-inch wide strips. Heat oil in a cast-iron skillet over high heat. Sauté 6 ounces or just more than half the chicken livers until brown, about a minute per side. Drain on paper towels. Sauté breast meat in same pan until seared on the outside and *raw* inside, ½ minute per side. Drain on paper towels.

Add thyme, cloves, nutmeg, remaining chicken livers, and eggs to marinated ground meat mixture. Dip bread in warm water to soften, squeeze out excess moisture, and add. Puree in batches in a food processor until very smooth. Return to a large bowl and stir in pistachios.

Preheat oven to 325°F.

Spread 1 cup duck puree evenly over bottom of a 9 x 5 x 3-inch glass or ceramic loaf pan. Top with alternating strips reserved sautéed duck breast and chicken livers. Repeat, alternating puree with duck breast and livers, until pan is full and top layer is puree. Garnish with alternating strips of bay leaves and whole garlic cloves.

Tap pan against a counter to firmly pack. Cover with 2 layers aluminum foil, tucking edges under to completely seal. Place inside a large pan and pour in boiling water until it rises halfway up the sides of the pâté. Bake for 2 hours 15 minutes. Set aside to cool.

Place cooled pâté on a baking sheet and cover with another baking sheet. Top with about 3 pounds of weights (canned goods or milk cartons are good) and refrigerate overnight or as long as 2 weeks.

To serve, remove and discard bay leaf and garlic garnish. To loosen, dip pan's bottom in warm water and run a knife along inside edges. Unwrap bacon and invert onto a serving platter. Cut into ½-inch slices and serve on lettuce leaves.

Makes 1 Loaf or 18 Appetizers

Brandade of Salmon with Warm Mustard Sauce

Brandade, a classic Mediterranean dish, traditionally made with cod, is a blend of pureed fish and potatoes, lightly flavored with garlic. Temperature is key when combining the ingredients. Everything should be uniformly warm, or the mixture will harden as it sets. This earthly yet sophisticated dish is a nice way to start a fall or winter dinner of Confit of Goose with Peppercorns and Thyme (page 122).

2	SMALL BAKING POTATOES, WITH SKINS
1	POUND SKINLESS SALMON FILLETS, IN ½-INCH CUBES
1½	TEASPOONS SALT
1½	TEASPOONS WHITE PEPPER
1	TABLESPOON UNSALTED BUTTER
4	SHALLOTS, SLICED
4	MUSHROOMS, SLICED
½	CUP DRY WHITE WINE
2	CUPS FISH STOCK (PAGE 76) OR CLAM JUICE
⅔	CUP HEAVY CREAM
⅔	CUP FRUITY OLIVE OIL
2	TABLESPOONS PUREED GARLIC (PAGE 250)
	DASH OF TABASCO
	WARM MUSTARD SAUCE, RECIPE FOLLOWS

Preheat oven to 350°F. Boil potatoes with enough water to cover until tender, about 50 minutes. Arrange salmon in a single layer in an ovenproof skillet, sprinkle with ½ teaspoon each of salt and pepper, and set aside.

While potatoes are cooking, melt butter in a medium saucepan over moderate heat. Cook shallots and mushrooms until tender, about 5 minutes. Add wine, turn heat to high, and reduce by half. Add Fish Stock and cook just until the liquid returns to a boil. Remove from heat.

Strain warm reduced liquid over salmon in pan. Cover with a sheet of buttered parchment and bake 3 to 4 minutes, until salmon is barely pink in center. Strain salmon, reserving cooking liquid for later use in Warm Mustard Sauce.

Puree salmon in a food processor until smooth.

Combine cream and olive oil in a small saucepan and bring it barely to a boil. Add to pureed salmon along with garlic and process until smooth. Stir in remaining salt, pepper, and Tabasco.

When potatoes are done, but still warm, peel and work through a ricer or strainer. Add to salmon mixture and process with short pulses until just combined. Transfer to top of a double boiler set over simmering water and keep warm while preparing Warm Mustard Sauce.

To serve, coat serving plates with warm sauce and sprinkle with chives. Fill a pastry bag fitted with a #6 star tip with warm brandade and pipe a generous spiral in the center of each plate. Serve immediately with toasted French bread.

6 Servings

Warm Mustard Sauce

3   TABLESPOONS UNSALTED BUTTER, COLD
6   SHALLOTS, THINLY SLICED
6   MEDIUM MUSHROOMS, THINLY SLICED
1   CUP DRY WHITE WINE
2   CUPS RESERVED COOKING LIQUID, FISH STOCK (PAGE 76), OR CLAM JUICE
1   CUP HEAVY CREAM
3   TABLESPOONS STONEGROUND MUSTARD, ROOM TEMPERATURE
   DASH OF TABASCO
   SALT AND FRESHLY GROUND PEPPER TO TASTE
   CHOPPED FRESH CHIVES FOR GARNISH

Melt 1 tablespoon butter in a medium saucepan over low heat. Cook shallots and mushrooms until soft but not brown, about 5 minutes. Add wine, turn heat to high, and cook until liquid is reduced by half. Pour in reserved cooking liquid or Fish Stock and reduce by half. Then add cream and reduce by half again.

Reduce heat. Cut remaining butter in small pieces. Add butter, all at once, and whisk until completely smooth and incorporated. Remove from heat.

Strain through a fine sieve, pressing with the back of a ladle to extract all juices. Whisk in mustard and Tabasco and season to taste with salt and pepper. Serve immediately.

Makes 2 Cups

Liver Flan with Tomato Coulis

Liver's distinctive flavor often gets lost in dishes that call for high heat. We think this light, velvety flan captures its more elegant side. Try serving this special dish before a dinner of Grilled Chicken with Roasted Peppers (page 116).

3	TABLESPOONS UNSALTED BUTTER, SOFTENED
1	POUND 3 OUNCES FATBACK
1	POUND CHICKEN OR DUCK LIVERS, TRIMMED
¾	CUP MADEIRA
½	CUP HEAVY CREAM
4	EGGS
1½	TEASPOONS SALT
½	TEASPOON WHITE PEPPER
¼	TEASPOON FRESHLY GRATED NUTMEG
2	SPRIGS THYME, LEAVES ONLY
	TOMATO COULIS (PAGE 47)

Preheat oven to 325°F. Using half the butter, butter eight 6-ounce ramekins or coffee cups and reserve in freezer.

Skin fatback and cut into 1-inch cubes. Blanch fat in a large pot of boiling water until water returns to a boil. With a slotted spoon, transfer fat to top of a double boiler or a bowl over simmering water. Add remaining ingredients and stir until lukewarm.

Puree in a blender until smooth. Pass puree through a medium strainer into a bowl, pressing with the back of a ladle to extract all juices.

Butter ramekins again with remaining butter and place in a large roasting pan. Fill with warm liver puree. Pour boiling water into pan so it rises halfway up the sides of ramekins to create a *bain-marie*.

Bake 20 minutes, or until a toothpick inserted in center comes out nearly clean. The center should feel firm when pressed. Remove from *bain marie* and set aside to cool 10 minutes. Flan may be kept warm on top of oven or stove, then reheated in a *bain-marie* at 325°F for 10 minutes.

To serve, coat each serving plate with warm Tomato Coulis. To release flan, invert, one at a time, in palm of your hand, and slide onto center of each plate. Serve immediately.

8 Servings

Liver Terrine

This exceptionally fine pâté is as buttery and smooth as foie gras. It can be made and served the same day—just allow a minimum of 6 hours to properly chill. For a special sandwich, try thin slices of the pâté on Brioche (page 87) with lettuce and tomato and our Horseradish and Mustard and Mayonnaise spread (page 193).

2	POUNDS 3 OUNCES FATBACK
½	CUP BRANDY
3	BAY LEAVES
2	SLICES DAY-OLD WHITE BREAD, CRUSTS REMOVED
14	OUNCES DUCK OR CHICKEN LIVERS, TRIMMED
2	EGGS
3	TABLESPOONS HEAVY CREAM
¾	CUP MADEIRA
2	TEASPOONS SALT
½	TEASPOON WHITE PEPPER
⅛	TEASPOON FRESHLY GRATED NUTMEG
3	SPRIGS THYME, LEAVES ONLY

Skin fat and cut into 1-inch cubes. Blanch in a large stockpot of rapidly boiling salted water until water returns to a boil. Drain in a colander, rinse with warm water to remove impurities, and reserve in a warm place.

Combine brandy and bay leaves in a small saucepan and cook over low heat until warm, about 5 minutes. (This is called an infusion.) Set aside to cool and remove and discard bay leaves.

While brandy is cooling, dip white bread in warm water to soften. Squeeze out excess moisture. Combine bread, fatback, livers, eggs, and cream in a large bowl. Place bowl over a saucepan of simmering water and stir constantly until mixture is at room temperature, about 2 minutes. You want to warm it *without* cooking. Remove from heat.

Stir in remaining ingredients, including brandy, and puree in a blender until smooth. Strain through a medium sieve and stir well to combine.

Preheat oven to 325°F.

Pour puree into an ungreased 9 x 5 x 3-inch glass or ceramic loaf pan. Cover with 2 layers aluminum foil, tucking edges under to completely seal. Place inside a larger pan and pour in boiling water until it rises halfway up the sides of the terrine. Bake 1 hour, or until the center is just set. Set aside to cool, then refrigerate a minimum of 6 hours.

To serve, dip pan's bottom into water to loosen. Run a knife along inside edges and invert onto a serving platter. Cut into ½-inch slices and serve on lettuce leaves or spread on toast points and garnish with thinly sliced red onion for canapés.

Makes 1 Loaf, 18 Appetizers or 100 Canapés

Country Pâté

Country Pâté, Susan's favorite, is rich with strong flavors and contrasting textures. To get the full impact of the deep, spicy tastes, allow 4 to 6 days for the final refrigeration. This extra time lets the flavors mingle and ripen.

1	POUND 1 OUNCE LEAN VEAL OR CHICKEN
8	OUNCES LEAN PORK
14	OUNCES FATBACK
2	TEASPOONS SALT
1	TEASPOON WHITE PEPPER
½	CUP APPLEJACK, CALVADOS, OR BRANDY
1	TABLESPOON VEGETABLE OIL
4	OUNCES CHICKEN LIVERS, TRIMMED
1	TABLESPOON PUREED GARLIC (PAGE 250)
¼	CUP BRANDY
2½	BAY LEAVES
1	SLICE DAY-OLD WHITE BREAD, CRUSTS REMOVED
2	TEASPOONS GROUND ALLSPICE
½	TEASPOON FRESHLY GRATED NUTMEG
3	SMALL EGGS
½	POUND BACON, SLICED
¼	POUND BAKED HAM
¼	POUND PICKLED TONGUE
4	BAY LEAVES FOR GARNISH
5	GARLIC CLOVES, PEELED

Trim veal or chicken and pork of excess fat and tendons. Skin fatback. Cut into 1-inch cubes and pass through the largest hole of a meat grinder. Transfer to a large bowl. Stir in salt, pepper, and applejack. Cover with plastic wrap touching the mixture and refrigerate at least 1 day or as long as 3.

After marinating, heat oil in a medium skillet over high heat. Sauté livers until well browned, about 1 minute per side. Remove from pan and set aside to cool. Add garlic and cook about ½ minute, being careful not to let it color. Reserve garlic with liver.

Add brandy and bay leaves to same skillet. Scrape bottom of pan to loosen brown bits and cook over low heat until warm, about 5 minutes. Set aside to cool and remove and discard bay leaves.

Dip white bread in warm water to soften. Squeeze out excess moisture. Add to the liver and garlic along with 2 cups marinated ground meat, allspice, nutmeg, and brandy. Stir to combine.

Transfer to a food processor, add eggs, and puree until a smooth paste is formed. This paste will bind the pâté. Place puree in a large bowl, add remaining ground meat, and combine well. (We recommend using your hands, not a spoon, to combine this dense mixture.)

Preheat oven to 325°F.

Line a 9 x 5 x 3-inch glass or ceramic loaf pan with bacon slices so they overhang lengthwise, about 3 inches on each end. Slice ham and tongue into 4 x ½ x ½-inch julienne strips.

Spread about a cup of pâté evenly over the bacon to cover the bottom. Arrange alternating strips of ham and tongue lengthwise, over the pâté. Repeat this procedure, alternating pâté with strips of ham and tongue, until pan is filled and top layer is pâté. (When the loaf is sliced you will see a regular pattern of solids and pâté.) Fold overhanging bacon over top. (The pâté may rise slightly over the top of the pan. That's OK.)

Tap pan against a counter to firmly pack. Garnish top with bay leaves and garlic cloves. Cover with 2 layers aluminum foil, tucking edges under to completely seal. Place inside a larger pan and pour in boiling water until it rises halfway up the sides of the pâté. Bake 2 hours 15 minutes. Set aside to cool.

Place cooled pâté on a baking sheet and cover with another baking sheet. Top with some 3 pounds of weights (canned goods or milk cartons are good) and refrigerate overnight or as long as 2 weeks. This compacts the pâté and makes it easier to slice.

To serve, remove and discard bay leaf and garlic garnish. To loosen, dip pan's bottom in warm water and run a knife along inside edges. Invert onto a serving platter. Cut into ½-inch slices and serve on lettuce leaves.

Makes 1 Loaf or 18 Appetizers

Cold Salmon Mousse
with Watercress Mayonnaise

*We like to serve cool, pink slices
of salmon mousse in a pool of
bright green watercress mayonnaise. Much thinner than an
ordinary mayonnaise, it provides the perfect tart counter-
point to the delicate salmon.
Make this dish a day or two in
advance, when you're not feeling rushed, since the technique
is demanding.*

1¼   POUNDS SKINLESS SALMON FILLET, CUT INTO ½-INCH
      CUBES
1   TEASPOON SALT
1   TEASPOON WHITE PEPPER
3   CUPS FISH STOCK (PAGE 76) OR CLAM JUICE
1   TABLESPOON UNSALTED BUTTER
½   CUP THINLY SLICED MUSHROOMS
3   SHALLOTS, THINLY SLICED
1   CUP BRANDY
2   TABLESPOONS UNFLAVORED GELATIN
     DASH OF TABASCO
2½   CUPS HEAVY CREAM, COLD
     WATERCRESS MAYONNAISE, RECIPE FOLLOWS

Preheat oven to 350°F. Place salmon in a single
layer in a medium ovenproof skillet. Sprinkle
with salt and pepper and set aside.

Bring Fish Stock to a boil. Pour over salmon and
cook over medium-high heat until stock returns to a
boil. Cover with a sheet of buttered parchment paper,
transfer to oven, and bake 1 to 2 minutes. The salmon
should remain dark pink inside. Strain, reserving
salmon and stock in separate bowls.

Melt butter in a medium saucepan over medium-
low heat. Cook mushrooms and shallots until tender,
about 2 minutes. Pour in brandy, turn heat to high,
and light alcohol with a match. Cook over high heat
until liquid is reduced by half. Add reserved stock
and reduce again by half. Remove from heat, sprinkle
in gelatin, and stir. Strain liquid, discarding solids.

Puree reserved salmon, strained liquid, and Tabasco in a food processor until smooth.

Whip cold cream until soft peaks form and reserve in refrigerator.

Transfer pureed salmon to a bowl nested in a
larger bowl of iced water. Stir until mixture cools to
room temperature, not colder. The temperature is
critical. Then stir in ¼ whipped cream to lighten.
Gently fold in remaining cream until white just disappears.

Pour into a 9 x 5 x 3-inch glass loaf pan. Cover
with plastic wrap and chill a minimum of 6 hours
until the mousse sets, or as long as 2 days.

To serve, run a knife along inside edge of pan. Dip bottom in hot water for a few seconds and invert onto a serving platter. Coat serving plates with Watercress Mayonnaise. Cut mousse into ½-inch slices or pipe through a pastry bag fitted with a #6 star tip onto coated plates. Serve with toasted baguette slices.

8 to 10 Servings

Watercress Mayonnaise

2	BUNCHES WATERCRESS, LEAVES ONLY, ROUGHLY CHOPPED
1	CUP SOUR CREAM
2	TEASPOONS FRESH LEMON JUICE
	DASH OF TABASCO
1	TEASPOON SALT
¼	TEASPOON WHITE PEPPER
½	CUP MAYONNAISE (PAGE 194)

Puree watercress, sour cream, lemon juice, Tabasco, salt, and pepper in a blender until smooth. Transfer to a bowl and stir in mayonnaise.

Makes 1½ Cups

Marinated Fish and Meats

Marinated foods are great for hot weather entertaining. All are easy to prepare, low in calories, and taste best served icy cold.

It is essential to use the freshest meat and fish for these simple dishes. If you live in the middle of the country, the availability of fresh food has vastly improved: Special airfreight companies are shipping Louisiana crayfish, Maine lobsters, and fish from both coasts, South America, Hawaii, and Europe daily to the Midwest. If you live along the coast, it's worth a trip to the local fish market, where the restaurant buyers shop.

Oysters on the Half Shell with Red Wine Sauce

Red wine vinegar and shallots, pureed in a matter of minutes in a blender, give oysters a more delicate, festive feeling than the usual sharp cocktail sauce. To serve the oysters extra cold, line the plates with crushed ice and sprinkle with Kosher salt. Then arrange oysters on the ice shell-side down, garnished with seaweed in the center.

6 SHALLOTS, PEELED AND SLICED
¾ CUP RED WINE VINEGAR
36 FRESH OYSTERS

Puree shallots and red wine vinegar in a blender until smooth. Set aside. (Do not make this simple sauce far in advance or the delicate flavors will fade.)

To shuck oysters, wash under cold, running water and scrub with a stiff brush to remove any surface sand, especially around seam. With a towel in the palm of your hand to protect it, press shell against a work counter. In the pointy end of the oyster insert tip of oyster knife, gently twist to break seal, and run knife around edges until shell opens. Discard empty top shells. Dab around oyster with tip of wet towel to remove any bits of broken shell or sand. You can further clean, if necessary, with a pastry brush dipped in icy salted water. Shucked oysters may be kept, covered with a wet towel, in the refrigerator up to an hour.

Loosen the muscle that holds the oyster to the shell by gently sliding a knife between the two. Arrange 6 oysters per serving on chilled plates. Spoon about 1 teaspoon sauce over each oyster to cover with a thin layer. Serve immediately.

6 Servings

Marinated Tuna
with Spiced Sprouts

These thin slices of tuna must be marinated very briefly to maintain the finest texture and taste. You can prepare bite-sized rolls by cutting small rectangular slices and wrapping each around a small bouquet of sprouts. With either presentation, spoon on the marinade just before serving.

1	POUND SKINLESS, BONELESS TUNA, SUCH AS HAWAIIAN YELLOW FIN
½	CUP BROWN RICE VINEGAR (PAGE 246) OR RICE WINE VINEGAR (PAGE 248)
2½	TABLESPOONS SOY SAUCE
2	TABLESPOONS MIRIN (PAGE 248)
2	TABLESPOONS FRESHLY GRATED GINGER (PAGE 249)
2	(2-OUNCE) PACKAGES DAIKON SPICED SPROUTS (PAGE 249), ROOTS TRIMMED
½	MEDIUM RED ONION, SHREDDED

Using a sharp, wet knife, thinly slice tuna along grain using a long, horizontal sawing motion. The easiest way to do this is to press the fish down with one hand and cut slices off the top. Cover four serving plates with tuna. The lined plates may be reserved in refrigerator, covered with plastic wrap, up to 4 hours.

Mix vinegar, soy sauce, mirin, and ginger in a small bowl and spread about 2 tablespoons over each serving, evenly coating fish. Divide sprouts and arrange in a small fan on the side of each plate. Divide the red onion and place a small mound at root end of sprouts. Spoon a bit of dressing over sprouts and serve immediately.

4 Servings

Avoid the temptation to release your frustrations when pounding raw beef. The best carpaccio is the result of gentle flattening, rather than aggressive pounding, which breaks down the fibers and dulls the taste.

Use the freshest beef, of course. Susan, a raw-beef fanatic, suggests serving carpaccio before an entrée of Rigatoni Stuffed with Chicken and Fennel (page 115) or Roasted Black Cod with Coulis of Horseradish (page 127).

Beef Carpaccio

1	POUND BEEF SIRLOIN, TRIMMED OF ALL FAT AND SINEW
¾	CUP OLIVE OIL
	JUICE OF 1 LEMON
8	LARGE SHALLOTS, FINELY DICED
1	TEASPOON SALT
1	TABLESPOON PLUS 1 TEASPOON CRACKED BLACK PEPPERCORNS (PAGE 249)
	JULIENNED PARMESAN CHEESE AND CHOPPED FRESH CHIVES FOR GARNISH

Chill 8 serving plates. Place meat in freezer about 10 minutes.

Whisk together olive oil, lemon juice, shallots, salt, and pepper in a small bowl and reserve.

Slice cold beef across grain into ⅛-inch slices. Then place each slice, one at a time, between 2 sheets plastic wrap and, using the smooth side of a meat pounder, flatten by gently pounding and pressing back and forth. Work from center out. Keep turning to flatten it evenly to about ¹⁄₁₆ inch. (You should spend about a minute on each slice.)

Entirely cover each chilled plate with thin slices beef. (At this stage, you can cover with plastic wrap and reserve in refrigerator for several hours.) Carefully spoon reserved dressing over meat to evenly cover. Garnish with Parmesan strips and chives, and serve immediately.

8 Servings

Gravlax with Dill Mayonnaise

2	TABLESPOONS WHOLE CORIANDER SEEDS
¼	CUP COARSE SALT
¼	CUP CRACKED BLACK PEPPERCORNS (PAGE 249)
⅓	CUP GRANULATED SUGAR
2	POUNDS SKINLESS SALMON FILLET
1	BUNCH DILL
	DILL MAYONNAISE, RECIPE FOLLOWS

Cook coriander seeds in a small dry sauté pan over moderate heat just until the aroma is released. Crush seeds using the bottom of a heavy pot or a mortar and pestle. Mix seeds with salt, pepper, and sugar in a small bowl and reserve.

Slice salmon in half across width and lay pieces side by side on counter, flesh-side up. Divide dry spice mixture in half and sprinkle one half over both pieces. Place half the dill sprigs on 1 piece salmon and top with remaining piece salmon to enclose the spices and herbs, as if making a sandwich. (Make the sandwich even by placing the thick end of salmon on top of thin end.)

Evenly coat outside of salmon sandwich with remaining spices and dill. Tightly wrap in 2 layers plastic wrap, place in a shallow baking dish, and top with weights (canned goods or milk cartons are good). Refrigerate 3 days, turning over every 12 hours.

To serve, scrape off spices and dill. Slice thinly and serve cold with Dill Mayonnaise and thinly sliced black bread.

4 to 6 Servings

Dill Mayonnaise

4	EGG YOLKS
1	TABLESPOON DIJON MUSTARD
3	TABLESPOONS TARRAGON VINEGAR
1	TABLESPOON GRANULATED SUGAR
1 ¼	CUPS OLIVE OIL
¾	CUP SOYBEAN OIL
1	BUNCH CHOPPED FRESH DILL LEAVES
½	TEASPOON SALT
½	TEASPOON WHITE PEPPER

In a bowl, combine egg yolks, mustard, vinegar, and sugar. Blend with whisk. Gradually add olive oil and soybean oil, a drop at a time, whisking constantly. As mayonnaise begins to thicken, add oils more generously. Whisk in dill, salt, and pepper. Adjust seasonings and store in refrigerator up to 4 days.

Makes 2 Cups

Fish Tartare

Here is a pretty dish combining the chunky texture and strong tastes of beef tartare with delicately flavored fish. Feel free to substitute according to availability and freshness. Tuna or scallops could replace the salmon, and any mild fish, such as red snapper or sole, could stand in for the halibut.

8	OUNCES SKINLESS, BONELESS SALMON
8	OUNCES SKINLESS, BONELESS HALIBUT
	JUICE OF 2 LIMES
1	EGG YOLK
1	TABLESPOON DIJON MUSTARD
1	TEASPOON SALT
½	TEASPOON WHITE PEPPER
½	CUP EXTRA VIRGIN OLIVE OIL
2	DASHES OF TABASCO
12	CORNICHONS, FINELY DICED
6	SHALLOTS, FINELY DICED
⅓	CUP CAPERS, DRAINED AND CHOPPED
3	TABLESPOONS CHOPPED FRESH PARSLEY LEAVES
3	TABLESPOONS CHOPPED FRESH CHIVES
	RED LEAF LETTUCE FOR GARNISH

Using a sharp, wet knife, cut fish into ¼-inch cubes. Combine fish and lime juice in a glass or ceramic bowl. Cover with plastic wrap and refrigerate a minimum of 5 minutes or as long as 15 minutes.

Whisk egg yolk, mustard, salt, and pepper together in a mixing bowl. Gradually add olive oil, whisking constantly, until mayonnaise is formed. (You can thin the mixture with a few drops of lime juice, if necessary.) Stir in Tabasco, cornichons, shallots, capers, parsley, and chives.

Drain fish in a colander. Combine with mayonnaise and toss to evenly coat. To serve, line plates with lettuce leaves. Top with a scoop of fish tartare and serve immediately with toasted French bread or crackers.

4 Servings

Lamb's Tongue
with Thyme Vinaigrette

9	LAMB'S TONGUES
2	BAY LEAVES
1	BUNCH FRESH THYME, LEAVES AND STEMS SEPARATED
2	TABLESPOONS BLACK PEPPERCORNS
1	TEASPOON SALT
2	SHALLOTS, FINELY DICED
⅓	CUP EXTRA VIRGIN OLIVE OIL
	JUICE OF 1 SMALL LEMON
	SALT AND FRESHLY GROUND PEPPER TO TASTE
	RED LEAF LETTUCE FOR GARNISH

Combine tongues, bay leaves, thyme stems, peppercorns, and salt in a large stockpot with about 1 gallon of water. Bring to a boil and reduce to a simmer. Cook, uncovered, until tongues easily slide off when pierced with a fork, about 1½ hours. Remove from heat. Reserve tongues in cooking liquid.

Peel tongues by dipping, one at a time, in a bowl of iced water. Immediately remove any skin or tough gristle with your fingers or a small paring knife. Place in a bowl, cover with plastic wrap, and chill for 1 hour.

While tongues are chilling make the vinaigrette. Combine shallots, oil, and lemon juice with half the chopped thyme leaves in a small bowl. Whisk thoroughly and season with salt, pepper, and additional thyme, to taste.

When properly chilled, slice tongues thinly across the grain. Toss with vinaigrette. Arrange a bed of lettuce leaves on each plate. Place a scoop of tongue vinaigrette in center of each and serve.

4 to 6 Servings

VARIATION: Broiled clams are delicious with thyme vinaigrette. Arrange open clams on the half shell on a baking sheet, open-side up. Spoon about 1 teaspoon thyme vinaigrette over each to completely cover. Broil about 2 minutes and serve hot.

Marinated Scallops and Watercress Salad

It doesn't take the skill of a sushi chef to prepare this luxurious scallop salad. We prefer large sea scallops, which are easy to slice with any sharp knife and their buttery consistency is enhanced by only a brief marinade.

1   POUND SEA SCALLOPS

MARINADE

½   CUP EXTRA VIRGIN OLIVE OIL
    JUICE OF 2 LIMES
6   SHALLOTS, FINELY DICED
2   SMALL BUNCHES CILANTRO, LEAVES ONLY, COARSELY
    CHOPPED
1 ¼ TEASPOONS SALT
¼   TEASPOON WHITE PEPPER

1   RECIPE WATERCRESS AND AVOCADO SALAD (PAGE 184)

Carefully clean scallops of any roe, muscle, or brown connective tissue, which can become tough when marinated. Cut scallops into ¼-inch horizontal slices.

Combine marinade ingredients in a small bowl. Add scallops and toss to coat. Marinate, covered, in refrigerator 5 minutes or as long as ½ hour. (Any longer and the acid in the lime juice would overcook the seafood.)

Meanwhile prepare Watercress and Avocado Salad, reserving avocados.

To serve, divide dressed watercress salad among 6 serving plates. Arrange a circle of scallops in center of each and garnish with avocado slices along the side. Spoon leftover marinade over scallops and avocado. Serve cold.

6 Servings

Vegetarian Appetizers

Our small vegetarian plates fulfill many needs at the restaurant. With the exception of the Avocado Grapefruit Salad (page 49), which is strictly a starter, all the dishes can be served as hearty appetizers or light main courses for lunch or dinner. All they need is a simple green salad and some bread to make a complete meal.

Cheese gives these dishes heartiness. We like to use strong, salty cheeses like feta, Parmesan, and goat cheese, almost as you would spices, to add body and flavor to milder foods.

Roasted Red Peppers with Feta

This easy appetizer contrasts sweet, meaty red peppers with tangy feta. Look for Bulgarian feta in your local cheese shop or ethnic delicatessan. It's softer and less salty than the Greek type.

12	OUNCES FETA CHEESE, PREFERABLY BULGARIAN (PAGE 246), ROOM TEMPERATURE
1	CUP OLIVE OIL
6	LARGE RED BELL PEPPERS
24	BASIL LEAVES
½	CUP EXTRA VIRGIN OLIVE OIL

Drain feta of any water. Crumble into a small bowl and marinate in olive oil, at room temperature, until peppers are ready.

Char peppers on all sides under a preheated broiler or directly over a gas flame. Transfer to a plastic bag, close tightly, and set aside to steam, about 10 minutes. Under cold running water, carefully peel and split peppers open to remove seeds and excess pulp. Cut each into 4 equal pieces.

On each of 12 salad plates or a large platter, place 12 smaller pieces of pepper, skinned-side down. Cover each with a basil leaf and spread with 1 heaping tablespoon feta. Cover with another basil leaf and top with a larger piece of pepper. Drizzle 1 teaspoon extra virgin olive oil over each and serve at room temperature.

12 Servings

VARIATION: For finger food, cut peppers into smaller pieces and roll with basil and feta into bite-sized roll-ups. At Christmastime we like to arrange platters of alternating red, green, and yellow peppers.

Glazed Eggplant

A special harmony exists in the earthy combination of eggplant, tomatoes, and Parmesan cheese. Although this recipe seems long, the Tomato Concassé (page 48) Hollandaise, and eggplant can all be made up to 3 hours in advance. This hearty appetizer is a good way to begin a dinner of your favorite roasted meat.

HOLLANDAISE

3	EGG YOLKS
1	TABLESPOON WATER
2	TEASPOONS FRESH LEMON JUICE
⅛	TEASPOON SALT
⅛	TEASPOON WHITE PEPPER
¾	CUP CLARIFIED BUTTER (PAGE 249), WARM

In a medium bowl over simmering water, vigorously whisk together egg yolks, water, lemon juice, salt, and pepper until mixture is thick and fluffy, 3 to 5 minutes. The yolks should leave a trail when you lift the whisk. Remove from heat.

Gradually add clarified butter, a few drops at a time, whisking constantly. After half has been incorporated, you can add larger amounts of butter. Reserve up to 3 hours in a warm place.

1	CUP OLIVE OIL FOR FRYING
1	MEDIUM EGGPLANT, WITH SKIN, CUT IN ½-INCH HORIZONTAL (ROUND) SLICES
¾	CUP TOMATO CONCASSÉ (PAGE 48), WARM
½	CUP HEAVY CREAM
½	CUP FRESHLY GRATED PARMESAN CHEESE

Preheat broiler.

Heat oil in a medium skillet over moderate heat. Sauté eggplant until lightly golden, 1 to 2 minutes per side. Drain on paper towels and arrange in 1 layer on a baking sheet or individually on the ovenproof plates it's to be served on. Spread about 2 tablespoons Tomato Concassé over each slice and reserve.

Whip cream until soft peaks form. Gently fold cream and Parmesan cheese into reserved Hollandaise. Spoon over Tomato Concassé, to cover each slice. Broil until golden and bubbly, about 2 minutes. Serve immediately.

6 Servings

Gnocchi Parmesan

Made with cream puff dough, these gnocchi are lighter and fluffier than the traditional Italian potato dumplings. Serve this comforting dish before a simple grilled entrée or as a main course with a watercress salad and a glass of red wine.

1   CUP MILK
7   TABLESPOONS UNSALTED BUTTER
¾   TEASPOON SALT
¾   CUP ALL-PURPOSE FLOUR
4   EGGS
2   CUPS HEAVY CREAM
1   CUP (4 OUNCES) FRESHLY GRATED PARMESAN CHEESE
¼   TEASPOON WHITE PEPPER
     CHOPPED FRESH CHIVES FOR GARNISH

Because you will need to cook the gnocchi quickly once the batter is ready, do the following before you begin the preparation. Bring a large stockpot of salted water to a boil and reduce to a simmer. Have a large bowl of iced water nearby.

Combine milk, butter, and ½ teaspoon salt in a medium-heavy saucepan. Bring to boil over high heat. Add flour and stir vigorously with a wooden spoon until mixture is nearly solid, about 2 minutes. The batter should be the consistency of mashed potatoes and should clear the sides of the pan to form a ball. Remove from heat.

Transfer to a large bowl and add eggs, one at a time, beating well after each addition. (An electric mixer is fine for this.) The batter should be very thick, shiny, and smooth. Fill a pastry bag, fitted with a large plain tip #8, with batter.

Holding pastry bag over simmering water, gently squeeze out dough, slicing into 1-inch lengths with a paring knife.

Working in 4 batches of about 20 pieces, cook gnocchi at a slow simmer, stirring occasionally, until they start to puff, about 5 minutes. They should resemble floating corks. To test for doneness, remove a dumpling and cut in half. The center should have tiny bubbles. With a slotted spoon, transfer gnocchi to the bowl of iced water to cool. Drain well in a colander. At this stage, you can store gnocchi in refrigerator up to 2 days.

Preheat oven to 450°F.

Bring cream to a boil in a medium ovenproof

skillet or casserole. Add Parmesan, pepper, ¼ teaspoon salt, and gnocchi. Return to a boil and transfer to oven. Bake until sauce is thick and bubbly and a slight crust forms on top, about 7 minutes. Garnish with chopped chives and serve immediately.

6 Appetizers or 4 Entrées

Goat Cheese Avocado

Marinated goat cheese adds just the right kick to the soothing taste and texture of avocado in this simple spread. We never grow tired of eating it—as an appetizer, on French bread sandwiches, or with chips and crackers, as a dip. We suggest you keep a stash in the refrigerator for summer snacks. Inspired by partner Barbara, this snack became a staple at Susan's house.

4 OUNCES MILD, SOFT GOAT CHEESE SUCH AS
   MONTRACHET
½ CUP OLIVE OIL
4 RIPE AVOCADOS, HALVED, SEEDED, AND PEELED
   JUICE OF 1 LEMON
4 DASHES TABASCO
⅛ TEASPOON WHITE PEPPER
   SALT TO TASTE
   TOMATO WEDGES, CUCUMBER SLICES, AND THIN
   ROUNDS OF FRENCH BREAD FOR GARNISH

Marinate goat cheese in olive oil, in a small covered container, at room temperature, at least a day. (You can add fresh herbs and spices such as basil, thyme, rosemary, and peppercorns, if you wish, to flavor cheese.) Goat cheese can marinate indefinitely, as long as completely covered with oil.

Before serving, lift cheese out of oil. Combine with avocados, lemon juice, Tabasco, and pepper in a large bowl. Mash with a fork until mixture is slightly lumpy, *not* a smooth purée. Season sparingly with salt, since goat cheese can be very salty.

To serve, center a scoop on small salad plates. Garnish with tomato wedges, thick cucumber slices, and thin rounds of French bread.

6 Servings

VARIATION: This is a great sandwich spread. At the restaurant we serve it warm open-faced on baguettes with tomato and cucumber slices on top.

Fried Brie with Tomato Coulis

This dish is a sensual combination of mild, runny cheese, crisp breading, and sweet, smooth tomato sauce. The key lies in working with ice-cold cheese, so it keeps its shape when it hits the hot oil.

1½   POUNDS BRIE CHEESE
3   EGGS
1   CUP ALL-PURPOSE FLOUR
1   CUP FINE DRY BREAD CRUMBS
4   CUPS PEANUT OIL FOR FRYING
     TOMATO COULIS, RECIPE FOLLOWS

Slice Brie into 6 wedges and refrigerate until very cold and firm. Beat eggs in a bowl and place flour and bread crumbs in individual bowls. When cheese is cold, dip each wedge, one at a time, in flour, patting off any excess. Then dip in eggs, drain, and coat with bread crumbs. Be meticulous about covering every spot of cheese. Reserve coated cheese on a platter in freezer for 10 minutes.

Dip each wedge in eggs and bread crumbs again, being careful to drain the eggs and thoroughly coat with bread crumbs. Place in freezer for another 10 minutes.

Preheat oven to 350°F.

Heat oil in a large stockpot or saucepan to deep-fry temperature (350°F). Fry wedges, three at a time, until golden brown, about 1 minute. Do not stir, since the breading is easily broken. Carefully remove with a slotted spoon and drain on paper towels. Transfer to a large roasting pan and bake for 5 minutes.

To serve, coat each plate with warm Tomato Coulis. Top with wedge of cheese and serve immediately.

6 Servings

VARIATION: For cocktail parties, follow the same procedure with cheese cut into ½-inch cubes.

Tomato Coulis

This smooth tomato puree made with Madeira is sweet and mellow.

3	TABLESPOONS UNSALTED BUTTER
½	SMALL ONION, THINLY SLICED
3	MUSHROOMS, THINLY SLICED
2	SHALLOTS, THINLY SLICED
1	SMALL LEEK, WHITE PART, THINLY SLICED
¼	TEASPOON SALT
1	TABLESPOON BRANDY
¼	CUP PLUS 1 TABLESPOON MADEIRA
1	CUP CHICKEN STOCK (PAGE 74) OR CANNED BROTH
3	RIPE TOMATOES, CHOPPED WITH SKINS
2	SPRIGS THYME
1	BAY LEAF
	SALT AND FRESHLY GROUND PEPPER TO TASTE

Melt 2 tablespoons butter in a medium skillet over low heat. Cook onion, mushrooms, shallots, leek, and salt until soft, about 7 minutes. Add brandy and ¼ cup Madeira. Turn heat to high and light alcohol with a match. Cook over high heat until liquid is reduced by half.

Add Chicken Stock, tomatoes, thyme, and bay leaf. Reduce the heat to low and simmer, uncovered, for 20 minutes. Puree in a food processor or blender and strain.

Return to pan and place over medium heat. Whisk in remaining tablespoon butter, broken in small pieces, and remaining tablespoon Madeira. Season with salt and pepper to taste and serve.

Makes 2 Cups

Zucchini Pancakes
with Tomato Concassé

This vegetable pancake becomes light and fluffy as the eggs gently cook. It's a favorite among our vegetarian customers and makes a lovely brunch dish served with a green salad and good, fresh bread.

1 LARGE ZUCCHINI, ENDS TRIMMED AND ROUGHLY GRATED WITH SKINS
3 EGGS
3 TABLESPOONS CHOPPED PARSLEY LEAVES
¾ TEASPOON SALT
½ TEASPOON WHITE PEPPER
2 TABLESPOONS UNSALTED BUTTER
TOMATO CONCASSÉ, RECIPE FOLLOWS
FRESHLY GRATED PARMESAN CHEESE FOR GARNISH

Preheat broiler.
Mix zucchini, eggs, parsley, salt, and pepper in a medium bowl. Melt 1 tablespoon butter in each of 2 small ovenproof skillets (preferably Teflon) over medium-high heat. Pour half the zucchini mixture into each skillet and reduce heat to low. Gently cook, shaking pan occasionally, until batter is loose in center and set around the edges, 3 to 5 minutes.

Transfer to broiler and cook until firm in center, but not browned, about 4 minutes.

To serve, slice each into 3 wedges and center on serving plates. Garnish with warm Tomato Concassé and Parmesan cheese, and serve immediately.

6 Appetizers or 2 Entrées

Tomato Concassé

This peasant sauce—roughly chopped and quickly cooked—makes a lively garnish for grilled vegetables.

3 TABLESPOONS OLIVE OIL
1 MEDIUM ONION, DICED
2 GARLIC CLOVES, MINCED
1 TEASPOON SALT
3 RIPE LARGE TOMATOES, PEELED, SEEDED, AND DICED (PAGE 249) OR 6 CANNED ITALIAN PLUM TOMATOES, SEEDS REMOVED
5 BAY LEAVES
1 TEASPOON CHOPPED FRESH THYME OF ½ TEASPOON DRIED
1 TEASPOON FRESHLY GROUND PEPPER

Heat oil in a medium skillet over moderate heat. Sauté onions, garlic, and salt until golden, about 10 minutes. Add tomatoes, bay leaves, thyme, and pepper. Reduce to a simmer and cook, uncovered, stirring occasionally, 15 to 20 minutes. Remove and discard bay leaves, and serve. Concassé may be stored in refrigerator up to a week.

Makes 2 Cups

Avocado Grapefruit Salad with Sour Cream-Honey Dressing

The grapefruit and avocado slices for this easy salad can be arranged in advance and refrigerated. To avoid breaking down the fruit, add the dressing right before serving. Leftover dressing is excellent on summer fruit salads.

3 PINK GRAPEFRUITS, CHILLED
3 RIPE MEDIUM AVOCADOS, HALVED, SEEDED, AND PEELED
¾ CUP SOUR CREAM
  JUICE OF 2 LARGE LIMES
3 TABLESPOONS HONEY
½ TEASPOON SALT
¼ TEASPOON WHITE PEPPER
  MINT LEAVES FOR GARNISH

Slice ends off grapefruits and stand upright on a counter. Cut away skin and membrane, exposing fruit. Working over a bowl to catch the juice, separate sections by slicing with a serrated knife between membranes. Remove and discard seeds. Slice avocado halves lengthwise in ½-inch slices. Arrange alternating grapefruit sections and avocado slices on 6 salad plates.

Whisk together sour cream, lime juice, honey, salt, and pepper in a small bowl. Just before serving, spoon about 2 tablespoons dressing in a stripe over each salad. Garnish with mint leaves and serve.

6 Servings

VARIATION: Toss chunks of avocado and supremes of grapefruit with salt, pepper, and olive oil.

2 Soups and Stocks

We aren't sure why people don't cook more soups at home. We suspect it has something to do with the mistaken notion that a soup has to simmer for a long time in order to taste good. Actually, some of our favorite creamed soups can be prepared in about half an hour. In fact, the key to their intense tastes lies in cooking the main ingredient very briefly, so the pure flavor shines through. Ultimately, homemade soups are convenient. They can be cooked in advance and reheated whenever you need a nourishing lunch or hearty starter.

One precaution: Keep in mind that the quantities of salt in the recipes are based on using homemade chicken stock. Adjust the amount accordingly if substituting a salty canned broth.

Creamed Soups

Creamed vegetable soups offer the stomach-filling satisfaction we sometimes yearn for in a soup. With their rich flavors and velvety consistency they can serve admirably as either starters or entrées, depending on the serving size. Don't hesitate to reduce the amount of cream in the recipes to suit your taste or diet. Half and half or milk may be substituted as desired.

Carrot Soup with Dill

This simple yet sophisticated soup is terrific with full-flavored foods like a roast leg of lamb. Use this recipe as your guide for making other creamed vegetable soups. Just substitute hard vegetables like broccoli, turnip, or cauliflower and omit the dill. The key is to chop the main vegetable very small and cook briefly, just until soft, so its flavor remains fresh.

2 TABLESPOONS UNSALTED BUTTER
1½ MEDIUM ONIONS, SLICED
2 TEASPOONS SALT
½ TEASPOON WHITE PEPPER
1 BUNCH FRESH DILL
4 CUPS CHICKEN STOCK (PAGE 74) OR CANNED BROTH
1 POUND CARROTS, PEELED AND FINELY CHOPPED
1 CUP HEAVY CREAM
1 CUP HALF AND HALF

Melt butter over medium-low heat in a large stockpot or Dutch oven. Cook onions with salt and pepper until soft, about 5 minutes.

Chop dill in half, reserving the leaves for garnish. Tie stems with string and place in pot. Add the Chicken Stock and cook over moderate heat, uncovered, about 15 minutes. Meanwhile, finely chop carrots in a food processor.

Remove and discard dill stems and add carrots. Bring to a boil, return to a simmer, and cook, uncovered, until the carrots are soft, about 10 minutes.

Puree in a blender or food processor until smooth. Strain back into pot, pressing with the back of a ladle to extract all juices. Add cream and half and half. Bring to a boil and remove from heat. Serve immediately, garnished with dill leaves.

4 to 6 Servings   ✕

Tomato and Fennel Soup

This is the most elegant and refined of our creamed vegetable soups. It's sweet and delicate, allowing a hearty entrée like Marinated Rib Eye with Gorgonzola Sauce (page 96) to follow.

1	LARGE FENNEL BULB WITH STEMS AND LEAVES
2	TABLESPOONS UNSALTED BUTTER
1	MEDIUM ONION, THINLY SLICED
2	TEASPOONS SALT
½	TEASPOON WHITE PEPPER
½	CUP PERNOD
2–3	RIPE TOMATOES, SEEDED, AND CHOPPED (PAGE 249)
2	CUPS CHICKEN STOCK (PAGE 74) OR CANNED BROTH
½	CUP HEAVY CREAM
½	CUP HALF AND HALF
	DASH OF TABASCO

Wash and trim fennel, discarding stems. Separate bulb into stalks and thinly slice. Reserve wispy inner leaves for garnish.

Melt butter over moderate heat in a large stockpot or Dutch oven. Cook onions with salt and pepper until soft, about 10 minutes. Add fennel, reduce heat to low, and cook an additional 5 minutes.

Turn heat to high and add Pernod. (Don't be alarmed if the alcohol flames. It will subside momentarily.) Cook until liquid is reduced by half. Add tomatoes and Chicken Stock. Reduce to a simmer and cook, covered, about 15 minutes.

Puree in a blender until smooth. Strain back into pot and add cream and half and half. Bring to a boil, remove from heat, and stir in Tabasco. Serve immediately, garnished with fresh fennel leaves.

6 to 8 Servings   ✕

Cream of Mushroom Soup

There is little to distract from the clean, pure taste of mushrooms in this rich soup. Since they are so absorbent, the best way to clean mushrooms is by wiping with a damp cloth or paper towel rather than immersing in water. You can slice the mushrooms roughly by hand or with the slicing disc in a food processor. Precision isn't important since they will be pureed later.

4   TABLESPOONS (½ STICK) UNSALTED BUTTER
1½ POUNDS MUSHROOMS, CLEANED AND THINLY SLICED
1   TABLESPOON SALT
1   TEASPOON WHITE PEPPER
3   CUPS CHICKEN STOCK (PAGE 74) OR CANNED BROTH
2   CUPS HEAVY CREAM
1   TABLESPOON PLUS 1 TEASPOON FRESH LEMON JUICE

Melt butter over high heat in a large stockpot or Dutch oven. Cook mushrooms, uncovered, with salt and pepper until nearly all moisture is evaporated, about 15 minutes.

Stir in Chicken Stock and cream, bring to a boil, and remove from heat. Puree in a blender until smooth. Return to pot and bring just to a boil. Remove from heat. Add lemon juice, season with salt and pepper to taste, and serve immediately.

6 to 8 Servings

Butternut Squash Soup

This basic creamed squash soup makes a terrific autumn lunch served with plenty of warm fresh bread and a green salad.

1   LARGE BUTTERNUT SQUASH, ABOUT 1½ POUNDS, CUT
     IN HALF LENGTHWISE AND SEEDED
2   TABLESPOONS UNSALTED BUTTER
2   MEDIUM ONIONS, SLICED
1½   TEASPOONS SALT
¾   TEASPOONS WHITE PEPPER
4   CUPS CHICKEN STOCK (PAGE 74) OR CANNED BROTH
1   CUP HEAVY CREAM
1   CUP HALF AND HALF
1   LIME FOR GARNISH

Preheat oven to 450°F. Bake squash, cut-side down, in a foil covered roasting pan with about 1-inch water, until soft, 45 to 60 minutes. When cool enough to handle, scrape out interior flesh and reserve.

Melt butter over moderate heat in a large stockpot or Dutch oven. Sauté onions with salt and pepper until golden, 10 to 15 minutes. Add squash and Chicken Stock. Bring to a boil, reduce to a simmer, and cook, uncovered, about 10 minutes.

Puree in a blender until smooth. Strain back into pot and add cream and half and half. Return to a boil and remove from heat.

Peel lime and remove sections. (Follow the method used for lemons (page 210.) Dice into small pieces. Serve soup immediately, garnished with diced lime.

6 Servings   ✕

Yam and Ginger Soup

This soup reminds us of sweet potato pie without the crust. It is so sweet and thick. It would make a great opener for a winter dinner of Turkey Breast with Lemon Butter (page 121) and Sautéed Mustard Greens (page 186).

1–2	LARGE YAMS, ABOUT 2 POUNDS
2	TABLESPOONS UNSALTED BUTTER
1½	MEDIUM ONIONS, SLICED
2½	TEASPOONS SALT
½	TEASPOON WHITE PEPPER
3	TABLESPOONS FRESHLY GRATED GINGER (PAGE 249)
3	CUPS CHICKEN STOCK (PAGE 74) OR CANNED BROTH
1	CUP HEAVY CREAM
1	CUP HALF AND HALF
	JUICE OF ½ LIME

Preheat oven to 350°F. Bake yam until thoroughly soft, about 1 hour. (The sugar will rise to the surface and form syrup droplets on the yam's skin when done.) When cool enough to handle, peel and cut into slices.

Melt butter over medium-low heat in a large stockpot or Dutch oven. Cook onions with salt and pepper until soft, about 10 minutes. Add ginger and cook an additional 3 minutes, stirring occasionally. Add yams and Chicken Stock. Bring to a boil, reduce to a simmer, and cook, uncovered, 10 minutes.

Puree in a blender until smooth. Strain back into pot and stir in cream and half and half. Bring to a boil and remove from heat. Stir in lime juice and serve immediately.

4 to 6 Servings   ✕

Cream of Lettuce Soup

This is the best use we know for leftover or wilted salad greens. Virtually any lettuce will do, including spinach or watercress, but try to anticipate the final result since a bitter green may yield a soup that is too tart for your taste.

2	TABLESPOONS UNSALTED BUTTER
1½	MEDIUM ONIONS, SLICED
1	SLICE BACON
1½	TEASPOONS SALT
½	TEASPOON WHITE PEPPER
1	MEDIUM RED POTATO, PEELED AND THINLY SLICED
4	CUPS CHICKEN STOCK (PAGE 74) OR CANNED BROTH
1	LARGE OR 2 SMALL HEADS LETTUCE, LEAVES SEPARATED, WASHED, AND ROUGHLY CHOPPED INTO SMALL PIECES
1	CUP HEAVY CREAM
1	CUP HALF AND HALF

Melt butter over medium-low heat in a large stockpot or Dutch oven. Cook onions with bacon, salt, and pepper until soft, about 10 minutes. Add potato and Chicken Stock. Bring to a boil, reduce to a simmer and cook, uncovered, about 15 minutes.

Remove and discard bacon. Return stock to a boil, reduce to a simmer, and stir in lettuce. Cook over moderate heat, uncovered, 3 to 4 minutes.

Puree in blender until smooth. Strain back into pot, pressing with a ladle to extract all juices. Stir in cream and half and half. Bring to a boil and remove from heat. Serve immediately.

6 Servings

VARIATION: For a thinner lettuce soup, use romaine and omit the cream and half and half. Garnish with a mixture of ¼ cup each Gorgonzola cheese and sour cream and 1 teaspoon cracked pepper.

4 Servings

Hearty Broths

These rustic, peasant soups are dearest to our hearts. While each has its own special charm, all are substantial and interesting enough to serve alone as a lunch or light dinner with nothing more than a salad, some bread, and wine.

Swiss Onion Soup

Unlike some onion soups where the cheese forms a tough, stringy mass at the top, the cheese in this hearty soup grows softer and sweeter as it simmers in the milky broth. It may not look great, but the taste is superb. You can refrigerate this homey soup for as long as 6 days with no loss of quality. When gently reheating it, remember to keep stirring.

8   TABLESPOONS (1 STICK) UNSALTED BUTTER
3   MEDIUM ONIONS, THINLY SLICED
2   TEASPOONS SALT
¼   TEASPOON WHITE PEPPER
½   DAY-OLD FRENCH BREAD OR 6 SLICES WHITE BREAD
1   TEASPOON GRANULATED SUGAR
½   GALLON MILK
1   POUND GOOD-QUALITY SWISS OR GRUYÈRE CHEESE, DICED

Melt butter over moderate heat in a large heavy stockpot or Dutch oven. Cook onions with salt and pepper until soft but not colored, 15 minutes.

Cut bread into medium dice and add to pot along with sugar. Stir constantly for about 1 minute, so bread absorbs butter.

Add milk and bring to a boil. Add cheese, stir, and reduce to a simmer. Cook, uncovered, stirring occasionally, about 1 hour 15 minutes. Serve immediately.

8 to 10 Servings

Thai Pork Dumpling Soup

This is the kind of one dish meal we love to eat at home. The broth is clear and strong with the distinctive tastes of black pepper and cilantro, and the bowl is brimming with interesting textures. Don't be daunted by the unusual ingredients—this is a simple dish to prepare.

THAI PESTO

½	BUNCH FRESH CILANTRO, STEMS REMOVED
½	TABLESPOON PALM SUGAR (PAGE 248) OR BROWN SUGAR
½	TABLESPOON FRESHLY GRATED GINGER (PAGE 249)
1	TEASPOON CRACKED BLACK PEPPER
1	TEASPOON PUREED GARLIC (PAGE 250)
1	TABLESPOON THAI FISH SAUCE (PAGE 248)
1	OUNCE CELLOPHANE NOODLES OR BEAN THREADS (PAGE 246)
¼	POUND FRESH OR DRIED BLACK FUNGUS (WOOD EAR MUSHROOMS) (PAGE 246)
10	OUNCES GROUND PORK
1	TABLESPOON THAI FISH SAUCE (PAGE 248)
1	TEASPOON PUREED GARLIC (PAGE 250)
1	TABLESPOON CORNSTARCH
10	CUPS CHICKEN STOCK (PAGE 74) OR CANNED BROTH FRESH GROUND BLACK PEPPER AND THAI FISH SAUCE TO TASTE
1	BUNCH SCALLIONS, WHITE AND GREEN PARTS, THINLY SLICED
½	BUNCH CILANTRO, LEAVES ONLY

To make Pesto, puree all ingredients in a food processor or blender until a fine paste is formed. Set aside. You can do this by hand by first chopping all ingredients, except Thai Fish Sauce, together on a board to form a paste. Then mix with fish sauce in a small bowl.

Follow directions on packages for reconstituting cellophane noodles and dried mushrooms, if necessary. Noodles usually need to soak in warm water for about 15 minutes; mushrooms about 30 minutes.

While ingredients are soaking, make dumplings by combining ground pork, Thai Fish Sauce, garlic, and cornstarch in a bowl. With your hands, form small meatballs, about the size of hazelnuts. Set aside.

When noodles and mushrooms are finished soaking, drain. Remove and discard the tough stems and slice mushrooms into julienne strips. Cut noodles into 2- to 3-inch lengths.

Place all ingredients near stove and bring Chicken Stock to a boil in a large stockpot. Reduce to a simmer and add pork balls, mushrooms, and noodles. Cook, uncovered, until pork is done, about 10 minutes. Stir in Pesto and adjust seasonings with pepper and Thai Fish Sauce. (We like this broth really peppery.) Ladle into serving bowls, sprinkle with sliced scallions and cilantro leaves, and serve immediately.

10 Servings

Black-Eyed Pea Soup

Black-eyed peas, or cowpeas, are less starchy and more flavorful than other dried beans. In all our bean soups we call for boiling, rather than soaking, the beans to soften them. These techniques can be used interchangeably.

2 CUPS DRY BLACK-EYED PEAS, WASHED
4 SLICES BACON, CUT IN SMALL SQUARES
2 MEDIUM ONIONS, DICED
2 STALKS OF CELERY, DICED
1 TEASPOON SALT
½ TEASPOON PEPPER
6 CUPS CHICKEN STOCK (PAGE 74) OR CANNED BROTH
1 SPRIG FRESH ROSEMARY
1 TOMATO, PEELED, SEEDED, AND DICED (PAGE 249)

Place beans in a medium saucepan and cover with a generous quantity of water. Bring to a boil and cook, uncovered, until beans are tender, about 1 hour. Drain and reserve.

Cook bacon in a large stockpot over low heat until tender, not crisp. Add onions, celery, salt, and pepper. Cook over low heat until vegetables are soft, about 10 minutes.

Add peas, Chicken Stock, and rosemary. Bring to a boil, reduce to a simmer, and cook, uncovered, 30 minutes. Remove and discard the rosemary, stir in tomatoes, and cook long enough to heat through. Serve immediately.

8 Servings

Lentil Soup

In this authentic Indian recipe, the onions and lentils are well-browned before the stock is added. The resulting broth is thick and earthy, with a lovely caramel color. You can easily adapt this recipe for vegetarians by substituting water for the Chicken Stock.

2	TABLESPOONS UNSALTED BUTTER
1	LARGE ONION, DICED
1	TEASPOON SALT
2	TABLESPOONS PUREED GARLIC (PAGE 250)
1½	TABLESPOONS FRESHLY GRATED GINGER (PAGE 249)
¼	TEASPOON FRESHLY GROUND BLACK PEPPER
1½	CUPS LENTILS, WASHED AND DRAINED
5	CUPS CHICKEN STOCK (PAGE 74), CANNED BROTH, OR WATER
	PLAIN YOGURT FOR GARNISH

Melt butter over medium-high heat in a large stockpot or Dutch oven. Sauté onions with salt until deep brown, about 10 minutes. Reduce heat to low and add garlic, ginger, and pepper. Cook until aromas are released, stirring constantly, about 2 minutes. Add lentils and cook an additional 3 minutes, constantly stirring so the beans are evenly cooked.

Add Chicken Stock, bring to a boil, reduce to a simmer, and cook, uncovered, about 1 hour 15 minutes. Stir soup regularly to ensure even cooking so that beans do not burn. When done, beans should be soft inside, with no chalkiness. Serve immediately, garnished with a dollop of yogurt.

6 Servings

Pistou

All the flavors of the garden ring out loud and clear in this light vegetable soup from southern France. You can substitute any vegetables that are available, or omit some, but make sure to have fresh basil on hand for the dollop of Pesto. At the restaurant, we serve this fragrant broth topped with a poached and sliced chicken breast at lunchtime.

The key to a good vegetable soup is twofold. First chop the vegetables evenly, then add them to the pot in the proper sequence. Harder vegetables (like potatoes and carrots) always precede softer vegetables (like tomatoes or zucchini), so they all cook to the same degree of tenderness.

⅓ CUP DRY WHITE BEANS (NAVY OR GREAT NORTHERN), WASHED

PESTO

2 GARLIC CLOVES, PEELED
3 TABLESPOONS EXTRA VIRGIN OLIVE OIL
1 BUNCH FRESH BASIL, LEAVES ONLY
1 CUP (4 OUNCES) FRESHLY GRATED GRUYÈRE OR PARMESAN CHEESE

2 SMALL RED POTATOES, WITH SKINS
1 LARGE CARROT, PEELED
1 SMALL ONION
1 SMALL ZUCCHINI, WITH SKIN
1 SMALL YELLOW CROOKNECK SQUASH, WITH SKIN
1 STALK OF CELERY, PEELED
1 LARGE TOMATO, PEELED, AND SEEDED (PAGE 249)
¼ POUND GREEN BEANS
8 CUPS CHICKEN STOCK (PAGE 74) OR CANNED BROTH
SALT AND FRESHLY GROUND PEPPER TO TASTE

Place beans in a small saucepan and cover with a generous amount of water. Bring to a boil and cook, uncovered, until beans are tender, about 1 hour. Drain and reserve. (To test a bean for doneness, choose a small one. Smaller beans take longer to cook because of their dense centers. The bean should taste creamy, rather than powdery, inside.)

Make Pesto by pureeing garlic, olive oil, and a few basil leaves in a blender. Gradually add remaining leaves until all are pureed. Transfer to a small bowl, add grated cheese, and stir. Set aside.

Cut each vegetable into even ½-inch dice and set aside. To avoid discoloration, reserve potatoes in a bowl of cold water.

Bring Chicken Stock to a boil in a large stockpot. Add white beans, potatoes, carrot, and onion. Return to a boil, reduce to a simmer, and cook, uncovered, 15 minutes. Add remaining vegetables and bring back to boil. Reduce to a simmer and cook an additional 10 minutes, uncovered. Season to taste with salt and pepper.

To serve, place a generous tablespoon Pesto in each bowl, add soup, and serve immediately.

6 Servings

Cold Soups

Cold soups are wonderful for warm weather entertaining. They can be prepared well in advance, then set in the refrigerator to chill while you prepare the rest of the meal or just relax. They're the ideal starter for summer barbecues as well as elegant dinner parties. And, they pack well for picnics.

Cold Sorrel Soup

Cooking the sorrel quickly, then combining it with minimal amount of stock preserves its elusive lemony flavor beautifully. This is an excellent choice for a summer dinner party where you plan to serve a strong-tasting meat like duck or lamb. This soup can also be served hot.

2	TABLESPOONS UNSALTED BUTTER
1	LARGE ONION, THINLY SLICED
2	TEASPOONS SALT
¼	TEASPOON WHITE PEPPER
6	BUNCHES SORREL, STEMS TRIMMED AND WASHED
1½	CUPS HALF AND HALF
2	CUPS WATER
	DASH OF TABASCO
1	TEASPOON FRESH LEMON JUICE

Melt butter over moderate heat in a medium stockpot or Dutch oven. Cook onion with salt and pepper until soft, about 15 minutes. Stir in sorrel and cook over moderate heat, uncovered, about 5 minutes. Stir occasionally so the sorrel is evenly cooked.

Add half and half, water, and Tabasco. Bring to a boil and remove from heat. Puree in a blender until smooth and strain through a medium sieve. Stir in lemon juice, adjust with salt and pepper, and refrigerate a minimum of 4 hours, or, to serve immediately, chill in bowl rested in another bowl of iced water. Serve cold.

6 Servings

Gazpacho

Our favorite cold soup—this smooth Gazpacho—is dressier and takes less time to prepare than the chunkier version. The vegetables can be randomly chopped since they are pureed in the food processor before being combined with a rich mayonnaise.

1	STALK OF CELERY, CHOPPED
1	TOMATO, CORED AND QUARTERED
1	SMALL GREEN BELL PEPPER, CORED AND SEEDED
1	LARGE CUCUMBER OR 4 PICKLING CUCUMBERS OR KIRBIES (PAGE 247), PEELED AND CHOPPED
5	GARLIC CLOVES, PEELED
1–2	SMALL JALAPEÑO PEPPERS, SEEDS OPTIONAL TO TASTE
2	SLICES DAY-OLD WHITE BREAD, CRUSTS REMOVED
1	(32-OUNCE) CAN TOMATO JUICE

MAYONNAISE

3	EGG YOLKS
1	TABLESPOON PAPRIKA
2	TABLESPOON TARRAGON VINEGAR OR WHITE WINE VINEGAR
1 ½	TEASPOONS SALT
1	CUP OLIVE OIL
	TABASCO TO TASTE

CHOPPED FRESH CHIVES FOR GARNISH

Process celery, tomato, bell pepper, cucumber, garlic, jalapeños, and bread in a food processor until fine. Transfer to a blender along with tomato juice and puree in batches until smooth. Strain and set aside.

Make mayonnaise by whisking together egg yolks, paprika, vinegar, and salt in a large bowl. Gradually add olive oil, one drop at a time, whisking constantly until an emulsion forms. (As the mixture thickens, you can begin adding the oil faster.) After mayonnaise is formed, start adding reserved vegetable puree ¼ cup at a time, *whisking constantly*, until thoroughly blended. Adjust with Tabasco and chill for a minimum of 2 hours. Serve in chilled bowls, with a sprinkling of chopped chives.

6 to 8 Servings

Cold Avocado Soup
with Fresh Tomato Salsa

This refreshing summer soup is as smooth and lovely as a ripe avocado. It is best served the same day, since avocados discolor quickly. For vegetarians, substitute water for the Chicken Stock.

3	RIPE AVOCADOS, HALVED, PEELED, AND SEEDED
2	TABLESPOONS OLIVE OIL
1	MEDIUM ONION, THINLY SLICED
2	CUPS CHICKEN STOCK (PAGE 74), CANNED BROTH, OR WATER
2	CUPS MILK
1½	TEASPOONS SALT
	DASH OF WHITE PEPPER
2	TABLESPOONS FRESH LIME JUICE
	FRESH TOMATO SALSA FOR GARNISH, RECIPE FOLLOWS

Roughly chop avocados and place in a large bowl. Heat oil over low heat in a large saucepan. Cook onions until soft, about 10 minutes. Add Chicken Stock, turn the heat to high, and bring to a boil. Then, pour over avocados and mix to combine.

Transfer to a blender and puree with remaining ingredients until smooth. Strain and chill for a minimum of 2 hours. Serve cold, garnished with a heaping tablespoon Fresh Tomato Salsa.

6 to 8 Servings

Fresh Tomato Salsa

2	TOMATOES WITH SKINS, SEEDS REMOVED, AND FINELY DICED
1	SMALL RED ONION, FINELY DICED
1–3	SERRANO CHILES, WITH SEEDS, FINELY DICED
1	BUNCH FRESH CILANTRO, STEMS TRIMMED AND CHOPPED
1	TEASPOON SALT
2	TABLESPOONS FRESH LIME JUICE

Mix ingredients together in a bowl and chill.

Makes 1 Cup

Cucumber Yogurt Soup

*This quick summer soup has
just enough cumin and garlic to
keep it from being ordinary. Be
fussy about choosing cucumbers,
since their flavor will determine
the overall quality of this dish.
We prefer the smaller, pale
green pickling cukes called kirbies to larger salad cucumbers.
Always trim and discard the
ends of cucumbers, where the
bitter oils collect.*

6   LARGE PICKLING CUCUMBERS OR KIRBIES (PAGE 247),
     PEELED AND ROUGHLY CHOPPED
2   TEASPOONS SALT
½   TEASPOON WHITE PEPPER
1½ TEASPOONS PUREED GARLIC (PAGE 250)
1½ TEASPOONS GROUND CUMIN
3   CUPS PLAIN YOGURT
     CHOPPED FRESH MINT LEAVES FOR GARNISH

P uree cucumbers, salt, pepper, garlic, cumin, and
     yogurt in a blender until smooth. Strain through
a medium sieve and chill a minimum of 2 hours.
Serve cold, garnished with mint.

6 Servings

Seafood Soups

From the elegant Crayfish Bisque (page 68) to the stout Geoduck Clam Chowder (page 67), each of these shellfish soups is a gem. They are a bit more demanding to prepare than other soups. Save them for an occasion when expectations are high and time is plentiful.

Clams in Cream and Thyme Broth

This is one of the simplest and best ways to cook clams. Just throw the ingredients into a pot and within minutes the shells are open and the cream is infused with the taste of the ocean and the earthy aroma of thyme. Use small tender clams, such as cockles or Manilla, for this dish. Littlenecks will do, but they are not quite as tender.

60	CLAMS, IN THE SHELL
1	CUP CLAM JUICE OR FISH STOCK (PAGE 76)
2	CUPS HEAVY CREAM
2	BUNCHES FRESH THYME, LEAVES ONLY, ROUGHLY CHOPPED
½	TEASPOON WHITE PEPPER
	SALT TO TASTE

Wash clams in cold running water and scrub with a brush to remove surface sand.

Place clams in a large saucepan with clam juice, cream, thyme, and pepper. Cover and cook over high heat, shaking occasionally, until shells open, 4 to 6 minutes. Remove from heat. Season with salt to taste. Ladle into soup bowls and serve at once.

4 to 6 Servings

Geoduck Clam Chowder

This sturdy broth is filled with the pure taste of clams. Geoducks, which measure about one foot from side to side and are available at specialty fish markets in most Chinatowns, have the most remarkable flavor we have ever tasted.

10	OUNCES FRESH CLAM MEAT, PREFERABLY GEODUCK, CUT IN 1-INCH PIECES
4	TABLESPOONS (½ STICK) UNSALTED BUTTER
1½	MEDIUM ONIONS, DICED
4	CUPS CLAM JUICE
2	CUPS HEAVY CREAM
1	LARGE CARROT, PEELED AND DICED
1	STALK OF CELERY, DICED
1	LARGE RED OR WHITE POTATO, PEELED AND DICED

BEURRE MANIÉ

½	TABLESPOON SOFTENED, UNSALTED BUTTER
1	TABLESPOON ALL-PURPOSE FLOUR

½	TEASPOON SALT
¼	TEASPOON WHITE PEPPER
2	DASHES OF TABASCO
	JUICE OF ½ LEMON

Grind clam meat in a meat grinder through large holes or food processor until roughly chopped and reserve.

Melt butter in a large stockpot over low heat. Cook onions until soft, about 5 minutes. Add clams and cook an additional 3 minutes, stirring occasionally to avoid browning.

Add clam juice, turn heat to high, and bring to a boil. Add cream, return to a boil, then reduce to a simmer. Add carrots, celery, and potato. Cook over medium-low heat, uncovered, until vegetables are tender, about 10 minutes.

Make *beurre manié* by mixing butter and flour together with your fingers to form a smooth paste. Press onto ends of a whisk and stir into soup until completely and evenly dispersed. Stir in remaining ingredients, taste and adjust seasonings, and serve immediately.

6 Servings

Crayfish or Lobster Bisque

*We learned this wonderfully re-
fined bisque while working at
Le Perroquet in Chicago, where
we each cooked the restaurant's
signature dish hundreds of
times. We can't imagine ever
growing tired of its silken texture and complex flavor. It's
pure heaven in a bowl.*

2	TABLESPOONS UNSALTED BUTTER
12	SHALLOTS, THINLY SLICED
12	MUSHROOMS, THINLY SLICED
1	CUP BRANDY
1	CUP MADEIRA
6	CUPS LOBSTER OR CRAYFISH STOCK (PAGE 69)

BEURRE MANIÉ

1	TABLESPOON SOFTENED, UNSALTED BUTTER
2	TABLESPOONS ALL-PURPOSE FLOUR

1½	CUPS HEAVY CREAM
¼	TEASPOON FRESH LEMON JUICE
	DASH OF TABASCO

Melt butter in a large stockpot over medium-high heat. Sauté shallots until golden, about 3 minutes. Add mushrooms and cook over high heat until slightly browned, about 2 additional minutes.

Remove from heat and add brandy and Madeira reserving ¼ cup of each for final seasoning. Cook over high heat until liquid is reduced by half. Add Lobster or Crayfish Stock and return to a boil. Reduce to a simmer and cook, uncovered, 15 to 30 minutes, depending on the strength of your stock. (Weaker stocks need to cook longer to concentrate their flavors.) Occasionally skim and discard foam that rises to top.

Make *beurre manié* by mixing butter and flour together with your fingers to form a smooth paste. Press onto ends of a whisk.

When broth has a strong, almost salty, lobster or crayfish flavor, add cream and bring it back to a boil, skimming foam occasionally. Then whisk in *beurre manié* until dissolved. Cook an additional 5 minutes over high heat, whisking occasionally.

Strain through a fine sieve, pressing with the back of a ladle to extract all juices. Season with lemon juice, reserved brandy and Madeira, and Tabasco, and serve immediately.

6 to 8 Servings

✕

Lobster or Crayfish Stock

This basic shellfish stock forms the base for Lobster and Vegetable Broth (page 72) and Crayfish or Lobster Bisque (page 68), as well as classic lobster sauce. We use lobster and crayfish interchangeably, although lobster has a slightly richer flavor. The stock can be refrigerated for up to 2 days or frozen indefinitely. Oftentimes, you'll find yourself with only a few lobster bodies. In that case, wrap well and reserve in the freezer until you've gathered 10 to 12.

4	(1½ POUND) LOBSTERS OR 4 POUNDS CRAYFISH
8	TABLESPOONS (1 STICK) UNSALTED BUTTER
¼	CUP OLIVE OIL
2	MEDIUM ONIONS, FINELY CHOPPED
2	CARROTS, PEELED AND CHOPPED
2	STALKS CELERY, PEELED AND CHOPPED
1½	TEASPOONS SALT
2	CUPS DRY WHITE WINE
1	CUP MADEIRA
5	CUPS FISH STOCK (PAGE 76), CLAM JUICE, OR WATER
3	CUPS TOMATO JUICE
1	HEAD GARLIC, WITH SKINS, CUT IN HALF HORIZONTALLY
½	BUNCH FRESH PARSLEY, WITH STEMS
1	TABLESPOON BLACK PEPPERCORNS
2	BAY LEAVES
1½	TEASPOONS DRIED TARRAGON
1	TEASPOON DRIED THYME
½	TEASPOON CAYENNE

Bring a large stockpot of water to a rolling boil, add lobsters, and cook at a fast boil until done, about 10 minutes. Transfer to a bowl of iced water to cool, then remove and reserve tail and claw meat for another use. Do this messy job over a bowl to reserve drippings. Crush shells, which will be the base for the stock, using a mallet or hammer, then grind as fine as possible with reserved drippings in a food processor.

Follow same procedure for crayfish, reserving tail meat and claws, if possible, then grinding shells.

Melt butter and oil in a large stockpot over medium-high heat. Cook onions, carrots, celery, and salt until golden, about 10 minutes. Stir in crushed shells, white wine, and Madeira. Turn heat to high and cook until liquid is reduced by half.

Add clam juice and tomato juice. Bring to a boil and carefully skim and discard foam that rises to surface. Add remaining ingredients and cook at a simmer, uncovered, 1 hour 15 minutes.

Strain through a fine sieve and refrigerate up to 2 days or freeze indefinitely.

Makes 6¾ Cups

✕

Mussel Bisque

*If you haven't cooked a bisque
before, this one is good to begin
with. Mussels are easy to work
with, and this recipe doesn't call
for a homemade stock. Try to
dice the vegetables as finely as
possible, so they don't distract
from the sweet silkiness of this
fine bisque.*

2	CUPS DRY WHITE WINE
1½	POUNDS MUSSELS, WASHED AND DEBEARDED (PAGE 250)
1	TABLESPOON UNSALTED BUTTER
4	MUSHROOMS, THINLY SLICED
4	SHALLOTS, THINLY SLICED
½	TEASPOON SALT
½	TEASPOON WHITE PEPPER
½	CUP PLUS 1 TABLESPOON APPLEJACK OR APPLE BRANDY
3	CUPS CLAM JUICE
3	CUPS HEAVY CREAM

BEURRE MANIÉ

½	TABLESPOON SOFTENED, UNSALTED BUTTER
1	TABLESPOON ALL-PURPOSE FLOUR

1	SMALL RED POTATO, WITH SKIN, FINELY DICED
1	SMALL STALK OF CELERY, FINELY DICED
½	CARROT, PEELED AND FINELY DICED
1	TEASPOON FRESH LEMON JUICE
	DASH OF TABASCO

Bring wine to a boil in a large saucepan. Add mussels, reduce to a simmer, and cook, covered, until shells open, about 4 minutes. Remove mussels and set aside to cool, covered with a wet towel. Strain remaining liquid through a layer of cheesecloth or towel, to remove sand, and reserve.

Melt butter in a large stockpot or Dutch oven over low heat. Cook mushrooms and shallots with salt and pepper until soft, about 5 minutes. Add ½ cup applejack, turn heat to high, and cook until liquid is reduced by half. Add clam juice and reserved liquid, and reduce by a quarter. Add cream and bring to a boil.

Meanwhile make *beurre manié* by mixing butter and flour together with your fingers to form a smooth paste. Press onto ends of a whisk.

When liquid is boiling, quickly whisk in *beurre manié* until completely and evenly dispersed. Simmer an additional 5 minutes, remove from heat, and strain. Return to pot, add remaining diced vegetables, and bring back to a boil, simmer until potatoes are tender, then remove from heat. Season with lemon juice, Tabasco, remaining tablespoon of applejack, and salt and pepper to taste.

Remove mussels from their shells and stir into the warm soup. Ladle into serving bowls and garnish each with an open shell.

6 Servings

Lobster and Vegetable Broth

There is nothing precious about this rich lobster broth. It is densely packed with noodles, vegetables, and large chunks of lobster or crayfish. What a great surprise to serve at a special lunch or light dinner with loaves of crusty French bread and a salad.

3	OUNCES VERMICELLI
6¾	CUPS LOBSTER OR CRAYFISH STOCK (PAGE 69)
3	OUNCES CHINESE SNOW PEAS OR GREEN BEANS, TRIMMED AND JULIENNED LENGTHWISE
1	LEEK, WHITE PART, WASHED, CUT IN HALF, AND THINLY SLICED ACROSS THE WIDTH
1	LARGE CARROT, PEELED AND FINELY JULIENNED RESERVED LOBSTER OR CRAYFISH MEAT FROM STOCK MAKING (PAGE 69)
4	TABLESPOONS (½ STICK) UNSALTED BUTTER, COLD
3	TABLESPOONS BALSAMIC OR SHERRY WINE VINEGAR

Bring a medium saucepan of salted water to a boil. Cook vermicelli just until al dente. Drain in colander and rinse with cold water. Reserve.

Combine Lobster or Crayfish Stock with vegetables in a large stockpot and bring to a boil. While stock is heating, cut reserved lobster tail into ½-inch slices, leaving claws whole. Add lobster or crayfish to stock and return to a boil.

Dip vermicelli into broth to warm. Divide vermicelli among serving bowls. Remove lobster meat with a slotted spoon and place on vermicelli. Ladle over broth, and garnish each with pea-sized pieces cold butter and an equal share of balsamic vinegar. Serve immediately.

8 Appetizers or 4 Entrées

Stocks

A full-bodied stock is indispensable for making terrific soups and sauces. At the restaurant, we begin each day by starting a 20-gallon pot of chicken stock and end by putting up 15-gallon pots of the brown stocks, to bubble through the night. Stocks should be as fresh and flavorful as every other ingredient.

For the best results, start with fresh vegetables. Always cook at a gentle simmer, not a boil, and skim the foam, or impurities, that rise to the top. Cook the approximate time called for, since it *is* possible to overcook stock, thereby muddling its flavors.

Before you eliminate the salt in these recipes, remember the amount in the finished product is minimal since the quantity is dispersed throughout about a gallon of stock. This salt extracts flavor from the aromatics and bones, and also acts as a preservative for stocks that are stored.

What home cooks need to learn is just how valuable the shells and bones of the meats/fish we eat are. Each time you bone chicken, duck, etc., save the bones in the freezer and then make stock. All the flavor then locked in the bones, sinews, and tendons is what makes food taste *so* good.

Chicken Stock

For great chicken soup, simply garnish this lovely broth with diced vegetables and chicken meat or, if you prefer, a starchy accompaniment like the gnocchi in Gnocchi Parmesan (page 44) or Spaetzel (page 160).

5   POUNDS CHICKEN BONES (ASK YOUR BUTCHER FOR FEET, NECKS, AND HEADS)
2   CELERY STALKS, CUT INTO 2-INCH LENGTHS
2   MEDIUM CARROTS, PEELED AND SLICED
2   MEDIUM ONIONS, QUARTERED
1   LEEK, WHITE PART, SLICED
½   BUNCH PARSLEY STEMS
2   TABLESPOONS SALT
1   TABLESPOON BLACK PEPPERCORNS
1   TABLESPOON DRIED THYME
8   BAY LEAVES

Combine chicken bones, celery, carrots, onions, leek, and parsley stems in a large stockpot. Add enough water to cover, about 2 gallons, and bring to a vigorous boil. Skim and discard foam that rises to top. Reduce to a simmer, add remaining seasonings and cook, uncovered, about 1½ hours.

Remember to check pot for foam and skim occasionally. If liquid is evaporating too rapidly, add a cup or two water. The finished stock should have the comforting flavor of good chicken soup. Strain by lifting liquid out with a ladle. Discard solids. Set aside to cool to room temperature. Store in sealed containers in refrigerator as long as 5 days or in freezer indefinitely. The fat that rises to top may be rendered (page 250) and saved for sautéing.

Makes 1½ Gallons

Brown Lamb or Veal Stock

Like chicken, lamb bones make a delicious broth or base for stews and soups. Veal stock forms the foundation for a wide range of sauces for dark meats such as beef, veal, and liver.

5	POUNDS LAMB OR VEAL BONES (ASK YOUR BUTCHER TO CRACK THE BONES FOR STOCK MAKING)
2	MEDIUM CARROTS, PEELED AND CUT INTO LARGE CHUNKS
16	WHOLE CLOVES
2	MEDIUM ONIONS, WITH SKINS, CUT IN HALF HORIZONTALLY
2	CELERY STALKS, ROUGHLY CHOPPED
1	HEAD GARLIC, WITH SKINS, CUT IN HALF HORIZONTALLY
1	LEEK, CHOPPED
2	TOMATOES, ROUGHLY CHOPPED
2	CUPS DRY WHITE WINE
1½	TABLESPOONS SALT
1	TABLESPOON DRIED THYME
1	TABLESPOON BLACK PEPPERCORNS
1	TEASPOON DRIED TARRAGON
6	BAY LEAVES

Preheat oven to 400°F. Arrange bones in one layer in a roasting pan and roast for ½ hour, until some liquid has been released. (If the pan is dry, you can add about 2 tablespoons vegetable oil to speed up the process.) Then add carrots and bake an additional ½ hour, turning carrots occasionally, until bones and carrots are thoroughly browned.

Insert 4 cloves into each onion half. Heat a dry cast-iron skillet until very hot, then char onions, flat-side down, until black.

Combine roasted bones, carrots, onions, celery, garlic, leeks, and tomatoes in a large stockpot with white wine. Bring to boil and reduce to half. Add enough water to cover, about 2 gallons. Bring to a vigorous boil. Skim and discard foam that rises to the top. Reduce to a simmer, add remaining seasonings, and cook, uncovered, skimming occasionally. Lamb stock cooks about 4 hours and veal about 8.

Strain by lifting liquid out with a ladle. Discard solids. Set aside to cool to room temperature and skim off any fat that rises to top. Brown stock may be kept in sealed containers in refrigerator up to a week or in freezer indefinitely.

Makes 3 Quarts

Fish Stock

2   TABLESPOONS UNSALTED BUTTER

1   MEDIUM WHITE ONION, SLICED

1   CELERY STALK, SLICED

1   LEEK, SLICED, WHITE AND LIGHT-GREEN PART ONLY

8   SHALLOTS, SLICED

½   BUNCH PARSLEY

1   TEASPOON SALT

2   CUPS DRY WHITE WINE

3   POUNDS FISH BONES, PREFERABLY NON-OILY TYPE LIKE HALIBUT, BASS, OR SNAPPER, WASHED AND CUT INTO CHUNKS

5   BAY LEAVES

1   TEASPOON DRIED THYME

1   TEASPOON DRIED TARRAGON

1   TEASPOON CRACKED PEPPERCORNS (PAGE 249)

Melt butter in a large heavy stockpot or saucepan over moderate heat. Cook onion, celery, leeks, shallots, parsley, and salt just until soft, about 5 minutes. Add wine, turn heat to high and reduce by half. Add bones and about 1½ gallons or enough water to cover. Bring to a boil. Skim off and discard foam that rises to top. Add remaining spices and cook at a simmer, uncovered, 1½ hours. Strain by lifting liquid out with a ladle. Discard solids. Set aside to cool to room temperature. Store in sealed containers in refrigerator 2 days or freeze indefinitely.

Makes 2 Quarts

Brown Duck Stock

CARCASSES, NECKS, FEET, AND HEADS FROM 2 DUCKS
2 CARROTS, PEELED AND CUT INTO LARGE CHUNKS
2 MEDIUM ONIONS, PEELED AND CUT INTO QUARTERS
2 CELERY STALKS, ROUGHLY CHOPPED
5 BAY LEAVES
1 BUNCH FRESH THYME OR 2 TEASPOONS DRIED
½ BUNCH FRESH TARRAGON OR 1 TEASPOON DRIED
1 BUNCH PARSLEY STEMS
1 HEAD GARLIC, CUT IN HALF HORIZONTALLY
1 TABLESPOON BLACK PEPPERCORNS
1 TABLESPOON SALT

Preheat oven to 350°F. Crack bones with a heavy cleaver and arrange in one layer on large baking sheet or roasting pan. Bake ½ hour. Add carrots and onions, and bake for an additional 15 minutes. The bones and vegetables should turn a deep brown.

Combine roasted bones, carrots, onions, and celery in a large stockpot with enough water to cover, about 2 gallons. Bring to a vigorous boil. Skim and discard foam that rises to top. Reduce to a simmer, add spices and garlic, and cook, uncovered, skimming occasionally, for 3 hours.

Strain by lifting liquid out with a ladle. Discard solids. Set aside to cool to room temperature. Skim off any fat that rises to top. Duck stock may be kept in sealed containers in refrigerator up to 5 days or in freezer indefinitely. The layer of fat that rises to top may be saved and rendered (page 250) for sautéing.

Makes 3 Quarts

3 Sandwiches and Breads

While the "serious" restaurants where we received our training—like Ma Maison and Le Perroquet—traditionally ignore sandwiches, we decided to highlight them at ours. We thought many of our customers would prefer a casual, quick meal to an appetizer and entrée in the middle of the day. We know we do.

Our sandwiches are big, messy affairs, bursting at the seams with contrasting tastes and textures. Most of them are made from ingredients we keep on hand and yet, each sandwich is special.

We hope our sandwiches will spark some ideas for using your favorite leftovers. Although sandwiches are considered a casual food, the details can make all the difference. Choose a flavorful bread and slice it thinly so people don't fill up on dough. Each bite must contain a taste of each ingredient. Serve sandwiches before they get soggy. Choose a few homemade condiments like sauerkraut, pickles, or a chutney to fill out the plate. Sandwich making (and eating) should be fun and we think these big, bold sandwiches illustrate that point well.

Sandwiches

Club Sandwich

Preheat grill. For 3 sandwiches, flatten 3 skinless, boneless slices of turkey breast (page 121). Salt and pepper generously and grill about 2 minutes per side. (Or, sauté the slices just as quickly in butter over high heat.) Cut a baguette into thirds crosswise, then in thirds lengthwise. Toast on grill or under broiler.

Fry 6 slices bacon until crisp.

Coat each slice bread with Horseradish and Mustard and Mayonnaise (page 193). On the 3 bottom pieces, place a serving of turkey, top with avocado slices, then the middle piece of bread. Cover each with 2 slices bacon, thinly sliced tomatoes, and green leaf lettuce. Top with remaining bread. Cut in half and serve with french fries, Cole Slaw (page 182), and pickles.

Fried Egg with Canadian Bacon and Mustard Greens

For 6 sandwiches, toast 12 pieces Potato Bread (page 88) and spread 6 with Horseradish and Mustard and Mayonnaise (page 193). Sauté one bunch julienned mustard greens in butter (page 186). Cook 18 slices Canadian bacon until heated through, about 1 minute per side.

Cover the 6 coated pieces toast with mustard greens, bacon, and thinly sliced tomatoes. Melt 1 tablespoon butter in a large skillet over moderate heat. Fry 6 eggs until yolks are just set, about 1 minute per side. Set each egg atop a plain piece toast. Place egg covered piece on top of tomato to form sandwich. Slice in half and serve with Cole Slaw (page 182), olives, and french fries.

Lamb with Sautéed Eggplant and Onion Marmalade on Naan

Make the Onion Marmalade and let cool.
For 6 sandwiches, marinate ½ pound Bulgarian feta cheese in olive oil (page 246). Slice a medium eggplant in ¼-inch rounds and sauté in ⅔ cup olive oil until golden brown.

Preheat oven to 350°F. Using a serrated knife, slice 6 pieces of Naan (page 89) in half horizontally. Transfer to large baking sheet, cut sides up. Generously spread 6 pieces with Horseradish and Mustard and Mayonnaise (page 193). Cover with eggplant and thinly sliced tomatoes.

Spread remaining 6 pieces with Onion Marmalade. Top with thinly sliced Herb Stuffed Leg of Lamb (page 98) and crumbled feta cheese. Cover each sandwich half with a damp paper towel. Cook until heated through, about 3 minutes. Remove paper towels and combine the halves to form sandwiches. Cut in half and serve immediately.

Onion Marmalade

½ STICK UNSALTED BUTTER
3 MEDIUM ONIONS, THINLY SLICED
1 TEASPOON SALT
1 TEASPOON WHITE PEPPER
⅓ CUP CHICKEN STOCK (PAGE 74)
1 TEASPOON PUREED GARLIC (PAGE 250)

Melt butter in a large skillet over moderate heat. Add onions, salt, and pepper. Cook until onions are deep, golden brown, stirring occasionally, about 20 minutes. Add garlic, sweat 1 to 2 minutes, then add Chicken Stock and reduce heat to low. Cook, stirring frequently, about 25 minutes or until mixture is the consistency of marmalade. Set aside to cool to room temperature. (You can make this a day in advance and reserve in refrigerator.)

Roasted Pork
with Two Cabbages

For 3 sandwiches, cut a baguette in thirds crosswise, then in half horizontally, or substitute 6
pieces of rye bread. Grill or toast bread in broiler
and spread both sides with Horseradish and Mustard
and Mayonnaise (page 193). Cover the 3 bottom
pieces with a layer of Sweet and Sour Red Cabbage
(page 190), then add warm, thinly sliced Roasted
Pork Shoulder (page 103). Cover the 3 top pieces
with about ¼ cup Sauerkraut (page 197), cover with
slices of Swiss cheese, and broil 2 minutes. Close the
bread to form sandwiches. Cut in half and serve.

Skirt Steak on Rye Bread

For 4 sandwiches, toast 8 slices of thickly sliced
rye bread and lightly butter. (If the grill is hot,
coat the bread with butter and toast on the grill.)
Spread about 1½ tablespoons Horseradish and Mustard and Mayonnaise (page 193) on each slice. Cover
4 slices with romaine lettuce, thinly sliced tomatoes,
then sliced Marinated Skirt Steak (page 95). Top with
remaining toast to form sandwiches. Cut in half and
serve with french fries and a watercress salad.

Smoked Chicken Salad and
Sweet and Sour Cabbage

For 3 sandwiches, cut a baguette crosswise into
thirds, then slice each third in half lengthwise.
Pull out about half the doughy center and reserve
for another use (i.e., fine dry bread crumbs). Spread
stoneground mustard over each piece. Cover 3 pieces
of bread with ¾ cup Sweet and Sour Red Cabbage
(page 190). Top with Smoked Chicken Salad (page
144), then romaine lettuce. Top with the remaining
bread to form sandwiches.

Hot Brisket of Beef Sandwiches

For 6 sandwiches, reheat thinly sliced Beef Brisket (page 97) in its sauce with 6 julienned Dill Pickles (page 199). Cut 2 baguettes in thirds crosswise, then in half horizontally. Arrange bread cut-side up on baking sheet and broil until toasted. Spread generously with Horseradish and Mustard and Mayonnaise (page 193). Place warm meat mixture over 6 slices of bread. Top with thinly sliced tomatoes and green leaf lettuce. Cover with remaining bread. Cut in half and serve warm with Greek Potato Salad (page 170) and Sweet and Sour Red Cabbage (page 190).

Grilled Chicken and Baba Ghanoush

Preheat grill or broiler. For 4 sandwiches, season 4 boneless chicken leg and thigh pieces (with skin) with salt and pepper. Grill about 5 minutes per side. Lightly butter 4 pita breads and toast on grill.

Cut off and discard about 2 inches off top of each pita. Spread ⅓ cup Roasted Eggplant and Sesame (baba ghanoush) (page 176) inside each pita. Slice chicken thinly, across grain. Arrange slices over baba ghanoush and top with thinly sliced tomatoes and romaine lettuce. Serve warm. Can also be served on our homemade buns.

Breads

Bread baking best captures the essential magic of cooking. It always seems amazing that by simply combining some yeast, flour and water with a few other ingredients, letting it sit for awhile, and applying heat, something as deeply satisfying as bread emerges.

Bread is such an important part of the meal, we suggest you choose it as carefully as the other courses. Here are a few of our specialty breads to get the ideas flowing.

Banana Nut Bread

It takes about *10* minutes to mix this basic quickbread. At the restaurant we serve it with a fruit plate and our own Home-made Yogurt (page *195*) at lunch. It's also nice at break-fast, spread with cream cheese.

8   TABLESPOONS (1 STICK) BUTTER, SOFTENED
1   CUP GRANULATED SUGAR
2   LARGE EGGS
3   RIPE BANANAS
1   TABLESPOON MILK
1   CUP WALNUTS, COARSELY CHOPPED
2   CUPS ALL-PURPOSE FLOUR
1   TEASPOON SALT
1   TEASPOON BAKING SODA
1   TEASPOON BAKING POWDER

Preheat oven to 325°F. Butter a 9 x 5 x 3-inch loaf pan.

Cream butter and sugar until light and fluffy. Add eggs, one at a time, beating well after each addition.

In a small bowl, mash bananas with a fork. Mix in milk and nuts.

In another bowl, mix together flour, salt, baking soda, and baking powder.

Add banana mixture to creamed mixture and stir until combined. Add dry ingredients, mixing just until flour disappears.

Pour batter into pan and bake 1 hour to 1 hour 10 minutes, until a toothpick inserted in center comes out clean. Set aside to cool on rack in pan about 15 minutes. Remove from pan, invert, and cool completely on rack.

Makes 1 Loaf

What could be better than fresh hamburger buns? These freeze well, so you can make the recipe, divide into individual balls, wrap, freeze, and defrost as needed. In addition to salt and pepper, try sprinkling the tops with sesame, poppy, or caraway seeds. And don't limit these lovely buns to vehicles for hamburgers. They're great for holding barbecued beef, sloppy Joe's, or plain old tuna salad.

Hamburger Buns

1	CUP WATER
5	TABLESPOONS UNSALTED BUTTER
2	TABLESPOONS GRANULATED SUGAR
1½	TEASPOONS SALT
1	TABLESPOON DRY YEAST
⅓	CUP WARM WATER
1	EGG
3½	CUPS ALL-PURPOSE FLOUR
1	EGG, BEATEN FOR WASH
	COARSE SALT AND CRACKED BLACK PEPPER FOR SPRINKLING

Bring water to a boil. In a large bowl, combine boiling water with butter, sugar, and salt. Set aside to cool to lukewarm, about 110°F.

Combine yeast and warm water. Stir and set aside until foamy. Add dissolved yeast to water and butter mixture. Add egg and 1 cup flour. Beat at low speed until batter is lump-free. Cover with plastic wrap and set aside in a warm place until doubled and foamy, about 30 minutes.

Add remaining flour and beat until mixture becomes elastic, about 5 minutes. Transfer to buttered plastic container, cover, and refrigerate overnight. Occasionally check dough and punch down.

The next day, divide dough into 9 pieces. Lightly knead each to form a bun and set aside to rest on parchment-lined baking sheet, at room temperature until doubled, ½ hour.

Preheat oven to 375°F. Brush tops with egg wash and sprinkle with salt and pepper. Bake 15 to 20 minutes, until lightly browned. Set aside to cool.

Makes 8 to 10 Buns

For hamburgers for 6: mix 3 pounds ground beef with 1 onion, diced, and 3 garlic cloves, minced. Divide into 6 patties, sprinkle with salt and pepper, and grill over high heat.

Brioche

For a perfect golden loaf of cakelike bread make sure your eggs and butter are the proper temperature and allow enough time for a long, slow rising. Thanks to its richness, this bread freezes well. At the restaurant we slice it thinly and spread with liver pâté or cream cheese, chives, and smoked fish for canapés. At home, it makes heavenly toast.

2   TEASPOONS DRY YEAST
¼   CUP WARM WATER
1   TABLESPOON GRANULATED SUGAR
1   TEASPOON SALT
4   EGGS, ROOM TEMPERATURE
2   CUPS ALL-PURPOSE FLOUR
12   TABLESPOONS (1½ STICKS) UNSALTED BUTTER, COOL
     BUT PLIABLE

Combine yeast and water. Stir to dissolve and set aside.

In a large bowl, stir together sugar, salt, and eggs. Add dissolved yeast mixture and flour. Using an electric mixer, slowly beat about 2 minutes. Increase speed to medium and continue mixing until dough is stringy, about 5 minutes.

With machine running, add butter, a small piece at a time, beating until incorporated. It is important that the butter be the perfect temperature here—not hard, not soft, but sort of plastic-feeling. The dough should be wet and sticky.

Place dough in a buttered bowl, cover with buttered plastic wrap, and set aside in warm place to rise about ½ hour. Punch down, return to bowl, and let rise slowly, in refrigerator, overnight.

On a generously floured board (you may need to flour your fingers—this dough is so sticky), gently knead dough just until a loaf can be formed. Butter a 9 × 5 × 3-inch loaf pan. Place dough in pan, cover with plastic, and set aside in a warm place to rise until doubled, about 45 minutes.

Meanwhile preheat oven to 375°F. Bake 35 to 40 minutes, until bread sounds hollow when tapped. Turn out and cool on a rack.

Makes 1 Loaf

Potato Bread

A potato gives this wonderful sandwich bread a crumbly, earthy quality and a surprisingly light texture. The recipe comes from the Milliken family's Irish side.

1	BAKING POTATO, PEELED AND CUT INTO LARGE CHUNKS, OR 1 CUP LEFTOVER MASHED POTATOES
1	CUP MILK
1½	TABLESPOONS LARD
1½	TABLESPOONS UNSALTED BUTTER
1½	TEASPOONS SALT
1	TABLESPOON GRANULATED SUGAR
1	TABLESPOON DRY YEAST
⅓	CUP WARM WATER
5	CUPS BREAD FLOUR

Boil potato until soft. Drain and reserve cooking liquid. Rice the potato through a food mill.

Scald milk and combine with ½ cup reserved cooking liquid. Combine liquids and potato with lard, butter, salt, and sugar in a large bowl. Set aside to cool to room temperature.

Meanwhile combine yeast and warm water, and set aside until foamy. When potato mixture has cooled, add yeast mixture. Add flour and knead with a dough hook, on an electric mixer, until smooth and glossy, about 7 minutes.

Transfer to a buttered bowl, cover with plastic wrap, and set aside in warm place to rise about ½ hour. Punch dough down and briefly knead. Butter a 9 × 5 × 3-inch loaf pan. Place dough in pan, cover with plastic, and let rise until doubled, about 45 minutes.

Preheat oven to 350°F. Bake 30 minutes, until bread sounds hollow when tapped.

Makes 1 Loaf

Naan

Naan—an Indian puffy bread—is traditionally baked on the sides of a red-hot tandoor oven. We've forfeited puffiness and developed a great sour flavor in this adaptation for the American kitchen.

1	CUP WARM WATER, 110°F
1	TABLESPOON GRANULATED SUGAR
1	TABLESPOON DRY YEAST
1	CUP PLAIN YOGURT
1	TABLESPOON SALT
4¾	CUPS BREAD FLOUR
¼	CUP YOGURT FOR SPREADING
	BLANCHED GARLIC SLIVERS, SAUTÉED DICED ONION, SESAME SEEDS, OR COARSE SALT FOR GARNISH

Combine water, sugar and yeast. Set aside until foamy.

In bowl of an electric mixer fitted with a dough hook, combine yogurt, salt, and yeast mixture. With the machine running at medium speed, add flour and knead until smooth and elastic, about 10 minutes.

Coat a bowl with butter. Transfer kneaded dough to bowl, cover with plastic wrap, and set aside to rise at room temperature, about 45 minutes.

Coat a sheet pan with vegetable oil. Punch down dough and divide into 12 equal pieces. Knead each by hand to form a roll and place on baking sheet. Cover with oiled parchment paper or plastic wrap and set aside to rise until doubled, about 15 minutes.

Preheat oven to 550°F.

Stretch each piece (or roll with a pin) to form a 5-inch long oblong. Let rise an additional 5 minutes. Before baking, transfer to a dry sheet pan. Spread a teaspoon yogurt in center of each and sprinkle with garlic, onion, or other toppings. Bake about 12 minutes, until golden.

Makes 12 Individual Breads

4 Entrées

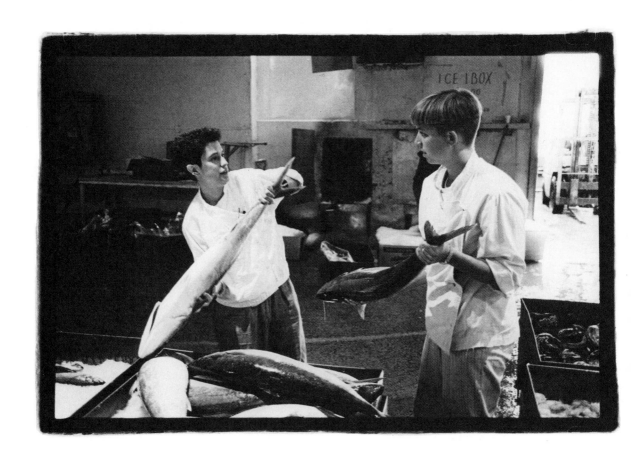

Beef, Lamb, Pork, Veal, and Other Meats

If there is a common theme to our meat entrées, it is the uncommon cut of meat. Our hearts inevitably go out to the neglected and often inexpensive cuts like lamb shank, pork shoulder, beef short ribs, and veal breast. While it takes more time and effort to cook them, they deliver the deep flavors and gaminess we look for in a meat.

A great advantage to using unusual cuts is that they allow us to offer our guests something they don't ordinarily cook at home, and in ample portions. Organ meats, like liver and kidney, are a great bargain. Properly cleaned of tendons (you can ask the butcher to do this) and cooked quickly, they can be as luxurious as the finest tenderloin, at one-quarter the price. We hope you'll give them a try.

Marinated Beef Short Ribs

Thin beef short ribs are first roasted and basted to break down tough tendons then marinated in a delicious Oriental barbecue sauce before a quick trip to the grill. We love to eat them in combination with Spicy Cold Soba Noodles (page 164) and Chopped Tofu with Parsley salad (page 156).

The key to this popular dish lies in the correct cut of short ribs. Ask a butcher to cut from the short plate, flanken style. The ribs should be cut across the bones in half-inch slices, leaving not a single rib, but a small cross section of about four ribs in each piece.

3¾   POUNDS BEEF SHORT RIBS, CUT IN ½-INCH SLICES
       WITH BONES
       SALT AND FRESHLY GROUND PEPPER TO TASTE
½   CUP WATER
2   TABLESPOONS FRESH LEMON JUICE
1   TEASPOON DRIED RED PEPPER FLAKES

MARINADE

¼   CUP HOISIN SAUCE (PAGE 247)
3   TABLESPOONS PLUM SAUCE (PAGE 248)
2   TABLESPOONS OYSTER SAUCE (PAGE 248)
2   TABLESPOONS SOY SAUCE
1   TABLESPOON PEANUT OIL
1   TABLESPOON SESAME OIL
1   TABLESPOON HONEY
1   TABLESPOON CHILI PASTE (PAGE 247)
1   TABLESPOON PUREED GARLIC (PAGE 250)
1   TABLESPOON FRESHLY GRATED GINGER (PAGE 249)
1   BUNCH CILANTRO, STEMS TRIMMED AND ROUGHLY
       CHOPPED
1   BUNCH SCALLIONS, FINELY CHOPPED

Preheat oven to 350°F.
Season ribs with salt and pepper. Lay across a rack in a roasting pan or baking sheet and bake 10 minutes. In a small bowl, combine water, lemon juice, and red pepper flakes. Brush over top side of ribs and bake an additional 10 minutes. Turn, brush again, and bake 10 minutes more. Set aside to cool.

Combine marinade ingredients in a large bowl. Add roasted ribs and toss to coat. Cover with plastic wrap and refrigerate a minimum of 4 hours or as long as 24.

Preheat grill or broiler. Grill for 2 minutes per side and serve immediately with Spicy Cold Soba Noodles (page 164) and Chopped Tofu with Parsley (page 156).

6 Servings

Grilled Pepper Steak
with Tamarind Chutney

Chutneys are often used in India, instead of elaborate sauces, to cool down a hot taste. In this barbecued dish, tart tamarind supplies the perfect complement to the steak's hot peppery crust. If you prefer a less spicy steak and more aromatic flavors, mix equal parts celery seed, cracked black peppercorns, mustard seeds, and sesame seeds. Rib eye is fattier than sirloin, but in our eyes much more flavorful.

6 (12-OUNCE) BEEF RIB EYE OR SIRLOIN STEAKS
½ CUP CRACKED BLACK PEPPERCORNS (PAGE 249)
SALT TO TASTE
TAMARIND CHUTNEY, RECIPE FOLLOWS

Preheat heavy-bottomed pan. Coat steaks generously on both sides with cracked peppercorns and sprinkle with salt. Sauté steaks, being careful not to burn the pepper, about 8 minutes per side, for medium rare. (We like to sear the edges of steak to brown the fat, thereby releasing more flavor.)

Spread a thin layer Tamarind Chutney on 6 serving plates. Place steaks on top and serve remaining chutney in ramekins.

6 Servings

Tamarind Chutney

If tamarind is not available, a sweet mango chutney would be good.

1 POUND DRY TAMARIND (PAGE 248) OR ½ CUP PULP
2½ TEASPOONS BROWN SUGAR
2 TEASPOONS FRESHLY GRATED GINGER (PAGE 249)
¼ TEASPOON SALT
DASH OF WHITE PEPPER

If using dry tamarind, extract pulp by first removing the hard outer pods. Place fruit in a medium saucepan and add enough water to cover. Bring to a boil and cook, uncovered, until flesh is soft, about 20 minutes. Push through a strainer and discard any seeds or bits of shell.

Combine pulp in a bowl with remaining ingredients. Chutney may be kept in refrigerator up to 5 days.

Makes ¾ Cup

Marinated Skirt Steak
with Horseradish Mustard

You can't go wrong with skirt steak for informal outdoor gatherings. This inexpensive, well-marbled cut benefits from long marination and cooking over high heat. Just slice it thinly and serve with simple accompaniments like baked potatoes or grilled corn and beer.

3	POUNDS SKIRT STEAK
1	CUP OLIVE OIL
2	TABLESPOONS RED WINE VINEGAR
½	CUP SOY SAUCE
2	TEASPOONS PUREED GARLIC (PAGE 250)
2	TEASPOONS DRY MUSTARD
2	TEASPOONS WORCESTERSHIRE SAUCE
1	TEASPOON TABASCO
1	TEASPOON CRACKED BLACK PEPPER
	HORSERADISH MUSTARD FOR GARNISH, RECIPE FOLLOWS

Trim steak of any outer pieces of fat or silver skin. Marbling within beef should remain. Combine remaining ingredients in a bowl. Place steak in a medium glass or ceramic roasting pan and add marinade, making sure beef is entirely covered. Cover with plastic wrap and refrigerate a minimum of 8 hours or as long as 2 days.

When marination is complete, grill or sauté meat. If grilling, a very hot, high fire is best. (We prefer a hardwood charcoal such as mesquite, oak, or cherry.) Grill meat 2 minutes per side, for rare. Or sear in a sauté pan, 2 minutes per side, in 2 tablespoons vegetable oil over high heat.

To serve, slice thinly, at an angle, across grain. Fan slices on serving plates and add small mounds of Fried Onions (page 104), Sweet and Sour Red Cabbage (page 190), and Horseradish Mustard.

6 Servings

Horseradish Mustard

1	CUP STONEGROUND MUSTARD
¾	CUP FRESHLY GRATED OR JARRED WHITE HORSERADISH

Mix and serve with Marinated Skirt Steak.

Makes 1¾ Cups

This hearty marinade marries well with the strong taste of beef and fragrant Gorgonzola and Madeira in the sauce. Serve along with our thin Roasted Potatoes (page 166) to meat and potato lovers.

Marinated Rib Eye
with Gorgonzola Sauce

4   (10-OUNCE) BEEF RIB EYE OR SIRLOIN STEAKS

MARINADE

1   CUP OLIVE OIL
2   TABLESPOONS DRY MUSTARD
1   TABLESPOON WORCESTERSHIRE SAUCE
1   TEASPOON MINCED GARLIC
1   TEASPOON SOY SAUCE
1   TEASPOON FRESH LEMON JUICE
    DASH OF TABASCO
    SALT AND FRESHLY GROUND PEPPER TO TASTE

4   TABLESPOONS (½ STICK) UNSALTED BUTTER, COLD
6   SHALLOTS, FINELY DICED
⅔   CUP MADEIRA
1½   CUPS BROWN VEAL STOCK (PAGE 75)
4–6   OUNCES (½ TO ¾ CUP) GORGONZOLA CHEESE, CRUMBLED

Trim steaks of all fat. Combine marinade ingredients in a large container. Add steaks, cover, and refrigerate at least 6 hours or as long as 24. Remove meat from refrigerator 2 hours before serving time to enhance flavors.

Preheat grill or broiler.

Melt 2 tablespoons butter in a medium skillet or saucepan over medium-high heat. Sauté shallots until brown. Add Madeira and cook until wine is reduced by half. Add Brown Veal Stock and reduce again by half. Reduce heat to moderate. Break remaining butter into small pieces and whisk into sauce until smooth. Whisk in crumbled cheese and remove from heat.

Grill or broil steaks 5 minutes per side for medium-rare. Place on warm serving plates, top with sauce, and serve immediately.

4 Servings

Beef Brisket

Brisket is easy to cook and great to have on hand for a comforting winter meal. It reheats beautifully for sandwiches or weeknight suppers with Mashed Potatoes (page 174) or potato pancakes and homemade Apple Sauce (page 198). If you prefer a thinner sauce, just ladle the broth over the sliced meat and chopped vegetables.

3½	POUNDS BEEF BRISKET
4	TABLESPOONS PAPRIKA
2	TEASPOONS SALT
1	TEASPOON WHITE PEPPER
¼	CUP ALL-PURPOSE FLOUR
½	CUP VEGETABLE OIL OR CHICKEN FAT
2	MEDIUM ONIONS, SLICED
4	CARROTS, PEELED AND SLICED
2	CELERY STALKS, SLICED
2	TABLESPOONS TOMATO PASTE
3	BAY LEAVES
1	TEASPOON DRIED THYME
½	TEASPOON CRACKED BLACK PEPPER
	SALT TO TASTE
3	QUARTS WATER

Preheat oven to 350°F. Sprinkle meat generously with paprika, salt, and pepper. Spread flour on a large platter and dip brisket to evenly coat.

Heat oil in a large Dutch oven over high heat. Brown meat on all sides until crusty. Remove from pan and reserve. Add onions, carrots, and celery, and cook until golden, about 5 minutes. Add tomato paste and cook 2 minutes. Add remaining ingredients and meat, and bring to a boil. Cover and transfer to oven. Bake 1 hour on each side or until the meat slips easily off a fork.

Transfer meat to cutting board and set aside 10 minutes before slicing. Carefully skim and discard fat from cooking liquid in pot. Discard bay leaves. Puree remaining sauce and vegetables in a blender. Strain through a sieve. Taste and adjust seasonings. Slice meat thinly across grain, top with warm sauce, and serve immediately.

6 Servings

Beef Stroganoff

Our updated Beef Stroganoff is easy and elegant—great for company. By using beef tenderloin to make this old favorite, preparation time has been cut dramatically. The simple creamed sauce can be made ahead and reheated while you prepare the noodles and sear the beef.

2½	POUNDS BEEF TENDERLOIN, TRIMMED
1	TABLESPOON UNSALTED BUTTER
2½	CUPS SLICED MUSHROOM CAPS
¼	TEASPOON SALT
	DASH OF PEPPER
1½	CUPS DILL PICKLES WITH 2 TABLESPOONS PICKLE JUICE, JULIENNED
2	CUPS HEAVY CREAM
	SALT AND FRESHLY GROUND PEPPER TO TASTE
2	TABLESPOONS VEGETABLE OIL

Remove any silver skin surrounding tenderloin and cut into 1-inch slices, across width. Slightly flatten slices by pressing with the palm of your hand. Set aside.

Melt butter in a medium skillet over medium-high heat. Sauté mushrooms with salt and pepper until golden, about 5 minutes. Add pickles and juice, and cook until juice evaporates slightly, about 2 minutes. Add cream and cook until reduced by half. While sauce is reducing, cook beef.

Season meat sparingly with salt and pepper, since sauce will be salty from the pickles. Heat a heavy large skillet over high heat, add oil and heat until it starts smoking. Sear meat briefly, two minutes per side for medium-rare. Serve beef over a bed of Homemade Fettuccine (page 163), with warm sauce ladled over all.

6 Servings

Herb Stuffed Leg of Lamb
with Pimento Sauce

By removing the center bone, leg of lamb is much easier to carve and serve to guests. Feel free to increase the amount of garlic and herbs to taste; this strongly flavored meat is enhanced by assertive seasonings.

1	(6-POUND) BONELESS LEG OF LAMB, WITH SHANK
	SALT AND FRESHLY GROUND PEPPER TO TASTE
3	TABLESPOONS PUREED GARLIC (PAGE 250)
½	CUP ASSORTED CHOPPED FRESH HERBS, SUCH AS PARSLEY, OREGANO, BASIL, THYME, CHIVES, MINT
2	TABLESPOONS OLIVE OIL
	PIMENTO SAUCE, RECIPE FOLLOWS

Ask a butcher to remove all bones, except shank, and to clean meat of all sinew and excess fat inside and out. Butterfly leg for stuffing.

Preheat oven to 375°F. Lay lamb flat on counter. Using a sharp knife, make several slits, about 2-inches long by ¼-inch deep, so seasonings can penetrate meat. Sprinkle generously with salt and pepper. Spread garlic evenly on top, then cover with herbs. Roll meat to enclose stuffing and tie with string at 1-inch intervals, keeping the diameter of the roll the same so that the roast cooks evenly. Shank bone will protrude at one end. Generously season outside with salt and pepper.

Heat oil in a large skillet over high heat. Brown lamb on all sides. Roast on rack in roasting pan 30 to 40 minutes for medium-rare, 1 hour for well done. (A meat thermometer inserted in center should read 160 to 165°F or a thin-bladed knife inserted to the center for 20 seconds should feel lukewarm on your lips.) Let sit at room temperature about 10 minutes before carving, so juices can run to center. Remove strings and slice meat thinly across the roll. Top with Pimento Sauce and serve with a side dish of City Ratatouille (page 192). To reheat carved lamb, place slices on a sheet pan, cover with a wet towel, and bake 5 minutes at 375°F.

Use leftovers for sandwiches (page 81).

6 Servings   ✕

Pimento Sauce

2   TABLESPOONS OLIVE OIL
5   SHALLOTS, FINELY SLICED
½   CUP MUSHROOMS, SLICED
¾   CUP DRY WHITE WINE
5   CUPS BROWN LAMB STOCK (PAGE 75) OR CANNED BEEF BROTH
1   TEASPOON TOMATO PASTE
3   TABLESPOONS PIMENTO OR ROASTED RED PEPPER PUREED IN BLENDER (WITH LAMB STOCK IF NECESSARY)
1   TEASPOON PUREED GARLIC (PAGE 250)
1   TABLESPOON UNSALTED BUTTER, COLD
    SALT AND FRESHLY GROUND PEPPER, TO TASTE

Heat oil in a medium saucepan over moderate heat. Cook shallots and mushrooms until golden. Add wine, turn heat to high, and reduce by half. Add Brown Lamb Stock and reduce again by a quarter. Whisk in tomato paste, pimento puree, and garlic. Break butter into small pieces and whisk into sauce until smooth. Adjust seasonings and strain through a fine sieve. Serve warm with sliced, roasted lamb or Moussaka.

Moussaka

MEAT FILLING

2   TABLESPOONS OLIVE OIL
1   LARGE ONION, DICED
2   POUNDS GROUND LAMB (LEFTOVER LAMB CAN BE
    GROUND AND USED)
2   TABLESPOONS PUREED GARLIC (PAGE 250)
4   TOMATOES, PEELED, SEEDED, AND DICED
½   CUP BRANDY
½   CUP TARRAGON VINEGAR
2   TABLESPOONS GROUND CUMIN
1   TABLESPOON SALT
½   TEASPOON WHITE PEPPER

Preheat oven to 400°F. Heat oil in a large ovenproof skillet over moderate heat. Cook onions
until soft. Add lamb and garlic, and cook until
browned, stirring occasionally. When meat is well-
browned, stir in remaining ingredients. Transfer to
oven and bake until quite dry, about 45 minutes. Set
aside to cool.

EGGPLANT

3   LARGE EGGPLANTS, WITH SKINS
    COARSE SALT
2   CUPS OLIVE OIL

Cut eggplants into ¼-inch slices, lengthwise. Sprinkle
with salt on both sides and let rest on a rack until
moisture rises to surface, about 30 minutes. Pat dry
with paper towels. Heat oil in a large skillet over
medium-high heat. Fry eggplant briefly, 1 to 2 minutes per side. Set aside to drain on paper towels.

VEGETABLE FILLING

3   CARROTS, PEELED AND THINLY SLICED
1   CUP (4 OUNCES) CHINESE SNOW PEAS
2   LEEKS, WHITE AND LIGHT GREEN PARTS, CUT IN HALF
3   CELERY STALKS, PEELED AND CUT INTO 1-INCH
    LENGTHS
2   CUPS MUSHROOM CAPS
4   TABLESPOONS (½ STICK) UNSALTED BUTTER
½   TEASPOON SALT

Wash and dry all vegetables, then cut into fine julienne. Blanch carrots and peas in a small saucepan of salted boiling water just until water returns to a boil. Refresh in cold water, drain, and reserve.

Melt butter in a medium skillet over moderate heat. Cook leeks along with salt 1 minute, add celery and cook 1 minute, then mushrooms and cook an additional minute. Set aside to cool. Toss all vegetables together in a large bowl and reserve.

CUSTARD

9	EGGS
2¼	CUPS HEAVY CREAM
1¼	TEASPOONS SALT
¼	TEASPOON WHITE PEPPER
¼	TEASPOON FRESHLY GRATED NUTMEG
¾	CUP GRATED PARMESAN CHEESE

Combine eggs, cream, salt, pepper, and nutmeg in a bowl. Whisk until smooth. Pass through a strainer to remove any stray eggshells. Whisk in Parmesan cheese and set aside.

1	RECIPE PIMENTO SAUCE (PAGE 99)

To assemble: Preheat oven to 350°F. Stir one-third custard into meat filling. Combine remaining custard with vegetable filling.

In a 9×13-inch roasting pan or casserole, arrange one-third eggplant slices to completely cover bottom. (The slices may overlap. That's fine.) Spread half meat filling on top, then cover with another third eggplant. Pour all vegetables in custard on top. Cover with remaining eggplant, then spread remaining meat mixture evenly over top.

Place pan inside a larger roasting pan and pour boiling water into roasting pan until it rises halfway up the sides of the moussaka pan. Bake, uncovered, until custard is set in center, about 1½ hours. You can test for doneness by sticking a knife in center, then pressing area around knife. If custard oozes out, cook longer.

Cut into individual portions and lift out with a spatula. Serve immediately, topped with Pimento Sauce. Moussaka can be made 1 or 2 days in advance and reheated in a 325°F oven 25 minutes.

10 to 12 Servings   ✕

Braised Lamb Shanks
with Oregano and Feta

Inexpensive cuts like the shank take longer to cook, but the resulting flavors are deeper and more satisfying than more expensive cuts. In this Greek peasant dish—similar to ossobuco—the meat flakes off the bone into a delicious tomato and herb broth.

6   LAMB SHANKS, TRIMMED OF EXCESS FAT
     SALT AND FRESHLY GROUND PEPPER, TO TASTE
1   CUP ALL-PURPOSE FLOUR
1   CUP VEGETABLE OIL
3   MEDIUM ONIONS, THINLY SLICED
3   QUARTS BROWN LAMB STOCK (PAGE 75) OR CANNED
     CHICKEN BROTH
4   BUNCHES OREGANO, STEMS AND LEAVES SEPARATED,
     LEAVES CHOPPED
¼   TEASPOON CAYENNE
2   LARGE TOMATOES, PEELED, SEEDED, AND DICED
     (PAGE 249)
1   CUP FETA CHEESE, CRUMBLED

Generously sprinkle shanks with salt and pepper, then dip in flour to lightly coat. Heat oil in a large Dutch oven over high heat. Brown shanks on all sides, transfer to a platter, and reserve.

Reduce heat to medium and cook onions in same pan, stirring occasionally, until golden brown. Return shanks to pan. Add Brown Lamb Stock, all oregano stems, half oregano leaves, and cayenne. (If shanks are not completely covered by liquid, add enough water to cover.) Bring to a boil, reduce to a simmer, and cook, covered, about 1½ hours, occasionally skimming foam and fat that rise to top. To test for doneness, pierce with a fork. If shank slides easily off fork, meat is tender. Remove from heat.

Using a slotted spoon and a fork, lift out lamb shanks. Cover with a damp towel and set aside in a warm place. Pass sauce through a fine sieve into a medium saucepan, pressing with a ladle to extract all juices. Skim fat from top and bring sauce to a boil. Stir in tomatoes and remaining oregano, and remove from heat.

To serve, arrange a shank on top a bed of bulgur wheat (page 246) in each serving bowl. Sprinkle feta cheese evenly over each shank, add sauce, and serve immediately.

6 Servings

Roasted Pork Shoulder

Caraway and mustard balance the strong flavor of pork, without overpowering it. We like to arrange warm platters of this comforting meat with accompaniments like Sweet and Sour Red Cabbage (page 190) and Sautéed Mustard Greens (page 186), or use it in sandwiches.

3½	POUNDS PORK SHOULDER, TRIMMED AND BUTTERFLIED
1½	TEASPOONS SALT
1	TEASPOON WHITE PEPPER
1	TABLESPOON DRY MUSTARD
1	TABLESPOON HONEY
2	TABLESPOONS PLUS ½ TEASPOON VEGETABLE OIL
½	TEASPOON WATER
2	TABLESPOONS CARAWAY SEEDS
10	TABLESPOONS (1 STICK PLUS 2 TABLESPOONS) UNSALTED BUTTER, COLD
6	TABLESPOONS MINCED SHALLOTS
¾	CUP RED WINE VINEGAR
¾	CUP BROWN VEAL STOCK (PAGE 75) OR CHICKEN STOCK (PAGE 74)
½	CUP HEAVY CREAM
	SALT AND FRESHLY GROUND PEPPER TO TASTE

Preheat oven to 400°F. Lay meat flat on counter and, using a sharp knife, make several slits about ¼-inch deep by 1-inch long. Sprinkle with salt and pepper.

In a small bowl, make a paste with mustard, honey, ½ teaspoon oil, and water. Spread mixture evenly over meat, then cover with caraway seeds. Press seasonings into slashes with your fingers to infuse meat with flavor. Roll meat, along the length, to enclose stuffing and tie with string at 1-inch intervals. Season outside with salt and pepper.

Heat remaining 2 tablespoons oil in a large skillet over high heat. Cook meat until brown all over, then transfer to rack in roasting pan. Bake, uncovered, 45 minutes, or until juices run clear when pierced with a sharp knife.

Just before serving, make sauce. Melt 4 tablespoons butter in a medium skillet over moderate heat. Sauté shallots until golden. Add vinegar, turn heat to high, and reduce by half. Add Brown Veal Stock and reduce again by half. Add cream, bring to a boil, and add remaining butter, in small pieces, whisking constantly until smooth. Adjust seasonings with salt and pepper.

Remove strings from pork and slice thinly across the roll. Arrange slices on serving plates, top with sauce, and serve immediately.

6 Servings

Lamb Curry
with Fried Onions

The key to a satisfying stew—and a curry is really just a spicy stew—is starting with large chunks of meat. The small pieces labeled as stewing meat in the supermarket become smaller and tougher as the stew bubbles on top of the stove. So please, start big!

4 POUNDS BONELESS, TRIMMED LAMB SHOULDER
   SALT AND FRESHLY GROUND PEPPER, TO TASTE
1 CUP VEGETABLE OIL
3 MEDIUM ONIONS, DICED
2 TABLESPOONS PUREED GARLIC (PAGE 250)
2 TABLESPOONS BLACK MUSTARD SEEDS (PAGE 246)
2 TABLESPOONS GARAM MASALA (PAGE 247)
2 TEASPOONS TURMERIC
2 TEASPOONS GROUND CARDAMOM
2 TEASPOONS GROUND CUMIN
1 TEASPOON DRIED RED PEPPER FLAKES
2 QUARTS BROWN LAMB STOCK (PAGE 75) OR CANNED
   CHICKEN BROTH
   PLAIN YOGURT AND FRIED ONIONS, RECIPE FOLLOWS,
   FOR GARNISH

Cut meat, as uniformly as possible, into 2 x 3-inch cubes. Generously sprinkle with salt and pepper.

Heat oil in a large Dutch oven over high heat. Cook meat until golden brown on all sides, then reserve on a platter. In same pot, cook onions, stirring occasionally, until golden. Reduce heat to medium, add garlic and all dry spices, and cook about 3 minutes, stirring constantly. Return meat to pan and pour in Brown Lamb Stock. Bring to a boil, reduce to a simmer, and cook, uncovered, 1 hour 15 minutes. Occasionally skim and discard fat that rises to top.

Ladle warm stew over a bed of Basmati Rice (page 166) and serve with Orange Dal with Ginger and Garlic (page 157). Garnish with yogurt and Fried Onions, and serve immediately.

6 Servings

Fried Onions

1   LARGE ONION
¼   CUP VEGETABLE OIL

Peel onion and slice as thinly as possible, more like a shave than a cut, across width. (You may need to use a meat slicer or food processor fitted with a 1 millimeter blade to slice it this fine.)

Heat oil over moderate heat in a small skillet. Working in small batches, fry onions, constantly shaking the pan, just until crispy and golden, about 3 minutes. Remove onions with tongs or a slotted spoon and drain on paper towels.

6 Servings

✕

Pork Schnitzel

We like the full flavor of pork rather than veal in this traditional, rich German dish. Since it requires last-minute attention, serve with a soup or salad that can be made in advance.

1¼   POUNDS PORK LOIN, TRIMMED
       SALT AND FRESHLY GROUND PEPPER TO TASTE
   1   CUP ALL-PURPOSE FLOUR
   3   EGGS, BEATEN
   2   CUPS FINE DRY BREAD CRUMBS
  ¼   CUP CLARIFIED BUTTER (PAGE 249)
   7   TABLESPOONS UNSALTED BUTTER
  ¼   CUP CAPERS, DRAINED
   1   BUNCH PARSLEY, STEMS TRIMMED, CHOPPED
   4   EGGS
   8   ANCHOVIES

Cut pork, across grain, into ¼-inch slices. Place between sheets of plastic wrap and pound to flatten to ⅛ inch. Season to taste with salt and pepper.

Dip pork cutlets one at a time in flour, vigorously patting off any excess. Then dip in eggs, drain, and lightly coat with bread crumbs.

Heat clarified butter in a large skillet over high heat. Sauté pork about 1 minute per side. Drain on paper towels and reserve.

In another skillet, melt 6 tablespoons butter over medium-high heat until brown bits form at bottom. Stir in capers and parsley, and remove from heat While butter is browning, melt remaining butter in another pan and fry eggs sunny-side up.

To serve, arrange 2 slices pork on each serving plate. Spoon caper butter evenly over pork. Place a fried egg in center of each and top with 2 anchovies, forming an X across the yolk. Serve immediately.

4 Servings

✕

Barbecued Baby Back Ribs

These are the messiest, juiciest, most delicious ribs ever. Serve with bowls of barbecue sauce for dipping. Our favorite accompaniments are mashed potatoes, apple sauce, grilled corn on the cob, and plenty of cold beer, of course. Leftover barbecue sauce, perfect for brushing over chicken, will keep about a week.

2	QUARTS WATER
1	CUP VINEGAR
½	CUP FRESH LEMON JUICE
1	TABLESPOON DRIED RED PEPPER FLAKES
⅛	CUP SALT
½	TEASPOON PAPRIKA
6	(12-RIB) RACKS BABY BACK RIBS

BARBECUE SAUCE

12	DRY ANCHO CHILES (PAGE 246)
1	CUP VINEGAR
3	CUPS WATER
¼	CUP VEGETABLE OIL
3	ONIONS, DICED
1½	TABLESPOONS PUREED GARLIC (PAGE 250)
1½	TABLESPOONS GROUND CUMIN
3	CUPS CHICKEN STOCK (PAGE 74) OR CANNED BROTH
¼	CUP PLUS 2 TABLESPOONS PACKED BROWN SUGAR
¼	CUP FRESH ORANGE JUICE
¼	CUP FRESH LEMON OR LIME JUICE
¼	CUP KETCHUP

Preheat oven to 350°F. Combine first six ingredients in a large roasting pan. Add ribs and marinate ½ hour.

Arrange ribs on rack in roasting pan, standing up if possible. Bake 2 hours, brushing every 20 minutes with water and vinegar marinade.

Meanwhile, make barbecue sauce. Split open chiles and remove seeds. Lightly roast over open flame or under broiler until brown and puffy, not black. Combine vinegar and water in a large bowl, add roasted chiles, and marinate about 2 hours. Transfer chiles and liquid to a food processor and puree until smooth, then strain.

Heat oil in a large skillet over medium-high heat. Sauté onions until brown. Add garlic, cumin, sauté a moment, then add pureed chiles, and Chicken Stock. Reduce to a simmer and cook 40 to 60 minutes.

Preheat grill or broiler to low. Combine remaining ingredients in a small bowl and make a paste. Whisk into sauce and cook an additional 15 minutes. Taste and adjust seasonings.

Dip roasted rib racks into barbecue sauce. Grill until warmed through and glazed, about 4 to 8 minutes per side.

6 to 8 Servings

Veal Kidneys
with Lemon and Soy

This smooth, rich meat has the most luxurious texture imaginable. Serve over a bed of crisp Fried Spinach (page 177), for just the right contrast.

6   (6-OUNCE) VEAL KIDNEYS
     SALT AND FRESHLY GROUND PEPPER, TO TASTE
¾   CUP FINE, DRY BREAD CRUMBS
6   TABLESPOONS (¾ STICK) UNSALTED BUTTER FOR
     SAUTÉING
2   TABLESPOONS SOY SAUCE
2   TABLESPOONS FRESH LEMON JUICE
6   TABLESPOONS BROWN VEAL STOCK (PAGE 75) OR
     CHICKEN STOCK (PAGE 74)
8   TABLESPOONS (1 STICK) UNSALTED BUTTER, COLD

Trim kidneys of all visible fat and sinew. Cut into ¾-inch horizontal slices, at an angle. Sprinkle with salt and pepper, then coat with bread crumbs.

Melt butter for sautéing in a large skillet over medium-high heat. Sauté kidneys until golden brown on each side, about 2 minutes per side. Transfer to a platter and set aside in a warm place.

In the same pan, combine soy sauce and lemon juice, and cook over moderate heat until slightly reduced. Pour in Brown Veal Stock and reduce by half. Break cold butter into small pieces and whisk into sauce until smooth. Pour any blood or juice that has drained from kidneys into sauce and mix.

Arrange kidneys on a bed of Fried Spinach (page 177) and spoon over sauce. Serve immediately.

6 Servings

Stuffed Veal Breast with Madeira and Wild Mushroom Sauce

The wild mushrooms in the stuffing and those in the sauce add an earthy quality usually lacking in veal. Veal breast, an unusually fatty cut, develops character and flavor as it slowly braises. It is important with these tougher cuts of meat to cook thoroughly for tenderness.

3	POUNDS BONELESS VEAL BREAST, TRIMMED
3	TABLESPOONS UNSALTED BUTTER
15	SHALLOTS, SLICED
3	TEASPOONS SALT
1	TEASPOON WHITE PEPPER
1	POUND WHITE MUSHROOMS, SLICED
2½	CUPS MADEIRA
1	POUND GROUND VEAL
2	EGGS
1	CUP FINE DRY BREAD CRUMBS
	SALT AND FRESHLY GROUND PEPPER TO TASTE
½	CUP VEGETABLE OIL OR CHICKEN FAT
3	QUARTS BROWN VEAL STOCK (PAGE 75) OR CANNED CHICKEN BROTH

Since veal breast is an uncommon cut, it is best to call a butcher in advance to order it. Ask him to cut a long, horizontal pocket for stuffing, leaving ends attached.

Melt butter in a large skillet over high heat. Sauté shallots with salt and pepper until limp and golden. Add mushrooms and cook, stirring occasionally, until the liquid evaporates and mushrooms brown slightly. Add Madeira and reduce until only a tablespoon liquid remains in pan. Transfer to a bowl and chill by placing over a larger bowl filled with ice. Stir to evenly cool. Add ground veal, eggs, and bread crumbs, and stir until well combined. The stuffing is now complete.

Preheat oven to 350°F.

Using a kitchen needle and string, sew 3 sides veal breast closed, leaving one end open for stuffing. Stuff with mushroom filling as evenly as possible, then finish sewing to seal breast. Season outside with salt and pepper.

Heat vegetable oil or chicken fat in a large Dutch oven over high heat. Brown meat on all sides. Add Brown Veal Stock, bring to a boil, and cover. Transfer to oven and bake 45 minutes per side. (The veal can then be refrigerated, in its juices, and served hot or cold the following day.)

To serve immediately, lift out meat and reserve in warm place. Skim and discard fat in pan and reserve 4 cups cooking liquid for sauce. Prepare sauce.

Remove string from veal breast and cut across grain into ¼-inch slices. (Cold slices can be placed on a platter, covered with a damp towel, and reheated in a 350°F oven about 15 minutes.) Arrange meat on serving plates, top with Madeira and Wild Mushroom Sauce, and serve immediately.

6 to 8 Servings

Madeira and Wild Mushroom Sauce

½ POUND WILD MUSHROOMS, SUCH AS CHANTERELLES
8 TABLESPOONS (1 STICK) UNSALTED BUTTER, COLD
16 SHALLOTS, MINCED
2 CUPS MADEIRA
4 CUPS RESERVED COOKING LIQUID OR BROWN VEAL STOCK (PAGE 75)

Cut mushrooms in ¼-inch slices. Melt 2 tablespoons butter in a medium saucepan and sauté mushrooms until slightly golden. In another saucepan, sauté shallots until golden, add Madeira, and cook over high heat until wine is reduced by half. Add reserved cooking liquid and reduce again by half. Break remaining butter into small pieces and whisk into sauce until completely smooth. Stir in sautéed wild mushrooms and serve.

Grilled Veal Chops
with Thyme Vinaigrette

This easy entrée captures the essence of good summer entertaining—just a cool sauce over simply grilled meat. The key to cooking veal outside is to let the grill cool down to a low, even fire and then almost roast, rather than sear, the meat.

6 (1-INCH THICK) VEAL CHOPS
SALT AND FRESHLY GROUND PEPPER TO TASTE
½ BUNCH FRESH THYME, LEAVES ONLY, CHOPPED
2 SHALLOTS, FINELY DICED
⅓ CUP EXTRA VIRGIN OLIVE OIL
JUICE OF 1 SMALL LEMON

Preheat grill or broiler. Season chops to taste with salt and pepper. When coals have cooled down, grill 8 to 10 minutes per side.

Meanwhile combine remaining ingredients in a small bowl to make a vinaigrette. Taste and adjust seasonings, and spoon over warm chops. Serve immediately.

6 Servings

Calf's Liver
with Port Wine and Ginger

This sweet, strong sauce stands up well to the distinctive flavor of liver. It is best to make the sauce first, and keep warm or reheat it while quickly cooking the meat. Most "bad" liver is simply overcooked.

PORT SAUCE

10 TABLESPOONS (1 STICK PLUS 2 TABLESPOONS) UNSALTED BUTTER, COLD
6 TABLESPOONS MINCED SHALLOTS
¾ TEASPOON SALT
2 HEAPING TABLESPOONS FRESHLY GRATED GINGER (PAGE 249)
1¼ CUPS RED PORT
1½ CUPS BROWN VEAL STOCK (PAGE 75) OR CANNED BROTH
1 CUP HEAVY CREAM

6 TABLESPOONS CLARIFIED BUTTER (PAGE 249) FOR FRYING (OPTIONAL)
6 (8-OUNCE) SLICES CALF'S LIVER, TRIMMED OF ALL SINEW AND CUT INTO ½-INCH SLICES
SALT AND FRESHLY GROUND PEPPER, TO TASTE

To make sauce, melt 2 tablespoons butter in a medium skillet over moderate heat. Sauté shallots with salt until golden. Add ginger and cook briefly, stirring occasionally, until aroma is released.

Remove from heat and add Port. Cook over high heat until reduced by half. Add Brown Veal Stock, reduce again by half, then add cream. Bring to a boil and add remaining butter, broken in small pieces. Whisk sauce until smooth and remove from heat. Strain to remove any "hairs" from ginger.

Preheat grill or heat clarified butter in a large skillet over high heat. Season liver with salt and pepper, and cook briefly, about 3 minutes per side. Serve immediately over Sautéed Onions (page 101) with Port sauce spooned on top.

6 Servings

Calf's Liver with Bacon, Sautéed Onions, and Mustard Sauce

In our most traditional liver dish, we combine the hearty flavors that liver fans expect with a slight twist. This would be a good dish to serve recent converts to this delectable meat.

12 OUNCES BACON, SLAB OR SLICED, IN 1 × ¼-INCH PIECES
10 TABLESPOONS (1 STICK PLUS 2 TABLESPOONS) UNSALTED BUTTER, COLD
 6 TABLESPOONS MINCED SHALLOTS
 ½ TEASPOON SALT
 ¾ CUP RED WINE VINEGAR
 ¾ CUP BROWN VEAL STOCK (PAGE 75) OR CHICKEN STOCK (PAGE 74)
 ¼ CUP STONEGROUND MUSTARD

 6 (8-OUNCE) SLICES CALF'S LIVER, TRIMMED OF ALL SINEW AND CUT INTO ½-INCH SLICES
    SALT AND FRESHLY GROUND PEPPER, TO TASTE
 6 TABLESPOONS (¾ STICK) SOFTENED UNSALTED BUTTER
    SAUTÉED ONIONS, RECIPE FOLLOWS

Fry bacon until crisp. Drain on paper towels and reserve.

Melt 4 tablespoons butter in a medium skillet over moderate heat. Cook shallots with salt until soft and nearly golden, about 3 minutes. Add cooked bacon, stirring briefly to rewarm. Add vinegar, turn the heat to high and reduce by half. Add stock and reduce again by half. Break remaining butter into small pieces and whisk into sauce until smooth. Whisk in mustard and remove from heat.

Preheat grill or a dry skillet. Season liver with salt and pepper, and coat both sides with softened butter. Grill or sauté about 3 minutes per side.

Arrange liver over a bed of Sautéed Onions on individual serving plates and spoon on sauce. Serve immediately.

Sautéed Onions

 6 TABLESPOONS (¾ STICK) UNSALTED BUTTER
 3 SMALL ONIONS, THINLY SLICED ACROSS WIDTH
 ½ TEASPOON SALT

Melt butter in a large skillet over high heat. Reduce heat. Sauté onions with salt, stirring occasionally, until golden brown, about 15 minutes.

6 Servings

In this sensuous pink dish, the tongue's velvety texture is accentuated by the sweet, smooth sauce. We like to reserve this showstopper for special occasions. Garnish the plates with thin slices of sautéed pear and serve champagne, for a celebration dinner.

Calf's Tongue
with Crayfish Sauce

1	PICKLED CORNED BEEF TONGUE, ABOUT 3 POUNDS
1	TABLESPOON BLACK PEPPERCORNS
1	TABLESPOON DRIED THYME
4	BAY LEAVES

CRAYFISH SAUCE

1	TABLESPOON UNSALTED BUTTER
3	MUSHROOMS, THINLY SLICED
3	SHALLOTS, THINLY SLICED
½	CUP BRANDY
1	CUP MADEIRA
4½	CUPS LOBSTER OR CRAYFISH STOCK (PAGE 69)
¾–1	CUP HEAVY CREAM

BEURRE MANIÉ

½	TABLESPOON SOFTENED, UNSALTED BUTTER
1	TABLESPOON ALL-PURPOSE FLOUR

DASH OF TABASCO
JUICE OF ¼ LEMON

Place tongue, peppercorns, thyme, and bay leaves in a large stockpot. Add water to cover. Bring to a boil, reduce to a simmer, and cook, uncovered, about 4 hours. Check pot occasionally, and add water, as needed, to cover. (The tongue may be made a day or 2 in advance and stored in refrigerator in its cooking liquid.)

To make sauce, melt butter in a medium saucepan over medium-high heat. Sauté mushrooms and shallots until golden. Remove from heat and add brandy and Madeira. Cook until reduced by half. Add Lobster or Crayfish Stock and reduce by about a quarter, until mixture tastes quite salty. Add cream and reduce again by half.

Meanwhile make *beurre manié* by mixing softened butter and flour together to form a paste. Press onto ends of a whisk and, when cream is reduced, quickly stir in. Strain through a fine sieve, pressing with the back of a ladle to extract all flavors. Season with Tabasco and lemon juice.

To serve, reheat tongue if made in advance. Remove skin and any excess fat. Slice thinly across width and fan on serving plates. Spoon warm sauce over meat and serve immediately.

6 Servings

Poultry

While chicken may be the most accommodating main course ingredient—even those on restricted diets will usually eat it—the challenge for the adventurous cook is how to avoid kitchen boredom. How many times can you grill a plain chicken breast? With that in mind, we've tried to select recipes with an eye toward ethnic diversity: There's a tropical duck curry from Thailand, a stuffed turkey breast from Italy, French duck confit, and a homey Mediterranean chicken in tomato and vegetable broth, to name just a few.

We suggest you explore the wide variety of types and cuts of poultry now available in your local supermarket. Boneless chicken thighs, for example, are great for grilling. They don't dry out as easily as the more expensive breasts and their dark meat is much more flavorful. Turkey, one of the most popular sellers at the restaurant, is another great buy. The breast meat, available boned and even sliced, is fat-free and can be used as a substitute for costly veal escalopes in quick sautés and grilled dishes. As for duck, that most luxurious bird, we've worked at reducing the amount of fat on the plate.

Chicken Stuffed
with Cilantro and Turmeric

6	BONELESS CHICKEN LEGS AND THIGHS, WITH SKIN
3	BONELESS WHOLE CHICKEN BREASTS, WITH SKIN
	SALT AND FRESHLY GROUND PEPPER TO TASTE
4	TEASPOONS TURMERIC
¼	CUP OLIVE OIL
3	BUNCHES CILANTRO, STEMS TRIMMED AND ROUGHLY CHOPPED
	FRESH TOMATO SAUCE, RECIPE FOLLOWS

Preheat oven to 400°F.

Run your fingers between the skin and meat of each piece of chicken, leaving one side attached, to create a pocket for stuffing. Season all over with salt and pepper.

Combine turmeric, 2 tablespoons olive oil, and cilantro in a small bowl to form a paste. Divide into 9 equal parts and spread evenly between skin and meat.

Heat remaining olive oil in a large ovenproof skillet over medium-high heat. Fry chicken, skin-side down first, until golden brown, about 2 minutes per side. Transfer to oven and bake 15 minutes.

Serve immediately, over a bed of bulgur wheat (page 246) or rice, with Fresh Tomato Sauce spooned on top.

6 Servings

Fresh Tomato Sauce

10	TABLESPOONS (1 STICK PLUS 2 TABLESPOONS) UNSALTED BUTTER, COLD
6	SHALLOTS, MINCED
3	CUPS PEELED, SEEDED, AND DICED TOMATOES (PAGE 249)
¾	TEASPOON SALT
¼	TEASPOON WHITE PEPPER
1	TEASPOON FRESH LEMON JUICE
3	TABLESPOONS CHOPPED FRESH PARSLEY

Melt 2 tablespoons butter in a medium sauté pan over moderate heat. Cook shallots just until golden. Add tomatoes, salt, and pepper, and cook an additional 3 minutes, uncovered. Break remaining butter into tablespoon-sized pieces and stir in, along with lemon juice. When smooth, remove from heat, stir in parsley, and serve.

Makes 4 Cups

Turmeric and cilantro lend a distinctive Indian flavor and brilliant golden color to roasted chicken. This is a wonderful stuffing to try with Cornish hens or other small birds like poussin.

Rigatoni Stuffed
with Chicken and Fennel

This creamy pasta, stuffed with a delicate combination of chicken and fennel seed, is among our most comforting and popular dishes. Serve as a pasta course or as a main dish at either lunch or dinner with a green salad. You can stuff the rigatoni as much as 2 hours in advance and keep warm over a pot of gently simmering water.

¾	POUND RIGATONI
¾	POUND GROUND CHICKEN, WHITE MEAT ONLY
1	TABLESPOON FENNEL SEEDS, ROUGHLY CHOPPED
1	EGG WHITE
1¼	CUPS HEAVY CREAM, COLD
1	TEASPOON SALT
½	TEASPOON WHITE PEPPER
2	DASHES OF TABASCO
1	TEASPOON OLIVE OIL

CREAM SAUCE

2½	CUPS HEAVY CREAM
½	CUP FRESHLY GRATED PARMESAN CHEESE
1	TEASPOON SALT
½	TEASPOON WHITE PEPPER
2	TABLESPOONS CHOPPED FRESH CHIVES FOR GARNISH

Cook rigatoni in a large pot of rapidly boiling salted water until al dente, about 8 minutes. Drain in a colander and chill in a large bowl of iced water. Drain chilled pasta until nearly dry and toss with 1 tablespoon olive oil to coat. Reserve.

Puree chicken, fennel, and egg white in a food processor until smooth, about 2 minutes. Transfer to a bowl nested inside a larger bowl half-filled with iced water. Stir until evenly chilled.

Add cream, a quarter-cup at a time, stirring vigorously with a wooden spoon after each addition, until all is added. Stir in salt, pepper, and Tabasco. (At this stage, the stuffing can be stored in refrigerator up to 24 hours.)

To stuff rigatoni, fill a pastry bag fitted with a #4 plain tip with chicken mixture and stuff rigatoni from both ends. Reserve.

Preheat oven to 400°F.

To make sauce, combine cream, Parmesan cheese, salt, and pepper in a medium ovenproof skillet. Bring to a boil. Add stuffed rigatoni, return to a boil, then transfer to oven. Bake until sauce is thick and bubbly, and rigatoni is cooked through, about 10 minutes.

Spoon into serving bowls or plates, sprinkle with chives, and serve hot.

4 Entrées or 6 Appetizers

Grilled Chicken
with Roasted Peppers

With their moist, dark meat, chicken legs can withstand the high heat of the grill without sacrificing flavor or texture. In this colorful summer dish, grilled chicken legs are awash in a lively tomato and bell pepper broth.

6   WHOLE CHICKEN LEGS WITH THIGHS
    SALT AND FRESHLY GROUND PEPPER TO TASTE
3   TABLESPOONS OLIVE OIL FOR BRUSHING
3   TABLESPOONS UNSALTED BUTTER
2   MEDIUM ONIONS, THINLY SLICED
1   TEASPOON SALT
1   TEASPOON FRESHLY GROUND PEPPER
2   GARLIC CLOVES, MINCED
1   TEASPOON PAPRIKA
2   EACH RED, GREEN, AND YELLOW PEPPERS ROASTED,
    PEELED, SEEDED, AND JULIENNED (PAGE 250)
1   TOMATO, PEELED, SEEDED, AND JULIENNED (PAGE 249)
1¼ CUPS CHICKEN STOCK (PAGE 74) OR CANNED BROTH

Preheat grill or broiler. Season chicken to taste with salt and pepper, and lightly brush with olive oil. Grill or broil, skin-side down first, about 10 minutes per side. (To mark skin with a crisscross pattern, begin cooking on the grill's hottest area until marks appear, then finish on the cooler area to avoid drying out meat.)

Melt butter in a medium skillet over medium-high heat. Cook onions with salt and pepper until soft and clear. Add garlic and paprika, and cook an additional minute, stirring constantly. Add remaining ingredients, bring to a boil, reduce to a simmer, and cook, uncovered, about 5 minutes.

Place chicken over individual beds of bulgur wheat (page 246), rice, or pasta. Ladle on sauce and serve immediately.

6 Servings

Chicken Breast
with Garlic and Parsley

Our favorite technique for stuffing chicken is to place the flavorings between skin and meat, so that every bite is infused with flavor. This simple garlic and parsley combination is just right in the summertime, especially with the added punch of the cool sauce. Plan in advance, since the Tomato Puree must be chilled before serving.

3 HEADS GARLIC, PEELED AND THINLY SLICED
6 BONELESS, WHOLE CHICKEN BREASTS, WITH SKIN
  SALT AND FRESHLY GROUND PEPPER TO TASTE
2 BUNCHES ITALIAN PARSLEY, STEMS TRIMMED AND
  ROUGHLY CHOPPED
3 TABLESPOONS CHICKEN FAT OR VEGETABLE OIL
  COOL TOMATO PUREE, RECIPE FOLLOWS

Preheat oven to 400°F. Blanch garlic in a small pot of rapidly boiling, salted water for 1 minute. Drain and set aside to cool.

Create a pocket for stuffing by running your fingers between the skin and meat of each breast, leaving one side attached. Season all over with salt and pepper.

In a small bowl combine chopped parsley and garlic. Divide into 6 equal parts and stuff each breast between skin and meat, spreading evenly.

Heat chicken fat or oil in a large ovenproof skillet over medium-high heat. Sauté chicken, skin-side down first, until golden brown, about 2 minutes per side. Transfer to oven and bake about 10 minutes. Set aside for 5 minutes, to redistribute juices before serving.

Whisk Cool Tomato Puree and coat 6 serving plates with it. Cut each breast into ½-inch slices, across the width. Arrange slices over puree and serve.

6 Servings

Cool Tomato Puree

7 MEDIUM, RIPE TOMATOES
⅔ CUP EXTRA VIRGIN OLIVE OIL
1 TEASPOON SALT
¼ TEASPOON WHITE PEPPER

Core tomatoes, cut in half horizontally, and remove seeds. Puree half the tomatoes in a blender until liquefied, then add olive oil, salt, and pepper. Puree until smooth. (Thin with a few tablespoons water if sauce seems thick.) Strain to remove any seeds and chill until serving time. Puree can be made a day in advance. Whisk before serving.

Makes 3 Cups

Spicy City Chicken

True Indian cooking is much more complex and subtle than the firey-hot westernized versions served in America. This fragrant chicken dish is sweet, sour, and spicy—all at once.

3	POUNDS BONELESS CHICKEN BREASTS AND THIGHS
	SALT AND FRESHLY GROUND PEPPER TO TASTE
2	TABLESPOONS VEGETABLE OIL
1	TABLESPOON FRESH LIME JUICE
6	SCALLIONS
2	TABLESPOONS UNSALTED BUTTER
6	SHALLOTS, DICED
6	LARGE MUSHROOMS, THINLY SLICED
1	BUNCH CILANTRO, STEMS AND LEAVES SEPARATED
1½	JALAPEÑO PEPPERS, CHOPPED WITH SEEDS
2	TABLESPOONS GROUND CUMIN
2	CUPS CHICKEN STOCK (PAGE 74) OR CANNED BROTH
1	CUP HEAVY CREAM
3	EGG YOLKS
3	TABLESPOONS PALM SUGAR (PAGE 250) OR BROWN SUGAR
¼	CUP RED WINE VINEGAR

Preheat broiler or prepare grill. Season chicken lightly with salt and pepper, since sauce will be spicy. Mix oil and lime juice in a small bowl and brush chicken and scallions with it.

Broil or grill thighs about 12 minutes, breasts about 9 minutes, and scallions about 2 minutes per side. Always grill chicken skin-side down first.

Meanwhile, make sauce by melting butter in a medium skillet over moderate heat. Cook shallots and mushrooms until soft and golden, about 10 minutes. Add cilantro stems, jalapeño peppers, and cumin, lower heat, and cook for 5 minutes. Add Chicken Stock. Turn heat to high and cook until liquid is reduced by half. Add cream and return to a boil. Remove from heat. Puree in a blender, strain, and return to heat.

Whisk egg yolks, sugar, and vinegar together in a small bowl. Pour one cup pureed sauce into egg mixture to temper. Then combine egg mixture and puree and cook over low heat, stirring constantly, until sauce is thick and smooth.

Arrange grilled chicken over a bed of Basmati Rice (page 166) and spoon sauce over all. Garnish with cilantro leaves and scallions, and serve immediately.

6 Servings

Sautéed Chicken
with Caraway and Cream

This creamy winter dish is long on flavor and short on cooking time. It takes about 30 minutes, from start to finish, and should be brought to the table piping hot and fragrant with caraway. A great meal for fireside dining.

6	SKINLESS, BONELESS WHOLE CHICKEN BREASTS
	SALT AND FRESHLY GROUND PEPPER TO TASTE
½	CUP VEGETABLE OIL
6	SHALLOTS, MINCED
2	TABLESPOONS CARAWAY SEEDS, CHOPPED
2	CUPS MADEIRA
4	CUPS CHICKEN STOCK (PAGE 74) OR CANNED BROTH
2	CUPS HEAVY CREAM
½	TEASPOON SALT
¼	TEASPOON WHITE PEPPER
3	DASHES OF TABASCO

Cut chicken into ½-inch wide strips and season with salt and pepper. Combine in a medium mixing bowl with 2 tablespoons vegetable oil. Toss to coat.

Heat remaining oil in a large skillet over high heat. Fry chicken strips until golden all over but pink inside, about 1 minute per side. Remove from pan and reserve.

In same pan, cook shallots over moderate heat until soft, about 2 minutes. Add caraway seeds and carefully cook just until aroma is released, about 1 minute. (It's very easy to burn the seeds.) Remove from heat. Add Madeira and cook over high heat until reduced by half. Add Chicken Stock, reduce again by half, and add cream. Reduce by about half, or until cream has thickened sauce to suit your taste.

Reduce heat, stir in remaining seasonings, and return chicken and juices to pan to reheat. When sauce returns to a boil, remove from heat, and serve. Spoon chicken over a bed of Spaetzel (page 160) or pasta. Ladle on sauce and serve immediately.

6 Servings

Paupiette of Turkey

These rich little turkey rolls are bursting with the flavors of Italy. It's best to stuff the turkey in advance to firmly set the filling and reduce last-minute preparation. The browned butter sauce is a snap.

2   TABLESPOONS OLIVE OIL

2   BUNCHES SPINACH, WASHED AND DRIED
    SALT AND FRESHLY GROUND PEPPER TO TASTE

1   (2½-POUND) SKINLESS, BONELESS TURKEY BREAST

6   SLICES PROSCIUTTO, CUT IN QUARTERS

1   CUP FRESHLY GRATED GRUYÈRE OR PARMESAN CHEESE

1   CUP ALL-PURPOSE FLOUR

4   EGGS, LIGHTLY BEATEN

2   CUPS FINE DRY BREAD CRUMBS

10 TABLESPOONS (1 STICK PLUS 2 TABLESPOONS)
    UNSALTED BUTTER, COLD

1   TABLESPOONS FRESH LEMON JUICE

2   TABLESPOONS CHOPPED FRESH PARSLEY

½   TEASPOON SALT

½   TEASPOON FRESHLY GROUND PEPPER

Heat olive oil in a large sauté pan over medium-high heat. Cook spinach with salt and pepper just until wilted, about 2 minutes. Set spinach in refrigerator to cool.

Carefully trim turkey of any tendons or cartilage. Slice across grain into ½-inch scallops. Place between 2 layers plastic wrap and flatten by pressing with flat side of a mallet until scallops are ¼-inch thick.

Arrange turkey on a counter and cover each scallop with a layer prosciutto and grated cheese. Squeeze moisture out of spinach, divide, and place evenly over cheese. Roll each to form a small, tight cylinder, enclosing filling.

Dip each roll in flour, patting off any excess. Then dip in eggs, drain, and coat with bread crumbs. Dip again in eggs and bread crumbs. Reserve in refrigerator at least ½ hour to set, or as long as 12 hours.

Preheat oven to 350°F. Melt 5 tablespoons butter in a large ovenproof skillet over medium-high heat. Sauté chilled turkey rolls until golden on all sides. Transfer to oven and bake for 15 minutes, until cheese begins to ooze.

Meanwhile, melt remaining butter in a medium skillet over medium-high heat, shaking pan occasionally to avoid browning. When butter is golden and foamy, about 5 minutes, remove from heat. Stir in lemon juice, parsley, salt, and pepper.

Arrange paupiettes on serving plates, spoon on butter sauce, and serve immediately.

6 Servings

Turkey Breast
with Lemon Butter

Somehow the occasion always seems special when turkey is served. Sliced thinly, turkey breast offers the elegance of veal, without the expense, and with a great deal more flavor. If you prefer, instead of sautéing, the turkey slices can be cooked about a minute per side on a very hot grill.

1	(2½-POUND) BONELESS, SKINLESS TURKEY BREAST
	SALT AND FRESHLY GROUND PEPPER TO TASTE
2	TABLESPOONS OLIVE OIL
7	TABLESPOONS UNSALTED BUTTER, COLD
10	SHALLOTS, FINELY DICED
	JUICE OF 1½ LEMONS
½	CUP CHICKEN STOCK (PAGE 74) OR CANNED BROTH
½	TEASPOON SALT
½	TEASPOON WHITE PEPPER
½	TEASPOON CHOPPED FRESH PARSLEY

Carefully trim turkey of any tendons or cartilage and slice across grain into ½-inch slices. Place between 2 layers of plastic wrap and flatten by pressing with flat side of a mallet until ¼-inch thick. Season all over with salt and pepper.

Heat olive oil in a large heavy skillet over high heat. Sauté turkey about 1 minute per side and set aside in a warm place.

Melt 3 tablespoons butter in a medium sauté pan over medium-high heat. Cook shallots until soft, about 2 minutes. Add lemon juice and Chicken Stock, and bring to a boil. Reduce by half. Break remaining cold butter into small pieces and whisk into pan until smooth. Remove from heat. Stir in salt, pepper, and parsley and reserve.

Arrange escalopes over individual beds of Sautéed Mustard Greens (page 186) or collard greens and spoon over lemon butter sauce. Serve immediately.

6 Servings

When meat is as flavorful and rich as goose, the best thing a cook can do is cook it correctly and serve it simply. We like to arrange mounds of condiments like Sweet and Sour Red Cabbage (page 190) and Marinated Mushrooms (page 198) on serving plates and simply slice the meat and serve, so guests can appreciate the pure, full flavor of goose.

Confit of Goose
with Peppercorns and Thyme

1   (11-POUND) GOOSE
2   TEASPOONS SALT
2   TABLESPOONS FRESH GROUND WHITE PEPPER
6   SPRIGS FRESH THYME, CHOPPED
6   CUPS RENDERED GOOSE, DUCK, OR PORK FAT (PAGE 250)
8   GARLIC CLOVES, PEELED

Remove legs and breasts from goose, saving remaining bones and wings for stock. With bones and skin attached, chop breast in half. Remove drumstick tips and reserve for stock.

Sprinkle all over with salt, pepper, and thyme, and set aside at room temperature 45 minutes. Then transfer to a heavy large pot with rendered fat and garlic. Cook over low heat, uncovered, until goose is tender when pierced with a fork, about 3 hours.

Transfer goose pieces to a medium baking dish or crock and add warm fat. Let cool to room temperature, cover with plastic wrap, and refrigerate a minimum of 24 hours or as long as 4 weeks. Before serving, lift goose pieces out of fat. Remove and discard skin and any excess fat. Follow same instructions as those for serving Confit of Duck (page 125). If you wish to serve a sauce, Madeira (page 125) would be fine.

6 Servings

Smoked Duck with Grapes

A handful of hickory chips thrown into the water before steaming imparts the most subtle smoky flavor, unlike commercially smoked products. With its sweet and sour sauce, this dish is lovely on a bed of crispy, puffed Oriental Rice Sticks (page 164).

1 (5-POUND) DUCK
  SALT AND FRESHLY GROUND BLACK PEPPER TO TASTE
1 CUP HICKORY-SMOKED WOOD CHIPS
10 TABLESPOONS (1 STICK PLUS 2 TABLESPOONS) UNSALTED BUTTER, COLD
6 TABLESPOONS MINCED SHALLOTS
¼ CUP GRANULATED SUGAR
1½ CUPS RED WINE VINEGAR
2 CUPS BROWN DUCK STOCK (PAGE 77) OR CHICKEN STOCK (PAGE 74)
1 POUND SEEDLESS GRAPES, PREFERABLY RED, WASHED, DRIED, AND CUT IN HALF
½ TEASPOON SALT

Trim duck of any excess fat. Generously season inside and out with salt and pepper. Make a steamer by filling a medium roasting pan or Dutch oven with about 2 inches of water. Add hickory chips. Place duck on rack over, but not touching, water and cover with a tight-fitting lid. (You may have to improvise here, since the lid should not touch the duck. We covered ours with another roasting pan, then sealed the edges with aluminum foil.) Place on a burner over high heat for 10 minutes, reduce to a simmer, and cook another 30 minutes. (The recipe can be made up to this point 24 hours in advance.) Meanwhile, preheat oven to 400°F.

Remove duck from steamer and transfer to another roasting pan with a rack. Bake, uncovered, 20 minutes. Turn heat to 500°F and bake an additional 20 minutes.

To make sauce, melt 2 tablespoons butter in a medium saucepan over moderate heat. Sauté shallots until golden brown, about 7 minutes. Stir in sugar and cook until it starts to caramelize, about 3 minutes. Add vinegar, turn heat to high, and reduce liquid by half. Add Brown Duck Stock and reduce again by half. (You may make the sauce, up to this point, in advance.)

Reduce heat to moderate, add grapes, and cook just long enough to warm, about 2 minutes. Break remaining butter into small pieces and whisk into sauce until smooth. Stir in salt and remove from heat.

To serve, carve duck and arrange on serving plates. Top with warm sauce and serve immediately.

2 to 4 Servings

Braised Duck
with Red Curry

Lime juice and coconut milk give this authentic Thai curry a fruity, almost tropical taste—compared to the earthier Indian curries. This bold stew needs nothing more than a generous bed of rice to balance its flavors.

2 (5-POUND) DUCKS
SALT AND FRESHLY GROUND PEPPER TO TASTE
¼ CUP RENDERED DUCK FAT OR VEGETABLE OIL
16 MEDIUM SHALLOTS, THINLY SLICED
8 GARLIC CLOVES, MINCED
2 TABLESPOONS FRESHLY GRATED GINGER (PAGE 249)
¼ CUP THAI RED CURRY PASTE (PAGE 249)
5 CUPS BROWN DUCK STOCK (PAGE 77) OR CHICKEN STOCK (PAGE 74)
¼ CUP THAI FISH SAUCE (PAGE 248)
1 (14-OUNCE) CAN COCONUT MILK (PAGE 247)
3 TABLESPOONS PALM SUGAR (PAGE 248) OR BROWN SUGAR
¼ CUP FRESH LIME JUICE
2 BUNCHES CILANTRO, CHOPPED, STEMS TRIMMED
2 LIMES, PEELED AND DICED
1 BUNCH SCALLIONS, THE WHITE AND ½ THE GREEN PART, TRIMMED, AND THINLY SLICED ALONG DIAGONAL

Bone ducks and remove the skin. (You can ask a butcher to do this, reserving the carcass for stock making and skin for rendering.) Cut breasts in half, then into about 3 pieces across the width. Chop legs and thighs into about 4 pieces each. (Remember: you want to start with generous pieces of meat, since they will shrink when cooked. Don't worry about cleaning the tendons, since they will soften with long cooking.) Sprinkle meat with salt and pepper.

Heat rendered fat in a large, heavy-bottomed Dutch oven over high heat. Brown duck on all sides, then transfer meat to a platter. Reduce heat to medium-low and cook shallots until brown. Add garlic and ginger, cook about a minute, then add curry paste. Cook, stirring constantly, about 3 minutes. Return duck meat to pot along with Brown Duck Stock and cook at a simmer, uncovered, until meat is tender, about 40 minutes.

With a slotted spoon, transfer meat to a platter and reserve in a warm place. Puree sauce in a blender and strain back into pot. Cook over high heat until liquid is reduced by one-third. Stir in Thai Fish Sauce, coconut milk, sugar, and lime juice, and remove from heat. Stir duck back into warm sauce. Ladle stew over Basmati Rice (page 166). Garnish with remaining ingredients and serve immediately.

6 Servings

Confit of Duck

Don't let the quantity of fat in this recipe alarm you. While the duck is slowly cooking, its interior fat melts, leaving the silky, smooth meat without a trace of grease. This technique, originally used for preserving, must be started at least a day in advance. The cooked duck can then be held as long as 4 weeks without any loss of quality. Use some for a Cold Confit of Duck Salad (page 148).

2	(5-POUND) DUCKS
2	TEASPOONS SALT
2	TABLESPOONS BLACK PEPPERCORNS, CRACKED
6	CUPS RENDERED DUCK OR PORK FAT (PAGE 250)
6	GARLIC CLOVES, PEELED

Remove ducks' legs and breasts, saving remaining bones and wings for Brown Duck Stock (page 77). Leaving bones and skin attached, chop breasts into halves. Remove tips of drumsticks to use in stock.

Sprinkle all over with salt and pepper, and set aside at room temperature 45 minutes. Then place duck pieces in a Dutch oven with rendered fat and garlic. Cook over low heat, uncovered, 1 ½ to 2 hours. To test for doneness, pierce with a sharp fork. It should fall off fork when shaken.

Transfer duck pieces to a medium baking dish and add the fat. Let cool to room temperature, cover with plastic wrap, and refrigerate at least 24 hours or as long as 4 weeks. Before serving, lift duck pieces out of fat. Remove and discard skin and any excess fat. Serve duck hot or cold.

6 Servings

Warm Confit of Duck with Madeira Sauce

Try this in place of roasted duck at a holiday dinner. It's much less greasy and, best of all, the duck can be made weeks in advance! We like to serve warm duck on top of Roasted Potatoes (page 166).

1	RECIPE CONFIT OF DUCK (ABOVE)
8	SHALLOTS, FINELY MINCED
1	CUP MADEIRA
2	CUPS BROWN DUCK STOCK (PAGE 77) OR BROWN VEAL STOCK (PAGE 75)
6	TABLESPOONS UNSALTED BUTTER, COLD

Preheat oven to 350°F. Arrange skinless pieces of duck in a roasting pan, cover with aluminum foil, and bake 30 minutes to reheat.

Meanwhile, cook shallots and Madeira in a medium saucepan over high heat until wine is reduced by half. Add stock and reduce again by half. Break butter into small pieces and whisk into sauce until completely smooth. Top with Madeira sauce.

6 Servings

Fish and Shellfish

It goes against our grain to give recipes for fish in the same style as we have for meat and poultry, since the key to fish cookery is its flexibility. Unlike a cut of meat that must be cooked a certain way, then served with a particular sauce, fish's mild flavor invites experimentation. So while we might specify swordfish, for example, with the mustard and chopped shallots, you could easily substitute salmon or tuna.

The best fish for grilling are the oily ones like tuna, swordfish, salmon, sturgeon, mackerel, or mahi mahi to name a few. Any of the cool, uncooked sauces—such as the ones on pages 149 and 151—served with grilled fillets make lovely, quick dinners.

For roasting or poaching, such as Cold Poached Salmon with Tomato and Herbs (page 149), use the flakier fish that tend to fall apart on the grill: red snapper, black cod, sea bass, salmon, whitefish, turbot, orange roughy, halibut, and monkfish. We dress them up with assorted mild vegetable-based cream sauces, called coulis, for more formal presentations. Once again, feel free to mix and match the sauces according to taste and what is available at your fish market. The best fish cookery is always the simplest.

Roasted Black Cod
with Coulis of Horseradish

Horseradish and lime make this a thin coulis that's a bit acidic—a good match for light, buttery black cod.

COULIS OF HORSERADISH

5	TABLESPOONS UNSALTED BUTTER, COLD
4	SHALLOTS, THINLY SLICED
4	MUSHROOMS, THINLY SLICED
1	TEASPOON SALT
¼	TEASPOON WHITE PEPPER
1½	CUPS DRY WHITE WINE
1½	CUPS CLAM JUICE OR FISH STOCK (PAGE 76)
1½	CUPS HEAVY CREAM
	JUICE OF 1 LIME
4	DASHES OF TABASCO
6	TABLESPOONS FRESHLY GRATED HORSERADISH
6	(7-OUNCE) BLACK COD FILLETS
	SALT AND WHITE PEPPER TO TASTE
4	TABLESPOONS (½ STICK) UNSALTED BUTTER
3	LIMES, THINLY SLICED, DAIKON SPICED SPROUTS (PAGE 247), AND FRESHLY GRATED HORSERADISH FOR GARNISH

Melt 2 tablespoons butter in a medium saucepan over low heat. Add shallots, mushrooms, salt, and pepper, and cook until soft. Turn heat to high, add wine, and reduce by half. Add clam juice and reduce again by half. Strain through a medium sieve back into pan.

Preheat oven to 450°F.

Return pan to high heat, add cream, and reduce by half, being careful not to overreduce. (If the sauce should break at this point, you can bring it back together with a quick turn in the blender.) Stir in lime juice, Tabasco, and horseradish. Break remaining 3 tablespoons cold butter into small pieces and whisk into sauce until smooth. Reserve in a warm place.

Season fillets all over with salt and pepper. Melt remaining 4 tablespoons butter in a large skillet over high heat. Sauté fish for 1 minute. Turn over, transfer to oven, and bake, uncovered, for 3 to 5 minutes.

Arrange fish on individual plates. Spoon on warm sauce and garnish with slices of lime, daikon spiced sprouts, and more fresh horseradish. Serve immediately.

6 Servings

Grilled Swordfish with Mustard

Our secret formula for last-minute summer entertaining—this entire dish can be put together in about 10 minutes. Use the freshest shallots and chives, however, so that each flavor is cool, clear, and refreshing.

5 TABLESPOONS DIJON MUSTARD
2 TABLESPOONS OLIVE OIL
6 TABLESPOONS CLAM JUICE
½ CUP MINCED SHALLOTS
½ CUP CHOPPED FRESH CHIVES
½ TEASPOON WHITE PEPPER
6 (7-OUNCE) SWORDFISH FILLETS
   SALT AND WHITE PEPPER TO TASTE
   OLIVE OIL FOR BRUSHING

Preheat grill as hot as possible.
Mix mustard, olive oil, clam juice, shallots, chives, and pepper in a small bowl. Cover with plastic wrap and reserve.

Season fish all over with salt and pepper. Grill about 3 minutes per side, brushing with olive oil after turning. Transfer onto serving plates, spoon sauce, place grilled fish on sauce, and serve immediately. Goes nicely with Sautéed Mustard Greens (page 166).

6 Servings

Roasted Sea Bass with White Port and Roasted Peppers

The sweetness of Port wine is balanced by the smoky roasted peppers and salty olives in this versatile warm fish sauce. It goes equally as well with roasted red snapper or halibut.

WHITE PORT AND ROASTED PEPPER SAUCE

2 TABLESPOONS UNSALTED BUTTER
6 MUSHROOMS, THINLY SLICED
6 SHALLOTS, THINLY SLICED
   SALT AND WHITE PEPPER TO TASTE
2 CUPS WHITE PORT WINE
2 CUPS CLAM JUICE OR FISH STOCK (PAGE 76)
2 CUPS HEAVY CREAM
2 RED BELL PEPPERS, ROASTED, PEELED, SEEDED, AND JULIENNED (PAGE 250)
2 CUPS KALAMATA OLIVES, SLICED OFF PIT AND JULIENNED

6 (7-OUNCE) SEA BASS FILLETS
   SALT AND WHITE PEPPER TO TASTE
4 TABLESPOONS (½ STICK) UNSALTED BUTTER
1 BUNCH CHIVES, CHOPPED, FOR GARNISH

Melt butter in a medium saucepan over low heat. Add mushrooms, shallots, salt, and pepper, and cook until soft, about 10 minutes.

Preheat oven to 450°F.

Raise heat to high, add Port, and reduce by half. Add clam juice or Fish Stock and reduce again by half. Add cream and reduce one more time by half. Remove from the heat, strain sauce, and stir in peppers and olives. Reserve in a warm place.

Season fillets all over with salt and pepper. Melt remaining 4 tablespoons butter in a large skillet over high heat. Sauté fish for 1 minute. Turn over, transfer to oven, and bake, uncovered, for 3 to 5 minutes.

Arrange fish on individual plates. Spoon on warm sauce and garnish with chopped chives. Serve immediately.

6 Servings

Grilled Tuna with Chopped Tomatoes and Spinach Pesto

We like to emphasize the simplicity of grilled fish by serving it with fresh, uncomplicated accompaniments like Chopped Tomatoes and Spinach Pesto. With its red and green stripes, this easy dish is a good-looking entrée.

Chopped Tomatoes

8	TOMATOES, PEELED, SEEDED, AND DICED (PAGE 249)
½	CUP OLIVE OIL
1½	TEASPOONS SALT
¼	TEASPOON WHITE PEPPER

Mix all ingredients in a bowl and reserve in the refrigerator.

Makes 4 Cups

Spinach Pesto

3	TABLESPOONS OLIVE OIL
2	BUNCHES SPINACH, STEMS TRIMMED, WASHED, AND DRIED
½	TEASPOON SALT
¼	TEASPOON WHITE PEPPER
2	TABLESPOONS PUREED GARLIC (PAGE 250)

Heat oil in a large skillet over high heat. Add spinach, salt, and pepper and cook briefly until spinach begins to wilt. Add garlic and cook, stirring constantly, until aroma is released. Puree in a food processor or blender, along with the liquid in pan, until smooth. Chill until serving time.

Makes 1 Cup

6	(7-OUNCE) TUNA FILLETS
	SALT AND WHITE PEPPER TO TASTE

Preheat grill as hot as possible. Season fish all over with salt and pepper, and grill 3 to 6 minutes per side. The centers should remain bright pink.

Coat serving plates with Chopped Tomatoes. Using a squirt bottle or a spoon, arrange Spinach Pesto in generous stripes over tomatoes. Top with grilled fish and serve immediately.

6 Servings

Grilled Whole Salmon

In this dramatic outdoor presentation, the entire fish is first wrapped in greens, then seared on a red-hot grill. The greens protect the fish and impart a delicate, tart flavor before they blacken and remain on the grill. Make sure your grill is extremely hot and well-seasoned before proceeding. Ideal for a summer buffet.

MARINADE

½   CUP CRACKED BLACK PEPPER
2   CUPS SAN BAI SU (PAGE 250)
½   CUP FRESH LEMON JUICE
¾   CUP SESAME OIL
6   TABLESPOON SESAME TAHINI

1   (7-POUND) SALMON, CLEANED, WITH HEAD AND
     TAIL ON
2   BUNCHES COLLARD GREENS, WASHED, UNTRIMMED
     JAPANESE WASABI POWDER AND WHITE VINEGAR FOR
     GARNISH (OPTIONAL)

Combine marinade ingredients in a glass or ceramic roasting pan. Whisk to combine. Using a sharp knife, score several diagonal lines along the length of fish, down to spine, on either side. Marinate 2 to 4 hours at room temperature.

After marination, preheat grill or broiler.

Blanch greens in a large pot of boiling, salted water, just until the water returns to a boil. Refresh with iced water and drain.

On a large baking sheet, arrange greens, overlapping, to form a rectangle as long as the fish and more than twice as wide. Place fish in middle and wrap with greens so only the head and tail are exposed. The dampness will make them cling.

Transfer fish to grill, reserving marinade. Cook 7 to 12 minutes per side, until greens, head, and tail blacken. It will take 2 spatulas, one at the head and one at the tail, to turn fish. Don't be concerned about greens sticking.

To test for doneness, try to pull out a dorsal fin from top of fish. If it slides out easily fish is done.

To serve, place whole fish on a serving platter. Using a dull knife and soup spoon, scrape off any remaining skin and remove fins. Spoon half reserved marinade over top. Cut along spine first and serve the top fillet. Lift tail, insert knife between bones and flesh, and run it along length. All (or most) bones should easily lift out. Spoon on remaining marinade and serve second fillet.

As an optional garnish, mix dry Japanese wasabi powder with a few drops of vinegar to form a paste. Serve small squares alongside fish or in ramekins with the marinade for dipping.

8 to 10 servings

*Monkfish, also known as lotte
or angler, has an exceptionally
strong flavor and meaty texture
that goes well with earthy turnips. Because turnips are so absorbent, keep your eye on this
sauce. It will reduce quickly.*

Roasted Monkfish
with Coulis of Turnips

COULIS OF TURNIPS

10	TABLESPOONS (1 STICK PLUS 2 TABLESPOONS) UNSALTED BUTTER, COLD
6	MUSHROOMS, THINLY SLICED
1	LEEK, WHITE AND LIGHT GREEN, CUT IN HALF AND THINLY SLICED
6	SHALLOTS, THINLY SLICED
½	TEASPOON SALT
¼	TEASPOON WHITE PEPPER
3	TURNIPS, PEELED, CUT IN HALF, AND THINLY SLICED
1	CUP DRY WHITE WINE
4	CUPS CLAM JUICE OR FISH STOCK (PAGE 76)
1½	CUPS HEAVY CREAM
	JUICE OF ½ LEMON
2	TABLESPOONS TABASCO
6	(7-OUNCE) MONKFISH FILLETS
	SALT AND WHITE PEPPER TO TASTE
4	TABLESPOONS (½ STICK) UNSALTED BUTTER
1½	OUNCES HARD SMOKED BEEF SAUSAGE, JULIENNED (OPTIONAL GARNISH)

Melt 2 tablespoons butter in a medium saucepan over low heat. Add mushrooms, leek, shallots, salt, and pepper, and cook until soft but not colored, about 10 minutes. Add turnips and continue cooking over low heat, stirring occasionally, until they begin to soften, about 5 minutes.

Add wine, turn heat to high, and reduce by half. Add clam juice and reduce again by half. Add cream, bring to a boil, and remove from heat.

Preheat oven to 450°F. Puree cream mixture in a blender until smooth. Pass through a medium strainer back into pan. Bring back to a boil. Break remaining cold butter into small pieces and whisk into sauce until smooth. (You can thin the sauce with additional clam juice or stock, if necessary.) Stir in lemon juice and Tabasco, and reserve.

Season fillets all over with salt and pepper. Melt remaining 4 tablespoons butter in a large skillet over high heat. Sauté fish 1 minute. Turn over, transfer to the oven, and bake, uncovered, for 3 to 5 minutes.

Slice fillets and arrange on individual plates. Spoon on warm sauce and serve immediately. For optional garnish, sauté sausage strips in a dry pan until warmed through and sprinkle over top.

6 Servings

Roasted Salmon
with Coulis of Red Grapes

COULIS OF RED GRAPES

1	POUND RED SEEDLESS GRAPES
2	TABLESPOONS UNSALTED BUTTER
1	LEEK, WHITE PART, CUT IN HALF LENGTHWISE AND THINLY SLICED
3	MUSHROOMS, THINLY SLICED
2	SHALLOTS, THINLY SLICED
1	TEASPOON SALT
¼	TEASPOON WHITE PEPPER
1½	CUPS DRY WHITE WINE
1½	CUPS CLAM JUICE OR FISH STOCK (PAGE 76)
1	CUP HEAVY CREAM
	DASH OF TABASCO

6	(7-OUNCE) SALMON FILLETS
	SALT AND WHITE PEPPER TO TASTE
4	TABLESPOONS (½ STICK) UNSALTED BUTTER
	RED GRAPES FOR GARNISH (OPTIONAL)

Remove grapes from stems and puree in a blender—reserving 6 small clusters for garnish later—until smooth. Strain to remove skins and reserve juice in another container. (Do not wash the blender yet.)

Melt butter in a medium saucepan over low heat. Add leek, mushrooms, shallots, salt, and pepper, and cook until soft, but not colored, about 5 minutes. Turn heat to high, add wine, and reduce by half. Add clam juice and reduce again by half. Add cream and reduce one more time by half.

Preheat oven to 450°F.

Puree cream mixture until smooth in the unwashed blender, then pass through a medium strainer. Pour back into pot and stir in reserved grape juice and Tabasco. (Since grape juice is so delicate it's important not to apply much heat once the purees are combined. Do not bring this sauce back to a boil. You can keep it warm in the top of a double boiler over simmering water or a *bain-marie*.)

Season fillets all over with salt and pepper. Melt remaining 4 tablespoons butter in a large skillet over high heat. Sauté fish for 1 minute. Turn over, transfer to oven, and bake, uncovered, for 3 to 5 minutes.

Arrange fish on individual plates. Spoon on warm sauce and garnish with additional grapes, if desired. Serve immediately.

6 Servings

Roasted Halibut
with Coulis of Leeks

Our vegetable coulis are rich and creamy sauces. Choose a light, flavorful starter like Thai Melon Salad (page 19) or Chinese Sausage Salad (page 22) if you are planning to serve this type of entrée at a dinner party.

COULIS OF LEEKS

2	LEEKS
6	SHALLOTS, SLICED
10	TABLESPOONS (1 STICK PLUS 2 TABLESPOONS) UNSALTED BUTTER, COLD
6	MUSHROOMS, THINLY SLICED
1	TEASPOON SALT
¼	TEASPOON WHITE PEPPER
1	CUP DRY WHITE WINE
2	CUPS CLAM JUICE OR FISH STOCK (PAGE 76)
1	CUP HEAVY CREAM
3	DASHES OF TABASCO
1	TEASPOON FRESH LEMON JUICE
6	(7-OUNCE) HALIBUT FILLETS
	SALT AND WHITE PEPPER TO TASTE
4	TABLESPOONS (½ STICK) UNSALTED BUTTER

Trim and discard dark green part of leeks and slice whites in half lengthwise. Wash in cold, running water and cut across width in ¼-inch slices.

Melt 2 tablespoons butter in a medium saucepan over low heat. Add leeks, shallots, mushrooms, salt, and pepper. Cook until soft but not colored, about 10 minutes. Add wine, turn heat to high, and reduce by half. Add clam juice and reduce again by half. Add cream, bring to a boil, and remove from heat.

Preheat the oven to 450°F.

Puree cream mixture in a blender until smooth, then strain. Return to pan and bring back to a boil. Break remaining cold butter into small pieces and whisk into sauce until smooth. Stir in Tabasco and lemon juice. Set aside in a warm place.

Season fillets all over with salt and pepper. Melt remaining 4 tablespoons butter in a large skillet over high heat. Sauté fish 1 minute. Turn over, transfer to oven, and bake, uncovered, for 3 to 5 minutes.

Arrange fish on serving plates. Top with sauce and serve immediately.

6 Servings   ✕

VARIATION: To add a touch of color and crunch, try deep-frying a leek as garnish for this white dish. Cut leek in thirds lengthwise, then finely julienne. Deep-fry in 2 cups vegetable oil, until golden, about 1½ minutes. Drain on paper towels, and serve alongside the fish.

Sauteed Shrimps
with Tomatoes and Pernod

It takes a strong shellfish like shrimp, or sea scallops, to stand up to the distinctive anise-flavored, French aperitif Pernod. Serve this soupy dish over a bed of fettuccine with plenty of crusty French bread to sop up the delicious sauce.

6	LARGE TOMATOES, PEELED, SEEDED, AND DICED (PAGE 249)
2	TABLESPOONS PERNOD
2	TEASPOONS SALT
½	TEASPOON WHITE PEPPER
2½	POUNDS MEDIUM SHRIMP, PEELED AND DEVEINED
	SALT AND FRESHLY GROUND PEPPER TO TASTE
8	TABLESPOONS (1 STICK) UNSALTED BUTTER, COLD
¼	POUND CHINESE SNOW PEAS, JULIENNED
1	BUNCH CHERVIL, STEMS TRIMMED, CHOPPED, FOR GARNISH

Puree tomatoes in a blender until smooth. If dry, add a tablespoon or two water. Pass through a medium strainer into a mixing bowl. Stir in Pernod, salt, and pepper. Reserve.

Season shrimps with salt and pepper. Melt 4 tablespoons butter in a large skillet over high heat. Sauté shrimps until pink-orange, about 1 minute per side. With a slotted spoon, transfer shrimp to a platter, leaving butter in pan.

Add reserved tomato sauce and julienned snow peas. Bring to a boil and cook until reduced by about one-third. Adjust seasonings to taste.

Break remaining butter in small pieces and stir into sauce along with shrimp. Once smooth, remove from heat, and ladle over bowls of warm fettuccine. Garnish with chervil and serve immediately.

4 Servings

Portuguese Mussel
and Cockle Stew

This dish is a great crowd pleaser. All the ingredients can be measured and chopped in advance. At the last minute, just add the liquids and boil for about 10 minutes for a great homemade fish stew.

2 POUNDS MUSSELS
2 POUNDS COCKLES (LITTLENECK OR OTHER SMALL CLAMS MAY BE SUBSTITUTED)
1 RED BELL PEPPER
1 GREEN BELL PEPPER
1 YELLOW BELL PEPPER
1 MEDIUM YELLOW SPANISH ONION
1 SMALL ZUCCHINI, WITH SKIN
1 SMALL YELLOW CROOKNECK SQUASH, WITH SKIN
1 HARD, SMOKED LINGUICA SAUSAGE (ABOUT 6 OUNCES) OR PROSCIUTTO
1 LARGE RIPE TOMATO, PEELED, SEEDED, AND DICED (PAGE 249)
½ CUP KALAMATA OLIVES, CUT FROM THE PIT AND JULIENNED
2 OR 3 CUPS WELL-SEASONED FISH STOCK (PAGE 76) OR CLAM JUICE
¾ CUP WHITE PORT WINE
   FRESHLY GROUND PEPPER TO TASTE
2 TABLESPOONS CHOPPED FRESH PARSLEY FOR GARNISH

Wash mussels and cockles or clams under cold running water and scrub with a stiff brush. Remove mussels' beards by sharply pulling. Place shellfish in a large bowl, cover with a wet towel, and reserve in refrigerator.

Core and seed bell peppers. Cut into fine julienne, about 2 inches long. Cut onion, zucchini, and yellow squash into similar julienne. Cut sausage or prosciutto into thin 2-inch lengths and finely julienne.

Combine shellfish, julienned vegetables, sausage, tomato, olives, Fish Stock, Port, and pepper in a large stockpot or Dutch oven. Cover and cook over high heat until shells open, about 8 to 10 minutes. Taste before adjusting seasons since shellfish and bottled clam juice are quite salty. Sprinkle with chopped parsley, ladle into soup bowls, and serve immediately.

6 SERVINGS

Crayfish Casserole

5	TABLESPOONS OLIVE OIL
2	MEDIUM ONIONS, DICED
1	TABLESPOON PUREED GARLIC (PAGE 250)
1	TEASPOON SALT
1	TEASPOON PAPRIKA
1	TEASPOON GROUND CUMIN
½	TEASPOON CAYENNE
½	TEASPOON FRESHLY GRATED NUTMEG
½	TEASPOON CINNAMON
¼	TEASPOON GROUND CLOVES
6	OUNCES SMOKED SAUSAGE OR SALAMI, JULIENNED
2	BELL PEPPERS, RED AND GREEN, JULIENNED
2	TOMATOES, PEELED, SEEDED, AND DICED (PAGE 249)
2	CUPS BOTTLED CLAM JUICE
1	CUP TOMATO JUICE
5	CUPS COOKED RICE
1½	POUNDS CLEANED, COOKED CRAYFISH TAILS OR MEDIUM SHRIMP
1½	CUPS FINE, DRY BREAD CRUMBS

Preheat oven to 350°F.

Heat 3 tablespoons oil in a large skillet over
medium-high heat. Sauté onions until golden. Add
all spices and cook just until aromas are released, 1
to 2 minutes.

Reduce heat to moderate. Add smoked sausage
or salami, bell peppers, tomatoes, clam juice, tomato
juice, rice, and crayfish or shrimp. Stir to combine.
Transfer to a 10-cup ovenproof casserole or 6 individual casseroles.

Mix bread crumbs with remaining 2 tablespoons
of oil to form a paste. Sprinkle evenly over top. Bake
until bubbly, about 20 minutes. Serve immediately.

6 Servings

Vegetarian Entrées

Here is a small sample of the vegetable dishes that we serve as entrées at the restaurant. They are all satisfying and special enough to serve to guests—and not necessarily vegetarians!

Pasta with Oyster Mushrooms

This easy pasta dish takes about 20 minutes to prepare. Use thin oyster mushrooms whole or, if you prefer smaller pieces, tear them by hand as you would tear lettuce leaves.

4	TABLESPOONS (½ STICK) UNSALTED BUTTER
1	POUND OYSTER MUSHROOMS, STEMS TRIMMED, WIPED CLEAN
2	TABLESPOONS PUREED GARLIC (PAGE 250)
1½	CUPS HEAVY CREAM
2	TEASPOONS FRESH LEMON JUICE
½	CUP PEELED, SEEDED, AND DICED TOMATOES (PAGE 249)
	SALT AND WHITE PEPPER TO TASTE
½	POUND HOMEMADE FETTUCCINE (PAGE 163) OR DRIED
¼	CUP PLUS 2 TABLESPOONS FRESHLY GRATED PARMESAN CHEESE

Melt butter in a large skillet over moderate heat. Cook mushrooms until soft. Add garlic and cook briefly, until the aroma is released. Add cream, turn heat to high, and reduce by half. Reduce heat and stir in lemon juice and tomatoes. Season to taste with salt and pepper, and keep warm.

Bring a large stockpot of salted water to a boil. Cook fettuccine until al dente and drain in a colander. Transfer to a large bowl. Sprinkle on Parmesan cheese, top with mushroom mixture, and toss well. Serve immediately.

2 Entrées or 6 Appetizers

Eggplant Spinach Curry

For a complete vegetarian meal, serve this light, flavorful stew over a bed of Basmati Rice (page 166) a dal, and a raita (page 196) and spicy Pickled Tomatoes (page 201).

1	LARGE EGGPLANT, DICED, WITH SKIN
2	TEASPOONS COARSE SALT FOR SPRINKLING
2	TABLESPOONS BLACK MUSTARD SEEDS (PAGE 246)
6	TABLESPOONS CLARIFIED BUTTER (PAGE 249)
1	LARGE ONION, DICED
½	TEASPOON SALT
2	TABLESPOONS PUREED GARLIC (PAGE 250)
2	TABLESPOONS FRESHLY GRATED GINGER (PAGE 249)
1	TEASPOON GROUND CUMIN
½	TEASPOON GROUND CORIANDER
½	TEASPOON GROUND CARDAMOM
½	TEASPOON GARAM MASALA (PAGE 247)
¼	TEASPOON TURMERIC
¼	TEASPOON GROUND CLOVES
¼	TEASPOON CAYENNE
2	TOMATOES, PEELED, SEEDED, AND DICED (PAGE 249)
1	CUP WATER
1	TABLESPOON PALM OR BROWN SUGAR (PAGE 248)
2	BUNCHES SPINACH, STEMS REMOVED, WASHED, AND CUT IN 2-INCH PIECES

Place eggplant in a colander, sprinkle with coarse salt, and let stand for 30 minutes to sweat. Pat dry with paper towels.

Place mustard seeds in a small, dry sauté pan and cook over moderate heat until they turn gray and start popping. Remove from heat and reserve.

Heat ¼ cup clarified butter in a large skillet over moderate heat. Sauté eggplant, stirring occasionally, until soft and golden. Remove from heat and reserve in a bowl with mustard seeds.

Heat remaining butter in a medium saucepan over medium-high heat. Add onions and salt. Sauté until onions are golden and soft. Add garlic and ginger, cook just until aromas are released, then stir in all spices. Cook an additional minute, stirring constantly, to blend spices and prevent scorching.

Add tomatoes, water, and sugar. Turn heat to high and bring to a boil. Add spinach, bring back to a boil, and stir in eggplant mixture. When eggplant is heated through, about 2 minutes, remove from heat and serve.

4 Entrées or 6 Accompaniments

Chanterelle Risotto

Woodsy chanterelle mushrooms underline the heartiness of risotto, the delicious short-grained Italian rice dish. Serve with a bitter green salad, such as watercress, for a satisfying supper.

1½	POUNDS CHANTERELLE MUSHROOMS
¼	CUP OLIVE OIL
4	TABLESPOONS (½ STICK) UNSALTED BUTTER
2	LARGE ONIONS, DICED
1	TEASPOON SALT
1	TEASPOON WHITE PEPPER
1	TABLESPOON PUREED GARLIC (PAGE 250)
½	CUP BRANDY
1	POUND ARBORIO RICE (AVAILABLE IN ITALIAN SPECIALTY SHOPS)
2	BAY LEAVES
9	CUPS CHICKEN STOCK (PAGE 74) OR CANNED BROTH, WARM
1	CUP PARMESAN CHEESE

Wipe mushrooms clean with a damp paper towel. Break into bite-sized pieces and reserve.

Heat oil and butter in a large saucepan over medium-low heat. Cook onions with salt and pepper until soft and translucent. Stir in garlic and cook until aroma is released. Add mushrooms and sauté until golden. Add brandy, turn heat to high, and scrape bottom of pan with a wooden spoon to release brown bits.

Light alcohol with a match. When flame subsides, add rice and sauté until slightly colored. Add bay leaves and 1½ cups Chicken Stock. Bring to a boil, reduce heat to medium, and cook until nearly dry.

Once the liquid is evaporated, briefly sauté rice. Then, add stock 1½ cups at a time, constantly stirring with a wooden spoon until absorbed. Repeat procedure, stirring constantly and briefly sautéing between additions, until all stock has been absorbed. You must *constantly* stir while cooking rice. When done, the rice should be glazed outside and soft throughout. It takes approximately 20 minutes to add all the stock. Stir in Parmesan cheese. Serve immediately.

4 to 6 Servings

Potato Pea Curry

In India, where cooks work with a limited number of native ingredients, spices are considered as important as the main ingredient. We urge you to keep on hand the dry spices listed here, in place of curry powder, to create your own curries. Remember, authentic curries are not necessarily hot—always adjust the seasonings to suit your taste.

3   LARGE BAKING POTATOES, PEELED
½   CUP CLARIFIED BUTTER (PAGE 249)
2   LARGE ONIONS, DICED
1   TABLESPOON PUREED GARLIC (PAGE 250)
1   TABLESPOON FRESHLY GRATED GINGER (PAGE 249)
2½   TABLESPOONS GROUND CUMIN
1   TEASPOON TURMERIC
½   TABLESPOON GROUND CORIANDER
½   TABLESPOON DRIED RED PEPPER FLAKES
3   TOMATOES, PEELED, SEEDED, AND DICED (PAGE 249)
3   CUPS CHICKEN STOCK (PAGE 74) OR WATER
1   TABLESPOON SALT
2   CUPS FRESH OR FROZEN PEAS, THAWED
1   TABLESPOON PALM OR BROWN SUGAR (PAGE 248)
¼   CUP FRESH LIME JUICE
1   BUNCH FRESH CILANTRO, ROUGHLY CHOPPED

Cut potatoes into ½-inch dice. Place in a bowl and rinse with cold running water until water runs clear, to remove excess starch.

Heat ¼ cup clarified butter in a medium saucepan over medium-high heat. Sauté onions until brown. At same time, heat remaining clarified butter in a large skillet over moderate heat. Fry potatoes until golden and add sautéed onions.

Add garlic and ginger, and cook just long enough to release their aromas. Remove from heat and add cumin, turmeric, coriander, and pepper flakes. Return pan to moderate heat. Stir in tomatoes, Chicken Stock or water, and salt.

Simmer, uncovered, until potatoes are soft, about 15 minutes. Add remaining ingredients and cook until peas are heated through. Adjust seasonings and serve immediately.

6 Entrées or 4 Accompaniments

Vegetable Vermicelli

Inspired by partner Sue, this dish has become a favorite of many customers. It is a colorful one-dish meal, an abundant array of fresh vegetables julienne cut to match the shape of the pasta. Although the ingredient list is long, this is an easy dish to prepare—one that meat eaters will love as much as vegetarians.

1	POUND WHITE OR ½ POUND OYSTER OR WILD MUSHROOMS
1	LARGE LEEK, WHITE AND LIGHT GREEN PARTS, WASHED
1	LARGE TURNIP, PEELED
1	LARGE CARROT, PEELED
1	ZUCCHINI, WITH SKIN
1	YELLOW CROOKNECK SQUASH, WITH SKIN
¼	POUND CHINESE SNOW PEAS
5	TABLESPOONS UNSALTED BUTTER, COLD
1½	TABLESPOONS PUREED GARLIC (PAGE 250)
1	TEASPOON CRACKED PEPPER
1½	TABLESPOONS SALT
1	LARGE TOMATO, PEELED, SEEDED, AND DICED (PAGE 249)
1½	CUPS TOMATO JUICE
1	TABLESPOON FRESH LEMON JUICE
1	CUP WATER
2	CUPS FRESHLY GRATED PARMESAN CHEESE
1½	POUNDS VERMICELLI
	GRATED PARMESAN CHEESE AND CHOPPED CHIVES FOR GARNISH

Clean all vegetables and slice into fine julienne, ¹⁄₁₆ inch by 3 inches.

Melt 3 tablespoons butter in a large skillet over medium-high heat. Cook mushrooms until slightly colored. Add garlic, cook briefly, and reduce heat to moderate. Add leeks with cracked pepper and cook about a minute. Then add salt, turnip, carrot, zucchini, yellow squash, and snow peas. Cook until vegetables soften, about 3 minutes.

Add tomatoes, tomato juice, lemon juice, and water. Bring to a boil and whisk in remaining 2 tablespoons butter. Remove from heat and stir in Parmesan cheese.

Meanwhile, bring a large stockpot of salted water to a boil. Cook vermicelli until al dente. Try to time it so that pasta is done just when vegetables are cooked. Drain, transfer to vegetable mixture, and toss to combine. Ladle into bowls and garnish with grated Parmesan and chives. Serve immediately.

6 Servings

Main Course Salads

Most of these recipes grew out of our feeling that more and more people are craving lighter, fresher, and healthier meals when they eat out. In other words, people are eating their vegetables. This selection best captures the way we feel people are eating now.

Smoked Chicken Salad

If you have a good-sized grill, you can easily smoke chicken or turkey outside. Build your fire on one side of the grill and place an oven thermometer on the grate on the other side. When it registers 350°F, place the chicken on the side opposite the fire, cover, and cook about 1½ hours. At the halfway point, you can toss a handful of water-soaked hickory chips on the coals for extra flavor. Or, use our fail-safe stove top method here.

1   CUP HICKORY CHIPS, SOAKED IN WATER 1 HOUR
3   CHICKEN LEGS, WITH THIGHS
    SALT AND FRESHLY GROUND PEPPER TO TASTE
2   SMALL GRANNY SMITH APPLES, PEELED AND CORED
3   SCALLIONS, WHITE AND LIGHT GREEN PARTS
2   CELERY STALKS, PEELED
½   CUP HOMEMADE MAYONNAISE (PAGE 194)
1   TABLESPOON RED WINE VINEGAR
½   HEAD GREEN LEAF LETTUCE, 1 BASKET CHERRY
    TOMATOES, 2 AVOCADOS, SLICED, 1½ CUPS SWEET AND
    SOUR RED CABBAGE (PAGE 190) FOR GARNISH

After soaking hickory chips, make a stove top smoker with that big old pot you've been meaning to throw away. (Or line a good pot with aluminum foil to keep it from aging quickly.) Place chips on bottom of pot and a rack above them.

Season chicken with salt and pepper. Place legs on rack, cover pot, and place on a burner over high heat. When chips start to smoke, reduce heat to moderate and cook chicken about ½ hour per side. The juices should run clear when pierced with a knife. Chill a minimum of 2 hours or as long as a day. When meat is chilled, remove skin and bone, and cut into ½-inch dice for the salad.

Cut apples and celery into ½-inch dice and thinly slice scallions across the width. Combine diced chicken, apples, and scallions with celery, mayonnaise, and vinegar in a large bowl and toss well. Adjust salt and pepper to taste.

Line each serving plate with a bed of lettuce. Divide chicken salad and place a mound in center of each plate. Garnish with cherry tomatoes, avocado slices, Sweet and Sour Red Cabbage, and any other crudités you may have in the refrigerator.

4 to 6 Servings

Squid or Octopus Salad

Since people tend to feel strongly about eating squid, we like to place an exotic, spicy salad like this one on a buffet, where people can politely take it or leave it. Another good idea is to serve this refreshing salad as an appetizer before a rich, creamy entrée.

1	POUND SQUID OR COOKED OCTOPUS, CLEANED AND THINLY SLICED
½	TEASPOON SALT
½	TEASPOON WHITE PEPPER
½	CUP THAI FISH SAUCE (PAGE 248)
1	CUP FRESH LIME JUICE
½	CUP WHITE VINEGAR
½	CUP CLAM JUICE
1	MEDIUM RED ONION, FINELY DICED
3	SERRANO CHILES, FINELY MINCED WITH SEEDS
2	LARGE TOMATOES, PEELED, SEEDED, AND DICED (PAGE 249)
2	PICKLING CUCUMBERS OR KIRBIES, DICED WITH SKINS (PAGE 247)
1	BUNCH FRESH CILANTRO, CHOPPED
	TABASCO, SALT, AND PEPPER TO TASTE

Sprinkle squid with salt and pepper. Blanch until water just returns to a boil. Drain and chill. (Octopus need not be blanched.)

Combine the fish sauce, lime juice, vinegar, clam juice, onion, serrano chiles, tomatoes, cucumbers, and cilantro, and toss well with chilled squid or octopus. Season to taste with Tabasco, salt, and pepper. Serve chilled over a bed of greens.

6 Servings

Scotch Eggs

In this old favorite, hard-cooked eggs are coated with sausage, then dipped in bread crumbs and deep-fried. Feel free to substitute store-bought breakfast sausage for the pork and sage mixture. Serve this hearty dish at an Easter brunch with homemade muffins and champagne.

1	POUND GROUND PORK
3	TABLESPOONS FENNEL SEEDS
½	BUNCH FRESH SAGE, CHOPPED
2	TEASPOONS SALT
1	TEASPOON WHITE PEPPER
8	HARD-COOKED EGGS, PEELED AND CHILLED
3	CUPS FINE, DRY BREAD CRUMBS
4	EGGS, BEATEN
4	CUPS VEGETABLE OIL
1	RECIPE WATERCRESS SALAD (PAGE 184) (MADE WITHOUT AVOCADOS)
2	TOMATOES, SLICED
	HORSERADISH AND MUSTARD AND MAYONNAISE (PAGE 193)

Mix together pork, fennel seed, sage, salt, and pepper. Divide into 8 equal portions. Form a patty in your hand with the first portion. Flatten patty, place egg inside, and keep rolling egg and meat in the palms of your hands, until a thin layer of meat coats the egg. Repeat this procedure until all eggs are coated with pork mixture. Chill 20 minutes.

Dip chilled, coated eggs first in bread crumbs, then in eggs and bread crumbs again. Chill 15 minutes. Dip again in eggs, then bread crumbs, and reserve in refrigerator.

Preheat oven to 375°F.

Heat oil in a large stockpot or saucepan to deep-fry temperature (350°F). Fry eggs, 2 or 3 at a time, until golden brown, 3 to 5 minutes. Drain on paper towels. Transfer to a roasting pan and bake 10 minutes.

To serve, arrange a bed Watercress Salad on each serving plate. Slice eggs in half and place 4 halves on top of each salad. Garnish with tomato slices and dollops of Horseradish and Mustard and Mayonnaise for dipping. Serve while eggs are warm.

4 Servings

Cold Poached Salmon
with Tomato and Herbs

One of several versatile un-cooked sauces that we serve with fish is Tomato and Herbs. This one can be served with grilled tuna as well as poached salmon. And, the oil can be omitted for even fewer calories. In the summertime, this elegant entrée appears on our Hollywood Bowl take-out menu with other good travelers like Roasted Red Peppers with Feta (page 42) and Parsnip Chips (page 177).

6   (6-OUNCE) SKINLESS SALMON FILLETS
SALT AND WHITE PEPPER TO TASTE
3   CUPS FISH STOCK (PAGE 76) OR CLAM JUICE

TOMATO AND HERBS

1   BUNCH OREGANO
1   BUNCH BASIL
1   BUNCH PARSLEY
1   BUNCH THYME
6   TOMATOES, PEELED, SEEDED, AND DICED (PAGE 249)
½   CUP EXTRA VIRGIN OLIVE OIL
1½ TEASPOONS SALT
¼   TEASPOON WHITE PEPPER

To poach salmon, preheat oven to 350°F.
Season salmon all over with salt and pepper. Bring stock or juice to a boil in a large ovenproof skillet. Add fish, so they are barely touching, and bring liquid back to a boil. Turn fish over, then cover with a piece of parchment paper coated with olive oil. Transfer to oven and bake 5 minutes. Turn fish over, cover again, and bake an additional 2 minutes. (Drain and reserve the liquid in the pan for use as stock.) Transfer fish to a platter, cover with plastic wrap, and chill until serving time.

To make dressing, remove stems and finely chop all herbs. If these fresh herbs are not available, substitute chives, mint, marjoram, or chervil. Watercress or the bright yellow leaves inside celery stalks are also preferable to dried herbs. Mix all ingredients in a small bowl and reserve in refrigerator.

To serve, arrange each fillet on a lettuce-lined serving plate. Spoon on Tomato and Herbs. We like to serve with various garnishes such as radishes, sliced avocado, pickles, or olives around the salmon.

6 Servings

Cold Confit of Duck Salad

This rich main-course salad mixes the provocative taste of goat cheese with that of mellow duck.

1   RECIPE MARINATED GOAT CHEESE ON RED CHARD
    (PAGE 181)
1   RECIPE CONFIT OF DUCK (PAGE 125)

MUSTARD VINAIGRETTE

1   TEASPOON DIJON MUSTARD
1   TEASPOON STONEGROUND MUSTARD
1   TEASPOON CRACKED BLACK PEPPERCORNS (PAGE 249)
2   TEASPOONS CHOPPED FRESH THYME
2   TABLESPOONS CHOPPED SHALLOTS
½   TEASPOON SALT
¾   CUP OLIVE OIL
¼   CUP RICE WINE VINEGAR (PAGE 248)

3   TOMATOES, SLICED, FOR GARNISH

Arrange marinated goat cheese salad on each of 6 large serving plates. Debone duck and thinly slice meat against grain. (It's easy to slice when cold.) Divide into 6 portions and fan the slices alongside salad.

Make vinaigrette by whisking together ingredients in a small bowl. Spoon vinaigrette on duck, garnish with tomato slices, and serve with toast points.

6 Servings

Marinated Mussel Salad

Diced assorted bell peppers add the right touch of color and flavor to mild steamed mussels. We suggest tapping each mussel before using. If any sound solid, they are probably filled with sand and should be discarded.

2   CUPS DRY WHITE WINE
4½   POUNDS FRESH MUSSELS, WASHED AND DEBEARDED
       (PAGE 250)
1   RED BELL PEPPER
1   GREEN BELL PEPPER
1   YELLOW BELL PEPPER
½   CUP EXTRA VIRGIN OLIVE OIL
1   TABLESPOON BALSAMIC VINEGAR
¼   TEASPOON SALT
       PINCH OF WHITE PEPPER

1   RECIPE WATERCRESS AND AVOCADO SALAD (PAGE 184)
       CRACKED BLACK PEPPER TO TASTE

Bring wine to a boil in a large saucepan. Add mussels, reduce to a simmer, and cook, covered, until shells open. Remove mussels, cover with a wet towel, and set aside to cool.

Meanwhile, core and seed bell peppers. Cut into fine julienne, 1/16 inch, then finely dice. Mix remaining vinaigrette ingredients in a small bowl and stir in diced peppers. Prepare salad.

Arrange salad on 6 serving plates. Remove mussels from shells and dip, one at a time, in bell pepper vinaigrette to coat. Place in a circle over salad, leaving center bare. Spoon on additional bell pepper vinaigrette to taste. Garnish center with slices of avocado and sprinkle with cracked pepper. Serve immediately.

6 Servings

Grilled Tuna with Tomato and Olive Compote

Tuna's strong flavor stands up well to this zesty Spanish-style sauce. If you don't feel like heating the grill to briefly cook the fish, you can sear it in a very hot cast-iron pan instead.

TOMATO AND OLIVE COMPOTE

3/4	CUP OLIVE OIL
3	MEDIUM ONIONS, JULIENNED
1	TEASPOON SALT
1/2	TEASPOON WHITE PEPPER
6	TOMATOES, PEELED, SEEDED, AND DICED (PAGE 249)
2	BUNCHES OREGANO, LEAVES ONLY, CHOPPED
1	CUP SMALL GREEN OLIVES, WITH PITS
3	TABLESPOONS CAPERS, CHOPPED WITH JUICE
6	(6-OUNCE) SKINLESS TUNA FILLETS
	SALT AND WHITE PEPPER TO TASTE

Heat 3 tablespoons oil in a medium skillet over moderate heat. Cook onions with salt until soft, about 10 minutes. Combine remaining ingredients in a bowl. Add cooked onions and chill.

Season tuna all over with salt and pepper. Cook on a very hot, clean grill, about 3 minutes per side. The inside should be bright pink. Transfer to a platter and chill.

To serve, arrange fillets on individual plates. Spoon over Tomato and Olive Compote and serve cold.

6 Servings

Spinach Salad
with Yogurt Dressing

Yogurt dressing with garlic and lemon juice—a variation on ranch dressing—accentuates the light, refreshing quality of fresh spinach leaves.

2   BUNCHES TENDER SPINACH LEAVES, WASHED AND
    DRIED
1   CUP WHITE MUSHROOM CAPS, SLICED
    YOGURT DRESSING, RECIPE FOLLOWS
6   SLICES BACON
3   HARD-COOKED EGGS
2   RED BELL PEPPERS, ROASTED, PEELED, AND SEEDED
    (PAGE 250)
1   RIPE LARGE TOMATO, CUT IN WEDGES
½   CUP FETA CHEESE, CRUMBLED

Break spinach into bite-sized pieces and combine in a large bowl with mushrooms. Add enough Yogurt Dressing to coat leaves and toss well. Divide salad among 6 serving plates.

Fry bacon until crisp, drain on paper towels, then break into 1-inch long strips. Cut eggs in half and slice peppers thinly, lengthwise.

Garnish each salad with bacon strips, bell pepper, tomato wedges, cheese, and half an egg.

6 Servings

Yogurt Dressing

1   TABLESPOON DIJON MUSTARD
1   TABLESPOON PUREED GARLIC (PAGE 250)
2   TABLESPOONS FRESH LEMON JUICE
1   TEASPOON SALT
½   TEASPOON WHITE PEPPER
½   CUP OLIVE OIL
1   CUP PLAIN YOGURT

Mix mustard, garlic, lemon juice, salt, and pepper in a bowl. Gradually whisk in olive oil. Stir in yogurt.

Makes 1½ Cups

Caesar Salad

Mary Sue's husband, Josh's, idea of heaven consists of an evening at home with a Caesar Salad, some martinis, a James Bond movie, and Mary Sue. If you want something more, we suggest Tomato and Fennel Soup (page 53) to start.

CAESAR SALAD DRESSING

5	ANCHOVIES
1	TEASPOON CRACKED BLACK PEPPERCORNS (PAGE 249)
½	CUP EXTRA VIRGIN OLIVE OIL
½	CUP FRESHLY GRATED PARMESAN CHEESE
1	EGG
3	TABLESPOONS RED WINE VINEGAR
2	TABLESPOONS FRESH LEMON JUICE
1	TABLESPOON PUREED GARLIC (PAGE 250)
2	TEASPOONS DRY MUSTARD
1	TEASPOON CELERY SALT
3	DASHES OF TABASCO
3	DASHES OF WORCESTERSHIRE SAUCE
½	LOAF SOURDOUGH OR HEARTY FRENCH OR ITALIAN BREAD, WITH CRUST, DICED FOR CROUTONS
2	MEDIUM HEADS ROMAINE LETTUCE

Combine anchovies, black pepper, and olive oil in a blender. Puree about 5 minutes until very smooth. Add grated Parmesan and blend briefly to combine. Measure and reserve one-third cup for use with croutons.

Bring a small saucepan of water to a boil. Place a refrigerated egg on a slotted spoon and into boiling water. Cook 1½ minutes, remove, and reserve.

Place remaining dressing ingredients in a large bowl and whisk in anchovy mixture. Crack open egg and spoon (including the parts that are uncooked) into mixture. Whisk until well combined. The dressing may be refrigerated at this stage.

Combine reserved anchovy mixture with diced bread in a bowl and toss to coat. Heat a dry cast-iron skillet over medium-high and cook croutons, stirring constantly, until golden and crisp.

Wash and dry lettuce and break into bite-sized pieces. Place in a salad bowl along with dressing and toss well. Add toasted croutons, toss again, and serve.

6 Servings

*A buttery fish like black cod,
salmon, or sturgeon is delicious
smoked. Served on a bed of
thinly sliced Potato Salad Vinaigrette, this one-dish meal is
great for a hot weather lunch.*

Cold Smoked Black Cod
with Potato Salad Vinaigrette

1   CUP HICKORY CHIPS

BRINE

½   CUP COARSE SALT
½   LARGE ONION, SLICED
3   TABLESPOONS BROWN SUGAR
3   BAY LEAVES
1   TABLESPOON DRY MUSTARD
1   1-INCH LENGTH FRESH GINGER, SLICED THINLY
1   TEASPOON BLACK PEPPERCORNS
¼   TEASPOON WHOLE ALLSPICE
¼   TEASPOON WHOLE CLOVES
¼   TEASPOON FRESHLY GRATED NUTMEG
2   CUPS WATER

6   (6-OUNCE) BLACK COD FILLETS
1   RECIPE POTATO SALAD VINAIGRETTE (PAGE 170)

Soak hickory chips in water for an hour. Meanwhile, combine brine ingredients in a medium
saucepan. Bring to a boil, strain into a ceramic or
glass roasting pan, and chill. When cool, marinate
fish about 15 minutes at room temperature.

Make a stove top smoker following the instructions for Smoked Chicken Salad (page 144). When
chips start smoking, place fish on rack, cover, and
cook over moderate heat 10 minutes. Transfer fish
to a platter, cover with plastic wrap, and chill.

To serve, line 6 serving plates with a thin layer
Potato Salad Vinaigrette. Cover each with a chilled
fish fillet and serve.

6 servings

Warm Shredded Chicken Salad

Expect some smoke and splatter when you make this dish. It's important to heat the pan until it glows, so the marinated chicken gets crisp on the outside and remains tender and juicy inside. The results are delicious!

6   BONELESS, SKINLESS CHICKEN BREASTS

MARINADE

½   CUP SESAME OIL
2   TABLESPOONS PEANUT OIL
    JUICE OF ½ LEMON
¼   CUP SOY SAUCE
3   TABLESPOONS FRESHLY GRATED GINGER (PAGE 249)
1   TABLESPOON CORNSTARCH

1   RECIPE WATERCRESS AND AVOCADO SALAD (PAGE 184)
½   CUP PEANUT OIL FOR FRYING

Trim chicken of any excess fat or sinew. Slice, across grain, into 3 x ½-inch strips. Stir marinade ingredients together in a medium bowl. Add chicken strips and toss to evenly coat. Set aside at room temperature, uncovered, 30 minutes. It's important not to marinate any longer, or the acid in the lemon will break down the fibers of the chicken.

Meanwhile arrange Watercress and Avocado Salad on 6 serving plates. Reserve in refrigerator.

To cook chicken, heat a large dry cast-iron skillet, over high heat 15 minutes. (Yes, 15 minutes.) Heat peanut oil for frying. Lift chicken strips from marinade, one at a time, and add to pan, standing as far away as possible to avoid splatters. Fry until dark golden brown and crisp, about 1 minute per side. Arrange about 8 hot chicken strips on each salad in a spoke pattern. Serve immediately.

4 Servings

Accompaniments

These are the small dishes that round out a meal. At the restaurant, we serve these vegetable accompaniments with each platter— a puree, a chip, and a sautéed or baked vegetable—to give diners a variety of tastes and textures to try.

At home, however, these dishes can meet a wide variety of needs. Many can easily be served as starters, salads, or even weeknight suppers with perhaps some bread or fruit and cheese. Be creative. Why limit yourself to a meat and vegetable for dinner when you can get your protein just as well from a beautiful Thai Bean Salad (page 158)? Have fun.

Beans

Lentil and Walnut Salad

This inexpensive salad combines the earthiness of lentils and nuts with a refreshing vinaigrette. It can be prepared entirely in advance.

2	CUPS LENTILS
¼	CUP RED WINE VINEGAR
¾	CUP EXTRA VIRGIN OLIVE OIL
½	TABLESPOON DRY MUSTARD
½	TEASPOON SALT
¼	TEASPOON WHITE PEPPER
2	BUNCHES SCALLIONS, THINLY SLICED
2	CUPS WALNUTS, ROUGHLY CHOPPED

Pick over lentils to remove dirt or pebbles, then rinse in cold, running water until water runs clear. Place lentils in a large pot, add enough water to cover, and bring to a boil. Reduce to a simmer and cook, uncovered, 15 to 20 minutes, until beans are done but not pasty. Drain in a colander.

Whisk red wine vinegar, olive oil, mustard, salt, and pepper together to form a vinaigrette.

While lentils are still warm, combine with scallions and walnuts in a large bowl. Pour on dressing and toss. Chill until serving time.

6 Servings

Chopped Tofu with Parsley

Tofu is great for offsetting strong, spicy foods. The parsley in this recipe adds a fresh flavor to the tofu and garlic. At the restaurant, we serve it with our Spicy Cold Soba Noodles (page 164) and Marinated Beef Short Ribs (page 93).

1	(14-OUNCE) PACKAGE SOFT TOFU
2	TABLESPOONS OLIVE OIL
2	TABLESPOONS PUREED GARLIC (PAGE 250)
1	CUP FINELY CHOPPED FRESH PARSLEY
¼	CUP MAYONNAISE (PAGE 194)
2	TABLESPOONS FRESH LEMON JUICE
1½	TEASPOONS SALT
½	TEASPOON WHITE PEPPER

Drain tofu of water, wrap in a thin kitchen towel or 4 layers of cheesecloth, and squeeze to remove any excess moisture. Roughly chop and reserve.

Heat oil in a small skillet over low heat. Cook garlic 2 to 3 minutes.

In a bowl, combine tofu, sautéed garlic, parsley, Mayonnaise, lemon juice, salt, and pepper. Mash with a fork until fine. Chill and serve in small ramekins or as a dip for crackers or toasts.

Makes 2 Cups

Orange Dal
with Ginger and Garlic

Orange dal has a lighter, sweeter quality than darker lentils. For a complete protein, vegetarian lunch at home, try combining the dal with rice, then topping it with a dollop of yogurt and some crisp fried onions.

2	CUPS ORANGE LENTIL DAL (PAGE 247)
2	TABLESPOONS CLARIFIED BUTTER (PAGE 249)
2	LARGE ONIONS, FINELY DICED
1	TEASPOON SALT
1	TEASPOON WHITE PEPPER
2	TABLESPOONS PUREED GARLIC (PAGE 250)
2	TABLESPOONS FRESHLY GRATED GINGER (PAGE 249)
2½	CUPS CHICKEN STOCK (PAGE 74), CANNED BROTH, OR WATER

Spread dal on a cookie sheet and pick out any stones or clumps of dirt. Place in a large bowl and wash under cold, running water until water runs clear, about 10 minutes. Drain in a colander.

Heat butter in a medium saucepan over moderate heat. Sauté onions with salt and pepper until golden brown. Add garlic and ginger, and cook 2 to 3 minutes, stirring occasionally. Add dal and Chicken Stock or water. Bring to a boil, reduce to a simmer, and cook, covered, 20 minutes. Serve immediately. Dal keeps well for 2 to 3 days. Reheat before serving.

6 Servings

Black Bean Salad
with Bell Peppers

This healthy salad has lots of visual appeal, with the finely diced, brightly colored peppers against a dark background. It also travels well for picnics or potlucks and keeps in the refrigerator about 2 days.

1½ CUPS DRIED BLACK BEANS, WASHED
3 BELL PEPPERS, PREFERABLY RED, YELLOW, AND GREEN
¾ CUP EXTRA VIRGIN OLIVE OIL
⅓ CUP RED WINE VINEGAR
1 TEASPOON SALT
1 TEASPOON FRESHLY GROUND PEPPER
1 LARGE RED ONION, DICED

Place beans in a large pot with a generous quantity of water. Bring to a boil, reduce to a simmer, and cook, uncovered, until tender, about an hour. Check pot occasionally and add water, if necessary, to cover. To test for doneness, taste a small bean as it will be the last to finish cooking. If tender and smooth inside, all beans are done. Continue cooking if the taste is at all powdery. Drain in a colander.

Meanwhile, core and seed peppers and finely dice. In a large bowl, whisk together olive oil, vinegar, salt, and pepper to form a vinaigrette. Toss in diced peppers and onion, and mix well. Add drained beans, toss again, and chill about 2 hours.

6 Servings

Thai Bean Salad

Mary Sue brought this recipe back from Bangkok, where vendors sell individual portions on the street as a between-meal snack. Serve it on a salad buffet with a strong entrée like Grilled Pepper Steak with Tamarind Chutney (page 9), or as a casual main course.

1 POUND CHINESE LONG BEANS, OR GREEN OR YELLOW
   BEANS, ENDS TRIMMED
2 TOMATOES, PEELED, SEEDED, AND DICED (PAGE 249)
1 SMALL ZUCCHINI, GRATED WITH SKIN
1 TABLESPOON PUREED GARLIC (PAGE 250)
¼ CUP PALM OR BROWN SUGAR (PAGE 248)
½ CUP THAI FISH SAUCE (PAGE 248)
½ CUP FRESH LIME JUICE
3 OR MORE SERRANO CHILES TO TASTE, STEMS REMOVED
   AND THINLY SLICED HORIZONTALLY, WITH SEEDS
3 KAFFIR LIME LEAVES (PAGE 2) CHOPPED, OR
   1 TEASPOON GRATED LIME ZEST
½ CUP DRIED SHRIMP (PAGE 247)
1 CUP ROASTED, UNSALTED PEANUTS

Blanch beans in a large pot of boiling, salted water until barely tender, about 1 minute. Immediately refresh in a bowl of iced water. If using long beans, tie each bean in a series of knots, 1 inch apart. Then cut between knots, so each piece has a knot in its center. (If this presentation doesn't appeal to you or long beans are not available, skip the knots. The dish tastes fine with beans cut diagonally into ½-inch lengths.) Combine beans with tomatoes and zucchini in a large bowl and reserve.

In another bowl, mix garlic, palm or brown sugar, Thai Fish Sauce, lime juice, serrano chiles, and lime leaves. Roughly chop shrimp and peanuts. Combine with fish sauce mixture.

Pour dressing over reserved vegetables and toss well. Serve immediately.

6 to 8 Servings

Cold Garbanzo and Cucumber Salad

Refreshing cucumbers lighten the hearty beans in this simple winter salad.

¾ CUP EXTRA VIRGIN OLIVE OIL
2 TABLESPOONS RED WINE VINEGAR
1½ TEASPOON SALT
1½ TEASPOONS WHITE PEPPER
2 CUPS CANNED GARBANZO BEANS, DRAINED
5 PICKLING CUCUMBERS OR KIRBIES (PAGE 247), PEELED AND DICED
1 MEDIUM RED ONION, DICED
2 TOMATOES, PEELED, SEEDED, AND DICED (PAGE 249)
1 BUNCH FRESH BASIL, CHOPPED

Combine olive oil, vinegar, salt, and pepper in a large bowl. Whisk to form a vinaigrette. Add remaining ingredients. Toss to combine and chill.

6 to 8 Servings

Green Beans with Scallions

The pureed scallions in the dressing give this green salad a forceful bite. The dressing and beans can be prepared in advance, but always combine at the last minute for the best crunch.

2   POUNDS GREEN AND YELLOW BEANS (IF AVAILABLE),
    CUT INTO 2-INCH LENGTHS DIAGONALLY
2   BUNCHES SCALLIONS, WHITE AND PART OF GREEN,
    SLICED
1   CUP SOUR CREAM
1   TABLESPOON FRESH LEMON JUICE
½   TEASPOON SALT
½   TEASPOON WHITE PEPPER
½   CUP MAYONNAISE (PAGE 194)

Blanch beans in rapidly boiling salted water until water returns to a boil. Immediately refresh in iced water until thoroughly chilled and drain.

In a blender, combine scallions, sour cream, and lemon juice. Pulse a few times to combine, then puree until smooth. Add salt, pepper, and Mayonnaise. Blend just to combine.

Toss beans with pureed scallion dressing. Serve immediately.

6 Servings

Noodles

Spaetzel

Here is a handy recipe that takes about 20 minutes from start to finish—great for last-minute emergencies. Serve these comforting little dumplings with any gravy or sauced dish like our creamy Sautéed Chicken with Caraway and Cream (page 119) or Beef Brisket (page 97).

2   EGGS
2   EGG YOLKS
½   CUP HEAVY CREAM
1   CUP ALL-PURPOSE FLOUR
½   TEASPOON SALT
¼   TEASPOON WHITE PEPPER
¼   TEASPOON FRESHLY GRATED NUTMEG

Mix eggs, egg yolks, and cream together in a bowl. Add remaining ingredients and mix just until moist.

Bring a large saucepan of water to a boil and reduce to a simmer. Hold a large-holed slotted spoon over simmering water and push about ¼ cup dough at a time through the holes to make dumplings. Sometimes a large-holed colander could suffice. Gently simmer until cooked through, 2 to 3 minutes. Remove with a slotted spoon and transfer to a bowl of iced water. Repeat until all dough is cooked. Reheat spaetzel in a small amount of cream, or butter with water.

Makes 1 Pound

Pasta Salad
with Black Olives and Feta

Pasta salads were a mainstay at our first restaurant, City Café, out of necessity. The kitchen was so tiny there was no room for an oven. Of the one hundred varieties we created there, this simple, strong salad remains a favorite.

1 TABLESPOON OLIVE OIL
2 TABLESPOONS SALT
1 POUND PASTA, SMALL TUBES OR SHELLS
¾ CUP EXTRA VIRGIN OLIVE OIL
1 CUP CRUMBLED FETA CHEESE
¾ CUP KALAMATA OLIVES
2 MEDIUM TOMATOES, PEELED, SEEDED, AND DICED (PAGE 249)
1 LARGE RED ONION, DICED
3 PICKLING CUCUMBERS OR KIRBIES (PAGE 247), PEELED AND DICED
2 BUNCHES OREGANO, LEAVES ONLY, CHOPPED
3 DASHES OF TABASCO
SALT AND FRESHLY GROUND PEPPER TO TASTE

Bring 1 gallon water to a rolling boil in a large stockpot. Add 1 tablespoon olive oil, salt, and pasta, and cook until al dente, about 6 minutes for fresh and 8 minutes for dry. Drain in a colander and immediately transfer to a large bowl of iced water to cool. Drain well, transfer to another bowl, and toss with ¼ cup extra virgin olive oil.

Mix all remaining ingredients in a bowl. Toss with pasta, adjust seasonings, and serve.

8 Servings

Pasta Salad with
Roasted Peppers and Onions

*Serve a rich, creamy salad like
this before a simple entrée like
Turkey Breast with Lemon Butter (page 121) or grilled fish.
Or serve it as a main course,
with the addition of salami.*

1	TABLESPOON OLIVE OIL
2	TABLESPOONS SALT
1	POUND PASTA, SMALL TUBES OR SHELLS
½	CUP EXTRA VIRGIN OLIVE OIL
6	RED AND/OR YELLOW BELL PEPPERS
3	MEDIUM ONIONS, JULIENNED
1½	TEASPOONS SALT
¼	TEASPOON WHITE PEPPER
1	TABLESPOON PUREED GARLIC (PAGE 250)
1	TABLESPOON PAPRIKA
3	LARGE TOMATOES, PEELED, SEEDED, AND DICED, WITH JUICE (PAGE 249)
1½	CUPS SOUR CREAM
3	DASHES OF TABASCO

Bring 1 gallon water to a rolling boil in a large
stockpot. Add 1 tablespoon olive oil, salt, and
pasta and cook until al dente, about 6 minutes for
fresh and 8 minutes for dry. Drain in a colander and
immediately transfer to a large bowl of iced water to
cool. Drain well, transfer to another bowl, and toss
with ¼ cup extra virgin olive oil. Cover with plastic
wrap and set aside at room temperature.

Roast peppers under a preheated broiler or directly over a gas flame until completely charred.
Transfer to a plastic bag, tightly close, and set aside
to steam about 10 minutes. Then, under cold running
water, peel and split open to remove core and seeds.
Julienne slice peppers and reserve.

Heat remaining ¼ cup oil in a large skillet over
high heat. Add onions, salt, and pepper, and cook
until golden brown. Lower heat to moderate, add
garlic, and cook 1 minute, then add paprika, and
cook 1 minute more. Add red peppers and tomatoes,
cook an additional minute, and remove from heat.

Transfer to a medium bowl and combine with
sour cream and Tabasco. Pour over reserved pasta,
toss well, and serve.

4 to 6 Servings   ✕

VARIATION: Add about half a pound Genoa salami,
sliced thinly and julienned, to sautéed onions before
adding garlic.

Homemade Fettuccine

Pasta making is labor-intensive work—great therapy for bad weather weekends. Once you start making your own, dry pasta will never taste the same.

5   CUPS SEMOLINA FLOUR
3   EGGS
3   EGG YOLKS
1   TEASPOON PLUS 1 TO 2 TABLESPOONS OLIVE OIL
1   TEASPOON PLUS 1 TABLESPOON SALT
1   TABLESPOON COLD WATER

Place semolina in a large bowl. In a small bowl, combine eggs, egg yolks, 1 teaspoon olive oil, 1 teaspoon salt, and water, and pour into flour. Stir with a wooden spoon until the flour clumps together and forms a dry, firm ball.

Knead 5 to 7 minutes, until smooth. Dough should be quite stiff. Cover with a damp cloth and set aside to rest 15 minutes. Divide dough into 4 equal pieces. Set 3 pieces aside, under cloth, and begin rolling fourth.

First flatten by hand. Then, with pasta machine at widest setting, roll through 3 times, folding in half lengthwise between turns. It should be smooth and as wide as the rollers. Reduce setting, rolling dough through once at each, until you reach the next to the thinnest setting.

Trim dough into 12-inch lengths, dust with flour, and cut with fettuccine blade. Fluff strands to separate and set aside on floured trays. Repeat procedure with remaining 3 portions.

To cook fresh fettuccine, bring about 3 gallons water to a rapid boil with 1 tablespoon salt. Cook pasta until al dente, about 3 minutes. Drain in a colander and serve. If making in advance, immediately transfer to a large bowl of iced water and chill. Drain and place in a plastic container. Toss with a tablespoon or two of olive oil and store in refrigerator until ready to use.

Finished pasta can be reheated in a shallow pan, on top of stove. Combine with 1 tablespoon oil, 3 tablespoons water, or a scant ¼ cup cream. Warm over moderate heat, shaking pan to avoid scorching.

Makes 2 Pounds

Rice Sticks

Rice Sticks are fun to make when children are in the house. In a remarkable transformation, these clear white noodles become crisp white clouds almost the moment they hit the hot oil. Use them to add crunch to Oriental salads, for snacks, or as a starch accompaniment.

1 ½ CUPS VEGETABLE OIL

3 OUNCES CHINESE OR JAPANESE RICE STICKS (PAGE 248)

Heat oil in a medium skillet over high heat until it just begins to smoke, about 5 minutes. Have paper towels ready for draining. To test oil, break off one rice stick and toss into oil. If it puffs immediately, oil is ready. (Cold oil will cause the rice sticks to harden when cooked, so don't let the oil cool down between batches.)

Divide rice sticks into about 6 parts, and add a batch at a time to oil. When they puff, turn with tongs, and cook an additional second. Drain on paper towels and season to taste with salt. Cooked rice sticks will remain crisp about a day in paper or plastic bags.

6 Servings

Spicy Cold Soba Noodles

Many of our newer recipes have been inspired by our trips to Asia, where people eat less meat. These Japanese buckwheat noodles are a complete protein when served with a Chopped Tofu with Parsley salad (page 156).

If Chinese chili oil is not available, you can make your own by combining ¼ cup of heated peanut oil with two tablespoons of dried red pepper flakes. Let sit about 3 minutes to infuse, and strain out the peppers.

⅓ CUP SOY SAUCE

1 TABLESPOON MOLASSES

¼ CUP SESAME OIL

¼ CUP TAHINI (PAGE 248)

¼ CUP BROWN SUGAR

¼ CUP CHILI OIL

3 TABLESPOONS BALSAMIC OR RED WINE VINEGAR

½ BUNCH SCALLIONS, WHITE AND GREEN PARTS, THINLY SLICED

SALT TO TASTE

½ POUND SOBA OR JAPANESE BUCKWHEAT NOODLES (PAGE 248)

Place soy sauce in a pan over high heat and reduce by half. Turn heat to low, stir in molasses, and warm briefly. Transfer to a mixing bowl. Add sesame oil, tahini, brown sugar, chili oil, vinegar, and scallions, and whisk to combine. Season to taste with salt, if desired.

Bring a large pot of salted water to a rapid boil. Add noodles, bring back to a boil, and cook, stirring occasionally, until they just begin to soften, about 3 minutes. (Soba noodles can overcook very quickly, so stay nearby.)

Have ready a large bowl of iced water. Drain noodles, plunge in iced water, and drain again. Place in a colander and rinse well under cold running water. Combine noodles and sauce, toss well, and chill.

6 Servings   ✕

Pasta Salad with Prosciutto and Peas

With its generous quantity of meat and rich Caesar Salad Dressing, this elegant pasta salad could easily be served as a main course. The key when preparing this or any other pasta salad is to mix the pasta with the other ingredients right before serving.

1   TABLESPOON OLIVE OIL
2   TABLESPOONS SALT
1   POUND PASTA, SMALL TUBES OR SHELLS
¾   CUP EXTRA VIRGIN OLIVE OIL
2   CUPS FRESH OR FROZEN PEAS
3   MEDIUM RED ONIONS, JULIENNED
¾   POUND PROSCIUTTO, SLICED TWICE AS THICK AS PAPER
     AND JULIENNED
½   RECIPE CAESAR SALAD DRESSING (PAGE 151)

B ring 1 gallon water to a rolling boil in a large stockpot. Add 1 tablespoon olive oil, salt, and pasta, and cook until al dente, about 6 minutes for fresh and 8 minutes for dry. Drain in a colander and immediately transfer to a large bowl of iced water to cool. Drain well, transfer to another bowl, and toss with ¼ cup extra virgin olive oil. Cover with plastic wrap and set aside at room temperature.

Cook peas. Immediately rinse with cold water and reserve.

Heat remaining ½ cup oil in a large skillet over high heat. Add onions and cook until golden. Remove from heat. Transfer to a medium bowl and set aside to cool. Stir in peas and Caesar dressing. Pour over reserved pasta, toss well, and serve.

4 to 6 Servings   ✕

Starches

Roasted Potatoes

*These potatoes are as thin and
habit forming as potato chips.
Serve with grilled steaks or
chops, or Warm Confit of Duck
(page 125).*

3 LARGE BAKING POTATOES, PEELED
¾ CUP CLARIFIED BUTTER (PAGE 249)
½ TEASPOON SALT
¼ TEASPOON WHITE PEPPER

Preheat oven to 450°F. Slice potatoes as thinly as
possible across length. (We like to use a mandolin, although a food processor fitted with a 2-
millimeter slicing blade will do just fine.) Rinse potatoes by placing in a large bowl, under cold running
water, until water runs clear, about 5 minutes. Drain
and pat dry with paper towels.

Combine potatoes with butter, salt, and pepper
in a medium bowl. Toss to coat.

Arrange potato slices in two or three layers on a
medium jelly roll pan or baking sheet. Bake 30 to 35
minutes, until the edges are golden brown. Tip pan
to drain off excess butter, cut into wedges, and serve
immediately.

6 Servings

Basmati Rice

*In India, where Basmati rice is
prized above all others, each
harvest is given a vintage, so
that people can request a specific year.*

2 CUPS BASMATI RICE (PAGE 246)
3 CUPS WATER
1 TEASPOON SALT
2 TEASPOONS UNSALTED BUTTER

Place rice in a bowl and rinse under cold, running
water, stirring occasionally, until water runs clear.
Drain well.

Combine water, salt, and butter in a medium saucepan and bring to a boil. Add rice, return to a boil, and cover. Reduce to a simmer and cook 10 minutes. Remove from heat and let stand, covered, 5 minutes. Serve immediately.

6 to 8 Servings

Fenneled Rice

Aromatic fennel and Pernod give rice a fresh, clean taste. This dish is superb with Chicken Breast with Garlic and Parsley (page 117).

1½	CUPS BASMATI RICE (PAGE 246)
1–2	FENNEL BULBS
2	TABLESPOONS OLIVE OIL
1	TEASPOON SALT
½	TEASPOON WHITE PEPPER
½	CUP PERNOD
2	CUPS CHICKEN STOCK (PAGE 74) OR CANNED BROTH
1	TOMATO, PEELED, SEEDED, AND DICED (PAGE 249)

Place rice in a bowl and rinse under cold, running water until water runs clear. Drain and reserve.

Remove wispy fennel leaves. Chop and reserve for garnish. Cut bulbs in half and slice thinly across width. Finely dice, discarding hard cores.

Heat oil in a medium saucepan over moderate heat. Add chopped fennel bulbs and stalks, salt, and pepper. Cook, uncovered, until soft. Add Pernod, turn heat to high, and light alcohol with a match. Continue to cook over high heat until liquid is reduced by half. Add reserved rice and Chicken Stock, and bring to a boil. Cover, reduce to a simmer, and cook 5 minutes. Remove from heat and let sit, with cover on, for 5 minutes.

Stir in tomato. Cover and steam an additional 2 minutes. Adjust seasonings, garnish with reserved fennel leaves, and serve warm.

4 to 6 Servings

Bulgur Pilaf

Bulgur, or cracked wheat, is available at health food and Middle Eastern markets. It has a wholesome nutty taste that we love. A great pilaf to serve beneath Grilled Chicken with Roasted Peppers (page 116).

1	CUP BULGUR WHEAT (PAGE 246)
1	CUP BOILING WATER
4	TABLESPOONS (½ STICK) UNSALTED BUTTER
3	OUNCES VERMICELLI, IN SMALL PIECES
1	SMALL ONION, DICED
1	CUP CHICKEN STOCK (PAGE 74), CANNED BROTH, OR WATER
½	TEASPOON SALT
½	TEASPOON WHITE PEPPER

Combine wheat and water in a bowl and set aside until reconstituted, about 10 minutes.

Melt butter in a medium saucepan over medium-high heat. Sauté onion until golden, about 10 minutes. Add vermicelli and sauté until golden. Stir in reconstituted bulgur, Chicken Stock, salt, and pepper. Reduce to a simmer and cook, covered, about 10 minutes.

4 to 6 Servings

VARIATION: Stir in a diced, roasted red pepper, along with reconstituted bulgur and stock, for some added color.

Rice Salad with Cumin and Squash

This pretty salad showcases cumin—an ingredient that usually appears in combination with hot spices. A great use for leftover rice, you can serve this versatile dish as a starter, a side dish, or on a salad buffet.

1	CUP OLIVE OIL
½	EGGPLANT, WITH SKIN, FINELY DICED
1	SMALL YELLOW CROOKNECK SQUASH, WITH SKIN, FINELY DICED
½	ZUCCHINI, WITH SKIN, FINELY DICED
1	LARGE RED ONION, DICED
2	TEASPOONS SALT
1	TABLESPOON PUREED GARLIC (PAGE 250)
2	TABLESPOONS GROUND CUMIN
1	LARGE TOMATO, PEELED, SEEDED, AND DICED
1½	CUPS COOKED RICE, PREFERABLY BASMATI (PAGE 166)
2	TABLESPOONS TARRAGON OR RED WINE VINEGAR

Heat ½ cup oil in a large skillet over moderate heat. Cook eggplant until soft, about 3 minutes. Add yellow squash and zucchini, and cook about 2 minutes more, stirring occasionally. Transfer vegetables to a bowl and reserve.

Add remaining oil to pan and turn heat to high. Sauté onions with salt until golden brown, about 5 minutes. Stir in garlic and cook briefly. Add cumin and cook an additional minute. Reduce heat to low.

Return vegetables to pan. Add tomato, cooked rice, and vinegar. Stir to combine and remove from heat. Serve warm as a vegetable accompaniment or chilled as a salad.

6 Servings

Spinach Pilaf

Here is a quick, easy pilaf that is terrific with grilled fish or sautéed squid.

4   TABLESPOONS (½ STICK) UNSALTED BUTTER

3   BUNCHES SPINACH, STEMS TRIMMED

2   TEASPOONS SALT

1   LARGE ONION, DICED

1   TABLESPOON GROUND CUMIN

1   TEASPOON GROUND CARDAMOM

1   TEASPOON GROUND CORIANDER

1   TEASPOON GROUND TURMERIC

2   CUPS COOKED RICE, PREFERABLY BASMATI (PAGE 166)

2   TOMATOES, PEELED, SEEDED, AND DICED

Melt 2 tablespoons butter in a large sauté pan over medium-high heat. Sauté spinach with salt just until leaves are wilted. Reserve.

Melt remaining butter in a medium saucepan over medium-high heat. Sauté onions until lightly browned. Reduce heat, add ground spices, and stir briefly. Add cooked rice, tomatoes, and reserved spinach. Cook just enough to heat rice through, stirring well to combine. Serve warm.

4 to 6 Servings

Greek Potato Salad

*We prefer smooth-textured red
potatoes for our light, thinly
sliced potato salads. Fresh thyme
or sage are good substitutes if
oregano is unavailable.*

2	POUNDS RED POTATOES, WASHED, WITH SKINS
1	CUP VIRGIN OLIVE OIL
3	SHALLOTS, CHOPPED
1½	BUNCHES OREGANO, LEAVES ONLY, CHOPPED
2	TEASPOONS FRESH LEMON JUICE
1	TEASPOON SALT
¼	TEASPOON WHITE PEPPER

Cut potatoes across width into ⅛-inch slices. Place in a large bowl and wash in cold, running water until water runs clear.

Bring a large pot of salted water to a boil. Add potatoes, bring back to a boil, and cook until slices are barely soft, about 3 to 5 minutes. Drain in a colander.

Combine remaining ingredients in a medium bowl. Add warm potato slices and toss to combine. Serve immediately or chill. Potato salad may be kept in a sealed container in refrigerator 2 to 3 days.

6 Servings

Potato Salad Vinaigrette

The potato slices are as thin and crunchy as lettuce leaves in this refreshing presentation. We serve it in smoked fish sand-wiches.

6	MEDIUM RED POTATOES, WITH SKINS, WASHED
½	MEDIUM RED ONION, THINLY SLICED
2	TABLESPOONS RED WINE VINEGAR
1	TABLESPOON PLUS 1 TEASPOON DIJON MUSTARD
½	CUP VIRGIN OLIVE OIL
1	BUNCH PARSLEY, LEAVES ONLY, CHOPPED
2	TEASPOONS PUREED GARLIC (PAGE 250)
1½	TEASPOONS SALT
	DASH OF WHITE PEPPER

Using a mandolin or food processor, fitted with a 2-millimeter slicing blade, slice potatoes across width as thinly as possible. Place in a large bowl and wash in cold, running water until water runs clear.

Bring a large pot of salted water to a boil. Add

potatoes, bring back to a boil, and remove from heat. Drain in a colander. In a medium bowl, toss potatoes with red onion and reserve.

Whisk remaining ingredients in a small bowl to form a vinaigrette. Pour over potatoes and onions, and toss to combine. Serve immediately or refrigerate as long as 2 days.

6 Servings

Rice Stick Pilaf

Chinese rice sticks develop a nutty, caramel flavor and rich consistency in this unusually good pilaf. Delicious with roasted poultry or a simple grilled veal chop.

2 TABLESPOONS UNSALTED BUTTER
1 CUP DICED ONION
½ TEASPOON SALT
½ TEASPOON FRESHLY GROUND PEPPER
1 CUP DICED WHITE MUSHROOMS
½ CUP DICED, ROASTED RED BELL PEPPERS (PAGE 250)
8 OUNCES RICE STICKS (PAGE 164), COOKED UNTIL GOLDEN
2 CUPS CHICKEN STOCK (PAGE 74), CANNED BROTH, OR WATER

Melt butter in a heavy medium saucepan over medium-high heat. Cook onions with salt and pepper until translucent, about 5 minutes. Add mushrooms and cook until soft. Add roasted red peppers, rice sticks broken into small pieces, and Chicken Stock. Bring to a boil and reduce to a simmer. Cook, uncovered, until nearly dry, about 10 minutes. Serve immediately.

8 Servings

Purees

Roasted Eggplant with San Bai Su

This flavorful puree can be served hot, chilled, or at room temperature. We use it to round out a plate of grilled chicken and rice or with warm pita triangles as an appetizer.

3   MEDIUM EGGPLANTS
6   TABLESPOONS OLIVE OIL
3   TABLESPOONS PUREED GARLIC (PAGE 250)
½   CUP SAN BAI SU (PAGE 248) OR ¼ CUP SOY SAUCE
1   TABLESPOON CAYENNE
1   TEASPOON SALT (OPTIONAL)

Preheat broiler. Place eggplants on a large baking sheet close to flame. Roast as you would peppers, until skin is charred all over and flesh is softened, about 40 minutes. Set aside to cool. Peel and roughly chop meat, reserving juice.

    Heat oil in a medium skillet over medium-low heat. Add garlic. Cook gently, stirring occasionally, 1 minute. Stir in remaining ingredients and remove from heat. Season to taste with salt and serve.

6 Servings

Butternut Squash Puree

Butternut squash is one of the most appealing autumn vegetables. When fresh and sweet, you can reduce the amount of butter.

4   SMALL BUTTERNUT SQUASH
    SALT AND FRESHLY GROUND PEPPER TO TASTE
8   TABLESPOONS (1 STICK) UNSALTED BUTTER, ROOM TEMPERATURE

Preheat oven to 375°F. Cut squash in half lengthwise and remove seeds. Generously sprinkle with salt and pepper. Spread about 1 teaspoon softened butter over each half. Place cut-side down in a jelly roll or roasting pan. Pour about ½ inch water in pan, cover with aluminum foil, and bake until soft, 1½ to 2 hours.

When cool enough to handle, scoop out meat with a spoon, discarding skins. Transfer to a food processor with remaining butter and puree briefly. Adjust seasonings and serve hot.

6 servings

Sweet Potato Puree with Honey and Lime

This hearty accompaniment is not too sweet—a great idea for Thanksgiving dinner. You can tell that sweet potatoes and yams are done baking when honeylike droplets form on the skin.

5 POUNDS SWEET POTATOES, UNPEELED
4 TABLESPOONS (½ STICK) UNSALTED BUTTER
1 CUP SOUR CREAM
2 TABLESPOONS FRESH LIME JUICE
2 TABLESPOONS HONEY
½ TEASPOON SALT
¼ TEASPOON WHITE PEPPER

Preheat oven to 400°F. Bake potatoes until soft, about 45 minutes. Set aside to cool. Then peel, roughly chop, and puree in a food processor, being careful not to overprocess.

Place butter and sour cream in a medium saucepan over medium-low heat. Stir in pureed potatoes and remaining ingredients. Adjust seasonings and serve immediately.

6 Servings

Mashed Potatoes

Our authentic all-American recipe for everyone's favorite puree—mashed potatoes. The key to fluffy, creamy potatoes is to combine the ingredients while warm. For richer potatoes, increase the butter and sour cream to taste.

2½ POUNDS BAKING POTATOES, PEELED AND QUARTERED
1½ TABLESPOONS SALT
1   CUP SOUR CREAM
8   TABLESPOONS (1 STICK) UNSALTED BUTTER
    SALT AND FRESHLY GROUND PEPPER TO TASTE
    CRACKED BLACK PEPPER FOR GARNISH

Place potatoes in a bowl and wash under cold, running water until water runs clear. Place in a medium saucepan with salt. Add enough water to generously cover. Bring to a boil, reduce to a simmer, and cook, uncovered, until soft, about 15 minutes. While potatoes are still warm, mash with a fork, in a food mill, or gently in a food processor.

In a medium saucepan, warm sour cream and butter. Fold warm sour cream mixture into potatoes, add salt and pepper to taste, and serve immediately. Garnish with cracked pepper.

6 to 8 Servings

Turnip Puree
with Brown Butter

Browned butter adds a rich, nutty flavor to one of our favorite root vegetables. All the purees can be reheated in a covered casserole in a 300°F oven or in a bain-marie.

1½ POUNDS TURNIPS, PEELED AND SLICED THINLY ACROSS
    THE WIDTH
½   CUP (1 STICK PLUS 3 TABLESPOONS) UNSALTED BUTTER
2   TEASPOONS SALT
¼   TEASPOON WHITE PEPPER
2   CUPS WATER

Combine turnips, salt, pepper, and water in a medium saucepan. Bring to a boil, reduce to a simmer, and cook, covered, until soft, about 15 minutes. Drain turnips and puree in a food processor.

In a small skillet melt butter over moderate heat until brown bits form. Remove from heat and fold into turnips. Serve immediately.

6 Servings

. . . .

Creamed Spinach

We never grow tired of this classic spinach puree.

3	TABLESPOONS UNSALTED BUTTER
3	BUNCHES SPINACH, WASHED AND STEMS REMOVED
1	SMALL ONION, DICED
1½	CUPS HEAVY CREAM
1	TEASPOON SALT
½	TEASPOON WHITE PEPPER
¼	TEASPOON FRESHLY GRATED NUTMEG

Melt 1 tablespoon butter in a large skillet over moderate heat. Add spinach and cook, tossing gently, until wilted and bright green. Drain in a colander and reserve.

Melt remaining 2 tablespoons butter in same skillet over moderate heat. Cook onion until soft, but not brown. Meanwhile chop spinach finely and add to onions. Add cream, bring to a boil, and cook until mixture thickens slightly, about 5 minutes. Stir in seasonings and serve immediately.

6 Servings

Carrot and Rutabaga Puree

In this puree of winter vegetables, the carrots sweeten and lighten the earthy rutabaga.

1   LARGE RUTABAGA
6   LARGE CARROTS
5   TABLESPOONS UNSALTED BUTTER
¼   CUP WATER
SALT AND FRESHLY GROUND PEPPER TO TASTE

Preheat oven to 350°F.
        Peel rutabaga and carrots, and cut into ½-inch slices. Combine with remaining ingredients in a medium saucepan. Cover and bake until tender, 15 to 20 minutes. Finely grind vegetables in a food processor or meat grinder. Adjust seasonings and serve hot.

6 Servings

Roasted Eggplant and Sesame

This puree, also known as baba ghanoush, is great as a dip with pita triangles or garlic Naan (page 89). At the restaurant we spread it on grilled chicken sandwiches (page 83).

1¾   POUNDS EGGPLANT
2   TABLESPOONS TAHINI (PAGE 248)
1   TABLESPOON FRESH LEMON JUICE
1   TABLESPOON EXTRA VIRGIN OLIVE OIL
1   TABLESPOON PUREED GARLIC (PAGE 250)
1   TEASPOON CAYENNE
DASH OF TABASCO
SALT AND FRESHLY GROUND PEPPER TO TASTE

Preheat broiler. Place eggplant on a baking sheet and broil, turning occasionally, until charred all over and softened, about 40 minutes. Set aside to cool.
        When cool enough to handle, peel eggplant and roughly chop, reserving liquid. Transfer to a large bowl. Mix in remaining ingredients and season to taste with salt and pepper. Serve chilled or at room temperature.

4 to 6 Servings

Fried Vegetables

Fried Spinach

We use this technique to fry other greens, such as cilantro and parsley. The key is to expose the fragile leaves to hot oil just long enough to extract the water and turn them bright green and crispy, just like chips. We love to surprise people and serve our crispy spinach in bowls at parties or as an accompaniment to any dish that is not heavily sauced.

3 BUNCHES SPINACH, STEMS REMOVED
1 QUART VEGETABLE OIL
SALT TO TASTE

Wash spinach leaves thoroughly and pat dry with paper towels. Heat oil in a large stockpot or saucepan to deep-fry temperature (350°F). Fry a small handful of leaves at a time, until crisp, about 30 seconds. (Stand as far away as possible, since the water in spinach is bound to cause some splattering.) Remove with a slotted spoon, drain on paper towels, and sprinkle with salt. Serve immediately or reserve up to 2 hours at room temperature.

6 Servings

Parsnip Chips

A trademark of our restaurant, these crisp chips are similar to potato chips, only sweeter. The combination of starch and sugar in parsnips makes them perfect for frying.

1½ POUNDS PARSNIPS
1 QUART PEANUT OIL
SALT TO TASTE

Peel parsnips. Using a mandolin or food processor fitted with 2-millimeter slicing blade, cut into ¹⁄₁₆-inch slices, lengthwise.

Heat oil in a large stockpot or saucepan to deep-fry temperature (350°F). Fry parsnips, a handful at a time, until pale golden and crisp. Remove with a slotted spoon, drain on paper towels, and sprinkle with salt. Serve immediately or reserve a day or 2 in plastic bags.

6 Servings

Onion Rings

Beer batter gets lighter and fluffier as it sits. You can mix it as much as a day in advance.

1   CUP ALL-PURPOSE FLOUR
¾   TABLESPOON GRANULATED SUGAR
1   TEASPOON SALT
1   TEASPOON BAKING POWDER
1   TEASPOON CAYENNE
1   CUP BEER, ROOM TEMPERATURE
3   LARGE ONIONS
1   QUART PEANUT OIL
    SALT TO TASTE

Combine ¾ cup flour, sugar, salt, baking powder, and cayenne in a medium bowl. Add beer all at once and whisk until smooth. Cover with plastic wrap and set aside at room temperature at least an hour.

Peel onions and cut across width into ¼-inch slices. Separate slices to form individual rings.

When batter is ready, heat oil in a large saucepan to deep-fry temperature (350°F). Dust a handful of onion rings with flour, then dip into batter to coat evenly. Deep-fry until golden brown, being careful not to crowd the pan. Remove with slotted spoon, drain on paper towels, sprinkle with salt, and serve immediately.

6 Servings

Shoe String Fries

These thin little sticks are fully fried. It is important to remove them from the oil the moment they turn golden. They can burn within seconds.

6   SMALL BAKING POTATOES
1   QUART PEANUT OIL
    SALT TO TASTE

Peel potatoes. Using a mandolin or food processor fitted with a 6-millimeter julienne blade, cut into ¹⁄₁₆-inch julienne, or matchsticks. Place in a large bowl and rinse under cold running water until water runs clear. Drain and pat dry with paper towels.

Heat oil in a large stockpot or saucepan to deep-fry temperature (350°F). Fry potatoes, a handful at a time, until pale golden and crisp. Drain on paper towels and sprinkle with salt. Serve immediately or reserve up to 2 hours.

6 Servings

Cool Greens

Parsley Salad
with Garlic Vinaigrette

Our customers are usually shocked to learn what the ingredients are in this special salad. Blanching garlic creates a wild and buttery flavor. Since parsley leaves are so durable, this is one of the few salads that can be dressed in advance. Parsley, by the way, is exceptionally high in vitamin C.

12	GARLIC CLOVES, PEELED AND THINLY SLICED
1	CUP VIRGIN OLIVE OIL
2	TABLESPOONS FRESH LEMON JUICE
1	TEASPOON SALT
¼	TEASPOON WHITE PEPPER
2	BUNCHES CURLY PARSLEY

Bring a small pot of water to a boil. Blanch garlic about 3 minutes and drain. Combine garlic with olive oil, lemon juice, salt, and pepper and whisk to combine.

Remove stems and wash and dry leaves. Place in a bowl, add dressing, and toss to coat evenly. Serve small portions as an accompaniment.

4 Servings

Curly Endive, Apple, and Gorgonzola Salad

This rich little salad is special enough to start a dinner party. Follow it with something simple like Portuguese Mussel and Cockle Stew (page 137) or Confit of Duck (page 125).

3	SMALL HEADS CURLY ENDIVE, PREFERABLY FRISSÉ
3	LARGE GRANNY SMITH APPLES
1½	CUPS HEAVY CREAM
¾	CUP RED WINE VINEGAR
3	OUNCES GORGONZOLA, CRUMBLED
1½	TEASPOONS SALT
¼	TEASPOON WHITE PEPPER

Separate endive leaves and wash well in cold running water. Trim and discard stems, break leaves into bite-sized pieces, and pat dry. Set aside in a bowl.

Peel and core apples and cut into thin slices. In another bowl, combine remaining ingredients. Add apple slices to cream mixture. (The apples can now be reserved in the refrigerator as long as 4 hours.)

At serving time, pour apple and cream mixture onto endive. Toss well to coat and serve immediately.

6 Servings

Molded Broccoli and Cauliflower Salad

Alternating stripes of broccoli and cauliflower dotted with diced red pepper makes a colorful party presentation. Skip a green vegetable when serving this salad.

1	SMALL HEAD CAULIFLOWER
1	SMALL BUNCH BROCCOLI
1	CUP OLIVE OIL
½	CUP TARRAGON VINEGAR
3	SHALLOTS, FINELY DICED
1	BUNCH TARRAGON, LEAVES ONLY, CHOPPED
1	TEASPOON SALT
½	TEASPOON FRESHLY GROUND PEPPER
1	RED BELL PEPPER, SEEDED AND DICED (OPTIONAL)

Trim and separate cauliflower and broccoli into florets. Bring a large pot salted water to a boil and blanch vegetables separately until crunchy but fork tender, 3 to 6 minutes. Immediately refresh in iced water and drain.

Have ready 6 coffee cups or 1-cup molds. Placing florets with stem toward center, arrange alternating layers of broccoli and cauliflower in each cup. When cups are full, press down to remove air and pack florets tightly. Cover with plastic wrap and reserve in the refrigerator.

Meanwhile, make dressing by mixing remaining ingredients together in a bowl. To serve, invert each cup onto a lettuce-lined salad plate. Divide dressing, spoon over salad, and serve.

6 to 8 Servings

Red Chard and Hazelnut Salad

This luxurious salad can be made even richer by adding marinated goat cheese, as in the variation below.

2	BUNCHES RED CHARD, STEMS TRIMMED, WASHED AND DRIED
¼	CUP ROASTED, SKINNED, AND CHOPPED HAZELNUTS (PAGE 250)
⅔	CUP EXTRA VIRGIN OLIVE OIL
3	TABLESPOONS SHERRY WINE VINEGAR
¾	TEASPOON SALT
¼	TEASPOON WHITE PEPPER

Stack red chard leaves, roll, and slice across width in fine julienne. Combine chard and hazelnuts in a bowl and toss. Whisk remaining ingredients together in a bowl to form a vinaigrette. Toss dressing with salad just before serving.

6 Servings

VARIATION: Top with rounds of marinated goat cheese for a main course lunch salad or elegant starter. We marinate a log soft, unripened goat cheese from France, like Montrachet, in enough olive oil to cover, along with whole garlic cloves, 1 tablespoon peppercorns, about 5 bay leaves, and fresh herbs such as parsley, mint, basil, thyme, oregano, chives, and rosemary. This mixture can sit at room temperature, in a covered container, as long as a month. The cheese will keep absorbing flavor. Place ½-inch thick rounds over individual salads and serve.

Cole Slaw

We like our Cole Slaw clean and refreshing, without a hint of mayonnaise. If the quantity is too large, you can cut the recipe in half.

1	LARGE OR 2 SMALL GREEN CABBAGES, ABOUT 2 POUNDS
1	CUP VEGETABLE OIL
¼	CUP GRANULATED SUGAR
⅓	CUP WHITE VINEGAR
1	TABLESPOON STONEGROUND MUSTARD
1	TABLESPOON CELERY SEEDS
1½	TABLESPOONS GRATED HORSERADISH, PREFERABLY FRESH
1	TEASPOON SALT
¼	TEASPOON WHITE PEPPER

Cut cabbage in quarters, lengthwise. Remove and discard cores and slice as finely as possible across width. Reserve in a large bowl.

Combine remaining ingredients in another bowl. Add, half a cup at a time, to shredded cabbage just until well moistened. You don't want a pool of dressing at bottom of bowl. Toss well and store in refrigerator.

Makes 6 Cups

Limestone Lettuce with House Dressing

Our house dressing—stronger than most—is a unique combination of ethnic ingredients. It stands up well to any strong-tasting vegetable.

6	SMALL HEADS LIMESTONE LETTUCE OR OTHER GREENS
1	LARGE CARROT, PEELED
2	PICKLING CUCUMBERS OR KIRBIES (PAGE 247), PEELED
1	SMALL DAIKON RADISH

HOUSE DRESSING

2	TABLESPOONS THAI FISH SAUCE (PAGE 248)
1	TABLESPOON FRESH LEMON JUICE
1	TABLESPOON RICE WINE VINEGAR (PAGE 248)
2	TABLESPOONS VEGETABLE OIL
1	TABLESPOON SOY SAUCE
1	TABLESPOON PERNOD
2	TABLESPOONS SESAME OIL
2	TEASPOONS FINELY GRATED FRESH GINGER (PAGE 249)

Thoroughly wash and dry lettuce. Break into bite-sized pieces and place in a large salad bowl. Julienne-slice carrot, cucumbers, and radish, and toss with greens.

Whisk dressing ingredients together in a bowl. Toss with salad just before serving.

8 to 10 Servings

This easy green salad won't wilt. A good choice for a picnic.

Broccoli with Peanut Vinaigrette

4½   CUPS BROCCOLI FLORETS
½   CUP ROASTED, UNSALTED PEANUTS
½   CUP OLIVE OIL
¼   CUP RED WINE VINEGAR
½   CUP WATER
½   TEASPOON SALT
⅛   TEASPOON FRESHLY GROUND PEPPER

Bring a medium saucepan salted water to a boil. Blanch broccoli about 3 minutes. Immediately refresh in a bowl of iced water and drain.

Grind nuts in a blender or food processor until fine, being careful not to overprocess. Whisk nuts with remaining ingredients in a bowl until a vinaigrette is formed. Add broccoli, toss, and serve. The tossed salad may be stored in refrigerator for 6 to 8 hours.

6 Servings

Watercress and Avocado Salad

With its bitter bite, watercress is a good foil for rich foods. This is the salad we serve beneath Warm Shredded Chicken Salad (page 153) and Marinated Scallops (page 40).

½ CUP EXTRA VIRGIN OLIVE OIL
2 TABLESPOONS FRESH LEMON JUICE
¾ TEASPOON SALT
¼ TEASPOON FRESHLY GROUND PEPPER
5 LARGE BUNCHES WATERCRESS, STEMS REMOVED, LEAVES WASHED AND WELL DRIED
2 RIPE AVOCADOS, HALVED, SEEDED, AND PEELED

Whisk together olive oil, lemon juice, salt, and pepper in a bowl. Tear watercress into bite-sized pieces and toss with dressing. Divide salad among 6 serving plates. Thinly slice avocado halves into strips lengthwise. Garnish center of each salad with avocado and serve.

6 Servings

City Cucumber Salad

This refreshing summer salad is a lovely accompaniment to a simple meal of grilled fish or chicken.

6 CUCUMBERS OR 15 PICKLING CUCUMBERS OR KIRBIES (PAGE 247), PEELED AND TRIMMED
2 LARGE RIPE TOMATOES
1 MEDIUM RED ONION, DICED
½ CUP EXTRA VIRGIN OLIVE OIL
¼ CUP RED WINE VINEGAR
1 TEASPOON SALT
½ TEASPOON FRESHLY GROUND PEPPER

Cut cucumbers in half lengthwise. Slice across width in ¼-inch pieces. (If using large cucumbers, remove seeds. They can remain in pickling cucumbers.) Cut tomatoes in half across width. Remove seeds and roughly chop.

Mix oil, vinegar, salt, and pepper together in a large bowl. Add chopped tomatoes, cucumbers, and onion. Toss well and chill as long as 6 hours.

4 to 6 Servings

Hot Greens

Sautéed Okra with Cumin

The key to keeping okra fresh-tasting is to wipe it clean with a damp cloth, then cook quickly, before it has a chance to absorb too much liquid and get gummy.

6	TABLESPOONS (¾ STICK) UNSALTED BUTTER
1½	POUNDS OKRA, STEMS TRIMMED, WASHED
1	TEASPOON SALT
½	TEASPOON WHITE PEPPER
1½	TEASPOONS GROUND CUMIN

Melt butter over high heat in a medium sauté pan. Sauté okra with all seasonings 2 or 3 minutes. Reduce heat to moderate and cook, stirring occasionally, an additional 5 minutes. Serve hot.

6 Servings

Rapini with Garlic and Soy

Rapini is leafier and more pungent than ordinary broccoli. This simple preparation is delicious with either one.

6	TABLESPOONS (¾ STICK) UNSALTED BUTTER
2	TABLESPOONS PUREED GARLIC (PAGE 250)
1½	POUNDS RAPINI OR BROCCOLI, PEELED AND ROUGHLY CHOPPED
2	TABLESPOONS SOY SAUCE

Melt butter in a medium skillet over medium-low heat. Cook garlic gently to release oils but not to brown, about 3 minutes. Add rapini and cook over moderate heat until bright green, about 2 to 4 minutes. Stir in soy sauce and serve immediately.

6 Servings

Braised White Cabbage

Warm, tender cabbage enriched with butter is a comforting accompaniment to wintery dishes like Roasted Pork Shoulder (page 103) or Beef Brisket (page 97).

1	LARGE HEAD WHITE CABBAGE
1	CUP DRY WHITE WINE
2	BAY LEAVES
1½	TEASPOONS SALT
¼	TEASPOON WHITE PEPPER
8	TABLESPOONS (1 STICK) UNSALTED BUTTER, COLD

Preheat oven to 450°F. Cut cabbage in quarters, remove core, and shred finely.

Place wine and bay leaves in a large heavy saucepan. Bring to a boil and reduce by half. Add cabbage, salt, and pepper, and bring back to a boil. Cover with a tight-fitting lid and transfer to oven. Bake 30 to 35 minutes, until cabbage is thoroughly limp. Check pot after about 15 minutes and stir down cabbage.

Break butter into small pieces and stir into warm cabbage. Adjust seasonings and serve immediately or reheat in a 350°F oven 15 minutes.

6 Servings

Sautéed Mustard Greens

You can use this technique for collard, beet, or dandelion greens. Speed is essential, so the vegetables remain bright, flavorful, and full of vitamins. We like to serve this as an accompaniment with several dishes, such as Fried Egg Sandwich with Canadian Bacon (page 80) and Grilled Swordfish and Mustard and Chopped Shallots (page 128).

4	BUNCHES MUSTARD GREENS
2	TABLESPOONS UNSALTED BUTTER
½	TEASPOON SALT
½	TEASPOON WHITE PEPPER

Trim greens of any tough stems. Wash and dry. Roll leaves into a tight, long cylinder and cut across roll in ¼-inch slices.

Melt butter in a medium sauté pan over high heat. Sauté greens with salt and pepper just until wilted, about 2 to 3 minutes. Serve immediately.

6 Servings

Peapods with Ginger and Soy

Here is a simple, fast side dish that most people love.

¾ POUND CHINESE SNOW PEAS OR SNAP PEAS
4½ TABLESPOONS UNSALTED BUTTER
4 TEASPOONS FRESHLY GRATED GINGER (PAGE 249)
4 TEASPOONS SOY SAUCE
⅛ TEASPOON FRESHLY GROUND BLACK PEPPER

Trim peapods of any strings or tough ends. Heat butter in a medium skillet over high heat. Sauté peapods until they begin to soften, about 2 minutes. Add ginger, soy sauce, and pepper. Toss lightly and serve immediately.

6 Servings

Sautéed Spinach with Parmesan Cheese

It takes only 3 minutes to prepare this lush dish. Though we are not miniature vegetable fans, baby spinach tastes wonderful prepared this way.

3 BUNCHES SPINACH
1½ TABLESPOONS UNSALTED BUTTER
1½ TABLESPOONS PUREED GARLIC (PAGE 250)
¾ TEASPOON SALT
¼ TEASPOON FRESHLY GROUND PEPPER
2 SMALL TOMATOES, PEELED, SEEDED, AND DICED (PAGE 249)
1¼ CUPS FRESHLY GRATED PARMESAN CHEESE

Thoroughly wash and dry spinach and remove stems.

Melt butter in a medium skillet over moderate heat. Sauté garlic about a second. Add spinach and stir until evenly wilted, about 2 minutes. Add salt, pepper, and tomatoes. Cook an additional minute. Stir in grated Parmesan, remove from heat, taste and adjust seasonings. Serve immediately. If spinach releases too much water, you can drain mixture in a colander before serving. Taste and adjust seasonings again after draining.

6 Servings

Zucchini Boats

4	LARGE FIRM ZUCCHINIS, WITH SKINS
2	TABLESPOONS UNSALTED BUTTER
¾	CUP GROUND ALMONDS
½	CUP HEAVY CREAM
½	TEASPOON SALT
⅛	TEASPOON WHITE PEPPER
¾	CUP GRATED PARMESAN CHEESE
¼	CUP FINE DRY BREAD CRUMBS

Trim and discard zucchini ends. Working with the 3 widest, cut across width into 2-inch lengths. Using a melon baller or small spoon, scoop out inner meat and seeds of each 2-inch piece, leaving a thin base at bottom so "boat" stands for stuffing. Place scooped-out centers into a food processor.

Roughly chop remaining zucchini. Add to food processor and puree until smooth.

Bring a medium pot salted water to a boil. Blanch zucchini boats just until they begin to soften, about 3 minutes. Immediately refresh in a bowl iced water. Drain and arrange, flat-side down, in a large jelly roll pan or roasting pan.

Preheat oven to 375°F.

Melt butter in a medium saucepan over medium-high heat. Add reserved zucchini puree and sauté until liquid is evaporated, about 15 minutes. Stir in nuts, cook for 1 minute, then add cream, salt, and pepper. Bring to a boil. Cook until cream thickens, about 3 minutes. Add ½ cup Parmesan cheese and all bread crumbs. Remove from heat and stir until smooth.

Using a tablespoon or pastry bag fitted with a plain tip, stuff zucchini boats with cream mixture. Pour boiling water into pan containing filled zucchini boats until it rises about ¼-inch, to form a water bath. Bake 15 minutes.

Heat broiler. Sprinkle remaining Parmesan cheese over tops and place under broiler until slightly golden, about 1 minute. Serve immediately.

6 Servings

Leeks with Caraway

In this satisfying side dish, savory leeks are cooked just long enough to lose their crunch and become enriched with butter and wine.

6   LEEKS
4   TABLESPOONS (½ STICK) UNSALTED BUTTER
2   TABLESPOONS CARAWAY SEEDS, CHOPPED
1   TEASPOON SALT
½   TEASPOON WHITE PEPPER
½   CUP DRY WHITE WINE

Trim roots and dark green portion of leeks. Cut in half lengthwise and wash thoroughly under cold running water. Cut into ¼-inch diagonal slices, across width.

Melt butter in a medium skillet over medium-high heat. Add leeks, caraway, salt, and pepper, and cook until leeks are soft, about 2 minutes. Add wine, reduce heat to low and cook, covered, 3 to 5 minutes. Serve immediately.

6 Servings

Shredded Brussels Sprouts

This sweet, crunchy vegetable is always a surprise to our customers who ordinarily hate Brussels sprouts. Guaranteed to convert even the most determined detractor.

1½   POUNDS BRUSSELS SPROUTS
4   TABLESPOONS (½ STICK) UNSALTED BUTTER
½   TEASPOON SALT
¼   TEASPOON WHITE PEPPER
2   TEASPOONS WATER
     JUICE OF ½ LIME

Soak whole sprouts in a large bowl of cold, salted water to clean. Then trim and discard ends and any bitter outer leaves. Cut each in half lengthwise, then slice thinly across width.

Melt butter in a large skillet over medium-high heat. Sauté sprouts with salt and pepper until they start to brown. Add water and cook until barely limp, about 4 minutes. (The water changes the action from sautéeing to steaming.) Stir in lime juice and serve immediately.

6 to 8 Servings

Vegetable Combinations

Sweet and Sour Red Cabbage

Although it can be eaten hot or cold, the flavor of this sweet and sour accompaniment benefits from a few days in the refrigerator. We use it to garnish almost anything: sandwiches, smoked fish, pâtés, salads, brisket, pork, or even liver. And it can always be found at Thanksgiving at Mary Sue's mom's house.

1	LARGE HEAD RED CABBAGE
2	LARGE ONIONS, THINLY SLICED
½	CUP GRANULATED SUGAR
1	CUP RED WINE VINEGAR
1	TABLESPOON CARAWAY SEEDS
1	BAY LEAF
1½	TEASPOONS SALT
¼	TEASPOON PEPPER
½	CUP RENDERED DUCK FAT (PAGE 250), PREFERABLY, OR CLARIFIED BUTTER (PAGE 249)

Cut cabbage in quarters, core, and finely julienne. Combine all ingredients, except the fat, in a large bowl. Stir to blend.

Heat fat in a large heavy skillet or Dutch oven over moderate heat. Add cabbage mixture and reduce heat to a simmer. Cover and cook, stirring occasionally, until cabbage is tender, about 1 hour. Serve hot or cold. Sweet and sour cabbage may be stored in refrigerator up to 5 days and may also be reheated.

10 to 12 Servings

Roasted Onion Compote

Sweet white onions with cream and bacon are irresistible, especially with a holiday dinner of turkey or roast beef. You can make this dish the day before and reheat with no loss of flavor.

1¾	POUNDS SMALL WHITE ONIONS, WITH SKINS
½	POUND THICKLY SLICED BACON
½	CUP BRANDY
1½	CUPS HEAVY CREAM
½	TEASPOON WHITE PEPPER

Preheat oven to 350°F. Arrange onions in an even layer on a large baking sheet. Bake, shaking pan occasionally to ensure even roasting, about 40 minutes. The largest onion should feel soft when pressed. Set aside to cool. Trim ends and peel.

Slice bacon across width into ¼-inch pieces. Fry until crisp in a large skillet. Drain off half fat, leaving bacon in pan. Remove from heat. Pour in brandy, turn heat to high, and light alcohol with a match. When flame subsides, add cream, reserved onions, and pepper. Cook until cream is reduced by half. Serve immediately.

6 servings

Sweet and Sour Eggplant

This hearty eggplant dish goes well with simple grilled foods or a roast, like Herb Stuffed Leg of Lamb with Pimento Sauce (page 98).

3½	POUNDS EGGPLANT, PREFERABLY JAPANESE
1	TABLESPOON COARSE SALT
1	CUP OLIVE OIL
2	LARGE ONIONS, DICED
2	TABLESPOONS PUREED GARLIC (PAGE 250)
½	CUP RED WINE VINEGAR
1½	TABLESPOONS TOMATO PASTE
⅓	CUP CAPERS WITH JUICE
½	CUP BROWN SUGAR
	SALT AND TABASCO TO TASTE

Trim ends of eggplants. Cut across width into ¼-inch slices, leaving skins on. (If you are using regular eggplants, cut into quarters lengthwise before slicing.) Place in a colander, sprinkle with coarse salt and let sweat 30 minutes. Pat dry with paper towels.

Heat oil in a large skillet over high heat. Sauté eggplant in batches until lightly brown, about 1 minute per side. Set aside to drain on paper towels.

In same pan, sauté onions until golden. Reduce heat, add garlic, and cook just long enough to release its aroma. Add tomato paste and cook 2 minutes. Stir in remaining ingredients. Continue cooking another 3 minutes. Taste to adjust seasonings. Serve immediately or chill a minimum of 2 hours or up to 2 days.

6 Servings

*In our ratatouille the vegetables
are neatly diced, then sautéed
individually so each retains its
own distinctive flavor.*

City Ratatouille

1	MEDIUM EGGPLANT, WITH SKIN
1	LARGE ZUCCHINI, WITH SKIN
1	YELLOW CROOKNECK SQUASH, WITH SKIN
3	BELL PEPPERS, PREFERABLY RED, YELLOW, AND GREEN, SEEDED
1	LARGE ONION
1	CUP OLIVE OIL
2	TEASPOONS PUREED GARLIC (PAGE 250)
1	CUP KALAMATA OLIVES, CUT FROM PIT IN SLICES
5	BAY LEAVES
1	TEASPOON CHOPPED FRESH THYME
1	TEASPOON CHOPPED FRESH OREGANO
1	TEASPOON SALT
½	TEASPOON FRESHLY GROUND PEPPER
1	CUP BROWN LAMB STOCK (PAGE 75) OR CHICKEN STOCK (PAGE 74) OR TOMATO JUICE
2	LARGE TOMATOES, PEELED, SEEDED, AND DICED (PAGE 249)

Trim ends and cores of eggplant, zucchini, yellow squash, and peppers. Cut each into ½-inch dice. Reserve separately. Trim end of onion and cut into ½-inch dice.

Place a large heavy skillet over high heat to heat dry pan. When you add oil, it should heat immediately. First, sauté eggplant until golden. Remove with a slotted spoon and reserve on paper towels. Then sauté zucchini and crookneck squash until golden and set aside to drain.

Reduce heat to moderate. In same pan, cook onions until soft and translucent. Add bell peppers and garlic, and cook until peppers soften, about 2 minutes. Add olives, bay leaves, thyme, oregano, salt, and pepper. Cook an additional minute.

Add Brown Lamb Stock, tomatoes, and reserved vegetables. Simmer, uncovered, about 5 minutes. Remove and discard bay leaves and serve hot or chilled.

6 Servings

Spaghetti Squash and Tomato Sauté

Tomatoes bring out the acidity of this lovely crunchy squash. This goes with just about everything.

1	SPAGHETTI SQUASH, ABOUT 2 POUNDS
4	TABLESPOONS (½ STICK) UNSALTED BUTTER
1½	TEASPOONS SALT
½	TEASPOON WHITE PEPPER
1	TOMATO, PEELED, SEEDED, AND DICED (PAGE 249)

Preheat oven to 350°F. Cut squash in half lengthwise and remove and discard inner seeds. Coat insides with 1 tablespoon butter and sprinkle with ½ teaspoon salt. Place cut-side down in a roasting pan and add about an inch of boiling water. Cover with aluminum foil and bake 30 minutes. Set aside to cool.

When cool enough to handle, scoop out meat with a spoon, discarding skins. Fluff hot strands with a fork to separate.

Melt remaining 3 tablespoons butter in a large skillet over medium-high heat. Sauté squash with remaining salt and pepper about 5 minutes. Add tomato and cook briefly, to evenly heat. Serve immediately.

6 Servings

Condiments

Horseradish and Mustard and Mayonnaise

The perfect sandwich spread. We use it on practically everything.

1	CUP MAYONNAISE (PAGE 194)
½	CUP FRESHLY GRATED HORSERADISH
½	CUP DIJON OR STONEGROUND MUSTARD
	WHITE PEPPER TO TASTE

Mix ingredients together and season to taste with pepper.

6 Servings

Mayonnaise

Question: How do you hold the
bowl, pour in the oil, and whisk
all at the same time?
   Answer: Gather a damp
towel snugly around the bowl's
bottom. The towel will keep the
bowl still—or at least on the
counter.

2   EGG YOLKS
1   TEASPOON RED WINE VINEGAR
    JUICE OF ½ LEMON
½   TEASPOON SALT
¼   TEASPOON WHITE PEPPER
    DASH OF TABASCO
    DASH OF WORCESTERSHIRE SAUCE
1   CUP VEGETABLE OIL

In a bowl, combine egg yolks, vinegar, lemon juice,
salt, pepper, Tabasco, and Worcestershire. Blend
with a whisk. Gradually add oil, a drop a time, whisking constantly. As mixture begins to thicken and looks
more like mayonnaise, you can add oil more generously. Adjust seasonings and store in refrigerator as
long as 4 days.

Makes 1½ Cups

Pantry Pickles

*Susan's mother's recipe for
homemade pickles takes about
20 minutes from start to finish.
(You can use a food processor
for the slicing.)*

6   PICKLING CUCUMBERS OR KIRBIES (PAGE 247), WITH
    SKINS
1   ONION, THINLY SLICED ACROSS THE WIDTH
1   RED BELL PEPPER, CORED, SEEDED, AND JULIENNED
2   CUPS RICE WINE VINEGAR (PAGE 248)
½   CUP GRANULATED SUGAR
1   TABLESPOON COARSE SALT

Cut cucumbers across width into ½16-inch slices,
diagonally. Combine all ingredients in a medium
saucepan. Bring to a boil, reduce to a simmer, and
cook, uncovered, 10 to 15 minutes. Store in pickling
liquid, in refrigerator.

Makes 1 Generous Quart

VARIATION: Add diced red, yellow, and green bell
peppers for canned Christmas gifts.

Hamburger Relish

*This is another wonderful
Ruthie Feniger recipe.*

3	RIPE TOMATOES, PEELED AND SEEDED (PAGE 249)
¼	HEAD GREEN CABBAGE, CORED
2	SMALL GREEN BELL PEPPERS, SEEDS REMOVED
2	MEDIUM ONIONS
1	QUART WHITE VINEGAR
1¼	CUPS GRANULATED SUGAR
2	TEASPOONS DIJON MUSTARD
1	TEASPOON CELERY SEEDS
1	TEASPOON GROUND CLOVES
1	TEASPOON CINNAMON
½	TABLESPOON TURMERIC

Place tomatoes, cabbage, peppers, and onions in a food processor fitted with steel blade and pulse until roughly chopped, or dice vegetables by hand.

Combine remaining ingredients in a large saucepan and bring to a boil. Add chopped vegetables, bring back to a boil, and reduce to a simmer. Cook, uncovered, until thick, about 1 hour. Relish keeps in refrigerator about 3 weeks.

Makes 1 Quart

Homemade Yogurt

*Homemade yogurt has a tart
freshness and rich creaminess
impossible to find in store-
bought. If you have the time
(and it doesn't take much), it's
worth the trouble to make your
own.*

1	QUART MILK
1	CUP HALF AND HALF
1	TABLESPOON PLAIN YOGURT

Combine milk and half and half in a medium saucepan. Bring to a boil over low heat. Remove from heat and transfer to a clean bowl. Set aside to cool to 115°F. Add yogurt and vigorously whisk.

Cover bowl with plastic wrap, then wrap well with heavy towels or a blanket. Set aside in a warm place for 6 to 8 hours, or longer according to taste. The longer yogurt sits, the more acidic it will become. Store in sealed containers in refrigerator.

Makes 5 Cups

Three Raitas

A raita is a natural accompaniment to any of our curries. They are all derived from Indian cuisine, where these flavored, textured yogurts provide a break from the spicier tastes of the meal. Each is distinctive: The banana is sweet and crunchy. The cucumber is the most refreshing. (Try increasing the proportion of cucumbers to yogurt for a salad.) And, the smoky eggplant is substantial enough to serve as a vegetable side dish.

Banana Raita

2	TABLESPOONS BLACK MUSTARD SEEDS (PAGE 246)
1	LARGE RIPE BANANA
¼	CUP FRESH, OR DRY UNSWEETENED, GRATED COCONUT
1	CUP PLAIN YOGURT
	PINCH OF SALT AND WHITE PEPPER

Place seeds in a small dry sauté pan and cook over moderate heat until seeds turn gray and start popping. Remove from heat.

Coarsely mash banana in a medium bowl. Add mustard seeds, grated coconut, yogurt, salt, and pepper. Stir to combine and serve at room temperature or chilled. May be stored in the refrigerator about a day.

Makes 1½ Cups

Cucumber Raita

1½	TEASPOONS OLIVE OIL
2	TEASPOONS PUREED GARLIC (PAGE 250)
2	TEASPOONS GROUND CUMIN
2	PICKLING CUCUMBERS OR KIRBIES (PAGE 247), WITH SKINS, FINELY DICED
½	CUP PLAIN YOGURT
¼	BUNCH CILANTRO, STEMS REMOVED, CHOPPED
¼	TEASPOON SALT
	PINCH OF WHITE PEPPER
2	DASHES OF TABASCO

Heat oil in a small skillet over moderate heat. Cook garlic, stirring occasionally, until aroma is released, about 2 minutes. Add cumin and cook briefly, just to combine flavors. Remove from heat.

Transfer to medium bowl. Add remaining ingredients and stir to combine. Serve at room temperature or chilled.

Makes 1 Cup

Eggplant Raita

1   SMALL EGGPLANT
1   TEASPOON OLIVE OIL
1   TABLESPOON PUREED GARLIC (PAGE 250)
1   TOMATO, WITH SKIN, SEEDED AND DICED
½   BUNCH CILANTRO, STEMS REMOVED, CHOPPED
1   CUP PLAIN YOGURT
½   TEASPOON SALT
    PINCH OF WHITE PEPPER

Preheat broiler and place tray as far as possible from flame. Place eggplant on a baking sheet and roast, turning occasionally, until charred on all sides and thoroughly soft, about 45 minutes. Set aside to cool.

Heat oil in a small skillet over moderate heat. Cook garlic, stirring occasionally, until aroma is released, about 2 minutes. Transfer to a medium bowl along with tomato, cilantro, yogurt, salt, and pepper. Hold eggplant over and squeeze juices into bowl. Peel and finely chop eggplant. Add to yogurt mixture, stir well, and serve at room temperature or chill.

Makes 2½ Cups

Sauerkraut

Here's a well-kept secret: Sauerkraut is incredibly easy to make. Just combine the ingredients and wait 5 days—no cooking needed!

1   (3½-POUND) GREEN CABBAGE
3   TABLESPOONS COARSE SALT

Cut cabbage into quarters and remove core. With a mandolin or food processor fitted with a 2-millimeter slicing blade, slice as thinly as possible. Place in a large bowl with salt and toss to combine.

Transfer to a large glass or ceramic container and tap down by hand so liquid rises to top. Cover with a damp towel touching cabbage and top with a 3-pound weight. Cover again with a layer of plastic wrap and set aside in a warm place 5 days to ferment. Sauerkraut may be kept in a sealed container in refrigerator as long as 3 weeks.

Makes 4 Cups

Apple Sauce

We love the crunch and bite of Granny Smith apples for home-made apple sauce. Delicious with short ribs or potato pancakes, of course.

6   GREEN APPLES, PEELED, CORED, AND CUT INTO CHUNKS
1 ½ CUPS WATER
1   CUP GRANULATED SUGAR
⅓   CUP FRESH LEMON JUICE

Combine ingredients in a large heavy saucepan. Cover and bring to a boil. Reduce heat to a simmer and cook until apples are soft, about ½ hour. Remove from heat and stir with a wooden spoon or whisk until texture suits your taste. Chill.

Makes 3 Cups

Marinated Mushrooms

Mushrooms are great for marinating. They are as absorbent as sponges! Keep these on hand for salads, sandwiches, and easy hors d'oeuvres.

1   POUND LARGE WHITE MUSHROOMS, STEMS REMOVED

MARINADE

1   CUP OLIVE OIL
½   CUP FRESH LEMON JUICE
2   SHALLOTS, CHOPPED
1   TEASPOON PUREED GARLIC (PAGE 250)
1   TEASPOON DRY MUSTARD
½   TEASPOON CRACKED BLACK PEPPERCORNS (PAGE 249)
¼   TEASPOON GROUND GINGER
1   BAY LEAF
1   TEASPOON SALT

Clean mushrooms by washing briefly under cold running water. Carefully pat dry with paper towels.

Combine marinade ingredients in a large bowl. Add mushrooms and toss to evenly coat. Transfer to a container and press mushrooms down until the liquid rises to top. Cover with plastic wrap and a heavy weight, and refrigerate 2 to 5 days.

Makes 3 Cups

Dill Pickles

*If you like pickled vegetables,
try substituting small onions,
carrots, and cauliflower for the
cucumbers.*

15	PICKLING CUCUMBERS OR KIRBIES (PAGE 247)

PICKLING LIQUID

3	CUPS WATER
2	CUPS WHITE VINEGAR
¼	CUP COARSE SALT
2	TABLESPOONS GRANULATED SUGAR
¾	TEASPOON GROUND CUMIN
½	TEASPOON GROUND GINGER
1	TEASPOON BLACK PEPPERCORNS
½	TEASPOON TURMERIC
2	WHOLE CLOVES
1	BAY LEAF
1	MEDIUM ONION, SLICED
1	CELERY STALK, SLICED
½	CARROT, PEELED AND SLICED
1	JALAPEÑO PEPPER, SLICED WITH SEEDS
8	GARLIC CLOVES, PEELED
1	BUNCH DILL
1	SPRIG THYME

Bring a large stockpot water to a boil. Add cucumbers, immediately remove from heat, and drain in a colander. Rinse with cold water and reserve.

Combine pickling liquid ingredients in a medium saucepan and bring to a boil. Place cucumbers in a large container along with remaining vegetables and herbs. Pour hot pickling liquid over cucumber mixture and set aside to cool. Tap down solids until liquid rises to top. Cover with plastic wrap and let stand at room temperature 1 day. Transfer to a sealed container and refrigerate 3 days before serving. Store indefinitely.

Makes 15 Pickles

Spicy Apple Chutney

This sweet chutney is delicious with curries or as a spread for breakfast toast. If you are a chutney fan, see Mint and Cilantro Chutney (page 16) and Tamarind Chutney (page 94) for more ideas.

4	GREEN APPLES
2	TABLESPOONS VEGETABLE OIL
1	TABLESPOON MUSTARD SEEDS
1	MEDIUM ONION, DICED
1	RED BELL PEPPER, CORED AND DICED
1	TEASPOON SALT
2	TEASPOONS PUREED GARLIC (PAGE 250)
1	SERRANO CHILE, DICED WITH SEEDS
1	TEASPOON GROUND GINGER
1	TEASPOON GROUND ALLSPICE
¼	CUP RAISINS
1	CUP PACKED BROWN SUGAR
¾	CUP RED WINE VINEGAR
1	CUP WATER

Peel apples and cut into quarters. Remove cores, roughly chop, and reserve.

Heat oil in a large saucepan over high heat. Add mustard seeds, cover, and cook until popping stops. Reduce heat and add onion, red pepper, and salt. Cook, uncovered, stirring occasionally, until onions are translucent. Stir in garlic, serrano chile, ginger, and allspice, and cook an additional minute.

Add remaining ingredients, including reserved apples. Cook, uncovered, over moderate heat, until mixture is soft and aromatic, about 40 minutes. Chill before serving.

Makes 3 Cups

Curry Popcorn

We keep huge bowls of this bright orange popcorn at the bar at all times. You will want to adjust the spices to taste—this is definitely spicy!

½	TEASPOON CAYENNE
½	TEASPOON GROUND CUMIN
½	TEASPOON TURMERIC
1	TEASPOON CRACKED BLACK PEPPERCORNS (PAGE 249)
1	TEASPOON SALT
¼	CUP VEGETABLE OIL
½	CUP UNPOPPED POPCORN

Measure spices onto a plate and place near stove. Place oil and one kernel popcorn on a burner. Turn heat to high, cover pot, and cook until kernel pops. Then add popcorn and cover again. When corn starts popping, quickly add spices. Cover and cook, shaking constantly, until the popping stops.

Be careful not to breath in the spiced fumes as they can burn your throat.

Makes 12 Cups

Pickled Tomatoes

Packed into attractive jars, these extremely potent, sweet and spicy tomatoes make lovely Christmas gifts. We serve small ramekins of this Indian dish with Spicy City Chicken (page 118) and on vegetarian platters at the restaurant.

1½	POUNDS TOMATOES, PEELED (PAGE 249)
1	BUNCH SCALLIONS, WHITE AND GREEN, SLICED
3–5	SERRANO CHILES, WITH SEEDS, SLICED
¾	CUP WHITE VINEGAR
¼	CUP BROWN SUGAR
1	TABLESPOON COARSE SALT
2	TABLESPOONS FRESHLY GRATED GINGER (PAGE 249)
2	TABLESPOONS PUREED GARLIC (PAGE 250)
1	TABLESPOON BLACK OR YELLOW MUSTARD SEEDS (PAGE 246)
1	TABLESPOON CRACKED BLACK PEPPERCORNS (PAGE 249)
1	TABLESPOON GROUND CUMIN
2	TEASPOONS CAYENNE
1	TEASPOON TURMERIC
¾	CUP OLIVE OIL

Slice tomatoes into 6 wedges each. Reserve in a large bowl with scallions and serrano chiles.

In a medium saucepan bring vinegar to a boil. Add sugar and salt, and cook until dissolved, about 1 minute. Remove from heat and reserve.

Measure ginger, garlic, mustard seeds, cracked peppercorns, cumin, cayenne, and turmeric onto a plate and place near stove. In another medium saucepan heat oil over moderate heat until smoking. Add spices and cook, stirring constantly with a wooden spoon, until aromas are released, about 2 minutes. Remove from heat and stir in vinegar mixture.

Immediately pour over reserved vegetables. Mix well, cover with plastic wrap, and refrigerate a minimum of 3 days.

Makes 3 Cups or 6 Side Dishes

6

Desserts and Beverages

Everyone seems to crave something sweet after a meal—be it a simple fruit tart or an extravagant chocolate cake—and so do we. At the restaurant we try to satisfy that urge. Each day we provide a choice of twenty-five fresh cakes, pies, tarts, cookies, cupcakes, custards, and assorted sweets—there's something for everyone.

Since baking was Mary Sue's first love—she worked at a pastry shop for five years while attending chef's school—she has a few suggestions for home bakers. The trick to overcoming nervousness is to repeat recipes. Rather than try a new dessert each time you give a dinner party, master two or three favorites. Develop your confidence before going on to something new. Make the dessert in advance, away from the storm and strife of last-minute preparations. Remember, your guests will always be impressed by something fresh—however humble.

Chocolate

Black Velvet

This sophisticated cake is dense with ground nuts and whiskey. With its shiny top coat and feathery white lines, this glamorous chocolate cake is a good choice for a grownup's birthday party.

14	OUNCES SEMISWEET CHOCOLATE, CHOPPED
1	CUP (2 STICKS) UNSALTED BUTTER, SOFTENED
¼	CUP WATER
½	CUP PLUS 2 TABLESPOONS FINELY GROUND HAZELNUTS, WITH SKINS
½	CUP PLUS 2 TABLESPOONS FINELY GROUND ALMONDS, WITH SKINS
½	CUP PLUS 2 TABLESPOONS PASTRY FLOUR
6	EGGS, SEPARATED
1⅓	CUPS GRANULATED SUGAR
½	CUP GOOD SCOTCH WHISKEY
	GANACHE, RECIPE FOLLOWS
	PURE WHITE FROSTING, RECIPE FOLLOWS

Preheat oven to 325°F. Butter and flour a 10-inch springform pan and line with parchment paper.

Melt chocolate in the top of a double boiler or in a bowl over simmering water and remove from heat. Add butter, a tablespoon at a time, stirring until smooth. Stir in water.

Combine hazelnuts, almonds, and flour in bowl and set aside.

With an electric mixer, beat yolks at medium speed until light and fluffy. Gradually add sugar, beating until very light. With a wooden spoon, gently fold into chocolate mixture.

Fold reserved nut mixture and Scotch whiskey into chocolate mixture in three stages, alternating ingredients.

In a clean bowl, whisk egg whites until soft peaks form. Gently fold into batter in two parts.

Spread evenly in prepared pan and tap on a counter to eliminate air pockets. Bake 45 to 50 minutes, or until a toothpick inserted in center comes out slightly moist. (The top may be cracked and the center wobbly.) Set aside to cool, in pan on rack, about 1 hour. Chill a minimum of 3 hours, preferably overnight.

Release and remove sides of pan. Invert onto a parchment or wax paper-coated counter or cake decorating table. Prepare Ganache and Pure White Frosting.

Pour Ganache over cold cake. Let it set a few seconds, then, using a cake spatula, spread evenly over top and sides.

Fill a pastry bag fitted with your finest tip, or a handmade paper cone with a closed tip, with frosting. Quickly draw parallel lines, ¾-inch apart, across ganache. Drag tip of a sharp paring knife through lines at 1-inch intervals, in a perpendicular fashion. Turn cake around and draw knife through white lines in opposite direction. The resulting pattern should be a feathery checkerboard of wavy white lines.

12 Servings

Ganache

6 OUNCES SEMISWEET CHOCOLATE, CHOPPED
¾ CUP HEAVY CREAM

Place chocolate in a medium bowl. Bring cream to a boil. Pour into chocolate and stir until chocolate is completely melted. Let cool until mixture is less than body temperature.

Makes 1½ Cups

Pure White Frosting

⅔ CUP CONFECTIONERS' SUGAR
1 TABLESPOON MILK

Mix in a small bowl until smooth.

Makes ½ Cup

Cupcakes Hostess Style

Hostess cupcakes are our made-leines—one whiff and we are transported to childhood. While we improved the taste, the appearance remains classic Hostess. Milk is still the perfect accompaniment.

This is our favorite chocolate cake recipe. Use it for delicious layer cakes, with softened cream cheese and confectioners' sugar or whipped cream and sliced bananas, perhaps, between the layers.

For the best, moistest cupcakes, we bake them in ¼-inch-thick stoneware coffee cups.

5	OUNCES UNSWEETENED BITTER CHOCOLATE, CHOPPED
1	CUP PACKED BROWN SUGAR
1	CUP MILK
4	EGG YOLKS
8	TABLESPOONS (1 STICK) BUTTER, SOFTENED
1	CUP GRANULATED SUGAR
2	CUPS ALL-PURPOSE FLOUR
1	TEASPOON SALT
1	TEASPOON BAKING SODA
¼	CUP HEAVY CREAM
1	TEASPOON VANILLA EXTRACT
3	EGG WHITES
1	RECIPE PASTRY CREAM (PAGE 231)
½	RECIPE GANACHE (PAGE 205)
1	RECIPE PURE WHITE FROSTING (PAGE 205)

Preheat oven to 325°F. Butter and flour a 12-cup and a 6-cup muffin tin.

Melt chocolate in the top of a double boiler or in a bowl over simmering water. In another bowl, combine brown sugar, ½ cup milk and 2 egg yolks. Whisk until combined. Add to melted chocolate and stir constantly (while cooking over simmering water) until mixture is shiny and thick, about 3 minutes. Set aside to cool.

In a clean bowl, cream butter and granulated sugar until light. Add remaining 2 egg yolks, one at a time, beating well after each addition.

In another bowl, mix together flour, salt, and baking soda.

Combine cream, vanilla extract, and remaining ½ cup milk in a small bowl and reserve.

Pour cooled chocolate mixture into creamed butter and sugar. Whisk until smooth. Add combined dry ingredients and cream mixture in three stages, alternating liquid and dry ingredients, and ending with liquid.

Beat egg whites until soft peaks form. Gently fold, all at once, into batter. Spoon batter into muffin cups, about two-thirds full.

Bake 20 to 25 minutes, until a toothpick inserted in center comes out clean. Set aside to cool, in pan on rack, about 10 minutes. Invert and set aside on a lined sheet pan to cool, about an hour. Prepare Pastry Cream, Ganache, and Pure White Frosting.

Using the tip of a small paring knife, cut a small cone from bottom of each cupcake. Reserve cones. Scoop out about 1 teaspoon cake from center of each cupcake. Fill a pastry bag fitted with a plain tip with Pastry Cream. Pipe cream into cupcakes, then replace reserved cones. Place bottom-side down on a lined sheet pan and chill.

When Ganache is room temperature, dip cupcakes in to coat tops. Fill a plain-tipped pastry bag with frosting and decorate with a squiggle across each top, Hostess style. Store in refrigerator until serving time.

Makes 18 Cupcakes

VARIATION: For a layer cake, fill 2 buttered and floured 10-inch round pans and bake for 25 to 35 minutes, until a toothpick inserted in center comes out clean. Fill with softened cream cheese whipped with confectioners' sugar or with whipped cream and bananas.

City Chocolate
with Espresso Crème Anglaise

This sweet chocolate pâté works like a magnet—attracting chocolate lovers to the restaurant for dessert. A good choice for an elegant dinner party, it can be put together quickly and reserved in the refrigerator as long as 4 days.

3	TABLESPOONS BRANDY
½	CUP GOLDEN RAISINS
1	POUND 2 OUNCES SEMISWEET CHOCOLATE
1¾	CUPS (3½ STICKS) UNSALTED BUTTER
10	EGGS, SEPARATED
	ESPRESSO CRÈME ANGLAISE, RECIPE FOLLOWS

Line a 12½ x 4½-inch sharp-edged loaf pan with enough aluminum foil to hang over sides about 3 inches. Combine brandy and raisins in a small saucepan and warm over low heat. Reserve.

Chop chocolate into small pieces and melt with butter in the top of a double boiler or in a bowl over simmering water. Remove from heat and stir in reserved raisins and brandy. Whisk in yolks until combined.

Whisk egg whites until soft peaks form. Gently fold whites into chocolate mixture in two stages.

Pour into prepared pan, tap on counter to remove air gaps, smooth top, and cover with plastic wrap touching top. Chill 6 hours or overnight.

To serve, remove plastic wrap and invert onto a serving platter. The chocolate should release easily. Remove aluminum foil.

Coat dessert plates with Espresso Crème Anglaise. Top each with a slice of chocolate. This slices most easily with a long, thin knife that has been dipped into hot water.

14 Servings

Espresso Crème Anglaise

8	EGG YOLKS
1	CUP GRANULATED SUGAR
2	CUPS MILK
1½	TABLESPOONS FINELY GROUND COFFEE
1	TEASPOON VANILLA EXTRACT

In a large bowl, whisk together egg yolks and sugar. Line a sieve with a paper coffee filter. Combine milk and coffee in a medium saucepan and bring to a boil.

Pour hot milk and coffee through sieve and into egg mixture, whisking constantly. Return to saucepan. Cook over moderate heat, stirring constantly, until the mixture thickens slightly and coats the back of a wooden spoon, about 5 minutes. Remove from heat. Stir in vanilla and chill.

Tarts and Pies

Tarte Tatin

12	RED OR GOLDEN DELICIOUS APPLES
2	CUPS GRANULATED SUGAR
1	CUP WATER
8	TABLESPOONS (1 STICK) UNSALTED BUTTER
5	OUNCES PUFF PASTRY (PAGE 216) OR ⅓ RECIPE PIE DOUGH (PAGE 219)

Have ready an 8-inch x 2½-inch deep round sauté pan with straight sides and an ovenproof handle, or a *heavy* 8-inch cake pan. Peel apples, cut in half lengthwise, and remove cores.

Combine sugar and water in sauté pan. Cook over moderate heat until caramelized, about 15 minutes. Remove from heat. Using tongs, arrange a layer of apples upright and close together. Form a spiral with core sides touching curved sides from the center out. Fill pan as tightly as possible.

Cut butter into small pieces and sprinkle over apples in pan. Pile remaining apples, cut-side down, over butter. Cover with aluminum foil and place inside a 1- to 2-inch larger sauté pan (or roasting pan) to catch drippings.

Return to burner and cook over medium-low heat about 1 hour 20 minutes. Check pan every 20 minutes or so, pressing down apples on top. As apples cook, they shrink—eventually they will fit comfortably in pan. Also, pour any juices—as long as they're not burned—that spill into bottom pan back into apples. Set aside to cool about 15 minutes.

Preheat oven to 350°F.

On a lightly floured board, roll dough into a 9-inch circle, about ¼-inch thick. Let rest 15 minutes. Place over apples, allowing edges to hang over pan.

Bake about 35 minutes. Set aside to cool in pan ½ hour. Invert onto a serving platter and let sit, without lifting pan, 10 minutes. Remove pan and serve warm.

8 Servings   ✕

Lemon Hazelnut Tart

This is a sophisticated fruit tart. A dense cake layer is covered with lemon sections topped with a hazelnut-studded meringue. You can simplify the preparation by baking the cake a day in advance.

1	CUP FINELY GROUND HAZELNUTS
1	CUP FINELY GROUND ALMONDS
3	EGGS, SEPARATED
¾	CUP GRANULATED SUGAR
	GRATED ZEST OF 1 LEMON
1	TEASPOON VANILLA EXTRACT
1½	TABLESPOONS ALL-PURPOSE FLOUR
¼	TEASPOON SALT
	MERINGUE AND LEMON GARNISH, RECIPE FOLLOWS

Preheat oven to 350°F. Line a 10-inch round cake pan with parchment paper, butter, and flour.

Mix together hazelnuts and almonds, and reserve.

In an electric mixer, with whisk attachment, whip egg yolks and sugar until pale yellow. Add lemon zest and vanilla. Mix until light and fluffy, and reserve.

In a small bowl, combine 1 cup ground nut mixture with flour and set aside. Reserve remaining cup for meringue.

In another bowl, beat egg whites until foamy. Sprinkle in salt and continue beating until soft peaks form. Fold alternating thirds nut and flour mixture and whites into beaten egg yolk mixture. Pour into prepared pan.

Bake 25 to 30 minutes until lightly browned. Set aside to cool, in pan on rack, about 10 minutes. Run a knife along inside edge to loosen, invert onto platter, and remove parchment. While cake is cooling, prepare garnish.

MERINGUE AND LEMON GARNISH

3	LEMONS
4	LARGE EGG WHITES
1¼	CUPS GRANULATED SUGAR
1	CUP RESERVED GROUND NUT MIXTURE
	CONFECTIONERS' SUGAR FOR GARNISH

Preheat oven to 300°F. Place cake layer on a baking sheet lined with parchment paper.

Slice ends off lemons and stand upright on a counter. Cut away skin and membrane, exposing fruit. Working over a bowl to catch the juice, separate sections by slicing with a serrated knife between membranes. Remove and discard seeds. Arrange sections evenly over cake and, using a small strainer, drizzle juice on top.

In a clean bowl of an electric mixer, whisk egg whites until foamy. Gradually add sugar, whisking continuously, until stiff peaks form. (It takes about 10 minutes of beating at high speed for the meringue to get shiny and thick.) Gently fold in reserved nuts.

Spread meringue evenly over cake and bake ½ hour. As meringue drys, it may start to crack—that's O.K. Set aside to cool on rack. Dust with confectioners' sugar before serving.

8 to 10 Servings

Pecan Tart

This traditional filling is so rich we like to serve it in a thin tart shell.

½ RECIPE PÂTE SUCRÉE (PAGE 220)
3 EGGS
¾ CUP PACKED BROWN SUGAR
½ CUP PLUS 1 TEASPOON DARK CORN SYRUP
2 TABLESPOONS HONEY
2 TABLESPOONS MOLASSES
6 TABLESPOONS (¾ STICK) UNSALTED BUTTER, MELTED
2 TEASPOONS VANILLA EXTRACT
1 TEASPOON SALT
2½ CUPS PECAN HALVES

Preheat oven to 325°F.
Use a 10-inch tart pan with a removable bottom. Roll Pâte Sucrée to ⅛-inch thickness and line pan. Chill 15 minutes. Bake empty shell about 15 minutes. Meanwhile make filling.

In a large bowl, whisk together eggs, brown sugar, corn syrup, honey, molasses, butter, vanilla, and salt. Add pecans and mix to evenly coat.

Pour filling into prebaked tart shell and bake until center is set, 35 to 40 minutes. Set aside to cool on rack.

8 to 10 Servings

Linzer Tart

This is a fantastic dough—packed with fresh citrus zest, spices, and a fair share of butter. If you have difficulty working with such a rich dough, return it to the refrigerator whenever it softens.

1	CUP (2 STICKS) UNSALTED BUTTER, SOFTENED
1	CUP GRANULATED SUGAR
2	EGG YOLKS
	GRATED ZEST OF 1 LEMON
	GRATED ZEST OF 1 ORANGE
2½	CUPS ALL-PURPOSE FLOUR
1	CUP FINELY GROUND HAZELNUTS
1	TEASPOON BAKING POWDER
2	TEASPOONS CINNAMON
½	TEASPOON GROUND CLOVES
¼	TEASPOON SALT
1	CUP GOOD-QUALITY RASPBERRY PRESERVES

To make dough, cream together butter and sugar until light and fluffy. Add egg yolks, lemon zest, and orange zest. Beat until well-combined.

In another bowl, mix together remaining ingredients, except preserves, of course. Add dry mixture all at once to creamed mixture and mix briefly, until just combined. (This dough looks more like cookie dough than pastry.) Wrap in plastic and chill until firm, about 4 hours or overnight.

Before rolling dough, preheat oven to 350°F.

Divide dough in half. On a generously floured board, briefly knead 1 piece dough and flatten with the palm of your hand. Gently roll dough to ¼-inch thickness and use to line a 9 or 10-inch tart pan with a removable bottom. This rich dough patches easily. Chill about 10 minutes.

Meanwhile, roll second piece dough to form a 12 × 4-inch rectangle. Using a sharp knife or pastry wheel, cut lengthwise strips, about ⅓-inch wide. Remove lined tart shell from refrigerator and spread evenly with raspberry preserves. To create a lattice pattern with pastry strips, first lay some strips in parallel lines, ½-inch apart. Press to edges of crust to seal. Then lay a second row of strips at a 45° angle to first. Press to crust to seal. (Save leftover dough for cookies.)

Bake 45 minutes, until crust is golden brown and filling bubbly in center. Set aside to cool.

8 to 10 Servings

Walnut Caramel Tart

Don't worry if the quantity of filling seems excessive. It is supposed to form a huge, gooey, sticky dome between two pie shells. Definitely not for dieters, we recommend serving it warm with a scoop of vanilla ice cream.

3	CUPS GRANULATED SUGAR
1¼	CUPS WATER
1½	CUPS HEAVY CREAM
1	CUP (2 STICKS) UNSALTED BUTTER
6	CUPS WALNUT HALVES AND QUARTERS
1	RECIPE PIE DOUGH (PAGE 219)
1	EGG, LIGHTLY BEATEN, FOR GLAZE

To make filling, combine sugar and water in a large heavy saucepan. Bring to a boil. Cook over moderate heat until caramelized, about 12 minutes. Remove from heat. Gradually add cream, taking care to keep hands clear of the steam that escapes. Stir constantly with a wooden spoon until all lumps dissolve. Break butter into small pieces and add, all at once, to caramel. Whisk until smooth. Stir in walnuts and chill about 2 hours or overnight.

Divide Pie Dough in half. Roll one piece to ⅛-inch thickness and use to line a 9-inch tart pan with a removable bottom, leaving about 1 inch excess all around. Spoon in cooled filling, mounding it high in center. Cover with plastic wrap and set aside in refrigerator.

Roll second piece dough to form a 12-inch circle, ⅛-inch thick. Remove filled shell from refrigerator. Brush egg over overhanging dough. Place rolled dough over filling and carefully seal edges by gently pressing. (It is important to make this a solid seal.) Trim any excess dough with scissors. Flute the edges, using both top and bottom crusts.

Using a paring knife, cut and remove a ¼-inch circle in center of top crust for steam to escape. Brush top with egg and chill 2 to 3 hours, or preferably overnight.

Preheat oven to 350°F. Before baking, brush again with egg and check to make sure top and bottom crusts are sealed together.

Bake 50 minutes to 1 hour or until the edges are golden. Set aside to cool in pan several hours before serving.

10 to 12 Servings

Plum Streusel Tart

You can create an infinite variety of delicious fruit tarts with these basic components: Pâte Sucrée, almond cream, and streusel. Along with this recipe come a few suggestions.

½   RECIPE PÂTE SUCRÉE (PAGE 220)

ALMOND CREAM

½   CUP PLUS 1 TABLESPOON GRANULATED SUGAR
1   CUP SLICED ALMONDS, BLANCHED
9   TABLESPOONS (1 STICK PLUS 1 TABLESPOON) UNSALTED
     BUTTER, SOFTENED
1   EGG
1   EGG YOLK
2   TABLESPOONS RUM
1   TEASPOON VANILLA EXTRACT

To make almond cream, process sugar and almonds in a food processor until fine. Add butter, 1 tablespoon at a time, processing after each addition until smooth. Add remaining ingredients and process until smooth. Cover and refrigerate until ready to assemble. The almond cream may be made up to 4 days in advance.

STREUSEL

½   CUP PACKED BROWN SUGAR
7   TABLESPOONS UNSALTED BUTTER, ROOM TEMPERATURE
1   TEASPOON CINNAMON
¼   TEASPOON SALT
1   CUP PLUS 2 TABLESPOONS ALL-PURPOSE FLOUR

Cream together sugar and butter until smooth. Add cinnamon and salt, and mix until blended. Add flour. Mix with your fingers just until crumbly. Reserve.

6   MEDIUM PLUMS, ANY TYPE, RIPE

Roll Pâte Sucrée and use to line a 10-inch tart pan with a removable bottom. Chill ½ hour.

Preheat oven to 350°F. Bake empty tart shell 15 minutes. Remove from oven and spread almond cream in hot tart shell. Bake another 10 minutes. Remove from oven.

Meanwhile, cut plums in half and remove pits. Arrange plums, cut-side down, over baked almond cream; sprinkle with streusel and bake 20 to 30 minutes, until plums are soft and crust is golden brown. Set aside to cool in pan.

8 Servings

VARIATIONS: Use same formula for 10 to 12 ripe apricots—the streusel is optional. Or fan 5 or 6 ripe pears (thinly sliced lengthwise) over the almond cream—no streusel necessary. For berry tarts, garnish a fully baked almond cream tart with about 2½ pints fresh berries.

Rhubarb Pie

Mention fruit pies and we automatically think of rhubarb. However, don't hesitate to fill these shells with other fruits of the season. Peaches (peeled, pitted, and cut into wedges) or apples (peeled and diced) mixed with an equal amount of cranberries are delightful.

12   OUNCES OR ⅔ RECIPE PIE DOUGH (PAGE 219)
 3   POUNDS RHUBARB
1½–2 CUPS GRANULATED SUGAR TO TASTE
 3   TABLESPOONS TAPIOCA
 2   CUPS STREUSEL (PAGE 214)

Lightly butter a 10-inch pie plate.
On a generously floured board, roll dough to ⅛-inch thickness and line pie plate, leaving about ¼-inch overhang. Pinch up excess dough to form an upright fluted edge. Chill about an hour.

Preheat oven to 350°F. To prebake, line dough with a sheet of parchment paper or aluminum foil and fill with weights, beans, or rice. Bake 25 minutes, remove paper and weights, and set aside. Prepare filling.

Clean rhubarb and cut across width in ½-inch slices. Combine with sugar in a large bowl. Let sit at room temperature 15 minutes. Sprinkle on tapioca, toss well, and let sit an additional 15 minutes.

Pour filling into warm prebaked pie shell and sprinkle streusel over top. Bake until juices bubble, about 1 hour and 15 minutes. Set aside to cool on rack before serving.

8 to 10 Servings

Puff Pastry

It takes a certain state of mind to even want to make Puff Pastry at home. Choose a day when you won't feel rushed, preferably not the same day you plan on baking, since puff pastry benefits from an extra night in the refrigerator. It also freezes well. Be patient, follow these instructions precisely, and we guarantee spectacular results.

DOUGH

3½	CUPS ALL-PURPOSE FLOUR
½	CUP CORNSTARCH
2	TEASPOONS SALT
4	TABLESPOONS (½ STICK) UNSALTED BUTTER, SOFTENED
1	CUP PLUS 2 TABLESPOONS ICED WATER

Combine flour, cornstarch, salt, and butter in a large bowl. With your fingertips, mix until a coarse meal forms. Add the water, all at once, and knead by hand until a ball forms.

Transfer to a bowl of an electric mixer with a dough hook and knead until smooth and moist, about 5 minutes, or knead by hand about 15 minutes. Press dough into a 6 x 4-inch rectangle. Wrap with plastic and chill 4 hours or overnight.

BUTTER BLOCK

1¾	CUPS (3½ STICKS) UNSALTED BUTTER

Soften butter block with your hands or with an electric mixer until pliable enough to roll like dough—but not too soft. The key to rolling butter and dough is they must be warm enough to roll, but not warm enough to combine. The two parts should always remain separate.

On a floured board, roll cold dough, from center out, to form an 18 x 12-inch rectangle, keeping the thickness uniform, about 1/2 inch thick. Align dough so the length is parallel to the counter.

Imagine the dough divided in thirds along its width and spread butter over middle and right thirds, leaving a ½-inch margin uncovered on all sides. Fold dough in thirds, first left over middle, then right over left. Press edges together to seal in butter and press out any air.

Turn folded dough clockwise a quarter turn. You have now completed one turn. To make second turn, roll dough out again to an 18 x 12-inch rectangle. Fold in thirds again. As a reminder of turns completed, press 2 dots in dough with your fingertips. Wrap in plastic and chill ½ hour.

Roll, fold, and turn dough two more times. Press the dough with four dots, wrap, and chill ½ hour. Repeat the same procedure 2 more times, for a total of 6 turns. Wrap well in plastic and store in refrigerator overnight. Follow recipe for baking instructions. Puff Pastry may be frozen as long as 3 weeks.

Makes 3 Pounds   ✕

. . . .

Pithivers

In this simple yet elegant tart, the almond cream is surrounded by two layers of Puff Pastry. For the most impressive results, serve it fresh from the oven.

½ RECIPE PUFF PASTRY (PAGE 216)
1 RECIPE ALMOND CREAM (PAGE 214)
1 EGG, LIGHTLY BEATEN

Divide Puff Pastry in half. On a lightly floured board, roll each piece to a 10-inch square. Set aside in refrigerator ½ hour.

After chilling, assemble tart on a sheet pan lined with parchment paper. Lightly roll each piece so it returns to a 10-inch square. Place one pastry square on pan. Mound softened almond cream in a 5-inch circle about 2 inches high in center of square. Brush egg on exposed pastry.

Place second pastry square over almond cream, so corners align. Pressing out from center to release any air, seal in cream by pressing together top and bottom pastry. Cut a small hole in center of top layer using a paring knife. Press out excess air. Chill an additional hour or, preferably, overnight.

Preheat oven to 425°F.

Place a 10-inch round bowl over tart and, using a sharp paring knife, trim excess pastry to form a 10-inch circle. Do not drag knife. Press edges again to seal and carefully brush top with egg. Using a paring knife, make a pinwheel pattern by scoring dough from center out.

Bake, on lined sheet pan, 20 minutes. Reduce heat to 350°F and bake an additional ½ hour. Serve immediately.

8 to 10 Servings   ✕

Lemon Curd Tarts

Our nut crust is an easy dough to work with. We like the way it offsets the rich lemon custard in these tarts. Ideally, the crust should be as thick as the filling.

NUT CRUST

1	CUP (2 STICKS) UNSALTED BUTTER, SOFTENED
¼	CUP GRANULATED SUGAR
¾	CUP FINELY CHOPPED PECANS
1	EGG
1	EGG YOLK
1	TEASPOON SALT
2¾	CUPS ALL-PURPOSE FLOUR

Mix butter, sugar, pecans, whole egg, egg yolk, and salt with a wooden spoon until barely blended. Add flour and knead until a smooth ball forms. Wrap in plastic and chill about 4 hours.

After chilling dough, preheat oven to 350°F. Roll chilled dough to about ¼-inch thickness or divide into 8 parts and press into 8 individual tart pans, 3-inch round × 1-inch deep. The crust should be thick.

Bake empty tart shells 12 to 15 minutes, or until edges begin to brown. Set aside to cool. Meanwhile make lemon curd.

LEMON CURD FILLING

1	CUP (2 STICKS) UNSALTED BUTTER, MELTED
2	CUPS GRANULATED SUGAR
4	EGGS
1	SCANT CUP FRESH LEMON JUICE
¾	CUP FINELY CHOPPED PISTACHIO NUTS FOR GARNISH

Combine butter, sugar, eggs, and lemon juice in a bowl. Place over a pot of simmering water and stir constantly and gently with a spoon or a spatula, being careful not to incorporate air. Continue stirring until mixture is pale yellow and thickly coats the back of a spoon, 7 to 10 minutes. Strain and set aside to cool to room temperature.

Remove cooled tart shells from pans and fill with lemon curd. Garnish rims with pistachio nuts and serve.

8 Servings

VARIATION: For Passion Curd Tarts substitute 1 cup passion fruit juice for the lemon.

Pie Dough

When making Pie Dough, you should be able to see chunks of fat—whether lard, shortening, or butter—in the completed dough. In the oven, they will expand and release the steam that makes pie dough so flaky. All butter may be substituted for the lard, but for the best crust, we still use lard.

3	CUPS ALL-PURPOSE FLOUR
¾	CUP LARD
4	TABLESPOONS (½ STICK) UNSALTED BUTTER
1	TEASPOON SALT
½	CUP PLUS 2 TABLESPOONS ICED WATER

In a large bowl, combine 2½ cups flour with lard, butter, and salt. Mix lightly with your fingertips until dough forms pea-sized pieces. You should be able to see chunks of fat.

Stir in remaining flour, then stir in water. Lightly knead until dough forms a ball. It is important to handle this dough as little as possible.

Transfer to a plastic bag and form dough into a 6-inch log. Seal bag, pressing out any air, and refrigerate a minimum of 1 hour or as long as 3 days. Pie Dough may be stored in the freezer 1 week.

Divide log in thirds. To roll, soften dough by pressing it in your hands until malleable. Form each into a 4-inch round disk. On a generously floured board, roll from center out, lifting dough, turning it slightly, and occasionally flipping to prevent sticking. Roll dough to ⅛-inch thickness.

Lightly butter and flour a 10-inch pie pan and line with dough, leaving about ¼-inch overhang for shrinkage. Pinch up excess dough to form a rim. Flute edges by pressing the thumb of one hand between the thumb and first finger of the other to form a V pattern. Chill 1 hour.

To bake empty pie shell, preheat oven to 350°F. Line with a sheet of parchment paper or aluminum foil larger than the pan, and fill with pie weights, rice, or beans. Bake about 25 minutes, remove paper and weights, and follow pie recipe directions.

Makes Three 10-inch Pie Tops or Bottoms

Pâte Sucrée

Our tart pastry is sweet and rich, almost like cookie dough. If you are just learning to bake, this is a good, easy dough to start with. Excellent for fruit tarts as well as rolled sugar cookies.

8   TABLESPOONS (1 STICK) UNSALTED BUTTER, SOFTENED
1   CUP PLUS 6 TABLESPOONS CONFECTIONERS' SUGAR, SIFTED
1   EGG
1   TEASPOON SALT
1¾   CUPS ALL-PURPOSE FLOUR

In an electric mixer, cream together butter and sugar until light and fluffy. Add egg and salt, and beat until combined. Add flour, all at once, and slowly mix just until flour is evenly moistened. You don't want to mix until a ball forms around beaters.

Transfer to a plastic bag and form dough into a 6-inch log. Seal bag, pressing out any air, and refrigerate a minimum of 4 hours or as long as 4 days. (Well-wrapped Pâte Sucrée may be stored in the freezer a month.)

Divide log in half for one tart shell. To roll, soften dough by pressing it in your hands until malleable. Form a 4-inch round disk. On a lightly floured board, roll from center out, lifting dough, turning it slightly, and occasionally flipping to prevent sticking. Flour board as necessary. Roll dough to ⅛-inch thickness.

To line a tart pan, fold dough in half and lift. Place in pan, unfold, and gently press it evenly into bottom and up sides of pan. Create a lip at top by pressing dough between flutes of pan with your fingers as you pinch dough off at the edge. Then for an even crust, roll a rolling pin across top. Dough scraps can be used to patch short edges or holes, or for cookies. Chill ½ hour before baking.

To bake empty tart shell, preheat oven to 350°F. Bake 20 minutes for a fully baked shell or 15 minutes for a partially baked.

Makes Two 9- or 10-inch Tart Shells plus a Few Cookies

Baked Custards

Indian Pudding

Fresh squeezed ginger juice gives this homey American dessert additional zing. We love to serve it piping hot with a spoonful or two of cold cream or a scoop of vanilla ice cream.

2	CUPS MILK
½	CUP YELLOW CORNMEAL
¼	CUP GRANULATED SUGAR
¼	CUP PACKED BROWN SUGAR
½	CUP MOLASSES
1	TEASPOON SALT
2	TABLESPOONS UNSALTED BUTTER
¼	TEASPOON GROUND CLOVES
3	CUPS HALF AND HALF
1	3-INCH PIECE OF FRESH GINGER

Preheat oven to 325°F. Butter a 9 x 5 x 3-inch Pyrex loaf pan.

Combine milk and cornmeal in a medium stainless or enamel saucepan. Cook over moderate heat, whisking constantly, until mixture comes to a boil. Reduce heat to low and continue stirring until as thick as oatmeal. Remove from heat.

Add the granulated sugar, brown sugar, molasses, salt, butter, and cloves and 2 cups half and half. Stir to combine. Bring mixture back to a boil and transfer to prepared loaf pan.

Place inside a larger pan and pour in boiling water until it rises halfway up the sides of the loaf pan. Bake 1 hour, stirring after the first ½ hour.

Meanwhile, peel and grate ginger. Press against a fine sieve or squeeze through a piece of cheesecloth to extract a tablespoon or two juice.

After baking an hour, add ginger juice and remaining cup of half and half, and stir. Bake an additional hour, stirring each ½ hour. Serve immediately in small bowls or cups, or store in refrigerator and reheat over low heat.

8 Servings

Crème Caramel

One of the great rewards of cooking is making a perfect, velvety Crème Caramel—and then tasting it. The quintessential summer dessert, this delightfully simple dish can be prepared well in advance.

CARAMEL

2   CUPS GRANULATED SUGAR
1¼   CUPS WATER

CUSTARD

8   EGGS
4   EGG YOLKS
1   CUP PLUS 2 TABLESPOONS GRANULATED SUGAR
1   QUART HALF AND HALF
½   CUP TRIPLE SEC OR GRAND MARNIER
2   TEASPOONS VANILLA EXTRACT

Preheat oven to 325°F.

For caramel, combine sugar and ½ cup water in a medium saucepan. Be sure all sugar granules are washed down from pot sides. Cook over moderate heat, swirling pan occasionally, until color is golden brown and mixture smells like caramel. Often you need to cook it a bit darker than you would imagine. This should take 10 to 15 minutes. Pour enough caramel into a 9-inch round cake pan to coat bottom and sides. Swirl to coat and reserve.

Add remaining water to caramel in saucepan. Bring to a boil and cook over moderate heat until the sugar dissolves, about 5 minutes. Occasionally stir and brush down sides with a pastry brush dipped in cold water. This process prevents crystallization of the sugar. Set this caramel sauce aside at room temperature, then chill until serving time.

Combine all custard ingredients in a large bowl. Gently whisk together, being careful not to incorporate much air.

Strain half custard into prepared cake pan. Place inside a larger pan and pour in boiling water until it rises halfway up the sides of the cake pan. Set the roasting pan on the open oven door and strain in remaining custard.

Bake for 1 hour to 1 hour 15 minutes, until center feels just firm when pressed. Set aside to cool about 1½ hours. Cover with plastic wrap touching top. Refrigerate overnight or as long as 4 days.

To serve, run a knife along inside edge, 2 or 3 times, to loosen. When you press center, sides should pull away. Cover with a platter and quickly invert.

Carefully drain excess caramel into a bowl and strain into reserved cold sauce. Serve wedges of creme caramel on dessert plates. Top with chilled caramel sauce.

8 to 10 Servings

....

Cheesecake

We eliminated the crust in our otherwise classic cheesecake so that people could get right to the cheese. Serve it plain or with the fruit toppings suggested here.

½	CUP SLICED ALMONDS, TOASTED
2½	POUNDS CREAM CHEESE, SOFTENED
1	CUP PLUS 2 TABLESPOONS GRANULATED SUGAR
1½	TEASPOONS GRATED LEMON ZEST
⅓	CUP FRESH LEMON JUICE
3	EGGS
1½	TEASPOONS VANILLA EXTRACT

Preheat oven to 325°F. Butter a 9-inch round cake pan and line bottom and sides with almonds.

With an electric mixer at low speed, beat cream cheese until soft and smooth. With machine running, add sugar, lemon zest, and juice, beating well between additions. Add eggs, one at a time, beating well after each addition. Beat in vanilla. To ensure even mixing, be sure to scrape down bowl between additions.

Pour batter into lined cake pan. Tap it 3 or 4 times on the counter to eliminate air pockets. Place inside a larger pan and pour in boiling water until it rises halfway up the sides of the cake pan. Bake about 45 minutes, until center feels firm when pressed.

Set aside to cool on rack, then refrigerate 2 or 3 hours. To unmold, place pan over a low burner about 2 minutes. Invert onto a platter, then invert again—the nuts should be on the bottom. The completed cake may be kept in refrigerator up to 3 days.

8 to 10 Servings

VARIATIONS: To cut sweetness and add color, garnish with fresh berries—2 baskets of strawberries or blueberries. Brush with a glaze made from ¼ cup apricot jelly heated with 3 tablespoons water.

Bread Pudding
with Raspberry Sauce

The difference between good and great Bread Pudding lies in the standing time. It should be long enough for the bread to absorb the liquids before baking. Bread Pudding is delicious hot or cold.

6 EGGS
¾ CUP GRANULATED SUGAR
4 CUPS HALF AND HALF
¼ CUP TRIPLE SEC OR GRAND MARNIER
2 TEASPOONS VANILLA EXTRACT
   GRATED ZEST OF 1 ORANGE
6 CUPS DRY WHITE BREAD, CRUSTS REMOVED AND CUT
   INTO ½-INCH DICE
2 TABLESPOONS UNSALTED BUTTER, SOFTENED
1 TABLESPOON GRANULATED SUGAR PLUS 1 TEASPOON
   CINNAMON FOR SPRINKLING
   1 PINT FRESH RASPBERRIES
   RASPBERRY SAUCE, RECIPE FOLLOWS

Generously butter a 9 x 5 x 3-inch Pyrex loaf pan.

In a large bowl, whisk together eggs and sugar. Add half and half, Triple Sec, vanilla, and orange zest, and mix until combined. Add bread cubes and toss until the bread is evenly moistened. Transfer to prepared loaf pan and let stand at room temperature at least ½ hour, preferably 1 hour.

Preheat oven to 325°F.

Dot bread pudding with softened butter. Sprinkle on sugar and cinnamon. Place inside a larger pan and pour in warm water until it rises halfway up the sides of the loaf pan.

Bake 1 hour and 15 minutes to 1 hour and 30 minutes, until top is brown and crusty.

To serve hot, scoop and serve individual portions in bowls, topped with fresh berries. Or, chill 4 to 6 hours, invert onto a serving platter, and serve ½-inch slices with Raspberry Sauce.

10 Servings

Raspberry Sauce

1   CUP GRANULATED SUGAR
1   CUP WATER
1   PINT BASKET FRESH OR FROZEN RASPBERRIES

Combine sugar and water in a small saucepan and boil about 1 minute. Add raspberries, return to a boil, and cook, whisking constantly until the berries are smooth, about 3 minutes. Pass through a fine sieve and chill until serving time.

Makes 1½ Cups

Chocolate Chip Cheesecake

When the custard is baked, the chocolate chunks melt and form a marble pattern in this dense sweet cake.

½   CUP SLICED ALMONDS, TOASTED
2½   POUNDS CREAM CHEESE, SOFTENED
1   CUP PLUS 2 TABLESPOONS GRANULATED SUGAR
1½   TEASPOONS VANILLA EXTRACT
3   EGGS
6   OUNCES SEMISWEET CHOCOLATE, ROUGHLY CHOPPED

Preheat oven to 325°F. Butter a 9-inch round cake pan and line bottom and sides with almonds.

With an electric mixer at low speed, beat cream cheese until soft and smooth. With machine running, add sugar and vanilla. Add eggs, one at a time, beating well after each addition. To ensure even mixing, scrape down bowl between additions.

By hand, fold in chocolate chunks. Fill lined cake pan and tap 3 or 4 times on the counter to eliminate air pockets. Place inside a larger pan and pour in boiling water until it rises halfway up the sides of the cake pan. Bake about 45 minutes, until the center feels firm when pressed.

Set aside to cool on rack, then refrigerate 2 to 3 hours. To unmold, place pan over a low burner about 2 minutes. Invert onto a platter, then invert again—the nuts should be on the bottom. The completed cake may be kept in refrigerator up to 3 days.

8 to 10 Servings

Sweet Potato Flan

This is one of our most popular winter desserts. Why bother with a crust when you have a custard this dense and satisfying? For a pumpkin flan, substitute two cups of pureed pumpkin.

2   POUNDS SWEET POTATOES

CARAMEL

2   CUPS GRANULATED SUGAR
1¼   CUPS WATER

CUSTARD

1⅓   CUPS PACKED BROWN SUGAR
8   EGGS
2   CUPS HEAVY CREAM
3   TABLESPOONS BRANDY
2   TEASPOONS VANILLA EXTRACT
1   TABLESPOON FRESHLY GRATED GINGER (PAGE 249)
1   TEASPOON SALT
½   TEASPOON CINNAMON
¼   TEASPOON GROUND CLOVES
¼   TEASPOON GROUND ALLSPICE

Preheat oven to 350°F. Bake potatoes until soft throughout, about 1 hour. Set aside to cool, then peel and cut into chunks. Puree in a food processor, being careful not to overmix, and reserve. Reduce oven to 325°F.

Prepare caramel and sauce following the same method as for Crème Caramel (page 222). Line a 3-quart Pyrex loaf pan with caramel and set aside on a level surface. Chill sauce.

Combine custard ingredients in a large bowl and whisk to combine. Pour through a strainer into lined loaf pan.

Place inside a larger roasting pan. Pour in boiling water until it rises halfway up the sides of the loaf pan. Bake about 1 hour 50 minutes. The center should feel firm when pressed.

Set aside to cool about 1½ hours. Cover with plastic wrap touching top. Refrigerate overnight or as long as 4 days.

To serve, run a knife along inside edge, 2 or 3 times, to loosen. When you press center, sides should pull away. Cover with a platter and quickly invert. Carefully drain excess caramel into a bowl and strain into reserved cold sauce. Serve slices of flan on dessert plates. Top with chilled caramel sauce.

10 Servings   ✕

Cookies and Cakes

Chewy Date Bars

These great old-fashioned sandwich bars are crunchy on the top and bottom, and chewy inside. Use them to stuff lunch boxes, serve with a bowl of vanilla ice cream for dessert, or cut into small squares for afternoon tea.

1	POUND PITTED DRIED DATES, CHOPPED
1	CUP WATER
1	CUP GRANULATED SUGAR
½	CUP FRESH LEMON JUICE
3	CUPS ROLLED OATS
2½	CUPS ALL-PURPOSE FLOUR
1¾	CUPS PACKED BROWN SUGAR
¾	TEASPOON BAKING SODA
¾	TEASPOON SALT
1¾	CUPS (3½ STICKS) UNSALTED BUTTER, MELTED

Preheat oven to 350°F. Generously butter a 9 x 12-inch pan.

Combine dates and water in a saucepan. Cook at a low boil for 5 minutes, until mixture is as thick as mashed potatoes. Stir in sugar and remove from heat. Add lemon juice and set aside to cool.

In a large bowl, mix together oats, flour, brown sugar, baking soda, and salt. Add melted butter to dry mixture. Stir to evenly moisten.

Spread half oat mixture in baking pan to form an even layer. Cover evenly with all date mixture. Spread remaining oat mixture over top.

Bake about 40 minutes, until top is golden brown and pebbly. The edges should start caramelizing. Set aside to cool, in pan on rack, about 1 hour. Run a sharp knife along inside edges to loosen. Invert, trim edges, and cut into squares.

Makes 12 Large Squares

Mocha Almond Torte

9½	OUNCES (SCANT 3 CUPS) SLIVERED ALMONDS
¾	CUP PLUS 3 TABLESPOONS GRANULATED SUGAR
6	LARGE EGG WHITES
¼	TEASPOON SALT
1	TEASPOON VANILLA EXTRACT
	MOCHA BUTTERCREAM, RECIPE FOLLOWS
¾	CUP SLICED ALMONDS, TOASTED, FOR GARNISH
10	WHOLE COFFEE BEANS FOR GARNISH

Preheat oven to 350°F. Generously butter a 12 x 18-inch sheet pan. Line with parchment paper, butter again, and dust with flour.

Combine almonds and ¾ cup sugar in a food processor. Grind until fine and reserve.

Beat egg whites and salt with a whisk until foamy. Gradually add remaining sugar, whisking until soft peaks form.

Sprinkle ¼ almond mixture at a time over whites and gently fold. Fold in vanilla.

Pour batter into prepared sheet pan and spread evenly with spatula. Tap pan on the counter to eliminate air pockets. Bake 20 to 25 minutes, until golden and edges pull away from pan.

Set aside to cool in pan about 10 minutes. Run a knife along inside edges to loosen, then invert onto a parchment-lined sheet pan. With a serrated knife, cut cake into thirds, lengthwise, and reserve. Prepare mocha buttercream.

MOCHA BUTTERCREAM

1½	CUPS ESPRESSO CRÈME ANGLAISE (PAGE 208), ROOM TEMPERATURE
3	STICKS PLUS 2 TABLESPOONS UNSALTED BUTTER, ROOM TEMPERATURE

The temperatures of ingredients should be as uniform as possible, neither too hot nor too cold, but room temperature. Place Espresso Crème Anglaise in bowl of an electric mixer with a whisk attachment. With machine at medium speed, start adding butter, 1 tablespoon at a time, until all butter is added. Continue whisking an additional 5 minutes, until light, fluffy, and cool to the touch.

It is important to work quickly while assembling this torte, since the buttercream may start melting.

Stack the 3 lengths of almond cake on a counter and trim sides so they are uniform. Place first strip on a paper-lined serving platter and spread ¼ buttercream over cake. Repeat this procedure, alternating layers and evenly spreading mocha cream over top and sides to enclose cake.

Place remaining ¼ buttercream in a pastry bag fitted with a #2 plain tip. Pipe parallel lines side-by-side across width of cake. With a spatula, trim edges for a sharp, clean edge. Press toasted almonds along sides and decorate top with a center row of coffee beans. Serve at room temperature.

10 to 12 Servings

Brownies

These traditional brownies are great for taking along on picnics. They don't crumble or crack and everybody loves them.

5	OUNCES UNSWEETENED BITTER CHOCOLATE, CHOPPED
1¼	CUPS (2½ STICKS) UNSALTED BUTTER
½	TEASPOON SALT
2½	CUPS GRANULATED SUGAR
5	EGGS
1	TEASPOON VANILLA EXTRACT
1¼	CUPS ALL-PURPOSE FLOUR
2½	CUPS WALNUTS, ROUGHLY CHOPPED

Preheat oven to 325°F. Butter and flour a 9 x 12-inch pan and line with parchment paper.

Combine chocolate, butter, and salt in the top of a double boiler or in a bowl. Melt over simmering water and set aside to cool.

In a large bowl, combine sugar, eggs, and vanilla. Whisk until smooth. Add melted chocolate mixture and whisk to combine.

Fold in flour until it just disappears. Fold in walnuts. Spread batter evenly in pan.

Bake for about 35 minutes or until a toothpick inserted in center comes out clean. Set aside to cool, in pan on rack, 1 hour. Invert pan to release and cut into squares.

Makes 12 Large or 20 Small Brownies

Gâteau St.-Honoré

1	POUND (⅓ RECIPE) PUFF PASTRY (PAGE 216)

CREAM PUFFS

½	CUP MILK
3½	TABLESPOONS UNSALTED BUTTER
⅛	TEASPOON SALT
½	CUP PLUS 1 TABLESPOON ALL-PURPOSE FLOUR
2	EGGS

	PASTRY CREAM, RECIPE FOLLOWS
1½	CUPS SUGAR FOR CARAMEL
½	CUP WATER
½	RECIPE CITY CHOCOLATE (PAGE 208), OMITTING THE ESPRESSO CRÈME ANGLAISE
2	CUPS HEAVY CREAM, COLD
3	OUNCES SEMISWEET CHOCOLATE, MELTED

Roll Puff Pastry to form a 10-inch square and reserve in the refrigerator.

To make Cream Puffs, combine milk, butter, and salt in a medium-heavy saucepan. Bring to a boil. Add flour all at once. Mix quickly with a wooden spoon until a ball forms on the spoon and the flour is evenly moistened. Transfer to a bowl and add eggs, one at a time, beating well after each addition.

Preheat oven to 450°F.

Fill a pastry bag fitted with a large plain tip with dough and line a baking sheet with parchment paper. Pipe dough onto baking sheet to form small circles, about the size of quarters. With a finger dipped in cold water, flatten point on top of each puff. Drop pan on the counter to set puffs.

Bake until uniformly puffed and golden, about 10 minutes. Reduce heat to 375°F and bake an additional 15 to 20 minutes. You can test for doneness by opening a puff. The inside should be totally dry. Set aside to cool on a rack.

Turn heat up to 425°F. Place Puff Pastry on a parchment paper–lined baking sheet and, with a 10-inch round cake pan inverted over dough, trace a 10-inch circle using a sharp knife. This will be the base for the cake. Prick all over with a fork and set in refrigerator to rest 15 minutes. Then bake for 20 minutes, until puffed and golden. Reserve at room temperature.

Meanwhile make Pastry Cream. Fill a pastry bag fitted with a #2 tip with the cream. Make a hole in bottom of each puff using a small paring knife. Fill with Pastry Cream and reserve.

Combine sugar and water for caramelizing in a saucepan and cook until golden brown. Follow the method used for Crème Caramel (page 222). Immediately remove from heat. Using a fork, dip half of each cream puff into warm caramel and place on a tray lined with parchment paper. When caramel has set, turn puff and dip uncoated half in caramel. Immediately arrange puffs, flat-side up, along edge of cooled Puff Pastry to form an even wall.

Fill center of pastry with an even layer of City Chocolate. Whip cold cream until soft peaks form. Fold half of this cream into melted chocolate and set aside.

Spoon remaining whipped cream into a pastry bag fitted with a #8 plain tip. Pipe about 5 rows of Hershey's Kiss–shaped domes over chocolate filling, leaving even spaces between rows. Fill bag with chocolate-flavored cream and repeat, filling spaces between rows. Chill until serving time.

10 Servings

Pastry Cream

½   CUP GRANULATED SUGAR
¼   CUP CORNSTARCH
4   EGG YOLKS
2   CUPS MILK
½   TEASPOON VANILLA

Mix ¼ cup sugar and all cornstarch in a bowl until smooth. Add egg yolks and mix until a paste is formed. Stir in ½ cup milk.

Combine remaining milk and sugar in a saucepan and bring to a boil. Pour hot mixture into mixture in bowl, whisking constantly. Pour back into pan.

Cook over moderate heat, stirring constantly, until smooth and thick. Remove from heat and stir an additional minute. Stir in vanilla and transfer to a bowl. Cover with buttered parchment paper touching top and chill a minimum of 2 hours or as long as 2 days.

Makes 2½ Cups

Poppy Seed Cake
with Lemon Glaze

*Our customers love this classic
cake for dessert, but at home,
nothing beats a toasted slice
with morning coffee. The best
coffee cake ever—guaranteed.*

1	CUP POPPY SEEDS
1/3	CUP HONEY
1/4	CUP WATER
12	TABLESPOONS (1 1/2 STICKS) UNSALTED BUTTER, SOFTENED
3/4	CUP GRANULATED SUGAR
1	TABLESPOON GRATED LEMON ZEST
1	TEASPOON VANILLA EXTRACT
2	EGGS
2 1/4	CUPS ALL-PURPOSE FLOUR
1	TEASPOON BAKING SODA
1	TEASPOON BAKING POWDER
1	TEASPOON SALT
2 1/2	TABLESPOONS FRESH LEMON JUICE
1	CUP SOUR CREAM
	LEMON GLAZE, RECIPE FOLLOWS

Preheat oven to 325°F. Butter and flour a 10-inch tube pan.

Combine poppy seeds, honey, and water in a medium saucepan. Cook over moderate heat, stirring frequently, until water evaporates and mixture looks like wet sand. This will take about 5 minutes. Set aside to cool.

Cream together butter and sugar until light and fluffy. Mix in lemon zest and vanilla. Add eggs, one at a time, beating well after each addition.

In another bowl, combine flour, baking soda, baking powder, and salt.

When poppy seed mixture has cooled, stir in lemon juice. Pour into creamed butter mixture and stir until combined.

By hand, add dry ingredients and sour cream in 3 stages, alternating liquid and dry, and ending with sour cream. Spoon batter into prepared pan, smoothing top with a spatula, and tap vigorously on a counter to eliminate air pockets.

Bake about 1 hour and 15 minutes, until a toothpick inserted in center comes out clean. Set aside to cool, in pan on rack, about 15 minutes. Invert onto platter and prepare Lemon Glaze.

Brush hot Lemon Glaze all over bottom, top, and sides of cake to flavor it and seal in moisture.

8 to 10 Servings   ✕

Lemon Glaze

1   CUP GRANULATED SUGAR
½   CUP FRESH LEMON JUICE

Combine sugar and lemon juice in a small saucepan. Bring to a boil over moderate heat and cook a minute or two, until sugar is dissolved. Remove from heat.

Makes 1¼ Cups

Shortbreads

Shortbreads are quick and easy—nice to have on hand for afternoon coffee or tea.

1   CUP (2 STICKS) UNSALTED BUTTER, SOFTENED
⅓   CUP PACKED BROWN SUGAR
¼   CUP GRANULATED SUGAR
1   CUP ALL-PURPOSE FLOUR
1   CUP PASTRY FLOUR
¼   CUP CORNSTARCH
¾   TEASPOON SALT
⅓   CUP PECAN HALVES

Preheat oven to 325°F. Have ready an ungreased 10-inch tart pan with a removable bottom.

Cream together the butter, brown sugar and granulated sugar until light and fluffy.

In another bowl, mix together all-purpose flour, pastry flour, cornstarch, and salt. Add dry ingredients to creamed mixture and stir until combined.

With your fingers, spread dough evenly over pan, like a thick pie crust. (Occasionally dip your fingers into flour, if the dough is too sticky.) When you have an even layer, flute edges by pressing your fingers around rim to form 1-inch long ridges. Arrange pecans, flat-side down, in a circular pattern, in spaces between ridges. If you wish, you can decorate by pressing the tines of a fork into dough to form a pattern. Prick all over with a fork.

Bake until golden and slightly puffy, about 45 minutes. Set aside to cool on rack. Cut in wedges to serve.

10 Servings

Gâteau Benoit

At the restaurant, we like to top this simple, light cake with a generous pile of chocolate shavings, but feel free to simplify the presentation at home. This exceptionally moist cake is just as delicious with a sprinkling of confectioners' sugar or a dollop of whipped cream.

7½	OUNCES SEMISWEET CHOCOLATE, CHOPPED
11	TABLESPOONS (1 STICK PLUS 3 TABLESPOONS) UNSALTED BUTTER
4	EGGS, SEPARATED
½	CUP PLUS 1 TABLESPOON GRANULATED SUGAR
½	CUP ALL-PURPOSE FLOUR

Preheat oven to 350°F. Butter and flour a 10-inch round cake pan. Line with parchment paper.

Melt chocolate and butter together in the top of a double boiler or in a bowl over simmering water. Set aside to cool.

Beat egg yolks until light and fluffy, then slowly add sugar, beating constantly until pale yellow. Fold in melted chocolate mixture.

Sift flour over chocolate mixture and mix until flour just disappears.

Whisk egg whites until soft peaks form. Fold whites into chocolate mixture in two parts. Pour batter into pan, spread evenly, and tap once or twice on a counter to remove air.

Bake 20 to 25 minutes, until a toothpick inserted in center comes out with a few flakes clinging to it. Set aside to cool, in pan on rack, about an hour.

To release cake, run a knife along inside edge to loosen. Invert onto serving platter, peel off parchment, and invert again. Prepare chocolate curls.

Pile curls on top of cake in a circular pattern pointing outward from the center. Dust with confectioners' sugar.

CHOCOLATE CURLS

1-POUND OR LARGER BLOCK SEMISWEET CHOCOLATE
CONFECTIONERS' SUGAR FOR DUSTING

The key to making chocolate curls, or cigarettes, is the right temperature. Place chocolate in oven, with only the pilot light on, 10 to 20 minutes, until it softens slightly. Or place in an oven that's off but still warm until chocolate *just* begins to soften. In warm weather, this step may not be necessary.

Then, holding a heavy chef's knife between both hands and applying even pressure, pull blade across surface of block, toward you, at about a 60° angle. With some practice you can make either tight cigarette rolls or freeform ruffles. Leftover chocolate can be wrapped in plastic and used again.

8 Servings

···

Chocolate Chip Cookies

At home we like to keep a log of this rich dough in the refrigerator for midnight cravings. You can cut one-inch slices and bake small quantities as the occasion demands.

1	CUP (2 STICKS) UNSALTED BUTTER, SOFTENED
¾	CUP GRANULATED SUGAR
¾	CUP LIGHT BROWN SUGAR
1	TEASPOON VANILLA EXTRACT
2	EGGS
2½	CUPS ALL-PURPOSE FLOUR
1	TEASPOON BAKING SODA
1	TEASPOON SALT
6	OUNCES SEMISWEET CHOCOLATE, CHOPPED, OR CHOCOLATE CHIPS

Preheat oven to 350°F. Lightly butter and flour a cookie sheet or line with parchment paper.

Cream butter. Gradually add granulated and light brown sugars, continuing to cream until there are no lumps and the mixture is light and fluffy. Stir in vanilla. Add eggs, one at a time, beating well after each addition.

Mix flour, baking soda, and salt in another bowl. Add, all at once, to butter mixture and mix until combined. Fold in chocolate. Dough may be stored in the refrigerator wrapped in plastic 5 days.

Spoon about 1 tablespoon batter each for small cookies and 3 tablespoons each for jumbos onto prepared cookie sheets. Bake about 15 minutes for small—20 minutes for jumbo. The edges should just begin to turn golden. Set aside to cool on racks.

Makes 40 Small and 14 Jumbo Cookies

Old-Fashioned Peanut Butter Cookies

These childhood favorites are great for filling lunch boxes and cookie jars.

1   CUP (2 STICKS) UNSALTED BUTTER, SOFTENED
1   CUP GRANULATED SUGAR
1   CUP PACKED BROWN SUGAR
2   CUPS SOFT PEANUT BUTTER, SMOOTH OR CRUNCHY
2   EGGS
1   TEASPOON VANILLA EXTRACT
3   CUPS ALL-PURPOSE FLOUR
1   TEASPOON SALT
1   TEASPOON BAKING SODA

Preheat oven to 350°F. Lightly butter and flour a cookie sheet or line with parchment paper.

Cream together butter, granulated sugar and brown sugar. Stir in peanut butter until smooth. Add eggs and vanilla. Mix until well combined.

In another bowl, mix together flour, salt, and baking soda. Add to peanut butter mixture and stir just until flour disappears.

Spoon about 1 tablespoon batter each for small cookies and 3 tablespoons each for jumbos on prepared cookie sheets. Dip the tines of a fork into flour and score each cookie in a traditional crisscross pattern. Bake about 15 minutes for small cookies and 20 minutes for jumbos. The edges should just begin to turn golden. Set aside to cool on racks.

Makes 50 Small Cookies or 18 Jumbos

Oatmeal Rum Raisin Cookies

Rum-plumped raisins add an adult twist to another childhood favorite. We don't think kids will mind the change.

¾	CUP RAISINS
¼	CUP RUM
12	TABLESPOONS (1 ½ STICKS) UNSALTED BUTTER, SOFTENED
1 ½	CUPS PACKED BROWN SUGAR
½	CUP GRANULATED SUGAR
2	TABLESPOONS MOLASSES
2	EGGS
¼	CUP MILK
1	CUP GRATED UNSWEETENED COCONUT
2	CUPS ROLLED OATS
2 ½	CUPS ALL-PURPOSE FLOUR
½	TEASPOON BAKING POWDER
½	TEASPOON SALT

Preheat oven to 350°F. Lightly butter and flour a cookie sheet or line with parchment.

Combine raisins and rum in a small saucepan. Heat over low flame until most liquid has been absorbed. Set aside to cool.

Cream butter, brown sugar, granulated sugar, and molasses until light and fluffy. Add eggs, one at a time, beating well after each addition. Stir in milk.

In another bowl, mix together coconut, oats, flour, baking powder, and salt. Set aside.

Add raisins and rum to creamed mixture and briefly stir. Add dry ingredients and stir until well combined.

Spoon about 1 tablespoon batter each for small cookies and 3 tablespoons each for jumbos onto prepared cookie sheet. Bake about 15 minutes for small and 25 minutes for jumbos. The edges should just begin to turn golden. Set aside to cool on racks.

Makes 50 Small Cookies or 18 Jumbos.

Ice Cream Shells

It takes some practice to get the knack of molding these thin, crisp cookies. They make a delightful, light dessert filled with homemade ice cream and fruit.

1	TABLESPOON SOFT BUTTER AND 1 TABLESPOON FLOUR FOR COATING PAN
2	EGG WHITES
¼	CUP MILK
1	TEASPOON VANILLA EXTRACT
⅛	TEASPOON SALT
4	TABLESPOONS (½ STICK) UNSALTED BUTTER, MELTED
1	CUP CONFECTIONERS' SUGAR, SIFTED
¾	CUP ALL-PURPOSE FLOUR, SIFTED
¾	CUP SLICED ALMONDS

Preheat oven to 400°F. Combine the tablespoon each butter and flour to make a paste. Spread over a cookie sheet and set aside.

Combine egg whites, milk, vanilla, and salt in a bowl and let sit until room temperature. (You can speed the process by slightly warming mixture over a pan of hot water.)

Add melted butter. Whisk in sugar until evenly blended. Add flour and whisk until smooth.

Allowing about 6 inches for spreading, spoon 1½ tablespoons batter for each cookie onto prepared cookie sheet. With a spatula, spread batter to form a thin 5-inch circle, leaving about an inch between cookies.

Scatter some almonds over batter.

Bake about 3 to 5 minutes, until lightly golden all over. Immediately place each cookie over an inverted coffee cup. Cover with a dry cloth and press down to mold until stiff, 1 to 2 minutes. Continue until all cookies are baked. Serve immediately or store in airtight tins. A cookie sheet will hold about 3 cookies per batch. Coat the cooled sheet with butter and flour paste each time.

Makes 12 Cookies

Ice Creams

When it comes to ice cream, our tastes run to the pure and simple. All of these are luscious and easy to make with either a hand crank or an electric machine.

Lemon Ice Cream

7	LEMONS, WASHED
1½	CUPS HEAVY CREAM
2	CUPS HALF AND HALF
9	EGG YOLKS
1	CUP GRANULATED SUGAR
2	TEASPOONS VANILLA EXTRACT

Grate zest of all lemons, taking care to get only the yellow part—no white. Squeeze juice from 4 lemons and reserve.

Combine cream, half and half, and lemon zest in a medium-heavy saucepan. Bring to a boil.

In a large bowl, whisk together egg yolks and sugar until thick and pale yellow. Pour in boiling liquid and stir until combined. Stir in lemon juice and vanilla. Strain into a large container and refrigerate until cold, or place in a bowl nested in a larger bowl of ice water and stir occasionally until cold.

Pour into your ice cream maker and follow manufacturer's instructions. Store in freezer 1 to 2 days.

Makes 1½ Quarts

Chocolate Ice Cream

1½   CUPS HEAVY CREAM
2½   CUPS HALF AND HALF
5   EGG YOLKS
1¼   CUPS GRANULATED SUGAR
1   CUP COCOA

Combine cream and half and half in a medium-heavy saucepan. Bring to a boil.

Meanwhile, in a large bowl, whisk together egg yolks and sugar until thick and pale yellow. When cream mixture comes to a boil, stir in cocoa. Pour boiling liquid into egg mixture and stir until combined. Strain into a large container and refrigerate until cold, or place in a bowl nested in a larger bowl and stir occasionally until cold.

Pour into your ice cream maker and follow manufacturer's instructions. Store in freezer 1 to 2 days.

Makes 1½ Quarts

Vanilla Ice Cream

1   CUP HEAVY CREAM
1   CUP HALF AND HALF
1–2   VANILLA BEANS
5   EGG YOLKS
½   CUP GRANULATED SUGAR

Combine cream and half and half in a medium-heavy saucepan. Split vanilla beans in half lengthwise and, using tip of a knife, scrape out small black seeds. Add seeds and beans to cream mixture. Bring to a boil.

Meanwhile, in a large bowl, whisk together egg yolks and sugar until thick and pale yellow. Pour in boiling liquid and stir until combined. Strain into a large container and refrigerate until cold, or place in a bowl nested in a larger bowl of ice water and stir occasionally until cold.

Pour chilled mixture into your ice cream maker and follow manufacturer's instructions. Store in freezer 1 to 2 days.

Makes 3 Cups

Strawberry Ice Cream

2   CUPS VERY RIPE STRAWBERRIES, WASHED, HULLED,
AND SLICED
2   TABLESPOONS GRANULATED SUGAR FOR SPRINKLING
2   CUPS HEAVY CREAM
2   CUPS HALF AND HALF
9   EGG YOLKS
¾   CUP GRANULATED SUGAR
¼   CUP FRESH LEMON JUICE

Place berries in a bowl, sprinkle with sugar, and set aside.

Combine cream and half and half in a medium-heavy saucepan. Bring to a boil.

In a large bowl, whisk together egg yolks and sugar until thick and pale yellow. Pour in boiling liquid and stir until combined. Strain into a large container and refrigerate until cold, or place in a bowl nested in a larger bowl of ice water and stir occasionally until cold.

Stir in lemon juice and fold in sweetened berries. Pour into your ice cream maker and follow manufacturer's instructions. Store in freezer 1 to 2 days.

Makes 1½ Quarts

Caramel Ice Cream

This is Susan's favorite, especially with warm Chewy Date Bars (page 227).

CARAMEL CHUNKS

1	CUP GRANULATED SUGAR
½	CUP WATER

Combine sugar and water in a heavy saucepan. Cook over moderate heat until color turns deep brown and aroma is strong, about 10 to 15 minutes. You can use a pastry brush dipped in water to brush down any sugar crystals that cling to sides of pot. Immediately, and with great care, pour hot liquid onto a greased sheet of waxed or parchment paper on a baking sheet. Set aside until cool, then crack into ½-inch pieces. Reserve.

2½	CUPS HALF AND HALF
1½	CUPS HEAVY CREAM
9	EGG YOLKS
¾	CUP GRANULATED SUGAR
2	TEASPOONS VANILLA EXTRACT
1	CUP SOUR CREAM

Combine half and half and cream in a medium-heavy saucepan. Bring to a boil.

Meanwhile, in a large bowl, whisk together egg yolks and sugar until thick and pale yellow. Pour in boiling liquid and stir until combined. Add vanilla and stir. Strain into a large container and refrigerate until cold, or place in a bowl nested in a larger bowl of ice water and stir occasionally until cold.

Stir in sour cream and pour into your ice cream maker. Follow manufacturer's instructions. When ice cream is done, fold in reserved caramel pieces. Store in freezer 1 to 2 days.

Makes 1½ Quarts

Beverages

Lemon Ginger Tea

This spicy iced tea is the very best thirst quencher. Served hot with cinnamon sticks, it is great when you aren't feeling well.

1   QUART WATER
    JUICE OF 1 LEMON
¼   CUP FRESHLY GRATED GINGER (PAGE 249)
¼   CUP HONEY
    THIN SLICES OF LEMON AND LIME FOR GARNISH

Bring water to a boil. Add lemon juice, the squeezed lemon, and ginger. Let steep about 20 minutes. Stir in honey. Line a strainer with a thin wet cloth and strain tea into a pitcher. Chill thoroughly and serve on ice with thin slices of lemon and lime.

Makes 1 Quart

Yogi Tea

2   QUARTS WATER
¼   CUP MILK
¼   CUP HALF AND HALF
⅓   CUP GRANULATED SUGAR
2   CINNAMON STICKS
1   TEASPOON FRESHLY GRATED GINGER (PAGE 249)
2   TEASPOONS WHOLE CLOVES
2   TEASPOONS CARDAMOM SEEDS
½   TEASPOON FRESHLY GROUND BLACK PEPPER

Bring water to a boil, then reduce to a simmer. Add milk, half and half, sugar, and cinnamon, and simmer for 15 minutes. Add remaining ingredients and simmer an additional 30 minutes. Strain and serve hot or cold.

Makes 2 Quarts

City Herb Cooler

This cool, red drink is especially pretty garnished with thin slices of lime. Hibiscus flowers or rose hips, great sources of vitamin C, are available in Mexican and Armenian markets.

1   QUART WATER
¾   CUP DRIED HIBISCUS FLOWERS OR ROSE HIPS
¼   CUP HONEY
    THIN SLICES OF LIME FOR GARNISH (OPTIONAL)

Bring water to a boil. Add hibiscus flowers and let steep 15 minutes. Stir in honey. Line a strainer with a thin wet cloth and strain tea into a pitcher. Serve immediately, or chill and serve over ice with thin slices of lime.

Makes 1 Quart

Iced Mocha

Iced Mocha is thick like a milk shake but without the ice cream.

1   TABLESPOON CHOCOLATE SYRUP
1   CUP DOUBLE ESPRESSO OR VERY STRONG COFFEE, HOT
¼   CUP HALF AND HALF
4   ICE CUBES

Stir chocolate syrup into hot coffee until melted. Transfer to a blender, add half and half and ice cubes, and blend at high speed for 2 to 3 minutes. Serve immediately in a tall, cold glass.

Makes 1 Glass

Indian Iced Tea

2   CUPS HALF AND HALF
2   CUPS WATER
2   TABLESPOONS BLACK INDIAN TEA LEAVES, SUCH AS
    CEYLON
6   TABLESPOONS GRANULATED SUGAR

B ring half and half and water to a boil. Add tea
and simmer for 15 minutes. Stir in sugar, strain,
and chill. Serve over ice in a tall glass.

Makes 1 Quart

Egg Nog

Homemade Egg Nog is a cinch to make. Mix it at least 6 hours in advance to mellow the tastes and add rum or brandy as the occasion demands.

6   EGGS
1   CUP CONFECTIONERS' SUGAR
3   CUPS HALF AND HALF OR MILK
2   TABLESPOONS VANILLA EXTRACT
¼   TEASPOON SALT
     FRESHLY GRATED NUTMEG TO TASTE

I n an electric mixer, set at high speed, beat eggs
and sugar until light. Reduce speed to low. Add
half and half, vanilla, and salt, and continue beating
until thoroughly combined. Chill 6 to 8 hours. Serve
garnished with nutmeg.

Makes 1 Quart

Glossary of Ingredients and Techniques

Ingredients

Ancho Chile is a rich, mild-flavored dried poblano chile. It is medium-sized, with a triangular shape, deep mahogany color, and pebbly texture. Available in Mexican markets and some supermarkets.

Basmati is an aromatic, long-grained white rice grown at the base of the Himalaya mountains. It is distinguished by a small hook at one end and a nutty flavor. Available in Indian and health food markets and gourmet shops.

Black Fungus or **Wood Ear Mushrooms** are a rubbery, slightly crunchy fungus used to add color and texture in Thai and Chinese cuisines. Available in dehydrated form in Oriental markets and some supermarkets.

Black Mustard Seeds are the tiny, reddish brown seeds of the black mustard plant. Used in Indian cuisine, they are available in Indian or Middle Eastern markets. Yellow mustard seeds may be substituted.

Brown Rice Vinegar is a Japanese vinegar made from fermented brown rice. Available in Japanese and health food markets. Rice wine vinegar may be substituted.

Bulgarian Feta is a salty goat cheese, stored in brine. It is creamier and milder than the Greek variety. Available in good cheese shops and Armenian markets.

Bulgur Wheat is a coarse cracked wheat that has been cooked. It always needs to be reconstituted. Available in Middle Eastern and health food markets in a variety of grinds.

Cellophane Noodles or **Bean Threads** are thin translucent Chinese noodles made from ground mung beans. Available in the Oriental section of most supermarkets.

Chick-pea Flour is a fine, powdery flour made from milled, dried garbanzo beans. Available in Indian, Middle Eastern, and health food markets.

Chili Paste is a bottled sauce of red chiles, garlic, and salt. Available in Oriental markets and supermarkets.

Chinese Sausage (Lop Cheung) is a very firm, slightly bumpy pork sausage with a sweet smoky flavor. Available in Oriental markets.

Coconut Milk (unsweetened) is a Thai product made by grinding fresh coconut with water. It is available in cans in Oriental markets and in some supermarkets.

Dal is the Indian name for the inside of any whole, dried bean. Urid dal, black bean dal, and orange dal are three varieties available in Indian or Middle Eastern markets. Lentils may be substituted.

Daikon Spiced Sprouts are sprouted Japanese daikon radish seeds. Available in Japanese markets and fine produce markets.

Dried Shrimp are tiny, shelled, salty shrimp used as a spice. Available in Oriental and Mexican markets.

Garam Masala is blend of Indian dried spices which varies, like a curry, according to taste. Usually contains a combinaton of finely ground black pepper, cumin, coriander, and cardamom. Available in Indian and some health food markets or try making your own with ground spices.

Geoduck Clams are huge, long-necked clams from the Pacific Northwest. They are usually ground and used in chowders. Available in Oriental fish markets.

Hoisin Sauce is a thick, soybean-based, sweet Chinese sauce usually mixed with other condiments for marinades and sauces. Available in bottles or cans in Oriental markets and supermarkets.

Kaffir Lime Leaves are the dried leaves of the Thai kaffir lime tree. These brittle, bitter leaves are available in Thai markets or by mail order.

Kirbies or Pickling Cucumbers are small, pale green cucumbers with fewer seeds and a milder flavor than larger cucumbers. Available in supermarkets.

Mirin is a sweet Japanese cooking wine made with rice wine (sake) and sugar. Available in Japanese markets and the Oriental section of supermarkets.

Oyster Sauce is a thick, salty Chinese sauce made from oyster extract, soy sauce, and sugar. It is available in bottles in Oriental markets and supermarkets.

Palm or Coconut Sugar is a very sweet, hard-packed brown sugar made from the coconut palm tree. Imported from Thailand, it is available in cans in Oriental markets. Brown sugar may be substituted.

Plum Sauce is a sweet and sour Chinese sauce made from plums, vinegar, sugar, ginger, and garlic. It is available in bottles in Oriental markets and supermarkets.

Rice Sticks are dried, white Chinese vermicelli made from rice and water. They can be boiled in water until translucent and soft, or deep fried in oil until puffy and crisp. Available in Oriental markets and supermarkets.

Rice Wine Vinegar is a full-flavored, yellow Japanese vinegar made from rice wine. Available in Oriental markets and supermarkets.

San Bai Su is a Japanese seasoning sauce made from equal parts mirin, soy sauce, and brown rice vinegar. Available in bottles at Japanese markets or mix your own.

Soba Noodles are thin, dark Japanese noodles made from buckwheat flour. Available in Japanese and health food markets.

Tahini is a paste made from ground sesame seeds. Available in Middle Eastern markets and supermarkets.

Tamarind is a brittle, brown seed pod that grows on trees. When the dried pod is peeled, soaked, and strained it produces a thick paste with a unique sweet and tart flavor. The paste is used in chutneys, soft drinks, and meat sauces. Available in Mexican markets and some supermarkets.

Thai Fish Sauce or *Nam Pla* is a salty brown sauce, similar to soy sauce, made of anchovy, fish or shrimp extract and salt. Available in Oriental markets and supermarkets.

Thai Red Curry Paste is a hot paste of ground red chiles, onion, garlic, lemon grass, lime peel, and shrimp paste. It is available in Thai markets and by mail order.

Techniques

Beurre manié is a paste made of equal parts softened butter and flour. Mix it with your fingertips then gradually whisk into sauces or hot soups to thicken.

Clarified butter has a higher burning point than ordinary butter because the milk solids are removed. To separate the solids, melt butter in heavy saucepan over moderate heat. Simmer until the butter foams, then skim and discard the white froth that forms at the top. Carefully pour the remaining butter through a cheesecloth, allowing the white sediment to remain at the bottom of the pan. By clarifying, the volume is reduced by one quarter.

To crack peppercorns, place the whole peppercorns on a work counter. Place the bottom of a heavy skillet or saucepan on top and push down and away from you.

To grate fresh ginger in quantity, first peel the root, then cut into thin slices. With the machine running, drop through the feed tube of a food processor fitted with metal blade. Combine with a small amount of rice wine vinegar and store in the refrigerator as long as 2 weeks.

To make bread crumbs, first dry the bread (French or Italian loaves, with crust, are good) in a 300°F oven for 20 to 30 minutes. Cut into chunks and blend in a food processor until fine. Sift through a fine sieve and store in a cool, dry place.

To peel tomatoes, remove the cores and score an X on the underside. Blanch for 15 seconds in boiling water and immediately plunge into iced water to prevent cooking. Peel with a paring knife. Cut in half across the width and squeeze to remove the seeds or scoop them out with a spoon.

To puree garlic in quantity, break the bulbs apart and peel, first by flattening the cloves with the flat side of a heavy knife or cleaver, then removing the skin. Puree with a small amount of olive oil, in a food processor fitted with a metal blade or in a blender. Store in the refrigerator as long as 2 weeks.

To render fat, boil at a slow simmer until the solids settle to the bottom and water evaporates. The remaining clear liquid can be stored in the refrigerator and used for sautéeing.

To roast seeds (like mustard), cook in a dry sauté pan over medium-low heat, shaking occasionally, until the seeds smoke slightly and release their aroma. Or place on a baking sheet in a 250° F oven for 10 to 15 minutes, shaking the pan occasionally.

To roast peppers, place on a baking sheet under a preheated broiler and cook, turning occasionally, until the peppers are evenly charred. Transfer to a plastic bag, tie a knot at the top, and set aside to steam about 10 minutes. Peel under cold, running water.

To toast and skin nuts, spread the nuts on a sheet pan and cook for 10 to 15 minutes in a 350° F oven, shaking occasionally. Wrap in a clean, damp towel for 10 minutes. Remove the towel and rub the nuts between your hands to remove the husks.

To debeard mussels, pinch the hairlike beard and slide up and down until it releases.

A Few Mail-Order Sources

JAPANESE

Ai Hoa Market
860 North Hill Street
Los Angeles, CA 90012
213-629-8121

INDIAN AND ARMENIAN

Bezjian Grocery
4725 Santa Monica Boulevard
Los Angeles, CA 90029
213-663-1503

THAI

Bangkok Market
4757 Melrose Avenue
Los Angeles, CA 90029
213-662-9705

Index

A

B

AMERICAN WESTERN COOKING

from the

AMERICAN
WESTERN
COOKING

from the

ROBERT McGRATH

Photography by
Mary Herrmann
and
Michael Mertz

Lone Star Books®
An imprint of Gulf Publishing Company

AMERICAN WESTERN COOKING

from the

ROARING FORK

Lone Star Books®
An imprint of Gulf Publishing Company
Book Division
P.O. Box 2608 □ Houston, Texas 77252-2608

10 9 8 7 6 5 4 3 2 1

Library of Congress Cataloging-in-Publication Data

McGrath, Robert.
    American Western cooking from the Roaring Fork
  Restaurant / Robert McGrath.
      p.   cm.
    ISBN 0-87719-350-9 (alk. paper)
    1. Cookery, American—Western style.   2. Roaring Fork
  Restaurant.   I. Roaring Fork Restaurant.   II. Title.
  TX715.2.W47 M377 2000
  641.5978—dc21   99-050077

Printed in Hong Kong.

Printed on acid-free paper (∞).

Cover/book design and creative direction by Roxann L. Combs.

Front cover photo by Michael Mertz.

*Photos on pages xxii–1, 5, 7, 12, 16–17, 25, 28, 32–33, 46–47, 64–65,
68, 73, 82, 86–87, 96, 100–101, 113, 116–117, 122, 125, 146–147,
150, 157, 183, 188, 194–195, 208, 210–211, 227, 230–231, 241, 248
and cover back flap by Mary Herrmann. Food styling by Lee Stanyer.*

Photos on pages ii, vi–vii, xix, 77, 135, 165, and 170 by Michael Mertz.

Photos on pages 34, 103, and 197 by Roxann L. Combs.

Unless otherwise indicated, spot photos from Corbis and Photodisc.

This book is dedicated to:

The joy of my wife—Amy

The lives of my children—Melissa, Jason, and Montana

The memory of my mother and father—Carolyn and Robert

The support of my brothers—Tim, Jeff, and Doug

The pride of the staff of the Roaring Fork restaurant
&
Erin O'Brien, Patrick Boll, and Dan Rutland

The friendship of too many people to list
(you know who you are)

The music of Dan Hicks

CONTENTS

PERSONAL FAVORITES

STANDARD PREPARATIONS
(Some Basics for Us All)

RELISHES, DRESSINGS, & SAUCES

Cucumber Relish, 48

Carrot Salsa, 48

Avocado and Orange Relish, 49

Corn Relish, 49

Tomatillo Salsa, 50

Papaya Chile Relish, 50

Salsa Fresca, 51

Roasted Tomato Salsa, 51

Red Bell Pepper Ketchup, 52

Shrimp Remoulade, 53

Chipotle Mayonnaise, 53

Buttermilk and Goat Cheese Dressing, 54

Blue Cheese Vinaigrette, 55

Sun-Dried Tomato Vinaigrette, 55

Lemonade Vinaigrette, 56

Green Chile Buttermilk Dressing, 56

Tomato and Roasted Garlic Dressing, 57

Red Chile Adobo Sauce, 58

Barbecue Sauce, 59

Fire-Roasted Red Onion Sauce, 60

Chile Guajillo and Lemon Sauce, 60

Roasted Corn Sauce, 61

Green Chile and Mustard Sauce, 62

Wild Mushroom and Chile Pasilla Sauce, 63

SOUPS & STEWS

Smoked Beef and Roasted Onion Chili with Thickened Lime Cream, 66

Rustic Soup of Butternut Squash with Roasted Garlic, 67

Roasted Carrot Soup with Cilantro, Tofu, and Pepitas, 68

Corn Stew with Crabmeat, Mussels, and Grilled Shrimp, 69

Sweet Corn and Rock Shrimp Chowder with Apple Fritters, 70

A Clear Chowder of Roasted Corn and Leeks with Lump Crab Cake, 72

Green Chile Stew, 74

Lobster and Roasted Corn Chili
with Cream Cheese-Green Onion Quesadilla, 75

Pan-Roasted Mussels with Red Curry, White Wine, and Smoked Bacon, 76

Barbecued Onion Soup with Jalapeño Jack Cheese, 78

Doug's Posole, 79

Rustic Chowder of Red Snapper and Salt Cod
with New Potatoes, Leek, and Oregano, 80

Tortilla Soup with Roasted Chicken and Avocado Relish, 81

Chilled Watermelon Soup with Pineapple and Habanero Salsa, 83

Rock Shrimp Gazpacho with Cucumber Salsa and Watercress, 84

Yellow Tomato Gazpacho with Smoked Scallop Salsa, 85

SALADS

Organic Arugula in "Cowboy" Flat Bread with Spiced Lemon Vinaigrette, 88

Caesar Salad with Cornmeal Croutons, 89

Chicken Breast Salad on Romaine Leaves with Margarita Vinaigrette, 90

A Salad of Duck Fajitas, Avocado, and Roasted Peppers, 91

Iceberg Lettuce with Blue Cheese and Ranch Dressing, 92

Organic Lettuces and Herbs in a Jicama Tortilla
with Sun-Dried Tomato Vinaigrette, 93

Cracked Blue Crab with Avocado, Arugula, and Radishes, 94

Spinach Leaves with Texas Peanut Dressing
and Fried Sweet Buttermilk Onions, 95

Spinach Leaves with Almond-Crusted Goat Cheese
and Red Onion Vinaigrette, 97

Grilled Shrimp on a Spinach Leaf Salad with Mustard Dressing, 98

Grilled Beef Sirloin on Romaine Leaves
with Black Pepper and Tomato Dressing, 99

SANDWICHES

Achiote Chicken Breast Sandwich with Indian Grill Bread, 102

Southwestern Corn "Doggie," 104

Pastrami with Green Chiles, Chipotle Mayonnaise, and Pepper Jack Cheese, 105

Grilled Hamburger with Onion Rings and Red Bell Pepper Ketchup, 106

Roasted Peppers, Avocado, and Portabello Mushroom Sandwich
with Spiced Cream Cheese, 108

Hickory-Roasted Rabbit and Cornbread Sandwich
with Rosemary Apple Butter, 109

Seared Catfish Baked in a White Corn Tortilla with Red Chile Sauce, 111

Grilled Flat Bread with Rock Shrimp and
Salsa of Papaya, Avocado, and Red Onion, 112

Cracker-Crusted Pork Loin Sandwich with Chipotle Mayonnaise, 114

Flank Steak Fajitas on Home-made Tortillas, 115

SMALL COURSES

Steamed Artichoke with Smoked Trout Remoulade, 118

Crabmeat Skillet Cake with Greens and Iceberg Lettuce, 119

Cast Iron-Cooked Foie Gas
with Grilled Pineapple and Red Lentil "Chowchow," 121

Warm Goat Cheese on a Beefsteak Tomato with Verbena-Black Bean Sauce, 123

Peppered Goat-Cheese Ravioli
with Mild Green Chile Sauce and Pumpkin Seeds, 124

Grilled Lamb Skirt Steak with Pinto Bean Ravioli and Poblano Cream Sauce, 124

Lump Crab Cake with Local Citrus and Organic Greens, 127

"Dallas" Mozzarella with Pickled Onions and Avocado, 128

Portabello Mushroom in a Cornmeal Crepe
with Sweet Onions and Avocado Relish, 129

Grilled Quail, Foie Gras, and Endives, 131

Barbecued Quail Baked in Cornmeal Custard with Green Pea Guacamole, 132

Smoked Salmon Cheesecake with Watercress Salad, 134

Smoked Salmon on Buttermilk Corn Griddle Cakes
with Corn Milk Mascarpone, 136

Shrimp Cocktail with Bacon Horseradish Sauce
and Sweet Onion and Corn Slaw, 137

Grilled Shrimp and Pickled Cabbage with Red Chile-Whiskey Sauce, 138

Spinach Enchiladas with Red Bell Pepper Sauce, 139

Spiced Turkey Confit and Cracked Corn Stuffing
with Dried Figs and Country Ham, 141

Barbecued Wild Boar Empanadas with Spiced Mint Honey, 142

Barbecued Chicken in a Blue Corn Crepe with Spiced Pickled Onions, 144

MAIN COURSES

Skillet-Seared Ahi Tuna with Smoked Ham Hock and Three-Bean Salad, 148

Pan-Roasted Dorado with a Smoked Tomato Vinaigrette, 149

Pan-Roasted Black Grouper in Gumbo with Rock Shrimp Remoulade, 152

Pan-Roasted Lobster with Apple-Cured Bacon, Celery Leaves, and Lime, 154

Crisp Rainbow Trout on "Cowboy Couscous"
with Carrot Juice-Lemon Dressing, 155

Filet of Salmon Cooked Campfire-Style
with Pears, Cucumber, and Pickled Beets, 156

Steamed and Seared Scallops
with Cilantro Leaves, Dandelion Greens, and Ginger, 158

Grilled Shrimp with Chipotle-Creamed Leeks on a Golden Cornmeal Cake, 159

Spit-Roasted Chicken Marinated in Lemon and Garlic
with Warm Potato Salad, 160

Green Bean Casserole, 228

Sautéed Spinach, 228

Pinto Bean Ravioli, 229

BREADS AND DESSERTS

Jalapeño Spoonbread, 232

Rustic Baked Biscuits with Roasted Chiles and Corn, 233

Milk Bread with Marigold Mint and Onions, 234

Southwestern Green Chile Cornbread, 235

Blue Cheese Lavosh Cracker, 236

Indian Flat Bread, 237

Chile-Spiked Apples and Blueberries, 238

Grilled Fruit Brochette and Chilled Berry Consommé with Pineapple Sorbet, 239

Strawberries and Spiced Honey, 240

Cranberry and Jalapeño Ice, 240

A Tart of Peaches, Dired Chiles, and Mint, 242

Blackberry Pie, 243

Peach and Huckleberry Cobbler with Pecan Ice Cream, 244

Chile-Spiked Fig Cakes with Butterscotch and Clove Cream, 245

Toffee Chocolate Pecan Pie, 246

Chocolate "Mole" Empanadas with Fruit Salsa, 247

Grilled Pound Cake with Vanilla Syrup and Blueberry "Chowchow," 249

Chocolate Bread Pudding with Candied Pecans and Whiskey Sauce, 250

Vanilla Cream Custard with Raspberries and Pecans, 251

White Bean Cake with Milk Chocolate Sauce and Strawberries, 252

ACKNOWLEDGMENTS

This book owes a great deal of its existence to Helaine Dworkin. Her hard work helped transform an unpolished collection of recipes into a readable cookbook. Her attention to detail throughout this endeavor never wavered. I enjoyed the refreshing afternoon critiques of the work in progress, because the meetings always broke the tedium, which resulted in a fresh attitude for me. One of our dear friends . . . a big thanks from me to you.

I would like to thank Barbara Fenzl for being the person to bring me to Arizona nine years ago and for supporting my culinary adventures in Scottsdale. Barbara has been a driving force in educating and enlightening the diners (and myself!) in our region of the United States. Barb, thank you.

Great things are not possible without great people. This entire effort would not have been possible without the superlative management team at the Roaring Fork restaurant in Scottsdale, Arizona. The general manager, Erin O'Brien; the chef de cuisine, Patrick Boll; and the head bartender and cellar master, Dan Rutland, all put forth a tireless effort at the restaurant to enable me to take the time to put this book together. I would also like to thank Franck Guyot, our pastry chef, who gives us fresh bread and our seasonal desserts at the restaurant, and who has done so since we opened the doors at the Roaring Fork.

I would like to gratefully acknowledge all my guests at the Roaring Fork and the J-Bar. Everyone's support has given me the belief that what we are doing is something good, maybe even special. They get a very big, fat (hee-hee) thank you.

The Roaring Fork restaurant owes its existence to Paul Fleming and Guy Villavaso. Paul and Guy let me run with the idea, and it seems to be working. Paul is the founder of P. F. Chang's China Bistro and Fleming's Prime Steakhouse and Wine Bar, and Guy is one of the founders of the Z'Tejas and Brio Vista restaurants. Thank you.

I think it is important to give credit where it's due. There is no real way to thank Roxann Combs enough for this beautiful book. As Creative Director, she is the individual who designed and executed the layout of my book. I think you will agree that she did a helluva job. Teamed up with Ralph Smith Photography (Go Mary Go!) and photographer Michael Mertz, Roxann put all of the components together with great style. Unfortunately for her, she has now become a very dear friend of mine. Much obliged.

And to the Cowboy . . . thanks.

Rarely in life does one's true enjoyment and passion intertwine with one's work. When this congruence takes place, it can be a lot of fun! I truly love cooking, and I have been lucky in my professional career. My favorite way of enjoying some downtime is usually associated with the great outdoors, most frequently somewhere in the American West. Whether you're taking a five-day rafting trip down the Rio Grande through remote Big Bend National Park in West Texas, fly-fishing "the Flats" on the Frying Pan River in Colorado, or camping along the breathtaking Mogollon Rim in Northern Arizona, your adventure can be enjoyed with great food and wines. The outdoors can be a beautiful dining room! In addition, much of the food is cooked over campfires and a lot of it in cast-iron cookware. So the flavor of the meal is not limited to the taste of the cuisine or the wine; the flavor of the meal is more attributable to the combination of the beautiful terrain and vistas, the primitive way the food is cooked, and the satisfaction of cooking a meal in a manner of which nature would approve. These experiences combine to form the foundation of my restaurant—the Roaring Fork. That foundation is the synergy of bringing foods in from the rugged outdoors to a comfortable restaurant and then preparing them in a style that reflects a combination of rustic glory and contemporary elegance.

The goal of this cookbook is to bring some of these wonderful recipes to your home kitchen (and your outdoor "kitchen"), and to share with you the magic that America's West brings to the table.

What is American western cuisine? In my eyes, American western cuisine is created by a combination of several factors. First of all, it is dependent on using foods that are indigenous, or native, to the American West. The term native food, however, does not mean that these foods have been in the American West since the beginning of time. A lot of foods were brought to this part of the world during mankind's exploratory phase, and some were able to thrive in this geographic region. One important fundamental in cooking is using local ingredients. Why? If we use local ingredients, we are keeping the time and distance between their harvest and their usage to a minimum. This ensures that the freshest, most flavorful, and least expensive ingredients are used in your meal. When products are in season, they are priced the most reasonably, and their flavors are the most definitive. In more contemporary times, with agri-

cultural acreage shrinking, it has also become imperative to respond to our self-generated destruction of food-producing land by creating an awareness of sustainable farming, organic farming, and animal husbandry. The pioneering spirit must be maintained and directed toward the preservation of our natural resources.

Second, American western cuisine is greatly influenced by the cultures of the people who are responsible for establishing this geographic region. This includes Native Americans, Hispanics, and certainly the cowboys and pioneers who brought this region into modern times. The Native Americans (and the Hispanics, for that matter) gave us knowledge about corn, local fish, native plants, squash, beans, herbs, and the philosophy of taking care of the land that provides for all. The Hispanics shared their vast knowledge regarding chiles, tomatoes, spices, and herbs such as epazote, cilantro, and cumin. The cowboys and pioneers taught us about curing and drying meats and smoking foods (which they probably learned from the Native Americans), as well as about chiles, beans, and all the European vegetables they brought with them that found the climate just right.

Last, a certain intangible that cannot be denied contributes immensely to American western cuisine: *spirit!* The western part of the United States is typified by a boldness of spirit and the ability to pioneer new directions. A thin geographical line divides the East from the West, and here, the old and the new, the tried and the untried meet and reshape each other. This line is never stationary; it is always moving, with the cutting edge of civilization behind it. It only makes sense that the cuisine of the West personifies the same characteristics—cuisine that reflects the integrity of the balance of nature and that is also fun to prepare and fun to eat. Western cuisine is not a ceremony; it's a celebration! The robust flavors, the courage to try something a little different, the determination necessary to bring the crops in from seed, and the wholesomeness to see things through clean eyes are the characteristics the American West brings to the table.

Now it is up to us, the present inhabitants of the West, to be responsible for maintaining the quality of the environment. This responsibility mandates that we, as the consumers and chefs, increase awareness about organic and self-sustaining farming. With this awareness, we must become active players in our support of the organizations and businesses that will keep our fields and oceans from dying. We are now pioneers of a different sort. If we choose to take a complacent stance about sustainability, our children will become victims of our own irresponsibility. You clean your room, you clean your home, you clean your yard—please help us keep our lands and seas clean.

COCKTAILS

YOU GO WITH YOUR STRENGTH. **S**IMPLE AND STRAIGHTFORWARD. So when I decided to include a chapter in this book about cocktails, I asked Dan Rutland, our bartender and cellar master at the Roaring Fork restaurant, to write it with me. Dan has twenty-five years of experience behind the bar and a wealth of knowledge regarding the construction of a cocktail. We also work together closely on the wine program. We taste every wine, and we must both agree on the wine before it makes it to the wine list. Our wine list continues to evolve as our knowledge is fed by all the wineries available to us. We feel the wines are worthwhile for our guests, but cocktails are fun! We want our guests to have fun. We wanted to recreate for our guests the feeling that the J-Bar (a little bar in the Hotel Jerome in Aspen, Colorado) instills in us every time we quench our thirst there. Dan has the technology and is therefore the majority contributor to this chapter; I only have a couple of years of experience on the other side of the bar. We strongly urge that while enjoying these cocktails, you drink responsibly.

Art of the Cocktail

Although the final product may be looked upon as art, the science of building a cocktail is the essence of *mixology* [miks-AHL-ah-jee], which is the art or skill of preparing mixed drinks. We have compiled some old favorites, some original works, and some helpful hints to enhance your mixology skills. Here are some ideas to help you enjoy the fruits (and grains) of your labor.

Sour Mix

makes 3 cups

Several drinks included in this section will call for sour mix, sweet-and-sour, or lemonade. You may use frozen lemonade, frozen limeade, or a combination of the two. I, however, prefer using fresh ingredients whenever possible. I recommend you do the same. Here is a solid recipe for sour mix.

The first step in making the sour mix is to make simple syrup. Bring the water to a boil, add the powdered sugar, and then stir until the sugar is dissolved. Remove from the heat and allow to cool to room temperature. (This can be stored in the refrigerator for up to one week.) Stir the lime juice into the simple syrup, and you have sour mix. To enjoy the maximum flavors, use immediately after mixing. However, this can be stored, covered, for up to two days.

1	CUP WATER
1	CUP POWDERED SUGAR (GRANULATED SUGAR MAY BE USED, BUT IT DOES NOT DISSOLVE AS WELL)
2	CUPS FRESH LIME JUICE

MARGARITAS

Lovely 'Ritas

serves 2 to 4

1	LIME WEDGE (FOR RIMS OF GLASSES)
	KOSHER SALT (FOR RIMS OF GLASSES)
	ICE CUBES
4	OUNCES TEQUILA
4	OUNCES SOUR MIX (SEE RECIPE ON THIS PAGE)
1½	OUNCES TRIPLE SEC OR COINTREAU
2 TO 4	LIME WEDGES (FOR GARNISH)

Order a margarita and, chances are, you will immediately think of Jimmy Buffet. Although the margarita has its roots in Mexico, it has managed to embed itself in the southwestern United States. It holds its own when coupled with spicy food, it quenches a big Arizona thirst, and it is versatile. Although expensive 100 percent agave anejo tequilas are smooth and delicate enough to enjoy in a snifter or straight on the rocks, they are a waste of money in a margarita. Most moderately priced tequila will make a lovely 'rita. Quite often, the sour mix and not the tequila will make the difference between making your heart sing and making it burn. White, silver, blanco, or plata tequila is the preferred tequila by aficionados because it provides real tequila flavor. Most "gold" tequilas use molasses, or a similar substance, to attain the amber hue. This also softens and sweetens the tequila—not necessarily a bad thing but something to know and share. Dan recommends Sauza Hornitos.

Rub the rim of a frozen martini glass with a lime wedge. Dip into a shallow dish with a thin layer of kosher salt. Repeat with all glasses you plan to use; this will serve two large or four small people, depending on the size of the glass. In a large cocktail shaker filled with ice, add tequila, sour mix, and triple sec or Cointreau. Shake the ingredients vigorously, and then strain into the frozen, salt-rimmed martini glasses. Garnish each glass with a lime wedge.

If you prefer something a little lighter, then double the sour mix and serve on the rocks. You can also put the contents of the cocktail shaker in the blender and make a frozen margarita. Regarding that particular hint, we offer the next recipe for a poolside alternative.

Raging 'Rita

makes 1 blender full (approximately ½ gallon)

CRUSHED ICE TO
FILL BLENDER

2   CUPS SOUR MIX
    (SEE RECIPE ON PAGE 3)

1   CUP TEQUILA

3   OUNCES TRIPLE SEC

¼   CUP FRESH ORANGE JUICE

12 LIME WEDGES
    (FOR GARNISH)

Fill blender with ice. Add remaining ingredients except lime wedges to 2 inches below ice line. Start the blender on a low speed and steadily increase the blender speed until the margarita is smooth. Hold the lid down! Pour, garnish with lime wedges, and enjoy.

If tequila makes you hallucinate or bark at the moon, a Side Car is a wonderful variation. To make a Side Car, simply replace the tequila with brandy on any of the previous margarita recipes and use sugar on the rim instead of salt.

"Category 6" Lemonade

serves 1

The Roaring Fork River is known for white-water rafting. White-water rapids are rated for difficulty, with 6 being the most difficult and 1 being the least difficult. When a category 6 rapid is successfully run, it must be downgraded to a category 5. Playing on the strength of the category 6 rapids, Dan developed this next cocktail for a large contingent of my contemporaries who were in town for a culinary festival. The Roaring Fork restaurant was their second stop on a tour of five restaurants. Knowing they would be having several margaritas before and after our stop—and that they would be on a bus and therefore not driving—I wanted to serve them a drink they would remember, or that would make them forget.

1	OUNCE ABSOLUT CITRON VODKA
1	OUNCE ABSOLUT KURRANT VODKA
1	OUNCE STOLI ORANJH VODKA
1	OUNCE BACARDI LIMON RUM
½	OUNCE CHAMBORD RASPBERRY LIQUEUR
¾	OUNCE PUREED HUCKLEBERRIES (BLUEBERRIES OR BOYSENBERRIES CAN BE SUBSTITUTED)
4	OUNCES LEMONADE
	ICE CUBES
1	EACH OF LEMON SLICE, ORANGE SLICE, AND CHERRY (FOR GARNISH)

Mix the first seven ingredients in a shaker with the ice. Shake well to combine all the ingredients, and then pour into a pint glass. Garnish with a lemon slice, an orange slice, and a cherry. Be careful!

Huckleberry Lemonade

serves 1

Fill a Collins glass with ice cubes. Pour the vodka, huckleberries, and lemonade into a cocktail shaker, and then shake well to combine the ingredients thoroughly. Pour over the ice cubes into the Collins glass. Garnish the glass with a lemon slice and serve.

	ICE CUBES
1½	OUNCES YOUR FAVORITE VODKA
1½	OUNCES PUREED HUCKLEBERRIES (BLUEBERRIES OR BOYSENBERRIES CAN BE SUBSTITUTED)
2½	OUNCES LEMONADE
1	LEMON SLICE (FOR GARNISH)

The Desert Breeze

serves 1

ICE CUBES

1½ OUNCES YOUR FAVORITE VODKA

2 OUNCES CRANBERRY JUICE

2 OUNCES LEMONADE

1 LEMON SLICE (FOR GARNISH)

Fill a tall (Collins) glass with ice cubes. Pour the vodka, cranberry juice, and lemonade into a cocktail shaker, and then shake well to combine the ingredients thoroughly. Pour over the ice cubes into the Collins glass. Garnish the glass with a lemon slice and serve.

HERB AND JALAPEÑO COCKTAILS

Each of the following cocktails is made with a fresh herb—in this case, fresh mint—or with jalapeño peppers. The amount of flavor in the drink depends on the amount of mint or jalapeño used. The following recipes specify the quantities of mint and jalapeño that we use at the Roaring Fork, but the amount of these ingredients is up to you. These are simply guidelines to get you started.

The Mint Julep

Although this drink definitely has its roots in the southern United States, it tastes so fresh and crisp that we feel it is a great cocktail for warm climates and for summertime. Besides, we have fresh mint in abundance in the western United States. Prepare this delight twenty-four hours in advance by mottling (to mottle, mash with a wooden masher, like you would with a mortar and pestle) a half cup of coarsely chopped, fresh mint leaves into a cup of simple syrup (see Sour Mix, step 1, page 3). Refrigerate overnight and then strain out the mint leaves. Use the liquid as your mint julep base mix.

Our Mint Julep

serves 1

Fill a tall (Collins) glass with ice cubes. Add the mint julep base mix and bourbon, and then fill with water. Pour the contents of the glass into a cocktail shaker and shake well. Pour the shaken cocktail back into the glass. Garnish the glass with a fresh mint sprig and serve.

ICE CUBES

2 OUNCES MINT JULEP BASE MIX (SEE RECIPE UNDER THE MINT JULEP, PAGE 8)

2 OUNCES MAKER'S MARK OR ANY GOOD BOURBON

WATER

1 FRESH MINT SPRIG (FOR GARNISH)

Iced Tea with (Bacardi) Limon and Mint

serves 1

ICE CUBES

4 OUNCES MINT JULEP BASE MIX (SEE RECIPE UNDER THE MINT JULEP, PAGE 8)

1½ OUNCES BACARDI LIMON RUM

1 EACH LEMON WEDGE AND MINT SPRIG (FOR GARNISH)

Fill a tall (Collins) glass with ice cubes. Add the mint julep base mix and the rum. Pour the contents of the glass into a cocktail shaker and shake well. Pour the shaken cocktail back into the glass. Garnish the glass with a lemon wedge and mint sprig.

We have several drinks that call for jalapeño vodka. You can easily make this at home. Split two jalapeños into quarters and put them into your favorite kind of vodka. Warm the vodka (in its bottle) in a water bath that's heated to a light simmer; warm for 1 hour, and then remove the bottle and allow it to cool to room temperature. Set aside for at least 2 hours. The vodka will continue to get hotter as long as the jalapeños remain in the bottle. Use caution with the spice!

The Wrath of McGrath

serves 1

ICE CUBES

2½ OUNCES JALAPEÑO VODKA
(SEE RECIPE UNDER
JALAPEÑO COCKTAILS,
THIS PAGE)

2 JALAPEÑO-STUFFED OLIVES

Fill a cocktail shaker half full of ice cubes and pour the jalapeño vodka into the shaker. Shake well to chill the vodka, and then strain the chilled vodka into a frozen martini glass. Add the olives and serve.

Austin Cooler

serves 1

Pour the Shiner Bock beer into a pint glass and drizzle the jalapeño vodka over the surface of the beer. Squeeze the lime wedge over the drink and serve.

12 OUNCES ICE-COLD
SHINER BOCK BEER

1 OUNCE JALAPEÑO VODKA
(SEE RECIPE UNDER
JALAPEÑO COCKTAILS,
THIS PAGE)

1 LIME WEDGE

There are as many different recipes for Bloody Marys as there are bartenders and bars in the world. We would like to offer several ideas about the subject to you.

Basic Bloody Mary

serves 1

ICE CUBES

1½ OUNCES YOUR FAVORITE VODKA

¼ OUNCE WORCESTERSHIRE SAUCE

4 OUNCES V-8 JUICE OR TOMATO JUICE

2 TO 5 SHAKES OF TABASCO SAUCE (MORE OR LESS, TO YOUR TASTE)

CELERY SALT AND CRACKED BLACK PEPPER TO TASTE

1 EACH CELERY STALK (WITH THE LEAVES INTACT) AND LIME WEDGE

Fill a tall (Collins) glass with ice and add the vodka, Worcestershire sauce, V-8 or tomato juice, Tabasco sauce, celery salt, and cracked black pepper. Pour the contents of the glass into a cocktail shaker and shake well. Pour back into the glass. Garnish the drink with a celery stalk and lime wedge, and serve.

Here are a couple of variations on the Basic Bloody Mary:

Use beef bouillon instead of tomato juice for a Bloody Bull.

Use Clamato juice instead of tomato juice for a Bloody Caesar.

Dan's Bloody Mary Mix

makes 3 cups

Making a large batch of our mix can be a convenient way to have everything you need for a great Bloody Mary ready in your refrigerator. This mix includes all the necessary ingredients except the vodka, tomato juice, and ice. It will last for quite a while, and the longer it sits, the stronger the flavors become. A good Bloody Mary has flavor complexities, not unlike a nice sauce or mole. It is difficult at best to achieve that depth of flavors when making these drinks one at a time. Be creative with the garnishes you use for this drink. Everything from beef jerky to boiled shrimp has appeared on the rim of a Bloody Mary glass.

1	(2-CUP) BOTTLE OF WORCESTERSHIRE SAUCE
2	TABLESPOONS TABASCO SAUCE (ANY HOT SAUCE CAN BE SUBSTITUTED)
2	TABLESPOONS ROSE'S LIME JUICE
2	TABLESPOONS PREPARED HORSERADISH
2	TABLESPOONS A-1 STEAK SAUCE
2	TABLESPOONS BARBECUE SAUCE
1	TABLESPOON CRACKED BLACK PEPPER
1	TABLESPOON CELERY SALT
1	TEASPOON ONION POWDER
1	TEASPOON GARLIC POWDER
1	TEASPOON CHILI POWDER
1	TEASPOON GROUND CUMIN
1	TEASPOON GROUND CORIANDER
1	TEASPOON CAYENNE PEPPER

Combine all the ingredients and mix thoroughly. Funnel the mix into a bottle, and seal and store in the refrigerator. When you're ready to make a Bloody Mary, mix together one part Dan's Bloody Mary Mix, one part vodka, and three parts tomato juice. Then pour over ice.

The recent popularity of the martini has produced many hybrids that are quite removed from what a classic martini was intended to be—simple. As people argue about whether martinis are made with gin or vodka or whether they are shaken or stirred, we try to straddle the fence and just deliver a delicious cocktail. So, call it what you may, you will find it on our menu under Martinis. They taste good, they sell, so why not? We would rather taste them than talk about them.

Some particularly exceptional products are worth mentioning in regard to martinis. Citadelle, an extremely flavorful gin from France, has nineteen different aromatics that contribute to the unique flowery-yet-sophisticated flavor. Idaho, in America's West, gives us a true potato vodka that is triple distilled for smoothness. This vodka, Glacier, currently is available in the western United States. I am told it will be working its way east in the near future. There is an abundance of very high-quality vodkas and gins on the market now, and quite a few more will be available soon. Talk to your bartender about new and upcoming products to prevent yourself from dealing with trial-and-error selection, which can be costly.

The Quintessential Martini

serves 1

Early in Dan's career, an old Las Vegas bartender shared with him the secret to a good martini—a drop of scotch. Armed with this advice and the knowledge that James Bond (our hero!) prefers Lillet to Vermouth in his famous martinis, Dan set about to create the Quintessential

	SMALL ICE CUBES
2	OUNCES BOMBAY SAPPHIRE GIN
½	TEASPOON SINGLE MALT SCOTCH
½	TEASPOON LILLET
1	BLUE CHEESE-STUFFED OLIVE OR EXOTIC OLIVE OF YOUR CHOICE

Martini. He used Bombay Sapphire gin in this recipe because of its smoothness. This cocktail is mixology at work. The equal parts of Lillet and scotch blend so perfectly with the gin that the individual flavors are extremely subtle, and they impart a smoothness to the gin that a martini connoisseur will truly appreciate. This is a martini for a real martini drinker. Please feel free to use your favorite gin in this recipe.

In a shaker filled with ice, add gin, scotch, and Lillet. Shake well and strain into a frozen martini glass. Garnish with an olive.

These next martinis are of the new breed and lead us into dessert.

Chocolate Martini

serves 1

SMALL ICE CUBES

1 OUNCE YOUR FAVORITE VODKA

1 OUNCE STOLI VANIL VODKA

1 OUNCE GODIVA CHOCOLATE LIQUEUR

1 PARTIALLY FROZEN CHOCOLATE TRUFFLE

In a shaker filled with ice, add vodka and chocolate liqueur. Shake the ingredients well and strain into a frozen martini glass. Garnish with a chocolate truffle on a cocktail pick.

Espresso Martini

serves 1

Coat the rim of a frozen martini glass with granulated sugar. In a shaker filled with ice, add vodka, espresso, and Tia Maria or Kahlua. Shake the ingredients well and strain into martini glass.

GRANULATED SUGAR (FOR RIM OF GLASS)

SMALL ICE CUBES

1½ OUNCES YOUR FAVORITE VODKA

¾ OUNCE FRESH, CHILLED ESPRESSO (VERY STRONG COFFEE)

¾ OUNCE TIA MARIA (OR KAHLUA)

Forkless Dessert

serves 1

SMALL ICE CUBES TO FILL SHAKER

1 OUNCE BAILEY'S IRISH CREAM

1 OUNCE TIA MARIA (OR KAHLUA)

½ OUNCE CHAMBORD

This brings us to a dessert drink I call a Forkless Dessert. It is thick, rich, and decadent, and you do not need a fork.

Put all ingredients in a shaker and shake. Strain into a small parfait or cordial glass.

For a lighter dessert, pour the same amounts of Bailey's, Tia Maria or Kahlua, and Chambord into a tall glass filled with ice. Then fill the rest of the glass with sparkling water and stir.

I hope you enjoy these cocktails as much as I do. Drink well. Drink smart.

PERSONAL FAVORITES

EVERYONE HAS FAVORITES.

You have that one favorite breakfast, the one that helps you start your day with a dominant attitude. Maybe you have two favorite breakfasts. Wait a second—how can you have two favorites? There's that favorite meal on Sunday afternoon, the one you and your family, or friends, really enjoy. It's probably not a meal you will find in my restaurant, but that doesn't mean it's not good. It's just not a fine-dining type of food. These dishes are like your favorite pair of blue jeans and denim shirt. You feel totally comfortable in them, but you would not wear them to work.

In this world of personal tastes and big appetites (of all kinds), having two favorites is OK. As a matter of fact, this chapter is dedicated to some of my personal favorites. These are foods I love to eat although they are not necessarily fashionable dishes. You know what I mean. Everyone wants to be perceived as a knowledgeable diner, and dining to some is as much about impressing their guests and the restaurant's staff as it is about impressing their own taste buds.

Well, the recipes in this chapter are about eating. I hope that these dishes will become some of your favorite things to eat. From Amy's Queso to the Fish Tacos with Pickled Onions, which the staff of the restaurant devours, to the Pea and Carrot Salad, which accompanies our every cookout, these recipes are basic ideas. Good luck recreating these dishes and all the other recipes that follow. Remember that these recipes are suggestions and guidelines. Feel free to add or omit ingredients to satisfy your personal tastes. Be selfish about eating things you enjoy, about your personal favorites.

Amy's Queso

makes about 1½ quarts

1   POUND SPICY GROUND PORK SAUSAGE

1   CUP DICED YELLOW ONION

2   TABLESPOONS DICED JALAPEÑO

1   TABLESPOON MINCED GARLIC

1   (10-OUNCE) CAN ROTEL'S SPICY DICED TOMATOES
     AND GREEN CHILES, UNDRAINED

2   POUNDS VELVEETA PROCESSED CHEESE FOOD

¼   CUP CHOPPED CILANTRO

1   BAG TORTILLA CHIPS
     (YOU MAY SUBSTITUTE CORN OR FLOUR TORTILLAS)

Heat a heavy skillet over moderately high heat and sauté the spicy ground pork sausage until it starts to brown. Drain the excess oil from the sausage. Add the onion, jalapeño, and garlic, and then sauté with the sausage until tender. Add the Rotel tomatoes and green chiles. Cut the cheese into eight to ten pieces and add to the sautéed sausage and vegetable mixture. Stir the cheese frequently and add the cilantro. Let the cheese melt completely and serve with tortilla chips or tortillas.

Huevos Rancheros

serves 4

4 CUPS ALL PURPOSE FLOUR

1 TABLESPOON KOSHER SALT

⅓ CUP LARD (YOU MAY SUBSTITUTE VEGETABLE SHORTENING)

1 CUP WATER

1 TABLESPOON CORN OIL

¼ CUP + 1 TABLESPOON DICED WHITE ONION

2 TEASPOONS MINCED GARLIC

1½ CUPS COOKED PINTO BEANS
(SEE COOKING DRIED BEANS, PAGE 45)

¼ CUP TOASTED, SEEDED, AND PUREED CHILE ANCHO

KOSHER SALT AND CRACKED BLACK PEPPER TO TASTE

3 TABLESPOONS CHOPPED CILANTRO

½ CUP DICED RIPE TOMATO

1 TABLESPOON FINELY DICED JALAPEÑO

2 TABLESPOONS FRESH LIME JUICE

2 TABLESPOONS CLARIFIED BUTTER
(SEE PAGE 43)

8 LARGE EGGS

1 CUP CRUMBLED QUESO FRESCO
(WHITE COW'S MILK FARMER'S CHEESE)

To make the tortillas, combine the flour, 1 tablespoon salt, and lard; then mix together thoroughly. Slowly stir in the water to finish the dough. Knead the dough for 5 minutes into a firm, smooth ball. Allow the dough to rest for 15 minutes at room temperature. Cut the ball of dough into golf ball-size pieces, and then place each ball of dough between two pieces of wax paper and press in a tortilla press (you can roll out with a rolling pin also). Cook the tortillas one at a time in a cast-iron griddle or skillet over moderately high heat until lightly charred on the surface. Set tortillas aside, covered with a cloth towel or napkin.  Heat the corn oil in a heavy pan, and then over high heat, sauté the ¼ cup of white onion and 1 teaspoon of garlic until tender. Add the pinto beans and the chile ancho puree and cook for 10 minutes, stirring occasionally. Mash the beans by hand with a potato masher or with the back of a wooden spoon, and season to taste with kosher salt and cracked black pepper. Finish by stirring in 2 tablespoons of chopped cilantro and set aside in a warm place. Mix the tomato, 1 tablespoon of white onion, 1 teaspoon of garlic, jalapeño, lime juice, and 1 tablespoon of cilantro together and season to taste with salt and pepper. Set this salsa aside in a cool place. Over high heat, fry the eggs, one order at a time, in hot clarified butter in a nonstick skillet. You may fry the eggs over easy, sunny-side up, over well, or whatever way you prefer. I prefer either sunny-side up or over easy.

Salt and pepper the eggs. Spoon the beans onto the center of each plate (or individual little skillets). Sprinkle the crumbled queso fresco over the beans, and then melt the cheese slightly under the broiler. Place the fried eggs on the beans and top with a spoonful of the salsa. Roll the tortillas and place on the side of the plates, and then serve.

Fish Tacos
with Pickled Onions

serves 4

1	TABLESPOON DARK CHILE POWDER
1	TEASPOON GRANULATED GARLIC
1	TEASPOON GRANULATED ONION
1	TEASPOON KOSHER SALT
½	TEASPOON TOASTED AND GROUND CUMIN SEED
½	TEASPOON CAYENNE PEPPER
1	CUP SEASONED RICE VINEGAR
2	TABLESPOONS PICKLING SPICE, TIED IN CHEESECLOTH
2	CUPS VERY FINE JULIENNE OF WHITE ONION
1½	POUNDS LARGE-DICED MAHI MAHI (OR ANY FIRM-FLESHED WHITE FISH)
2	TABLESPOONS CORN OIL
½	CUP DICED POBLANO
½	CUP DICED RIPE TOMATO
½	CUP CILANTRO LEAVES
	KOSHER SALT AND CRACKED BLACK PEPPER TO TASTE
8	(6-INCH) FLOUR TORTILLAS
2	CUPS FINE CHIFFONADE OF GREEN CABBAGE (SEE NEXT PAGE)
1	CUP CHIPOTLE MAYONNAISE (SEE PAGE 53)
1	CUP TOMATILLO SALSA (SEE PAGE 50)
1	TABLESPOON CRUSHED RED CHILE FLAKES

Combine the chile powder, granulated garlic, granulated onion, 1 teaspoon of salt, ground cumin seed, and cayenne pepper and then set aside. This will be your chile powder seasoning mix. Bring the rice vinegar to a boil with the pickling spice in cheesecloth. Allow to cool to room temperature and pour over the julienne of white onion. Let the onions sit in the pickling brine for 1 hour in the refrigerator. Dust the mahi mahi with the chile powder seasoning mix. Heat the corn oil in a heavy skillet over moderately high heat and sauté the poblanos, tomatoes, and mahi mahi for 5 minutes. Then finish by sprinkling the cilantro leaves over the top. Season to taste with salt and pepper. Heat the tortillas,

and lay some pickled onions and chiffonade (a chiffonade is a very fine julienne cut of a leaf vegetable) of green cabbage down the center of one tortilla. Spoon some of the sautéed mahi mahi mixture on the cabbage and pickled onions, and then roll the tortilla around the mahi and vegetables. Repeat the procedure for the second taco. Crisscross the two tacos on the plate, and serve the Chipotle Mayonnaise and the Tomatillo Salsa in small ramekins on the plate. Sprinkle the red chile flakes over the plate. Repeat to make six more tacos and serve.

Pea and Carrot Salad

serves 8

¾ CUP SMALL-DICED CARROT

½ CUP FINELY DICED RED ONION

¾ CUP MAYONNAISE

¼ CUP SWEET PICKLE RELISH

½ CUP COARSELY CHOPPED HARD-COOKED EGG

1¼ CUPS COOKED SMALL, FRESH PEAS
(LeSEUR EARLY PEAS CAN BE SUBSTITUTED)

KOSHER SALT AND
CRACKED BLACK PEPPER TO TASTE

Mix all the ingredients together except the peas, salt, and pepper. Add the peas last, season to taste, and refrigerate for 30 minutes.

Simple Jalapeño and White Onion Slaw

serves 4

Toss the cabbage, onion, cilantro, and jalapeño together. In a separate bowl, combine the mayonnaise, vinegar, and lime juice and then whisk thoroughly. Pour the slaw dressing over the tossed vegetables and mix well. Season to taste and chill in the refrigerator before serving.

1 CUP FINE CHIFFONADE OF GREEN CABBAGE
(SEE FISH TACOS WITH PICKLED ONIONS,
PAGE 23)

1 CUP FINE JULIENNE OF WHITE ONION

½ CUP COARSELY CHOPPED CILANTRO LEAVES

¼ CUP VERY FINE JULIENNE OF JALAPEÑO

¼ CUP MAYONNAISE

¼ CUP SEASONED RICE VINEGAR

2 TABLESPOONS FRESH LIME JUICE

KOSHER SALT AND
CRACKED BLACK PEPPER TO TASTE

Deviled Eggs

serves 6

Roast the garlic cloves in the olive oil in a 325º oven for 10 minutes, until golden brown. Mash the roasted garlic cloves until smooth, and then combine with the mayonnaise. Split the cooked eggs lengthwise and separate the egg yolks from the whites, keeping the whites intact. Mash the cooked egg yolks with a fork until smooth. Add the roasted-garlic mayonnaise, Dijon mustard, Durkee's spread, and cayenne pepper to the mashed yolks. Season to taste. Carefully spoon the deviled-egg filling into the egg whites. Cover and chill in the refrigerator. Top with the chervil sprigs immediately before serving.

1	TEASPOON MASHED GARLIC CLOVES
½	TEASPOON EXTRA-VIRGIN OLIVE OIL
2	TABLESPOONS MAYONNAISE
12	HARD-COOKED EGGS
2	TABLESPOONS DIJON MUSTARD
2	TABLESPOONS DURKEE'S SANDWICH SPREAD
¼	TEASPOON CAYENNE PEPPER
	KOSHER SALT AND CRACKED BLACK PEPPER TO TASTE
24	SMALL CHERVIL SPRIGS

Helaine's Best Chocolate Minis

serves 8

3	OUNCES SEMISWEET CHOCOLATE
1	OUNCE UNSWEETENED CHOCOLATE
2	STICKS UNSALTED BUTTER
1	TEASPOON VANILLA EXTRACT
1½	CUPS GRANULATED SUGAR
1	CUP ALL PURPOSE FLOUR
4	EGGS AT ROOM TEMPERATURE
1	CUP CHOPPED PECANS

Preheat your oven to 325º. Melt the chocolates and butter together in a heavy pan over very low heat, stirring frequently. Remove from the heat. Add the other ingredients to the chocolate mixture one at a time, making sure each ingredient is completely incorporated into the mixture before the next ingredient is added. Mix well—but do not beat. Fill a mini-muffin tin with little paper muffin liners. Spoon the mixture in the muffin papers so that each is ¾ full. Bake for 20 minutes, until the tops are puffed up and just dry. Allow to cool to room temperature and serve.

Barbecue Brisket of Beef

serves 8

1 CUP GRANULATED SUGAR

1 CUP DARK CHILE POWDER

½ CUP KOSHER SALT

½ CUP CRACKED BLACK PEPPER

¼ CUP PAPRIKA

½ CUP CAYENNE PEPPER

1 (10-POUND) TRIMMED BEEF BRISKET

1½ CUPS BEER

½ CUP CIDER VINEGAR

½ CUP FINELY DICED YELLOW ONION

¼ CUP MINCED GARLIC

¼ CUP WORCESTERSHIRE SAUCE

2 TABLESPOONS PUREED CHIPOTLE CHILES IN ADOBO SAUCE

Mix the sugar, chile powder, salt, black pepper, paprika, and cayenne pepper together thoroughly. Rub this dry cure over all the meat, and allow the brisket to cure in the refrigerator for 24 hours. Repeat the procedure every couple of hours during the curing process. Allow the brisket to come to room temperature before cooking. Combine the beer, vinegar, onion, garlic, Worcestershire sauce, and chipotle chiles in adobo sauce. Bring to a boil and remove from the heat. Wood roast the brisket over hickory wood at 225° for 10 hours. Roast the brisket in the coolest side of the grill, with the fat side up. If you use a Texas Hondo barbecue grill, build the fire in the heat box and keep the brisket in the grill chamber. Brush the sauce on the brisket every hour or so. Allow the brisket to rest for 5 minutes before carving. Remove the fat cap, and slice the beef very thin at an angle across the grain. Serve warm.

Asparagus
with Roasted Garlic and Sherry Vinegar

serves 4

2	TABLESPOONS WHOLE GARLIC CLOVES
¼	CUP + 1 TEASPOON EXTRA-VIRGIN OLIVE OIL
	KOSHER SALT AND CRACKED BLACK PEPPER TO TASTE
32	PEELED ASPARAGUS SPEARS, 4½ INCHES LONG
	WATER
	ICE
¼	CUP AGED SHERRY VINEGAR

Preheat your oven to 325°. Roast the garlic cloves in the teaspoon of olive oil and a sprinkling of salt for 10 minutes, until they are golden brown. Mash the cloves into small pieces with the back of a fork. Blanch the asparagus spears in lightly salted and boiling water for 90 seconds. Chill the spears in ice water to stop them from cooking. When the spears are thoroughly chilled, drain them. Drizzle the 1 teaspoon of olive oil, the sherry vinegar, and the roasted garlic over the spears. Allow the asparagus to sit in the dressing for 15 minutes. Chill in the refrigerator, season to taste with salt and pepper, and serve.

Alaskan King Crab and Avocado Salad

with Roasted-Garlic Mayonnaise

serves 4

2	TABLESPOONS WHOLE GARLIC CLOVES
1	TABLESPOON EXTRA-VIRGIN OLIVE OIL
¾	CUP MAYONNAISE
2	TABLESPOONS FRESH LEMON JUICE
½	CUP DICED RIPE TOMATO
1	CUP CILANTRO LEAVES
2	CUPS AVOCADO CUT INTO ½ INCH CUBES
1	POUND CLEANED MEAT FROM KING CRAB
	KOSHER SALT AND CRACKED BLACK PEPPER TO TASTE
2	CUPS ARUGULA LEAVES

Roast the garlic cloves in the olive oil in a 325° oven for 10 minutes, until the cloves are golden brown. Mash the garlic cloves with a fork until smooth. Add the roasted garlic mash to the mayonnaise with the lemon juice. Combine the diced tomato, cilantro, avocado, and crabmeat with the mayonnaise mixture, and then season to taste. Spoon the crabmeat-avocado salad on the arugula leaves and serve.

The Ultimate Fish Sandwich

serves 4

¾   CUP MAYONNAISE

¼   CUP SWEET PICKLE RELISH

1   TEASPOON PUREED CHIPOTLE CHILES
     IN ADOBO SAUCE

1   CUP ALL PURPOSE FLOUR

     KOSHER SALT AND
     CRACKED BLACK PEPPER TO TASTE

4   (6-OUNCE) BONELESS GROUPER FILETS
     (SEA BASS CAN BE SUBSTITUTED)

3   BEATEN EGGS

1   CUP DRIED BREAD CRUMBS

¼   CUP + 2 TABLESPOONS CORN OIL

2   CUPS JULIENNE OF YELLOW ONION

2   CUPS SLICED BUTTON MUSHROOMS

2   TABLESPOONS MINCED GARLIC

3   TABLESPOONS SLICED JALAPEÑOS

4   LARGE ONION ROLLS

4   YELLOW CHEDDAR CHEESE SLICES

Mix the mayonnaise, sweet pickle relish, and chipotle puree together and chill in the refrigerator. Season the flour with salt and pepper. Dust each filet of grouper with the seasoned flour, and dip into the beaten eggs. Allow the excess egg to drip off, and then dredge the grouper in the breadcrumbs. Heat the ¼ cup of corn oil in a heavy skillet over moderately high heat and fry the breaded grouper filets for 2 minutes on one side; then turn over and cook for 2½ minutes. Remove from the oil and place on paper towels to absorb any excess oil.

Heat the other 2 tablespoons of corn oil in a heavy skillet over high heat (you may use the same skillet, but it needs to be wiped clean). Sauté the onion, mushrooms, garlic, and jalapeño until they are tender. Toast the onion rolls (halved, sandwich-style) in your toaster, if it's big enough, or under the broiler in your oven, and spread the chipotle tartar sauce on the rolls. Place a pan-fried grouper filet on the bottom half of each onion roll and spoon the sautéed onion-mushroom mixture over the fish. Cover the fish and the sautéed onion-mushroom mixture with a slice of cheddar cheese, and lightly brown under the broiler. Top with the other half of the roll and serve.

STANDARD PREPARATIONS

(SOME BASICS FOR US ALL)

Smoke Roasting, Smoking, and Grilling

The two necessary components in smoke roasting, or barbecue cooking, are a low cooking temperature and smoke. You need to have enough heat, usually about 200°, to cook the food. The temperature in the wood-burning oven is the principal difference between smoke roasting and smoking. Smoke roasting is best applied to tough cuts of meat, such as beef brisket, spareribs, and short ribs. The smoke flavor you want in smoke roasting should come from the wood, not the meat's fat dripping onto the hot coals. Use a drip pan under the cooking meat to collect the dripping fat.

Smoking is a method of preserving food and is usually a combination of some type of a salt cure and wood smoke. In smoking foods, the temperature should not get above 100°. When you cold smoke foods, the temperature should not exceed 80°; this can be controlled by using pans filled with ice. Place the pans of ice between the racks of the foods you are cold smoking, if you have a vertical smoker. If you are using a conventional bowl-shaped grill or a Hondo cooker, which has the firebox on the side of the grill, place the ice between the smoking wood and the food you are cold smoking.

Grilling foods is all about heat. The principle behind grilling is searing the meat on the outside to hold the juices on the inside. Grilling works most effectively on more tender cuts of meat, such as steaks, chops, and poultry. Dry cures can infuse flavors for grilling some foods, but be careful that the cures don't burn and become bitter.

The Wood and Equipment

Log fires tend to burn a little hotter and produce denser smoke than fires made using wood chips, or chunks of wood. I prefer to use hickory wood, but pecan wood is an excellent alternative. Hickory wood has a great robust flavor and burns well when properly dried. Pecan wood burns cooler than hickory, yet it still has a rich flavor like a mellow hickory wood. Mesquite wood burns very hot and leaves an acrid aftertaste, and I don't feel it is a worthwhile substitute.

For those of you who are interested in obtaining an excellent log pit, the best is from Pitt's and Spitt's in Houston, Texas (call 800-521-2947 for more information). For a more cost-effective alternative, I suggest the Hondo model from the New Braunfels Smoker Company (call 800-232-3398 for more information). Both of these log pits are extremely versatile and well designed. The steel plate on the Pitt's and Spitt's firebox is thicker than the plate on the New Braunfels Smoker Company firebox, but other than that, the design and functions are basically the same. You can smoke roast, smoke, or grill with both of these models. For smoke cooking on your stove top, I recommend the stainless steel smoker from C.M. International, the Cameron model (call 719-390-0505 for more information), which utilizes a convection type of smoke cooking. This smoker comes with a hardwood hickory dust (as well as alder, cherry, apple, and pecan), which is used in the smoking process.

The Fire

When using a log fire, you will want to start the fire at least an hour before you plan to begin cooking. When building a log fire, make a stack of dried hardwood kindling, and then arrange the logs so that plenty of air can circulate through the fire. Avoid using any fluid fuel to start the fire because the smell of the fuel will permeate the wood.

For smoke roasting, build the fire in the firebox on the models like the Hondo; for grilling, build the fire in the main compartment. For smoking, build the fire smaller. I use wadded newspaper when no dried kindling is available. If you are using a conventional grill for smoke roasting, build the fire as far as possible from where the food will be cooked. If you are using a conventional grill for grilling, then build the fire on one side of the grill instead of covering the entire bottom of the grill with the wood chunks or charcoal. This gives you a cool side of the grill, where you can rest meats or roast vegetables. Conventional grills will not last long if they are burning log fires because the metal walls on the grills are thinner than those on the Hondo, but they will perform well and last a little longer burning wood chunks. Once the fire is burning, allow the flames to die down and the logs to become embers. Then refuel the fire as needed with a small log for smoke roasting. For grilling, refuel the fire with a small log, and then allow it to burn down to embers. For smoking, do not refuel the smaller fire with logs; instead use small chunks of wood that have been soaked in water for 30 minutes.

If you are cooking with a charcoal fire, plan on starting the fire about 40 minutes before you want to cook. I suggest using the metal chimneys designed for this purpose. Fill the bottom of the chimney with crumpled newspaper, and fill the top with standard charcoal briquettes or lump hardwood charcoal. You must be careful trying to control the temperature with the lump hardwood charcoal because it burns hotter than briquettes. The charcoal is ready for grilling when it is completely covered with a thin layer of gray ash. The charcoal is ready for smoke roasting when it is covered with a thick layer of ash and no red glow is visible. Then, keeping the temperature at 200°, cover part of the fire with chunks of pecan wood that have been soaked in water for at least 1 hour. The best source for natural charcoals and hardwoods is a company called Nature's Own, and its products are available by mail order from Peoples Smoke-n-Grill (call 800-729-5800 for more information).

Stocks

Every cookbook you have ever picked up has probably told you that stocks are the foundation of cooking. I'm here to tell you that those authors and chefs were not lying to you.

Soups, sauces, and braising liquids are, for the most part, all based on stocks. Any serious cook wants to coax every possible nuance of flavor from the ingredients that are the focus of the dish. Stocks set that process in motion. Cooking is a type of progression—flavors are layered on top of each other or through each other. Stocks serve as the base for the progression.

As far as seafood stocks are concerned, they can either be very good or very average. Just trying to be nice. I really enjoy stocks made from crustaceans (shrimp, lobster, crab, or crawfish) for the richness of flavor and for the hint of sweetness they leave on your palate. Fish stocks should only be made from non-oily, white-fleshed fish (such as grouper, snapper, sea bass, etc.). Oily-fleshed fish tend to leave a strong fish taste in the stock, and that fishy taste carries over to the soups, or sauces, during the layering process.

Vegetable stocks can be quite versatile. You can roast the vegetables for a richer, more rustic flavor. You can use the vegetables in the raw state for a lighter, crisper-tasting stock. There is a tremendous variety of ingredients from which to choose in the building of the foundation of a particular soup or sauce. You can use everyday scraps for a stock, for example, which might include your ripe tomatoes and some sweet onions, or the trimmings from some portabello mushrooms and garlic, or roasted fennel and leek—I'm sure you get the idea. There are dozens of fresh, and dried, herbs that can be used to finish the different stocks.

I tend to use chicken stock most frequently because it offers a fairly neutral background for building a sauce or in which to cook other foods. I even prefer to use chicken stock in sauces for fish, or fish soups, because it is so neutral. By using chicken stock, the fish flavor does not become too intense from layering fish flavor on top of fish flavor. If you braise diced pork in water it still gets cooked, but by using chicken stock instead of water you reinforce the flavors instead of diluting them. It can create another layer of flavor.

Veal stock is probably the most complex of the stocks. It offers a smaller margin of error; that is, you have to pay attention. That can be tough for some of us. You need to roast the bones and vegetables properly so that the resulting stock does not become bitter. Veal stock can be reduced down in volume to create other sauces such as glace de viande (beef glaze, or "shellac" in this book) or demi-glace, which is the finished veal stock reduced in volume by half. Many soups and sauces can be derived from these by-products of the veal stock. Don't be intimidated by these stocks; they taste great, and you know what's in them.

Chicken Stock

yields 1 gallon

3½   GALLONS WATER

2   (3-POUND) CHICKENS, CUT INTO QUARTERS,
     INTERNAL ORGANS AND EXCESS FAT REMOVED

4   CUPS COARSELY CUT YELLOW ONION

4   CUPS COARSELY CUT CELERY
     (RESERVE THE LEAVES FOR ANOTHER RECIPE)

4   CUPS COARSELY CUT CARROT

½   CUP COARSELY CHOPPED GARLIC

½   CUP BAY LEAVES

¼   CUP BLACK PEPPERCORNS

¼   CUP COARSELY CHOPPED FRESH THYME

¼   CUP COARSELY CHOPPED FRESH PARSLEY

    KOSHER SALT AND
    CRACKED BLACK PEPPER TO TASTE

Place all the ingredients except 1 gallon of water in a large, heavy pot and bring to a boil. Let cook at a full boil for 45 to 50 minutes. Add the other gallon of water and bring to a boil. Cook at a full boil for 45 to 50 minutes. Allow to cool slightly, and strain. When you are straining the stock, reserve the chicken meat for another recipe. Bring to a boil again, and continue boiling until the liquid has reduced in volume to 1 gallon of stock. Season to taste. Allow the stock to cool to room temperature before refrigerating. This stock can be held for two weeks if it is sealed and kept in a refrigerator. Cook until the stock has reduced by ⅓ and strain. To get a broth, strain the stock through a fine chinois or cheesecloth.

Veal Stock

yields 1 gallon

¼	CUP CLARIFIED BUTTER (SEE PAGE 43)
5	POUNDS SPLIT VEAL SHANK BONES (HAVE YOUR BUTCHER SPLIT THEM)
3	POUNDS BEEF SCRAPS
4	CUPS COARSELY CUT PEELED YELLOW ONION
4	CUPS COARSELY CUT CELERY
4	CUPS COARSELY CUT CARROT
2	CUPS TOMATO SCRAPS
1	CUP COARSELY CHOPPED PARSLEY
½	CUP COARSELY CHOPPED GARLIC
½	CUP BAY LEAVES
½	CUP COARSELY CHOPPED FRESH THYME
¼	CUP WHOLE BLACK PEPPERCORNS
6	CUPS PINOT NOIR (ANY RICH RED WINE CAN BE SUBSTITUTED)
4½	GALLONS WATER
	KOSHER SALT AND CRACKED BLACK PEPPER TO TASTE

Heat the clarified butter in a heavy roasting pan in a 400° oven. Add the veal bones and beef scraps; roast for 10 minutes, or until they are just beginning to stick to the pan. Reduce the oven temperature to 350° and add the onion, celery, and carrot. Roast for another 15 minutes, stirring occasionally to keep everything from sticking to the pan too much. Move the roasting pan to the stove top, over moderately high heat, and add the tomato, parsley, garlic, bay leaves, fresh thyme, and peppercorns. Stir the meats and vegetables for 3 minutes, and then add the pinot noir. Cook until the wine has reduced in volume by ½, and then transfer the roasted bones, scraps, and vegetables into a heavy pot. Add 2½ gallons of water and bring to a boil. ⓇⓅ Cook at a full boil for 1 hour. Add the other 2 gallons of water and continue cooking at a full boil for 45 to 50 minutes. Reduce the heat to a strong simmer and cook for another 20 minutes. Strain. Return to the stove top and cook at a strong simmer until the volume has been reduced to 1 gallon. Season to taste, but do not salt heavily because the flavors will intensify in future reductions. Pass through a fine strainer and cool to room temperature before refrigerating.

Veal Demi-Glace

yields ½ gallon

ⓇⓅ Bring the finished veal stock (1 gallon) to a boil. ⓇⓅ Boil until the stock has reduced in volume by ½. This Veal Demi-Glace is used as the base for brown sauces for red meat.

Shellac
(Glace de Viande)

yields 1 cup

ⓇⓅ Bring the finished veal stock (1 gallon) to a boil in a heavy pan. ⓇⓅ Reduce the heat to a strong simmer, and simmer until stock has reduced in volume to 1 cup. Cool to room temperature before refrigerating. This shellac was originally intended to be a glaze for steaks and meats by itself, but with some imagination, it can carry other flavors with it to the meat. It is best applied with a small spoon (tablespoon) or a pastry brush. Once you use a brush with the shellac, it will not be usable for anything else.

Crawfish Stock

yields 1 gallon

¼	CUP CLARIFIED BUTTER*
5	POUNDS CLEANED CRAWFISH SHELLS (LOBSTER BODIES, CRAB BODIES, OR SHRIMP SHELLS WILL WORK WELL ALSO; CLEAN BY REMOVING MEAT AND GLANDS AND THEN RINSING UNDER COLD WATER)
3	CUPS COARSELY CUT PEELED YELLOW ONION
3	CUPS COARSELY CUT CELERY
3	CUPS COARSELY CUT CARROT
½	CUP COARSELY CHOPPED GARLIC
½	CUP COARSELY CHOPPED PARSLEY
½	CUP BAY LEAVES
¼	CUP BLACK PEPPERCORNS
2	CUPS BRANDY
4	CUPS CHARDONNAY (ANY FULL-BODIED WHITE WINE WILL WORK)
2½	GALLONS WATER
1	CUP TOMATO PASTE
	KOSHER SALT AND CRACKED BLACK PEPPER TO TASTE

Heat the clarified butter in a heavy roasting pan on the stove top over high heat. Add the crawfish shells, onion, celery, carrot, garlic, parsley, bay leaves, and peppercorns. Sauté until the shells are bright red and the vegetables are just beginning to stick to the pan. Deglaze** the roasting pan with the brandy, burn the brandy to lower the alcohol content (allow the brandy to catch fire from the stove or by using a long, wooden skewer), and cook until the brandy has reduced in volume by ½. Add the chardonnay and reduce in volume by ½. Transfer the contents of the roasting pan to a heavy pot, and add the water. Add tomato paste to the stock. Reduce in volume by ½ and strain. Return the strained stock to the stove top and bring to a boil. Then reduce heat to a strong simmer and cook until stock has reduced in volume to 1 gallon. Season to taste and cool to room temperature before refrigerating. (This stock can be thickened with a roux [equal parts of flour and butter cooked together in a pan on the stove top over moderately high heat until the butter is completely absorbed by the flour] to the desired consistency, and softened with the addition of heavy cream.)

*Clarified butter is quite useful in the kitchen and simple to prepare. Bring 1 pound of whole butter to an active simmer. The salts will rise to the surface (this takes approximately 5 minutes), where you should skim them off. The waters and milk will fall to the bottom of the pan. Very carefully pour the pure butterfat through cheesecloth, not allowing any of the milky liquid or sediment from the bottom of the pan to get to the cheesecloth. The strained butter is now clarified and has a much higher tolerance of heat. This makes a little more than 1 cup of clarified butter.

**To deglaze, you will dissolve the small particles of food remaining on the bottom of the pan by adding a liquid and heating.

Fish Stock

yields 1 gallon

Bring all the ingredients except the lemon rind, the chardonnay, and the salt and pepper to a boil in a heavy pot. Boil until liquid has reduced in volume by ½, and then strain. Add the lemon rind and the chardonnay. Bring the liquid to a boil and reduce in volume again by ¼. Season to taste; then strain again and cool to room temperature before refrigerating.

*Fish scraps include trimmings, heads, and bones but no internal organs.

2½	GALLONS WATER
3	POUNDS FISH SCRAPS* FROM A RED SNAPPER (OR OTHER NON-OILY, WHITE-FLESHED FISH, SUCH AS GROUPER, SEA BASS, ETC.)
4	CUPS COARSELY CUT PEELED YELLOW ONION
4	CUPS COARSELY CUT CELERY
2	CUPS COARSELY CUT CARROTS
½	CUP COARSELY CHOPPED GARLIC
½	CUP COARSELY CHOPPED PARSLEY
½	CUP BAY LEAVES
¼	CUP BLACK PEPPERCORNS
¼	CUP LEMON RIND, WITHOUT ANY OF THE WHITE PITH
2	CUPS CHARDONNAY (ANY FULL-BODIED WHITE WINE WILL WORK)
	KOSHER SALT AND CRACKED BLACK PEPPER TO TASTE

Chiles

Before we get into the various aspects of chiles, allow me to mention a few ongoing debates about them. First, there is the debate about the spelling of the word *chile* (as in chile pepper). Everybody has an opinion. Second, people disagree about the cadence of the word *chile*—whether it should come before or after the type of chile that it is. Again, everybody has an opinion. Third, we have the issue of whether the dish chili (as in a steaming bowl of four-alarm Texas chili) is spelled with an *e* or an *i*. It can go on and on. A lot of the opinions are attributable to people living in different regions. Some are not. Is whoever yells the loudest right? Not even.

Here are my opinions and explanations about these ongoing discrepancies, based on what I have learned over the years in this region of the country and what we practice at the Roaring Fork. If I am talking about the vegetable, such as chile chipotle, the word *chile* is spelled with an *e*. Regarding syntax, the word *chile* should follow the type of fresh chile, and the word *chile* should precede the type of dried chile. For example, poblano chile is a fresh chile, and chile ancho is a dried chile. Now does this affect the flavor of the chile? No. Does this affect the level of heat in the chile? No. The quality of the dish? No. Well, what does it affect? Absolutely nothing. By the way, the meat dish from Texas is spelled with an *i*. Chili!

I strongly suggest investing a couple of dollars in a box of latex gloves for handling chiles. These are available at any drugstore. Be careful not to touch your eyes or any other sensitive place, like your face or lips.

When buying fresh chiles, select ones that are firm, shiny, smooth to the touch, and heavy. Always wash the outside of the chiles with cold water and dry them with a towel before cooking with them. Always taste a small piece of the chile you are planning to use because the heat level (the amount of capsaicin) varies depending on the amount of water the chile plant has had. The less water, the hotter the chile. The greatest concentration of capsaicin is found in the seeds and ribs of the chile; therefore, removing the seeds and ribs will lower the amount of heat in the chile. When buying dried chiles, select the ones that are pliable, are whole, are not discolored, and have a rich chile scent. The dried chile most commonly used in this book is the chile ancho, which is a dried poblano chile. Store the fresh chiles in the vegetable crisper in your refrigerator, and the dried chiles in an airtight container in a cool, dry place.

Roasting fresh chiles (or bell peppers) creates a completely different flavor for the chile. Roast the chile on your grill or under your electric broiler until the skin is charred. Place the chile in a bowl and cover with plastic food wrap to trap the steam from the chile. This steam allows the skin to be peeled off easily. I do not suggest washing the skin off the chile because the water washes some of the flavor away. Split the chile's flesh with your fingers and remove the seeds. This roasted chile now can be pureed or diced and used. You can puree the roasted chile in a blender with just enough fluid (water or chicken broth) to allow the blender blades to puree the chile.

Cooking Dried Beans

When cooking dried beans, you need to start the night before. Carefully pick through the beans to remove any small stones or sticks. This is important because these little intruders can cause serious damage to your teeth or mouth. Rinse the beans in a colander, and then put them in a heavy pot. Cover the beans with twice as much water as the volume of beans, and allow to sit overnight. Drain the beans, and then cover them with 1½ times the amount of Chicken Stock. Add 1 smoked ham hock for every gallon of Chicken Stock and beans combined. Add 2 diced white onions for every gallon of Chicken Stock and beans combined. Add 2 tablespoons of chopped garlic for every  gallon of Chicken Stock and beans combined. As far as the amount of specific seasonings—such as salt, pepper, chiles, etc.—it is subjective, and they should be added to satisfy your personal tastes near the conclusion of cooking the beans. The length of time it takes to cook the beans depends greatly on whether you are using a Crockpot, a campfire, or a pot on the stove top. The altitude will affect the cooking time as well. I would count on approximately 45 minutes to 1 hour. I suggest bringing the Chicken Stock and beans to a boil and then lowering the heat and simmering actively until the beans are tender. It is a good idea to have a little extra Chicken Stock in the pot so you do not have to stir the beans so much, which will break the beans up. Then drain the beans if necessary and serve, or mash for your particular usage

RELISHES, DRESSINGS, & SAUCES

Cucumber Relish

serves 4

½ CUP PEELED, SEEDED, AND DICED CUCUMBER

1 TABLESPOON FINELY DICED POBLANO CHILE

1 TABLESPOON FINELY DICED RED BELL PEPPER

1 TABLESPOON FINELY CHOPPED RED ONION

1 TABLESPOON FINELY CHOPPED CILANTRO

2 TABLESPOONS FRESH LIME JUICE

KOSHER SALT TO TASTE

Combine all the ingredients except salt. Season to taste. Set aside in a cool place, or refrigerate. This relish is best if used on the day that it is made.

Carrot Salsa

serves 4

½ CUP DICED, LIGHTLY STEAMED, AND STILL SLIGHTLY CRUNCHY CARROTS

1 TABLESPOON FINELY DICED RED ONION

1 TABLESPOON FINELY DICED RED BELL PEPPER

1 TABLESPOON FINELY DICED YELLOW BELL PEPPER

1 TABLESPOON CHOPPED CILANTRO

1 TEASPOON FINELY DICED JALAPENO

1 TABLESPOON FRESH LIME JUICE

KOSHER SALT AND CRACKED BLACK PEPPER TO TASTE

Combine all the ingredients except salt and pepper. Season to taste. Set aside in a cool place, or refrigerate. This relish will last for three days covered in the refrigerator.

Avocado and Orange Relish

serves 8

1 CUP DICED AVOCADO

¼ CUP HALVED RED SEEDLESS GRAPES

¼ CUP ORANGE SECTIONS

2 TABLESPOONS FINELY DICED RED ONION

2 TABLESPOONS CHOPPED CILANTRO

2 TABLESPOONS FRESH LIME JUICE

1 TABLESPOON FINELY DICED JALAPENO

KOSHER SALT TO TASTE

Carefully combine all the ingredients except the salt, taking care that the avocado doesn't get smashed. Then season to taste, and chill in the refrigerator. This relish is best if used the day it is made.

Corn Relish

serves 4

½ CUP ROASTED SWEET CORN KERNELS*

2 TABLESPOONS FINELY DICED RED ONION

2 TABLESPOONS SEASONED RICE VINEGAR

1 TABLESPOON FINELY DICED RED BELL PEPPER

1 TABLESPOON CHOPPED CILANTRO

1 TEASPOON FINELY DICED JALAPENO

1 TEASPOON MINCED GARLIC

KOSHER SALT AND
CRACKED BLACK PEPPER TO TASTE

Combine all the ingredients except the salt and pepper. Then season to taste, and chill in the refrigerator. This relish will last two days covered in the refrigerator.

Husk the corn and roast in a hot oven for 5 minutes. Then remove the kernels from the ear.

Tomatillo Salsa

serves 8

1	CUP PEELED AND QUARTERED TOMATILLO
¼	CUP COARSELY CUT WHITE ONION
2	TABLESPOONS COARSELY CHOPPED JALAPEÑO
2	TABLESPOONS COARSELY CHOPPED GARLIC
2	TABLESPOONS CHOPPED CILANTRO
1	TABLESPOON FRESH LIME JUICE
	KOSHER SALT AND CRACKED BLACK PEPPER TO TASTE

In a very hot cast-iron skillet, char everything except the cilantro, lime juice, salt, and pepper. Puree the charred ingredients and then stir in the cilantro and lime juice. Season to taste and chill in the refrigerator. This relish will last for three days covered in the refrigerator.

Papaya Chile Relish

serves 8

1	CUP PEELED, SEEDED, AND DICED PAPAYA
3	TABLESPOONS FINELY DICED RED ONION
3	TABLESPOONS SEASONED RICE VINEGAR
2	TABLESPOONS FINELY DICED RED BELL PEPPER
2	TABLESPOONS FINELY DICED POBLANO CHILE
2	TABLESPOONS CHOPPED CILANTRO
	KOSHER SALT TO TASTE

Combine all the ingredients except salt. Season to taste. This relish will last for two days covered in the refrigerator.

Salsa Fresca

serves 4

½	CUP DICED RIPE TOMATOES
2	TABLESPOONS FINELY DICED WHITE ONION
2	TABLESPOONS FRESH LIME JUICE
1	TABLESPOON FINELY DICED JALAPEÑO
1	TABLESPOON CHOPPED CILANTRO
1	TABLESPOON MINCED GARLIC
	KOSHER SALT TO TASTE

Mix all the ingredients except salt together. Season to taste and refrigerate. This relish will last for three days covered in the refrigerator.

Roasted Tomato Salsa

serves 8

¾	CUP COARSELY CUT RIPE TOMATOES
¼	CUP COARSELY CUT WHITE ONION
2	TABLESPOONS COARSELY CHOPPED GARLIC
2	TABLESPOONS COARSELY CHOPPED JALAPEÑO
3	TABLESPOONS CHOPPED CILANTRO
3	TABLESPOONS FRESH LIME JUICE
	KOSHER SALT AND CRACKED BLACK PEPPER TO TASTE

In a very hot cast-iron skillet, char everything except the cilantro, lime juice, salt, and pepper. Puree the charred vegetables in a blender. Finish the salsa by stirring in the cilantro and lime juice, season to taste, and then refrigerate. This salsa will last three days in the refrigerator.

Red Bell Pepper Ketchup

yields 3 cups

1 TABLESPOON CORN OIL

2 TABLESPOONS FINELY DICED CARROT

2 TABLESPOONS FINELY DICED YELLOW ONION

1 TABLESPOON FINELY DICED JALAPEÑO

1 TABLESPOON MINCED GARLIC

1½ CUPS ROASTED, PEELED, SEEDED, AND
PUREED RED BELL PEPPER*

¼ CUP MALT VINEGAR

2 TABLESPOONS BROWN SUGAR

1 TABLESPOON MOLASSES

1 TABLESPOON HONEY

1 TEASPOON GROUND CINNAMON

1 TEASPOON NUTMEG

1 TEASPOON CAYENNE PEPPER

1 TEASPOON GROUND CLOVES

KOSHER SALT AND
CRACKED BLACK PEPPER TO TASTE

Heat the corn oil in a heavy pan over moderately high heat and sauté the carrot, onion, jalapeño, and garlic until tender. Add the remaining ingredients except the salt and pepper, and simmer for 30 to 35 minutes. Allow the mixture to cool to room temperature, and puree in a blender until smooth. Season to taste and chill in the refrigerator. This ketchup will last up to a week covered in the refrigerator.

*Roast the red bell pepper on the grill or under the broiler until the skin is charred.
Then cover in a bowl.*

Shrimp Remoulade

yields 2 cups

¾	CUP CLEANED AND COOKED ROCK SHRIMP
½	CUP MAYONNAISE
¼	CUP TOMATO KETCHUP
2	TABLESPOONS FRESH LEMON JUICE
2	TABLESPOONS FINELY DICED CARROT
2	TABLESPOONS FINELY DICED YELLOW ONION
1	TABLESPOON FINELY DICED JALAPEÑO
1	TABLESPOON FINELY CHOPPED CHIVES
1	TABLESPOON FINELY CHOPPED PARSLEY
1	TEASPOON TABASCO SAUCE
	KOSHER SALT AND CRACKED BLACK PEPPER TO TASTE

Combine all the ingredients except salt and pepper. Season to taste. This sauce will last for three days covered in the refrigerator.

Chipotle Mayonnaise

yields 1 cup

1	CUP MAYONNAISE
1	TABLESPOON PUREED CHIPOTLE CHILES IN ADOBO SAUCE

Mix together thoroughly. This will last for one week covered in the refrigerator. If you want the mayonnaise hotter, add another teaspoon of the chipotle puree.

NOTE: You can also use this mayonnaise as the base for tartar sauce.

Buttermilk and Goat Cheese Dressing

yields 2 cups

¾	CUP MAYONNAISE
½	CUP BUTTERMILK
½	CUP CRUMBLED GOAT CHEESE
2	TABLESPOONS FINELY CHOPPED CHIVES
2	TABLESPOONS GRANULATED SUGAR
1	TABLESPOON DIJON MUSTARD
1	TABLESPOON FRESH LIME JUICE
1	TABLESPOON DARK CHILE POWDER
1	TABLESPOON GRANULATED GARLIC
1	TABLESPOON GRANULATED ONION
	KOSHER SALT AND CRACKED BLACK PEPPER TO TASTE

Mix all the ingredients except salt and pepper together. Season to taste. This dressing will last covered in the refrigerator for one week.

Blue Cheese Vinaigrette

yields 2 cups

½ CUP EXTRA-VIRGIN OLIVE OIL

½ CUP CRUMBLED MAYTAG FARMS BLUE CHEESE*

¼ CUP SHERRY VINEGAR

¼ CUP FINELY DICED YELLOW ONION

2 TABLESPOONS MINCED GARLIC

2 TABLESPOONS FINELY CHOPPED CHIVES

2 TABLESPOONS FRESH LIME JUICE

2 TABLESPOONS CRACKED BLACK PEPPER

KOSHER SALT TO TASTE

Mix all the ingredients except salt together. Season to taste. This dressing will last covered in the refrigerator for one week.

Maytag Farms, in Newton, Iowa, produces one of the finest blue cheeses in the United States. For more information, call (515) 792-1133.

Sun-Dried Tomato Vinaigrette

yields 2 cups

½ CUP SEASONED RICE VINEGAR

¼ CUP CHOPPED SUN-DRIED TOMATO

2 TABLESPOONS TOMATO JUICE

2 TABLESPOONS MINCED GARLIC

2 TABLESPOONS FINELY CHOPPED SHALLOT

2 TABLESPOONS CHOPPED CILANTRO

½ CUP EXTRA-VIRGIN OLIVE OIL

KOSHER SALT AND
CRACKED BLACK PEPPER TO TASTE

Puree all the ingredients except the olive oil, salt, and pepper in a blender. Reduce the blender speed and slowly add the olive oil until the dressing becomes smooth. Season to taste, cover the dressing, and refrigerate. The dressing will last for a week.

Lemonade Vinaigrette

yields 2 cups

¾	CUP EXTRA-VIRGIN OLIVE OIL
½	CUP FRESH LEMONADE
¼	CUP FRESH LEMON JUICE
2	TABLESPOONS CRUSHED RED CHILE FLAKES
2	TABLESPOONS MINCED LEMON ZEST
2	TABLESPOONS CHOPPED CILANTRO
2	TABLESPOONS FINELY DICED SHALLOT
1	TABLESPOON CHOPPED PARSLEY
	KOSHER SALT AND CRACKED BLACK PEPPER TO TASTE

Mix all the ingredients except salt and pepper together. Season to taste. Cover and refrigerate. The flavors will fade away after three days.

Green Chile Buttermilk Dressing

yields 2 cups

¾	CUP MAYONNAISE
½	CUP BUTTERMILK
¼	CUP ROASTED, PEELED, SEEDED, AND PUREED POBLANO CHILE
2	TABLESPOONS CHOPPED CILANTRO
2	TABLESPOONS FINELY CUT GREEN ONION
2	TABLESPOONS FRESH LIME JUICE
1	TABLESPOON GRANULATED GARLIC
1	TABLESPOON GRANULATED ONION
1	TEASPOON DARK CHILE POWDER
	KOSHER SALT AND CRACKED BLACK PEPPER TO TASTE

Mix all the ingredients except salt and pepper together. Season to taste. Cover and refrigerate for up to a week.

Tomato and
Roasted Garlic Dressing

yields 2 cups

¾	CUP EXTRA-VIRGIN OLIVE OIL
¼	CUP COARSELY CUT AND ROASTED GARLIC CLOVES
¼	CUP COARSELY CUT AND SEEDED TOMATO MEAT
¼	CUP BALSAMIC VINEGAR
2	TABLESPOONS CHOPPED CHIVES
2	TABLESPOONS CHOPPED CELERY LEAVES
2	TABLESPOONS MINCED GARLIC
	KOSHER SALT AND CRACKED BLACK PEPPER TO TASTE

Mix all the ingredients except salt and pepper together. Season to taste. Cover and refrigerate for up to three days before the celery leaves fade in flavor.

Red Chile Adobo Sauce

serves 4

1	TABLESPOON CORN OIL
2	TABLESPOONS FINELY DICED WHITE ONION
2	TABLESPOONS TOASTED, SEEDED, AND MINCED CHILE ANCHO
¾	CUP CHICKEN BROTH
½	CUP CHOPPED RIPE TOMATOES
2	TABLESPOONS RED WINE VINEGAR
2	TABLESPOONS ACHIOTE PASTE (AVAILABLE IN THE MEXICAN FOODS SECTION)
2	TEASPOONS GRANULATED SUGAR
2	TEASPOONS PICKLING SPICE, TIED IN CHEESECLOTH
	KOSHER SALT AND CRACKED BLACK PEPPER TO TASTE

Heat 1 tablespoon of corn oil in a heavy pan over moderately high heat, and sauté the onion and chiles until tender. Add the remaining ingredients except salt and pepper, and bring to a boil. Boil until sauce has reduced in volume by ⅓, and then remove from the heat. Cool the sauce to room temperature, remove the pickling spice, and puree in a blender. Season to taste.

Barbecue Sauce

1	TABLESPOON CORN OIL
½	CUP DICED YELLOW ONION
2	TABLESPOONS DICED JALAPEÑO
1	TABLESPOON MINCED GARLIC
½	CUP TOMATO KETCHUP
¼	CUP CIDER VINEGAR
¼	CUP DR PEPPER SODA
2	TABLESPOONS MOLASSES
2	TABLESPOONS DIJON MUSTARD
	KOSHER SALT AND CRACKED BLACK PEPPER TO TASTE

Heat the corn oil in a heavy pan over high heat, and sauté the onion, jalapeño, and garlic until tender. Add the other ingredients except salt and pepper, bring to a boil, and boil until sauce has reduced in volume by ⅓. Lower the heat, season to taste, and set aside in a warm place.

Fire-Roasted Red Onion Sauce

serves 4

¾	CUP THICK SLICES OF RED ONION
2	TABLESPOONS CORN OIL
	KOSHER SALT AND CRACKED BLACK PEPPER TO TASTE
½	CUP CHICKEN BROTH
½	CUP CRANBERRY JUICE
¼	CUP COARSELY CUT COOKED BEETS (CANNED BEETS CAN BE USED)
2	TABLESPOONS GRANULATED SUGAR
2	TABLESPOONS MINCED GARLIC
2	TABLESPOONS FINELY CHOPPED SAGE

Rub the red onion slices with the corn oil, and season with salt and pepper. Grill them (with wood, charcoal, or an electric broiler) until they are lightly charred and tender. Place all the ingredients except sage into a heavy pan and bring to a boil. Remove from the heat and cool to room temperature. Puree in a blender and pass through a strainer. Add the sage, season to taste with salt and pepper, and set aside in a warm place.

Chile Guajillo & Lemon Sauce

serves 4

1	TABLESPOON CORN OIL
2	TABLESPOONS FINELY DICED WHITE ONION
2	TABLESPOONS MINCED GARLIC
2	TABLESPOONS FINELY DICED TOMATO
2	TABLESPOONS TOASTED, SEEDED, AND MINCED CHILE GUAJILLO
1	TABLESPOON TOASTED, SEEDED, AND MINCED CHILE ANCHO
2	TABLESPOONS MINCED LEMON ZEST
½	CUP WHITE WINE
1½	CUP FRESH LEMON JUICE
1	TABLESPOON GRANULATED SUGAR
3	CUPS CHICKEN BROTH
	KOSHER SALT AND CRACKED BLACK PEPPER TO TASTE

Heat the corn oil in a heavy pan over moderately high heat, and sauté the onion, garlic, tomato, dried chiles, and lemon zest until they are tender. Add the white wine and boil until the liquid has reduced in volume by ½. Add the lemon juice and sugar, and then reduce in volume by ½. Add the chicken broth and reduce in volume by ¾. Season to taste and set aside in a warm place.

Roasted Corn Sauce

serves 4

1	TEASPOON CORN OIL
2	TABLESPOONS FINELY DICED CELERY
2	TABLESPOONS FINELY DICED WHITE ONION
1	TEASPOON MINCED GARLIC
¼	CUP CHARDONNAY (ANY FULL-BODIED WHITE WINE WILL WORK)
1½	CUPS CHICKEN BROTH
¼	CUP PUREE OF SWEET CORN KERNELS
¼	CUP HEAVY CREAM
¼	CUP SWEET CORN KERNELS
	KOSHER SALT AND CRACKED BLACK PEPPER TO TASTE

Heat the corn oil in a heavy pan over moderately high heat and sauté the celery, onion, and garlic until tender. Add the chardonnay and boil until the sauce has reduced in volume by ½. Add the chicken broth and reduce in volume by ½. Allow it to cool to room temperature, and puree in a blender. Return to the stove top over moderate heat, and add the corn puree and cream. Simmer for 5 minutes. Add the corn kernels and season to taste. Set aside in a warm place.

Green Chile and Mustard Sauce

serves 4

1	TABLESPOON CLARIFIED BUTTER (SEE PAGE 43)
1	TABLESPOON FINELY CHOPPED SHALLOTS
1	TABLESPOON MINCED GARLIC
1	TABLESPOON GREEN PEPPERCORNS
¼	CUP BOURBON
2	TABLESPOONS ROASTED, PEELED, AND PUREED POBLANO CHILE
2	TABLESPOONS DIJON MUSTARD
½	CUP CHICKEN BROTH
¼	CUP VEAL DEMI-GLACE (SEE PAGE 41)
¼	CUP HEAVY CREAM
	KOSHER SALT AND CRACKED BLACK PEPPER TO TASTE

Heat the clarified butter in a heavy pan over moderate heat, and sauté the shallots, garlic, and peppercorns until tender. Deglaze* the pan with the bourbon and boil until sauce has reduced in volume by ½. Add the poblano puree, mustard, chicken broth, and demi-glace and then reduce in volume by ⅓. Add the cream and simmer for 5 minutes. Season to taste and set aside in a warm place.

To deglaze means to use a liquid to release all the food sticking to the inside of the pan.

Wild Mushroom and
Chile Pasilla Sauce

serves 4

1	TABLESPOON CLARIFIED BUTTER (SEE PAGE 43)
1	TABLESPOON MINCED GARLIC
1	TABLESPOON FINELY CHOPPED SHALLOT
1/4	CUP FINELY DICED WHITE ONION
1/4	CUP STEMMED, SEEDED, AND TOASTED CHILE PASILLA
1/4	CUP SLICED GOLDEN CHANTERELLES (OYSTER MUSHROOMS OR BUTTON MUSHROOMS CAN BE SUBSTITUTED)
1/4	CUP SLICED CEPES (SHIITAKE MUSHROOMS CAN BE SUBSTITUTED)
1/4	CUP DARK BEER
3/4	CUP CHICKEN BROTH
1/2	CUP VEAL DEMI-GLACE (SEE PAGE 41)
	KOSHER SALT AND CRACKED BLACK PEPPER TO TASTE
1	TABLESPOON UNSALTED BUTTER

Heat the clarified butter in a heavy pan over high heat, and sauté the garlic, shallots, onion, chile pasilla, and mushrooms until they are tender. Add the beer and boil until sauce has reduced in volume by ½. Add the chicken broth and demi-glace, and then reduce in volume by ⅓. Season to taste and set aside in a warm place. Whisk in the butter immediately before serving.

SOUPS & STEWS

Roasted Carrot Soup
with Cilantro, Tofu, and Pepitas

serves 4

In a heavy pot, combine all the purees with the chicken broth, ground cumin, jalapeño, and garlic. Bring to a soft boil, and then allow the mixture to simmer for ½ hour. Season to taste. Toss the toasted pumpkin seeds, the tofu cubes, and the rough-cut cilantro leaves together. For each serving, ladle the soup into a soup bowl or crock, and then spoon the tofu and pumpkin seed mixture in a small, off-center mound in the soup. Top with a cilantro sprig and serve.

1¼	CUPS ROASTED CARROT PUREE
¼	CUP ROASTED ONION PUREE
¼	CUP ROASTED RED BELL PEPPER STRIPS, PUREED
1½	CUPS CHICKEN BROTH
1	TEASPOON TOASTED AND GROUND CUMIN SEED
1	TABLESPOON FINELY CHOPPED JALAPEÑO
1	TABLESPOON FINELY CHOPPED GARLIC
	KOSHER SALT AND CRACKED BLACK PEPPER TO TASTE
¼	CUP TOASTED PUMPKIN SEEDS (PEPITAS)
¼	CUP TOFU CUBES
¼	CUP ROUGH-CUT CILANTRO LEAVES
4	CILANTRO SPRIGS

Corn Stew
with Crabmeat, Mussels, and Grilled Shrimp

serves 4

2	TABLESPOONS LARD (VEGETABLE SHORTENING CAN BE SUBSTITUTED)
½	CUP DICED WHITE ONION
¼	CUP DICED RED BELL PEPPER
¼	CUP DICED GREEN BELL PEPPER
¼	CUP DICED POBLANO CHILE
2	TABLESPOONS MINCED GARLIC
½	CUP DICED RUSSET POTATOES
2	CUPS FRESH SWEET CORN KERNELS (DRAINED CANNED CORN CAN BE SUBSTITUTED)
1	QUART WATER
2	TABLESPOONS TOMATO PASTE
12	SCRUBBED MUSSELS
	KOSHER SALT AND CRACKED BLACK PEPPER TO TASTE
¼	CUP GRANULATED SUGAR
¼	CUP DARK CHILE POWDER
2	TABLESPOONS KOSHER SALT
8	PEELED AND DEVEINED U-15 JUMBO SHRIMP (U-15 IS A SIZE DESIGNATION; IT REFERS TO THE NUMBER OF SHRIMP IN A POUND, AND IN THIS CASE IT MEANS THERE ARE LESS THAN 15 SHRIMP IN A POUND.)
1	CUP CLEANED LUMP CRABMEAT
¼	CUP CHOPPED CHIVES

In a heavy pot, heat the lard over high heat until hot. Sauté the onion, peppers, poblano chile, and garlic until they are just tender. Add the potatoes, corn kernels, and water and then simmer for 10 minutes. Add the tomato paste and the mussels, and then simmer for another 20 minutes. Season to taste. Mix the granulated sugar, dark chile powder, and salt together, and then rub the shrimp with this mixture. Grill the shrimp for 2 minutes on each side. Finish the stew by adding the crabmeat and the chives. Ladle the stew into four large soup bowls, arrange the shrimp on top of the stew, and serve.

Sweet Corn and Rock Shrimp Chowder
with Apple Fritters

serves 4

1	TABLESPOON CORN OIL
2	CUPS + ¾ CUP FRESH SWEET CORN KERNELS (DRAINED CANNED CORN CAN BE SUBSTITUTED)
1	CUP DICED WHITE ONION
1½	CUPS CHOPPED LEEK WHITES
3	TABLESPOONS MINCED GARLIC
½	CUP WHITE WINE
2	CUPS CHICKEN BROTH
1	TABLESPOON DARK CHILE POWDER
3	CUPS HEAVY CREAM
2	CUPS FRESH SWEET CORN PUREE
1	CUP CLEANED AND UNCOOKED ROCK SHRIMP
	KOSHER SALT AND CRACKED BLACK PEPPER TO TASTE
1½	CUPS ALL PURPOSE FLOUR
1	TEASPOON KOSHER SALT
2	TEASPOONS BAKING POWDER
¾	CUP APPLESAUCE
¼	CUP MILK
1	EGG
1	CUP DICED GOLDEN DELICIOUS APPLE
¼	CUP DICED RED BELL PEPPER
2	CUPS VEGETABLE SHORTENING (TO FRY THE FRITTERS)
¼	CUP FINE BIAS-CUT GREEN ONION

In a heavy pot, heat the corn oil over high heat and sauté the 2 cups of corn kernels, diced onion, leek whites, and garlic until just tender. Deglaze* the pot with the white wine, and then add the chicken broth and chile powder. Bring to a boil and cook until it has reduced in volume by ¼. Reduce the heat to a simmer and add the cream, corn puree, and rock shrimp. Allow the chowder to simmer for approximately 20 minutes. Season to taste and set aside in a warm place. To make the fritters, mix the flour, salt, and baking powder together. Then add the apple-sauce, milk, and egg to the dry ingredients; mix until there are no lumps. Fold the diced apples, the diced red bell pepper, and ¾ cup of sweet corn kernels into the batter. Heat the shortening to 350°. When making the fritters, use two table-spoons, one to scoop the batter and the other to slide the batter off the first spoon into the hot shortening. Fry each fritter until it floats on the surface and becomes golden brown. When each fritter is done, carefully remove it from the oil and place it on paper towels, to absorb any excess oil. This should make about twelve fritters. For each serving, ladle the chowder into a soup bowl and place two of the fritters in the center of the chowder (you should have a few extra fritters). Sprinkle the bias-cut green onions over the top and serve.

*To deglaze means to use a liquid to release all the food sticking to the inside of the pan.

71

A Clear Chowder of Roasted Corn and Leeks

with Lump Crab Cake

serves 4

½	GALLON CHICKEN BROTH
4	ROASTED AND SHUCKED EARS OF CORN, KERNELS REMOVED FOR GARNISH*
1	CUP ROASTED AND CHOPPED LEEK
½	CUP ROASTED, PEELED, AND CHOPPED POBLANO CHILE
2	TABLESPOONS MINCED GARLIC
	KOSHER SALT AND CRACKED BLACK PEPPER TO TASTE
2	TABLESPOONS MAYONNAISE
1	TABLESPOON FINELY CHOPPED GREEN ONION
1	TEASPOON FINELY CHOPPED JALAPEÑO
1	CUP CLEANED LUMP CRABMEAT
1	BEATEN EGG
½	CUP BREADCRUMBS
2	TABLESPOONS CLARIFIED BUTTER (SEE PAGE 43)
1	CUP BLANCHED** GLASS NOODLES (ANGEL HAIR PASTA CAN BE SUBSTITUTED)
1	CUP CORN KERNELS (FROM ROASTED EARS OF CORN, ABOVE)
½	CUP DICED, ROASTED RED BELL PEPPER
½	CUP DICED AVOCADO
¼	CUP CHIPOTLE MAYONNAISE (SEE PAGE 53)

In a heavy pot, bring the chicken broth, cleaned ears of corn, chopped leek, chopped poblano chile, and garlic to a boil. Boil until it has reduced in volume by ½, and then remove the corncobs and season to taste. Keep the chowder over low heat.

Ⓡ Mix the mayonnaise with the green onion and jalapeño, and then fold in the crabmeat. Season to taste with salt and pepper. Form the crabmeat mixture into four small patties and place in the freezer just long enough to firm them up. Dip the cakes in the beaten egg, and then dust with the breadcrumbs. Ⓡ Bring the chowder up to a light boil. Heat 1 tablespoon of the clarified butter in a heavy nonstick skillet over moderately high heat and sauté the crab cakes, all at once, until golden brown. Place the crab cakes on a paper towel to absorb any excess oil. Wipe out the nonstick skillet, and heat the other tablespoon of clarified butter over high heat; then sauté the noodles, corn kernels, and diced red bell pepper together. For each serving, spoon the noodle mixture into a small mound in the center of a shallow wide-rimmed soup bowl. Sprinkle the diced avocado around the mound. Place a crab cake on the mound of noodles and then top with a small dollop of the Chipotle Mayonnaise. Ladle the chowder around the perimeter of the noodles, vegetables, and crab cake.

NOTE: *If you are able to find baby leeks or baby corn shoots, they would make an excellent garnish for this soup.*

Remove the husks and roast the ears of corn in a moderately hot oven for 5 minutes.

**To blanch, boil in salted water until just tender. Drain, and ice to stop the cooking.*

Green Chile Stew

serves 4

Heat a heavy pot over moderately high heat, and render* the bacon. Add the diced carrots, onion, and garlic, and then sauté until just tender. Add the poblano chile puree, chicken broth, dried New Mexico chiles, and hominy, and bring to a boil. Reduce the heat and simmer for 30 minutes; then season to taste. For each serving, ladle into a soup bowl, or crock, and top with the grated Monterey Jack cheese. Lightly brown the cheese under your broiler and serve with warm flour tortillas.

1	CUP DICED, RAW HICKORY-SMOKED BACON
¼	CUP DICED CARROT
¼	CUP DICED WHITE ONION
2	TABLESPOONS MINCED GARLIC
1½	CUPS ROASTED, PEELED, AND SEEDED POBLANO CHILE PUREE
2	CUPS CHICKEN BROTH
2	TABLESPOONS MINCED, DRIED NEW MEXICO GREEN CHILES (OPTIONAL)
¼	CUP COOKED YELLOW HOMINY (CANNED VARIETIES ARE WIDELY AVAILABLE)
¼	CUP COOKED WHITE HOMINY (CANNED VARIETIES ARE WIDELY AVAILABLE)
	KOSHER SALT AND CRACKED BLACK PEPPER TO TASTE
½	CUP GRATED MONTEREY JACK CHEESE
4	(6-INCH) FLOUR TORTILLAS

*To render means to cook the fat until it is crisp or to melt the fat.

Lobster and Roasted Corn Chili

with Cream Cheese—Green Onion Quesadilla

serves 4

2	TABLESPOONS FINELY BIAS-CUT GREEN ONION
1½	TEASPOONS CHOPPED CHIPOTLE CHILE IN ADOBO SAUCE
¼	CUP CREAM CHEESE
4	(4-INCH) FLOUR TORTILLAS
2	TABLESPOONS CORN OIL
½	CUP ROASTED AND CHOPPED YELLOW ONION
½	CUP ROASTED CORN KERNELS
½	CUP TOASTED, SEEDED, AND PUREED CHILE ANCHO
2	CUPS CHICKEN BROTH
¼	CUP COOKED BLACK BEANS
2	TABLESPOONS DRY WHITE VERMOUTH
2	TABLESPOONS ORANGE ZEST
2	TABLESPOONS BROWN SUGAR
2	TABLESPOONS ORANGE JUICE CONCENTRATE
2	CUPS CUBED LOBSTER TAIL MEAT (UNCOOKED)
	KOSHER SALT AND CRACKED BLACK PEPPER TO TASTE

To prepare the quesadillas, mix the green onion and ½ teaspoon of the chopped chipotle chile in adobo sauce with the cream cheese. Spread this mixture on top of the flour tortillas and fold each in half, with the cream cheese sides together. Cover with plastic wrap (you may put these all on one plate and cover the plate with plastic wrap, as long as you don't stack them) and chill in the refrigerator for at least 1 hour. To make the lobster chili, heat a heavy pot with the corn oil over moderately high heat. Sauté the roasted onion and the corn kernels until just tender. Add the chile ancho puree and the chicken broth, and bring to a light boil. Now add the black beans, vermouth, orange zest, brown sugar, and orange juice concentrate. Reduce the heat to simmer and cook until liquid has reduced in volume by ⅓. Add the lobster meat and the teaspoon of the chipotle chile, and then season to taste. Heat a griddle, or nonstick skillet, over moderately high heat and lightly brown the quesadillas on both sides. Ladle the lobster chili into four large soup bowls, or crocks. Cut each quesadilla in half; place on the chili and against the rim of the bowl and serve.

Pan-Roasted Mussels
with Red Curry, White Wine, and Smoked Bacon

serves 4

1	CUP DICED, RAW HICKORY-SMOKED BACON
½	CUP LEEK WHITES
½	CUP CHOPPED FENNEL
1	CUP SLICED BUTTON MUSHROOMS
2	TABLESPOONS MINCED GARLIC
1	CUP DRY WHITE WINE
1	CUP COARSELY CHOPPED RIPE PLUM TOMATOES
2	TABLESPOONS RED CURRY PASTE (AVAILABLE IN ASIAN FOOD MARKETS)
64	FRESHLY SCRUBBED, CLOSED MUSSELS (WITH THE "BEARDS" REMOVED)
4	CUPS CHICKEN BROTH
½	CUP CHOPPED FRESH MINT
2	TABLESPOONS WHOLE UNSALTED BUTTER
	KOSHER SALT AND CRACKED BLACK PEPPER TO TASTE

Render (cook until the fat is beginning to crisp) the bacon in a heavy pot over moderately high heat. Add the leeks, fennel, mushrooms, and garlic, and cook until just tender. Deglaze* the pot with the white wine and then add the tomatoes and red curry paste. Add the mussels and chicken broth, and then cover the pot and shake it occasionally, until all the mussels have opened. Discard any unopened mussels. Finish the stew by stirring in the chopped fresh mint and whole butter. Season to taste and serve immediately by spooning the mussels into four large soup bowls and then ladling the broth and vegetables over the mussels.

NOTE: This dish tastes even better with warm, crusty bread.

*To deglaze means to use a liquid to release all the food sticking to the inside of the pan.

Barbecued Onion Soup
with Jalapeño Jack Cheese

serves 4

2	TABLESPOONS CORN OIL
1	CUP (½-INCH-THICK) SLICES OF SMOKE-ROASTED YELLOW ONION*
1	CUP (½-INCH-THICK) SLICES OF SMOKE-ROASTED WHITE ONION*
1	CUP SMOKED AND CHOPPED LEEK WHITES*
¼	CUP CHOPPED SHALLOT
¼	CUP ROASTED AND CHOPPED GARLIC
1	TABLESPOON DARK CHILE POWDER
2	TABLESPOONS BROWN SUGAR
2	TABLESPOONS BARBECUE SAUCE (SEE PAGE 59)
4	CUPS CHICKEN BROTH
	KOSHER SALT AND CRACKED BLACK PEPPER TO TASTE
1	CUP FINELY BIAS-CUT GREEN ONION
4	ROUND, TOASTED SOURDOUGH CROUTONS**
4	(¼-INCH-THICK) SLICES OF JALAPEÑO JACK CHEESE

Heat the corn oil in a heavy pot over moderately high heat, and sauté the onions, leeks, shallot, and garlic until golden brown. Then add the chile powder, brown sugar, and Barbecue Sauce. Add the chicken broth and simmer until the soup has reduced in volume by ⅓. Season to taste and finish by stirring in the bias-cut green onions. For each serving, ladle the soup into a crock, float a toasted crouton on the soup, and top it with a slice of jalapeño Jack cheese. Lightly brown the cheese under a broiler and serve immediately.

Some thoughts about techniques and preparations for smoke-roasting and smoking foods can be found on page 34.

** *To make round croutons, cut sliced sourdough bread with the open end of a glass (approximately 3 inches in diamater). Then toast.*

Doug's Posole

serves 4

2	TABLESPOONS CORN OIL
2	CUPS PORK LOIN, CUT IN THIN STRIPS (2 INCHES LONG X ¼ INCH THICK X ½ INCH WIDE)
	KOSHER SALT AND CRACKED BLACK PEPPER TO TASTE
½	CUP JULIENNE OF RED BELL PEPPER
½	CUP JULIENNE OF POBLANO CHILE
½	CUP JULIENNE OF WHITE ONION
2	TABLESPOONS MINCED GARLIC
2	TABLESPOONS SEEDED AND MINCED CHILE ARBOL
2	TABLESPOONS SEEDED AND MINCED CHILE ANCHO
8	CUPS CHICKEN BROTH
1	CUP COOKED AND DRAINED YELLOW HOMINY (CANNED VARIETY IS WIDELY AVAILABLE)
¼	CUP COARSELY CUT RIPE TOMATOES
2	TABLESPOONS MEXICAN OREGANO
2	TABLESPOONS CHOPPED CILANTRO
1	TABLESPOON TOASTED AND GROUND CUMIN SEED
½	CUP CRUMBLED QUESO FRESCO (WHITE COW'S MILK FARMER'S CHEESE)
½	CUP CILANTRO SPRIGS
½	CUP FINE CHIFFONADE* OF GREEN CABBAGE
1	LIME, CUT IN QUARTERS

Heat the corn oil in a heavy pot over high heat. Season the pork with the salt and pepper, and then brown the meat until it just begins to stick to the pot. Add the red bell pepper, poblano chile, onion, garlic, chile arbol, and chile ancho. Then sauté until just tender. Add the chicken broth, hominy, tomatoes, oregano, chopped cilantro, and cumin; then simmer for 1½ to 2 hours. Season to taste with salt and pepper. For each serving, ladle the posole into a large soup bowl and sprinkle the queso fresco on top. Set a mound of cilantro sprigs and cabbage in the center. Squeeze a lime wedge over the soup and serve hot.

A chiffonade is a very fine julienne cut of a leaf vegetable.

Rustic Chowder of
Red Snapper and Salt Cod
with New Potatoes, Leek, and Oregano

serves 4

¼	CUP DICED, RAW HICKORY-SMOKED BACON
½	CUP DICED LEEK WHITES
¼	CUP DICED WHITE ONION
¼	CUP DICED CARROT
¼	CUP DICED CELERY
1	CUP DICED NEW POTATOES
¼	CUP SEEDED AND DICED POBLANO CHILE
2	TABLESPOONS MINCED GARLIC
2	CUPS CHICKEN BROTH
1	CUP FISH STOCK (SEE PAGE 43)
2	CUPS V-8 JUICE
½	CUP DICED SALT COD
	KOSHER SALT AND CRACKED BLACK PEPPER TO TASTE
½	CUP COARSELY CHOPPED TOMATO
¼	CUP COARSELY CUT FRESH OREGANO
2	TABLESPOONS CORN OIL
4	(2-OUNCE) BONELESS RED SNAPPER FILETS

Render the bacon (cook until the fat is beginning to crisp) in a heavy pot over high heat. Add the leek, onion, carrot, celery, potatoes, poblano chile, and garlic; then sauté until just tender. Add the chicken broth, Fish Stock, V-8 juice, and salt cod and bring to a boil. Reduce the heat and allow the chowder to simmer for about 1 hour. Cook until the chowder has reduced in volume by ⅓. Season to taste, but be careful when adding salt to the chowder because of the salt content of the bacon and the salt cod. Finish the chowder by stirring in the chopped tomato and oregano, and then set aside in a warm place. Heat the corn oil in a skillet over moderately high heat and season the red snapper filets with salt and pepper (again, be careful with the amount of salt used). Sauté the red snapper filets for 90 seconds on each side. For each serving, ladle the chowder into a large soup bowl, trying to keep enough of the vegetables in the center of the bowl so that you are able to place a sautéed red snapper filet in the center of the chowder. Serve immediately.

Tortilla Soup
with Roasted Chicken and Avocado Relish

serves 4

Heat the corn oil in a heavy pot over high heat and sauté the onion, chile ancho, poblano chile, tomato, jalapeño, and garlic until just tender. Add the chicken broth and bring to a boil, cooking until the soup has reduced in volume by ¼. Add the toasted corn tortilla pieces and the chopped cilantro, and then season to taste. Reduce the heat and simmer for ½ hour. Puree the soup with a hand-held blender (when using a blender to puree, make sure you do not seal the blender airtight with a hot liquid in it while blending, or it might "explode," causing burns and, most certainly, a mess). Add the chicken to the soup and bring to a boil; then lower the heat to a simmer. For each serving, ladle the soup into a large soup bowl, or crock, and lay some strips of fried (or baked) tortilla across the soup. Spoon some diced avocado into the center of the soup and lay a cilantro sprig across the tortilla strips. Sprinkle dried Jack cheese over the soup, squeeze a lime wedge over it, and serve.

2	TABLESPOONS CORN OIL
½	CUP DICED WHITE ONION
¼	CUP TOASTED, SEEDED, AND MINCED CHILE ANCHO
¼	CUP DICED POBLANO CHILE
½	CUP COARSELY CHOPPED TOMATO
2	TABLESPOONS FINELY DICED JALAPEÑO
2	TABLESPOONS MINCED GARLIC
3	CUPS CHICKEN BROTH
1	CUP COARSE-CUT AND TOASTED CORN TORTILLAS, BROKEN INTO CHIP-SIZE PIECES
¼	CUP CHOPPED CILANTRO
	KOSHER SALT AND CRACKED BLACK PEPPER TO TASTE
1	CUP ROASTED AND SHREDDED CHICKEN MEAT*
2	(6-INCH) FLOUR TORTILLAS CUT IN LONG, THIN STRIPS AND FRIED (OR BAKED)
½	CUP DICED AVOCADO
4	CILANTRO SPRIGS
¼	CUP GRATED, DRIED MONTEREY JACK CHEESE (ANY HARD CHEESE, YELLOW OR WHITE, CAN BE SUBSTITUTED)
1	LIME, CUT INTO 4 WEDGES

Split the chicken and season with salt and pepper. Roast in a 400° oven for 25 to 30 minutes. Allow to cool and pull the meat from the bones.

Chilled Watermelon Soup
with Pineapple and Habanero Salsa

serves 4

¼	CUP RASPBERRY VINEGAR
¼	CUP GRANULATED SUGAR
1	CUP SEEDED, CHOPPED WATERMELON MEAT
1	CUP PEELED, SEEDED, AND CHOPPED CUCUMBER
¼	CUP PEELED, SEEDED, AND CHOPPED PAPAYA
¼	CUP PEELED, CORED, AND CHOPPED PINEAPPLE
2	TABLESPOONS CHOPPED MINT
2	TABLESPOONS CHOPPED CILANTRO
2	TABLESPOONS CHOPPED CHIVES
½	TEASPOON MINCED HABANERO CHILE*
2	TABLESPOONS GRILLED AND CHOPPED PINEAPPLE (GRILL OVER HIGH HEAT UNTIL GOLDEN BROWN)
2	TABLESPOONS GRILLED AND CHOPPED PAPAYA (GRILL OVER HIGH HEAT UNTIL GRILL MARKS ARE WELL DEFINED)
4	THINLY SLICED WATERMELON WEDGES
4	MINT SPRIGS
8	WHOLE CHIVES

Bring the raspberry vinegar to a boil and dissolve the sugar in it; then allow to cool to room temperature. Puree the watermelon, cucumber, papaya, and pineapple in a blender while slowly adding the raspberry vinegar and sugar mixture. Stir in the chopped mint, cilantro, and chives. Chill the soup in the refrigerator for at least 1 hour before serving. Mix the habanero chile, grilled pineapple, and grilled papaya together. Set aside in a cool place. For each serving, ladle the soup into a chilled martini glass. Garnish the soup by placing a thinly sliced watermelon wedge at an angle on the rim of the glass. Spoon the habanero-pineapple salsa onto the watermelon wedge next to the rim of the glass. Set a mint sprig and two whole chives into the salsa. Serve the glass by itself or on a plate with a folded napkin.

Please use care when handling habanero chiles—rubber gloves are a good call.

Rock Shrimp Gazpacho
with Cucumber Salsa and Watercress

serves 4

Preheat your oven to 350°. Toss the tomatoes, coarsely chopped cucumber, garlic, and coarsely chopped jalapeño in the ¼ cup of olive oil and roast in the oven for 10 minutes. Remove and let cool for 15 minutes. Pass the roasted vegetables through a food mill* to puree them. Season to taste and chill in the refrigerator for at least 1 hour before serving. Cook the rock shrimp in boiling, salted water for 30 seconds. Drain and ice the shrimp to stop the cooking process, but do not allow to sit in water. Mix the finely diced cucumber, minced jalapeño, chives, and lime juice together and set the cucumber salsa aside in a cool place. For each serving, ladle the gazpacho into a wide-rimmed soup bowl and arrange the watercress like a nest in the center of the bowl. Place the rock shrimp on the watercress and spoon the cucumber salsa on top of the shrimp. Top the salsa with a chervil sprig; then drizzle ¼ of the remaining 2 tablespoons of extra-virgin olive oil on top of the soup and serve.

2	POUNDS RIPE TOMATOES, CUT IN EIGHTHS
1	CUP COARSELY CHOPPED, PEELED CUCUMBER
½	CUP COARSELY CHOPPED GARLIC
¼	CUP COARSELY CHOPPED JALAPEÑO
¼	CUP + 2 TABLESPOONS EXTRA-VIRGIN OLIVE OIL
	KOSHER SALT AND CRACKED BLACK PEPPER TO TASTE
½	CUP PEELED, SEEDED, AND FINELY DICED CUCUMBER
1	TABLESPOON MINCED JALAPEÑO
2	TABLESPOONS FINELY CHOPPED CHIVES
1	TABLESPOON FRESH LIME JUICE
1	CUP WASHED, LARGE WATERCRESS SPRIGS
1	CUP CLEANED AND COOKED ROCK SHRIMP
4	CHERVIL SPRIGS

A food mill is a metal strainer with a paddle that turns by hand. The paddle purees the food by forcing it through the strainer. If you don't have a food mill, use a coarse strainer and force the food through with a rubber spatula. By using a food mill, you will retain the color of the tomatoes and achieve the proper texture; if you use a blender or food processor, you will lose the rich red color, and the texture will not be as full.

Yellow Tomato Gazpacho
with Smoked Scallop Salsa

serves 4

2	POUNDS RIPE YELLOW TOMATOES, CUT IN EIGHTHS
1	CUP COARSELY CHOPPED, PEELED CUCUMBER
½	CUP COARSELY CHOPPED GARLIC
2	TABLESPOONS COARSELY CHOPPED JALAPEÑO
¼	CUP EXTRA-VIRGIN OLIVE OIL
	KOSHER SALT AND CRACKED BLACK PEPPER TO TASTE
¾	CUP SMOKED AND DICED SCALLOPS*
2	TABLESPOONS DICED PLUM TOMATOES
1	TABLESPOON CHOPPED CILANTRO
2	TABLESPOONS FRESH LIME JUICE
1	TEASPOON FINELY DICED JALAPEÑO
1	CUP WASHED ARUGULA

Preheat your oven to 350°. Toss the yellow tomatoes, cucumber, garlic, and coarsely chopped jalapeño in the olive oil, and roast in the oven for 10 minutes. Remove the vegetables from the oven and allow them to cool for 15 minutes; then pass them through a food mill** to puree. Season to taste and chill in the refrigerator for at least 1 hour before serving. Toss the smoked scallops, plum tomatoes, chopped cilantro, lime juice, and finely diced jalapeño together, and then season to taste with salt and pepper. Set aside in the refrigerator. For each serving, ladle the gazpacho into a chilled margarita glass or a soup bowl, and place the arugula toward the rear of the glass, resting against the rim. Spoon the smoked scallop salsa against the arugula and serve.

*See page 34 for some thoughts about smoking food.

**By using a food mill, you will retain the color of the tomatoes and achieve the proper texture; if you use a blender or food processor, you will lose the rich yellow color, and the texture will not be as full. (See recipe for Rock Shrimp Gazpacho with Cucumber Salsa and Watercress, on page 84.)

SALADS

Organic Arugula in "Cowboy" Flat Bread
with Spiced Lemon Vinaigrette

serves 4

1⅔ CUPS ALL PURPOSE FLOUR

½ CUP YELLOW CORNMEAL

½ TEASPOON BAKING SODA

½ TEASPOON SUGAR

½ TEASPOON KOSHER SALT

½ TEASPOON GROUND BLACK PEPPER

1 TEASPOON CRUSHED RED CHILE FLAKES

1 TEASPOON MINCED GARLIC

1 TEASPOON MINCED ROSEMARY

⅓ CUP GRATED JALAPEÑO JACK CHEESE

⅓ CUP GRATED CHEDDAR CHEESE

½ CUP UNSALTED BUTTER

1½ TABLESPOON WHITE WINE VINEGAR

⅔ CUP COLD WATER

FOOD RELEASE SPRAY (TO GREASE SKILLET)

¼ CUP LEMONADE

¼ CUP FRESH LEMON JUICE

1 TEASPOON MINCED CHILE ARBOL

KOSHER SALT TO TASTE

¼ CUP EXTRA-VIRGIN OLIVE OIL

6 CUPS WASHED ARUGULA

2 TABLESPOONS FINE LEMON ZEST

Mix the flour, cornmeal, baking soda, sugar, ½ teaspoon salt, black pepper, crushed red chile flakes, garlic, and rosemary together in a bowl. Add the cheeses and butter to the flour mixture, and then mix thoroughly until the dough becomes a coarse crumble. Add the vinegar and water, and mix until the dough is slightly sticky. Refrigerate the dough for 1 hour. Preheat your oven to 375°. Then cut the dough into four pieces and form into balls. Roll dough out on a well-floured, hard surface to ¼ inch in thickness. Grease an 8-inch cast-iron skillet with food release spray and lay the rolled out dough in the 8-inch cast iron skillet. Carefully fit the dough into the edges and the sides of the skillet and bake in the oven until golden brown (approximately 12 to 14 minutes). You can bake the dough all at once, using four different skillets, or you can repeat the baking procedure four times, using one skillet. Allow the crust to cool to room temperature and remove from the mold. Mix the lemonade, lemon juice, chile arbol, salt to taste, and olive oil in a bowl. Set aside in a cool place until it cools to room temperature. Toss the arugula in the dressing. Place the "cowboy" flat bread in the center of four plates and fill with the dressed arugula. Top each salad with the lemon zest and serve.

Caesar Salad
with Cornmeal Croutons

serves 4

Bring the chicken broth and milk to a boil. Reduce heat to a simmer and add the finely ground yellow cornmeal. Stir continuously until the mixture is smooth (add a touch more milk for consistency if necessary), approximately 20 minutes. Stir in ½ cup of the Jack cheese. Spread the cornmeal mixture on a nonstick 10-inch roasting pan that has been greased with olive oil, and cool in the refrigerator. When cool, cut the cornmeal mixture into small cubes, about ¾ of an inch in size. To make the dressing, puree the lemon juice, red wine vinegar, anchovy paste, Worcestershire sauce, mustard, and 1 teaspoon salt together. Decrease the blender speed and slowly add 1 cup of olive oil. Finish the dressing with ½ cup of the Jack cheese and season to taste. Set aside in a cool place. Take the remaining 2 cups of Jack

3½	CUPS CHICKEN BROTH
1½	CUPS MILK
2	CUPS FINELY GROUND YELLOW CORNMEAL (POLENTA CAN BE SUBSTITUTED)
3	CUPS GRATED, DRIED MONTEREY JACK CHEESE (PARMESAN CHEESE CAN BE SUBSTITUTED)
	EXTRA-VIRGIN OLIVE OIL (FOR ROASTING PAN)
3	TABLESPOONS FRESH LEMON JUICE
2	TABLESPOONS RED WINE VINEGAR
1	TABLESPOON ANCHOVY PASTE
1	TABLESPOON WORCESTERSHIRE SAUCE
1	TABLESPOON DIJON MUSTARD
1	TEASPOON KOSHER SALT
1	CUP + 2 TABLESPOONS EXTRA-VIRGIN OLIVE OIL
	KOSHER SALT AND CRACKED BLACK PEPPER TO TASTE
6	CUPS CLEANED ROMAINE LEAVES, TORN INTO 1-INCH SQUARE PIECES
4	CUPS WASHED ROMAINE HEART PIECES (SMALL WEDGE OF ROMAINE)

cheese and make four thin, 6-inch-wide discs from the cheese (use just enough cheese to cover the surface) on a nonstick sheet pan (or a silicon mat, available at most cooking supply stores). Bake these in a 300° oven for 4 to 5 minutes, remove from the oven, and allow to cool to room temperature. You now have little cheese crisps for a garnish. (These will be more difficult to make in high-humidity regions of the country than in regions with lower humidity.) Heat the remaining 2 tablespoons of the olive oil in a heavy nonstick skillet over moderately high heat and lightly toast the surface of the cornmeal cubes (toasting should take about 3 to 4 minutes). Toss the romaine leaves in ¾ cup of the dressing. For each serving, place a mound of romaine leaves in the center of a chilled plate. Distribute cornmeal croutons around the salad, and then lean a romaine wedge against the mound of romaine leaves. Drizzle the other ¼ cup of the dressing over the wedge of romaine, top it with the little cheese crisp, and serve.

Chicken Breast Salad on Romaine Leaves
with Margarita Vinaigrette

serves 4

Mix the shredded chicken breast meat, celery, onion, poblano chile, celery leaves, cilantro, chives, egg, pickle relish, and mayonnaise together. Season to taste and chill in the refrigerator for at least an hour before serving. Puree the lime juice, lime zest, sugar, triple sec, and tequila in a blender, and then slowly add the olive oil. Season to taste with salt and pepper, and set aside at room temperature. Toss the romaine leaves in the margarita vinaigrette. For each serving, place leaves in the center of a chilled plate. Spoon the chicken breast salad onto the romaine leaves, sprinkle with cracked pepper, and serve.

2	CUPS GRILLED, SHREDDED CHICKEN BREAST MEAT
¼	CUP FINELY DICED CELERY
¼	CUP FINELY DICED WHITE ONION
2	TABLESPOONS FINELY DICED POBLANO CHILE
2	TABLESPOONS CHOPPED CELERY LEAVES
2	TABLESPOONS CHOPPED CILANTRO
2	TABLESPOONS CHOPPED CHIVES
½	CUP COARSELY GRATED HARD-COOKED EGG*
¼	CUP SWEET PICKLE RELISH
½	CUP MAYONNAISE
	KOSHER SALT AND CRACKED BLACK PEPPER TO TASTE
2	TABLESPOONS FRESH LIME JUICE
1	TEASPOON FINELY CHOPPED LIME ZEST
1	TEASPOON GRANULATED SUGAR
2	TABLESPOONS TRIPLE SEC
2	TABLESPOONS TEQUILA
¼	CUP EXTRA-VIRGIN OLIVE OIL
8	CUPS WASHED ROMAINE LEAVES
1	TEASPOON CRACKED BLACK PEPPER

To cook eggs, boil them for 20 minutes and then chill and peel the shells off.

A Salad of Duck Fajitas, Avocado, and Roasted Peppers

serves 4

Begin by marinating the duck breasts. Mix the dark beer, soy sauce, lime juice, Worcestershire sauce, 2 tablespoons of garlic, jalapeño, and 2 tablespoons of cilantro together; cover the duck breasts with this mixture. Marinate for 4 hours in the refrigerator. To make the vinaigrette, puree the chipotle in adobo sauce, adobo sauce, lemon juice, 1 teaspoon of garlic, shallots, 1 tablespoon of cilantro, and seasoned rice vinegar. Decrease the blender speed and slowly add the corn oil to the puree. Set aside in a cool place. Season the duck breasts and grill them to medium, approximately 3 minutes with the skin side down and 6 minutes on the other side. Then allow to rest for 3 minutes. Toss the mixed young lettuces with the chipotle vinaigrette. For each serving,

2	(8-OUNCE) BONELESS DUCK BREASTS
½	CUP DARK BEER
¼	CUP SOY SAUCE
½	CUP FRESH LIME JUICE
¼	CUP WORCESTERSHIRE SAUCE
2	TABLESPOONS + 1 TEASPOON CHOPPED GARLIC
2	TABLESPOONS CHOPPED JALAPEÑO
3	TABLESPOONS CHOPPED CILANTRO
1	TEASPOON CHIPOTLE CHILES IN ADOBO SAUCE
1	TEASPOON ADOBO SAUCE
2	TABLESPOONS FRESH LEMON JUICE
1	TEASPOON CHOPPED SHALLOTS
½	CUP SEASONED RICE VINEGAR
¾	CUP CORN OIL
	KOSHER SALT AND CRACKED BLACK PEPPER TO TASTE
8	CUPS MIXED YOUNG LETTUCES (MESCLUN)
½	CUP JULIENNE OF ROASTED AND PEELED RED BELL PEPPER
½	CUP JULIENNE OF ROASTED AND PEELED YELLOW BELL PEPPER
½	CUP JULIENNE OF ROASTED AND PEELED GREEN BELL PEPPER
2	AVOCADOS, SLICED
4	(6-INCH) FLOUR TORTILLAS
½	CUP CRUMBLED QUESO FRESCO (WHITE COW'S MILK FARMER'S CHEESE)

place a mound of lettuce on a chilled plate. Evenly distribute roasted peppers and sliced avocado over the top of the salad. Slice the duck breasts lengthwise and arrange some of the slices in a pinwheel on the top of the salad. Heat the tortillas, fold them, and lean one against each salad serving. Sprinkle the crumbled queso fresco over the salads and serve.

Iceberg Lettuce with Blue Cheese and Ranch Dressing

serves 4

To make the dressing, whisk the mayonnaise, buttermilk, sour cream, lemon juice, sugar, granulated onion, granulated garlic, kosher salt, and 1 tablespoon of cracked black pepper together and refrigerate for at least 1 hour before serving. For each serving, arrange the wedges of iceberg lettuce in a pinwheel fashion on a large, chilled plate and place the cilantro sprigs in the center of the pinwheel. Place a plum tomato wedge between each iceberg lettuce wedge. Sprinkle the blue cheese crumbles, the bias-cut green onions, and the red onion julienne over the salad. Dust the rim of the plate with the cracked black pepper and serve. Serve the ranch dressing on the side.

¾	CUP MAYONNAISE
½	CUP BUTTERMILK
¼	CUP SOUR CREAM
2	TABLESPOONS FRESH LEMON JUICE
2	TABLESPOONS GRANULATED SUGAR
1	TABLESPOON GRANULATED ONION
1	TABLESPOON GRANULATED GARLIC
1	TABLESPOON KOSHER SALT
1	TABLESPOON CRACKED BLACK PEPPER
2	CHILLED HEADS OF ICEBERG LETTUCE, CUT IN SIXTHS
1	CUP CILANTRO SPRIGS
2	RIPE PLUM TOMATOES, CUT IN SIXTHS
1	CUP CRUMBLED MAYTAG FARMS BLUE CHEESE*
½	CUP FINE BIAS-CUT GREEN ONION
1½	CUPS FINE JULIENNE OF RED ONION
2	TABLESPOONS CRACKED BLACK PEPPER

Maytag Farms, in Newton, Iowa, produces one of the finest blue cheeses in the United States. For more information, call (515) 792-1133.

Organic Lettuces and Herbs in a Jicama Tortilla
with Sun-Dried Tomato Vinaigrette

serves 4

¼ CUP SEASONED RICE VINEGAR

3 TABLESPOONS CHOPPED SUN-DRIED TOMATOES

2 TABLESPOONS TOMATO JUICE

1 TEASPOON MINCED GARLIC

1 TEASPOON CHOPPED SHALLOT

1 TEASPOON CHOPPED CILANTRO

½ CUP EXTRA-VIRGIN OLIVE OIL

KOSHER SALT AND CRACKED BLACK PEPPER TO TASTE

2 TABLESPOONS COARSELY CHOPPED BASIL

2 TABLESPOONS COARSELY CHOPPED CHIVES

2 TABLESPOONS COARSELY CHOPPED PEPPERCRESS

2 TABLESPOONS COARSELY CHOPPED OREGANO

6 CUPS MIXED YOUNG LETTUCES

4 VERY THIN SLICES OF JICAMA, 6 TO 8 INCHES IN DIAMETER

4 BLANCHED LEEK STRIPS, 9 INCHES LONG*

1 CUP JULIENNE OF TOMATO

¼ CUP TOASTED PINE NUTS

To make the dressing, blend the seasoned rice vinegar, sun-dried tomatoes, tomato juice, garlic, shallots, and cilantro together in a blender. Reduce the blender speed and slowly add the olive oil. Season to taste and set aside in a cool place. Toss the basil, chives, peppercress, oregano, and mixed young lettuces together, and then toss with ¾ of the dressing. Lay the thinly sliced jicama slices flat on a level surface and evenly distribute the lettuce mixture in a row in the middle of each jicama slice. Roll the jicama around the salad mix and secure each with a blanched leek strip. For each serving, lay a filled jicama "burrito" diagonally across a chilled plate and drizzle some of the remaining dressing over the plate. Randomly distribute the tomato julienne and toasted pine nuts around the plate and serve.

To blanch, dip very quickly in boiling, salted water, and then cool quickly with ice water.

Cracked Blue Crab
with Avocado, Arugula, and Radishes

serves 4

2	TABLESPOONS MAYONNAISE
2	TABLESPOONS CREOLE (OR WHOLE-GRAIN) MUSTARD
2	TABLESPOONS VERY FINELY DICED CARROT
2	TABLESPOONS CHOPPED CHIVES
1	TABLESPOON VERY FINELY DICED JALAPEÑO, WITHOUT SEEDS
1	TABLESPOON LEMON JUICE
1	CUP LUMP MEAT OF JUMBO BLUE CRAB (CLEANED BUT NOT SHREDDED)
1	CUP DICED AVOCADO
	KOSHER SALT AND CRACKED BLACK PEPPER TO TASTE
4	CUPS CLEANED ARUGULA
1	CUP SMALL, CURLY ENDIVE
1	CUP RADISH SPROUTS
1	CUP SHAVED RADISHES
1	AVOCADO, SLICED LENGTHWISE
¼	CUP EXTRA-VIRGIN OLIVE OIL

Mix the mayonnaise, mustard, carrots, chives, jalapeño, and lemon juice together. Carefully fold the crabmeat and diced avocado into the mayonnaise mixture and season to taste. Set aside in the refrigerator. Toss the arugula with endive, radish sprouts, and shaved radishes. For each serving, make a mound of the arugula mixture in the center of a chilled plate, and spoon the crabmeat-avocado mixture onto the mound of arugula. Lay the sliced avocado on top of the crabmeat salad. Drizzle olive oil over the arugula salad and serve.

Spinach Leaves with Texas Peanut Dressing
and Fried Sweet Buttermilk Onions

serves 4

To prepare the dressing, heat the peanut butter in a microwave, on high power, for 10 to 15 seconds. Mix the peanut butter, honey, and corn oil together. Add the raspberry vinegar, water, tarragon, and cilantro; then thoroughly mix. Set aside at room temperature. In the refrigerator, soak the white onion julienne in the buttermilk for ½ hour. Preheat the peanut oil to 360° for frying the onions. Mix the kosher salt and the cayenne pepper with the flour. Drain the buttermilk from the onions and toss the onions in the seasoned flour. Fry the onions until golden brown and lay on paper towels to absorb any extra oil. For each serving, place a radicchio "cup" in the upper left quarter of a chilled plate. Toss the spinach leaves and radicchio chiffonade in the peanut butter dressing, and then put some dressed spinach salad into each radicchio cup, with some of the salad coming out of the cup onto the plate. Place the fried onions on the plate next to the salad. Sprinkle bias-cut green onions and raspberries over the plate and serve.

¼	CUP PEANUT BUTTER
¼	CUP HONEY
¼	CUP CORN OIL
¼	CUP RASPBERRY VINEGAR
¼	CUP WATER
1	TABLESPOON CHOPPED TARRAGON
1	TABLESPOON CHOPPED CILANTRO
2	CUPS JULIENNE OF WHITE ONION
1	CUP BUTTERMILK
4	CUPS PEANUT OIL (FOR FRYING)
1	TABLESPOON KOSHER SALT
1	TEASPOON CAYENNE PEPPER
1	CUP ALL PURPOSE FLOUR
4	OUTSIDE CUPLIKE LEAVES FROM A HEAD OF RADICCHIO
6	CUPS WASHED SPINACH LEAVES
1	CUP CHIFFONADE* OF RADICCHIO
1	CUP FINELY BIAS-CUT GREEN ONIONS
1	CUP RASPBERRIES

*A chiffonade is a very fine julienne cut of a leaf vegetable.

Spinach Leaves with Almond-Crusted Goat Cheese
and Red Onion Vinaigrette

serves 4

For the vinaigrette, puree the seasoned rice vinegar, red onion puree, cranberry juice, and beet juice, and then decrease the blender speed and slowly add the corn oil to thicken the dressing. Season to taste and chill in the refrigerator. Gently scrub the pears with a plastic "scrubbie" (pot washer) to remove the peel lines and to give them a smooth appearance. Bring the red wine, port wine, sugar, chile ancho, and chile arbol to a boil, and then reduce the heat so the mixture is at a high simmer. Halve the pears lengthwise and poach them in the red wine and chile mixture until they are just tender; then remove from the liquid and cool to room temperature. Dip the chilled goat cheese slices into the olive oil and then into the finely chopped almonds. Lightly brown both sides of the slices in a nonstick skillet over

¼	CUP SEASONED RICE VINEGAR
¼	CUP PUREE OF ROASTED RED ONION
3	TABLESPOONS CRANBERRY JUICE
3	TABLESPOONS BEET JUICE
¼	CUP CORN OIL
	KOSHER SALT AND CRACKED BLACK PEPPER TO TASTE
2	PEELED AND CORED PEARS (PREFERABLY BARTLETT)
1	CUP RED WINE
1	CUP PORT WINE
¼	CUP GRANULATED SUGAR
2	TORN (CREDIT-CARD-SIZE) PIECES OF TOASTED, SEEDED CHILE ANCHO
2	WHOLE CHILE ARBOL
4	(1½-OUNCE) SLICES OF GOAT CHEESE, CHILLED
¼	CUP OLIVE OIL
½	CUP FINELY CHOPPED ALMONDS
8	CUPS WASHED SPINACH LEAVES
1	CUP BIAS-CUT GREEN ONIONS
½	CUP SLICED ALMONDS

moderate heat. Toss the spinach leaves in the red onion vinaigrette, and for each serving, place some spinach leaves in a mound in the center of a chilled plate. Slice the poached pears twice lengthwise (you are trying to achieve a "fan" effect with the pears, so slice them halfway up, lengthwise, with two cuts). Place them so they are leaning against the bottom right quarter of the salad (each salad should get ½ pear). Sprinkle bias-cut green onions and sliced almonds over the salad, and then top with a slice of the almond-crusted goat cheese and serve.

Grilled Shrimp on a Spinach Leaf Salad
with Mustard Dressing

serves 4

¼	CUP WHOLE-GRAIN MUSTARD
¼	CUP HONEY
¼	CUP SHERRY VINEGAR
2	TABLESPOONS CORN OIL
2	TABLESPOONS WATER
1	TEASPOON FINELY CHOPPED JALAPEÑO
2	TABLESPOONS FRESH LEMON JUICE
	KOSHER SALT AND CRACKED BLACK PEPPER TO TASTE
16	PEELED AND DEVEINED JUMBO SHRIMP
6	CUPS WASHED SPINACH LEAVES
1	CUP ROASTED CORN KERNELS*
1	CUP ROASTED RED ONION RINGS
1	CUP RADISH SPROUTS
2	TABLESPOONS BLACK SESAME SEEDS

To prepare the dressing, mix the whole-grain mustard, honey, sherry vinegar, corn oil, water, jalapeño, and lemon juice together; season to taste. Set aside in a cool place. Season the shrimp with salt and pepper, and then grill them (or broil in your oven) over moderately high heat for 2 minutes on each side. Toss the spinach leaves with the dressing, and for each serving, place some spinach leaves in a mound on a chilled plate. Evenly distribute the corn kernels, red onion rings, radish sprouts, and black sesame seeds over the top of each serving. Place four grilled shrimp on top of each individual salad and serve.

Shuck the corn and roast on a grill until the kernels are lightly browned. Then remove the kernels from the cob.

Grilled Beef Sirloin on Romaine Leaves
with Black Pepper and Tomato Dressing

serves 4

½	CUP EXTRA-VIRGIN OLIVE OIL
¼	CUP SHERRY VINEGAR
2	TABLESPOONS TOMATO JUICE
1	TEASPOON MINCED GARLIC
1	TEASPOON FINELY CHOPPED SHALLOTS
2	TABLESPOONS FRESH CRACKED BLACK PEPPER
2	TABLESPOONS FINELY CHOPPED CHIVES
	KOSHER SALT AND CRACKED BLACK PEPPER TO TASTE
2	(12-OUNCE) SIRLOIN STEAKS
8	CUPS TORN ROMAINE LEAVES
¼	CUP COARSELY CHOPPED TOMATO

To make the dressing, mix the olive oil, sherry vinegar, tomato juice, garlic, shallots, black pepper, and chopped chives. Season to taste and set aside at room temperature. Season the sirloin with salt and pepper and grill to the degree of doneness you prefer (for this salad, I suggest just over medium). Allow the steaks to rest for 3 to 4 minutes. Toss the romaine leaves and chopped tomato in the dressing, and place in a mound in the center of four chilled plates. Remove any gristle or fat, and thinly slice the sirloin across the grain. Arrange the sliced sirloin in a little nest on top of each salad and serve.

SANDWICHES

Achiote Chicken Breast Sandwich
with Indian Grill Bread

serves 4

½	CUP WORCESTERSHIRE SAUCE
¼	CUP SOY SAUCE
2	TABLESPOONS ACHIOTE PASTE (AVAILABLE IN THE MEXICAN FOODS SECTION)
2	TABLESPOONS FRESH LIME JUICE
1	TEASPOON CHOPPED JALAPEÑO
2	TEASPOONS MINCED GARLIC
2	TABLESPOONS CHOPPED CILANTRO
4	(6-OUNCE) BONELESS, SKINLESS CHICKEN BREASTS
1	CUP ALL PURPOSE FLOUR
¼	CUP NONFAT DRY MILK
⅛	TEASPOON BAKING POWDER
½	TEASPOON KOSHER SALT
2	TABLESPOONS LARD (VEGETABLE SHORTENING CAN BE SUBSTITUTED)
½	CUP WATER
	FLOUR (FOR ROLLING OUT DOUGH)
4½	CUPS WATER
1½	CUPS CIDER VINEGAR
1	CUP GRANULATED SUGAR
¼	CUP PICKLING SPICE
1	TEASPOON KOSHER SALT
½	CUP JULIENNE OF CHAYOTE, OR PEAR, SQUASH
½	CUP JULIENNE OF BUTTERNUT SQUASH
¼	CUP JULIENNE OF CARROT
¼	CUP JULIENNE OF POBLANO CHILE
¼	CUP SEASONED RICE VINEGAR
2	TABLESPOONS FRESH LEMON JUICE
1	TABLESPOON ADOBO SAUCE
1	TEASPOON PUREED CHIPOTLE CHILE IN ADOBO SAUCE
1	TEASPOON FINELY CHOPPED SHALLOT
½	CUP CORN OIL
1	CUP WATERCRESS SPRIGS

This sandwich takes a considerable amount of time to prepare, but it is well worth the effort for special lunches or brunches for family and friends.

⬡ Combine the Worcestershire sauce, soy sauce, achiote paste, lime juice, jalapeño, 1 teaspoon of garlic, and 1 tablespoon of chopped cilantro. Mix thoroughly and pour over the chicken breasts. Marinate the chicken in the refrigerator for at least 2 hours but no longer than 4 hours. ⬡ To make the Indian grill bread, mix the flour, nonfat dry milk, baking powder, and ½ teaspoon of salt together. Slowly add the lard and the ½ cup of water, kneading until the dough forms a ball. Cover the dough and allow to rest for 1 hour. Divide the dough into four pieces and roll each out on a lightly floured surface, making four discs that are 6 inches in diameter and ⅛ inch thick. Set aside, with wax paper separating the pieces of grill bread, in the refrigerator. ⬡ To make the vegetable escabeche (esskah-BEECH-ay), begin by bringing the 4½ cups of water, cider vinegar, sugar, pickling spice, and 1 teaspoon of salt to a boil. Cool this brine down to room temperature and add the chayote squash, butternut squash, carrot, and poblano chile. Marinate the vegetables in the refrigerator for 4 hours (you may want to let the vegetables marinate longer, depending on your individual taste). ⬡ To prepare the vinaigrette, puree the seasoned rice vinegar, lemon juice, adobo sauce, chipotle chiles in adobo sauce, remaining 1 tablespoon of cilantro, shallots, and remaining 1 teaspoon of garlic. Reduce the blender speed and slowly add the corn oil until the dressing is smooth. Set aside in the refrigerator. ⬡ Remove the chicken from the marinade and pat dry. Grill each chicken breast for 6 to 8 minutes on one side and 4 to 6 minutes on the other side. Grill the flat bread for 45 seconds on one side, and then turn it over and grill for about 10 to 15 seconds. Place the watercress sprigs on ½ of each slice of grill bread. Slice each chicken breast on the bias for a total of five or six pieces per breast, and lay the slices on the watercress. Drizzle the chipotle vinaigrette over the chicken and watercress. Top the chicken with escabeche (the marinated vegetables), fold the bread over, and cut each sandwich in half. Overlap the two halves on the plate and serve.

Southwestern Corn "Doggie"

serves 4

¼   CUP MASA HARINA
      (CORN FLOUR FOUND IN THE MEXICAN FOODS SECTION)

½   CUP ALL PURPOSE FLOUR

1   CUP YELLOW CORNMEAL

1   TABLESPOON DARK CHILE POWDER

1   TEASPOON KOSHER SALT

1   TEASPOON BAKING POWDER

1   TEASPOON GRANULATED GARLIC

½   TEASPOON CAYENNE PEPPER (OPTIONAL)

2   EGGS

1   CUP MILK

¼   CUP ROASTED, PEELED, AND PUREED POBLANO CHILE

½   CUP DIJON MUSTARD

4   CUPS CORN OIL (FOR FRYING)

4   (¼-POUND) HOT DOGS (YOUR PERSONAL FAVORITE)

4   WOODEN SKEWERS

To make the batter, combine the masa harina, flour, cornmeal, chile powder, salt, baking powder, granulated garlic, and cayenne pepper. Add the eggs and milk to the dry ingredients and mix thoroughly until the batter is smooth. Chill the batter in the refrigerator for 1 hour. Mix the roasted poblano puree with the Dijon mustard to make green chile mustard. Preheat the corn oil to 350° in a heavy pot. Place a hot dog on a wooden skewer, leaving at least 3 inches of the skewer exposed. Dip the hot dog into the batter, and holding the skewer, dip the battered hot dog into the hot oil (be careful!) until the batter begins to brown. Carefully release the skewer and let the hot dog submerge in the oil. Turn the hot dog occasionally with a set of tongs and fry the hot dog for 3 to 4 minutes. Carefully remove the hot dog from the oil and rest it on a paper towel to absorb any excess oil. Repeat with remaining hot dogs. Dip in the green chile mustard and enjoy.

Pastrami with Green Chiles, Chipotle Mayonnaise, and Pepper Jack Cheese

serves 4

1	TABLESPOON PUREED CHIPOTLE CHILES IN ADOBO SAUCE
1	CUP MAYONNAISE
4	(8-INCH) FLOUR TORTILLAS
12	OUNCES THIN-SLICED, PREMIUM-QUALITY PASTRAMI
8	SLICES PEPPER JACK CHEESE
1	CUP CHIFFONADE* OF GREEN CABBAGE
½	CUP VERY THINLY SLICED RED ONION
2	ROASTED, PEELED, AND SEEDED POBLANO CHILES, THINLY SLICED
1	CUP CILANTRO SPRIGS

Mix the chipotle puree with mayonnaise. Lay the tortillas on a flat surface and spread some of the chipotle mayonnaise on one side of each tortilla, reserving about ⅓ of the mayonnaise mixture. Lay the pastrami and the sliced cheese flat on the tortillas. Evenly distribute the chiffonade of cabbage over the pastrami and cheese. Spread a thin layer of the reserved chipotle mayonnaise over the cabbage. Evenly distribute the finely sliced red onion, sliced poblano chiles, and cilantro sprigs over the cheese. Now carefully roll each tortilla into a cylinder shape and rest the loose end of the tortilla on a plate. Microwave each tortilla on high power for about 15 to 20 seconds, cut in half on a bias, and serve.

A chiffonade is a very fine julienne cut of a leaf vegetable.

Grilled Hamburger
with Onion Rings and
Red Bell Pepper Ketchup

serves 4

1	TABLESPOON CORN OIL
2	TABLESPOONS FINELY DICED CARROT
2	TABLESPOONS FINELY DICED YELLOW ONION
1	TABLESPOON MINCED GARLIC
¼	CUP MALT VINEGAR
¼	CUP WATER
1	CUP ROASTED, PEELED, SEEDED, AND PUREED RED BELL PEPPER
1	TABLESPOON MOLASSES
1	TABLESPOON BROWN SUGAR
1	TABLESPOON HONEY
½	TEASPOON CAYENNE PEPPER
1	CUP ALL PURPOSE FLOUR
1	TEASPOON GRANULATED SUGAR
½	TEASPOON KOSHER SALT
½	TEASPOON CRACKED BLACK PEPPER
1	EGG
½	CUP BEER
½	CUP COLD WATER
4	(12-OUNCE) HAMBURGER PATTIES (85% BEEF AND 15% FAT)
	KOSHER SALT AND CRACKED BLACK PEPPER TO TASTE
4	CUPS CORN OIL (FOR FRYING)
20	(½-INCH-THICK) RINGS OF YELLOW ONION
4	LARGE HAMBURGER ROLLS
4	LARGE PIECES OF GREEN LEAF LETTUCE
1	BEEFSTEAK TOMATO, SLICED IN ½-INCH-THICK SLICES

To make the ketchup, heat the 1 tablespoon of corn oil in a heavy pan over moderately high heat and sauté the carrot, diced onion, and garlic until just tender. Add the malt vinegar and the water, and simmer until volume has reduced by ⅓. Add the red bell pepper puree, molasses, brown sugar, honey, and cayenne pepper; then simmer for 15 minutes. Puree and chill in the refrigerator for at least 1 hour. To make the batter for the onion rings, mix the flour, sugar, salt, and black pepper together. Add the egg, beer, and water and mix until smooth. Let the batter rest and chill in the refrigerator for ½ hour. Season the hamburger with salt and pepper and grill to the desired doneness. Heat the corn oil in a heavy pot over high heat to 360° for frying the onion rings. Dip the rings of onion in the batter. Carefully place them in the hot oil by holding them with tongs until they start to brown, and then releasing them, allowing the onion rings to submerge in the oil. Carefully remove the onion rings from the oil and place them on a paper towel to absorb any excess oil. Season with salt and pepper. Toast the hamburger rolls and liberally spread the red bell pepper ketchup on both halves of each roll. Place the hamburger patties on the rolls, and top each with the green leaf lettuce and tomato. Serve the hamburgers with the onion rings.

Roasted Peppers, Avocado, and Portabello Mushroom Sandwich
with Spiced Cream Cheese

serves 4

½	TEASPOON PUREED CHIPOTLE CHILE IN ADOBO SAUCE
½	CUP CREAM CHEESE
8	SLICES OF BUTTERMILK BREAD
1	CUP SLICED AND ROASTED RED ONION
1	CUP SLICED AND GRILLED ZUCCHINI
1	CUP JULIENNE OF ROASTED AND PEELED RED BELL PEPPER
1	CUP JULIENNE OF ROASTED AND PEELED YELLOW BELL PEPPER
1	CUP GRILLED AND SLICED PORTABELLO MUSHROOM
1	AVOCADO, SLICED LENGTHWISE
2	BEEFSTEAK TOMATOES, SLICED ¼ INCH THICK
	KOSHER SALT AND CRACKED BLACK PEPPER TO TASTE

Mix the chipotle chile puree with the cream cheese, and set aside covered at room temperature. Toast the bread and spread the cream cheese mixture on the toast. Layer the roasted red onion, sliced zucchini, julienne of roasted peppers, portabello mushroom, avocado, and sliced tomato on four pieces of toast. Top each sandwich with another slice of toast. Secure each sandwich with two sandwich picks, and then cut in half diagonally and serve.

Hickory-Roasted Rabbit and Cornbread Sandwich
with Rosemary Apple Butter

serves 4

2	CUPS WHITE CORNMEAL
1	TEASPOON KOSHER SALT
½	TEASPOON BAKING SODA
1	TEASPOON BAKING POWDER
1¼	CUPS BUTTERMILK
2	TABLESPOONS MELTED BUTTER
2	EGGS
1	TABLESPOON VEGETABLE SHORTENING
1	CUP PEELED AND DICED GOLDEN DELICIOUS APPLES
¼	CUP DARK BROWN SUGAR
1	TEASPOON GROUND CINNAMON
1	TABLESPOON CHOPPED ROSEMARY LEAVES
1	CUP CHICKEN BROTH
½	CUP APPLE JUICE CONCENTRATE
2	TABLESPOONS WHOLE-GRAIN MUSTARD
1	TABLESPOON FINELY CHOPPED SHALLOT
1	TABLESPOON TOASTED, SEEDED, AND MINCED CHILE ANCHO
2	CUPS HICKORY-ROASTED* AND SHREDDED RABBIT (OR CHICKEN) MEAT
4	ROSEMARY SKEWERS

Preheat the oven to 425° To make the cornbread, sift together the cornmeal, salt, soda, and baking powder. Add the buttermilk and melted butter, and then mix thoroughly. Add the eggs and mix until the batter is smooth. Grease a nonstick 9-inch square pan with the shortening and heat it before adding the batter. Pour the batter into the pan and bake for 20 minutes. Remove from the oven and allow to cool at room temperature for about 30 minutes. When the cornbread is cool, cut into four equal-size squares, and split each square horizontally so that each can be used for a sandwich. Cover with a breathable cloth and set aside at room temperature. ⓡ To make the rosemary apple butter, cook the apples, brown sugar, and cinnamon together for 1 hour, stirring regularly over moderate heat. Pass the cooked apple mixture through a food mill (or you can puree in a food processor, but the food mill keeps the mixture thicker; see Rock Shrimp Gazpacho recipe on page 84). Stir in the chopped rosemary leaves, and chill in the refrigerator for at least 2 hours. ⓡ To finish the rabbit (or chicken), bring the chicken broth, apple juice concentrate, whole-grain mustard, shallots, and chile ancho to a boil; boil until volume has reduced by ½. Reduce the heat and add the shredded rabbit meat to the sauce. Simmer for 10 minutes and set aside in a warm place. ⓡ Very carefully (so you don't break the cornbread) spread the rosemary apple butter on the inside of the split cornbread. Then spoon the rabbit meat on the dressed cornbread. Place the top piece of the cornbread on the sandwich, secure with the rosemary skewer, and serve.

Please see page 34 for some thoughts about techniques and practices of smoke roasting.

Seared Catfish Baked in a White Corn Tortilla
with Red Chile Sauce

serves 4

Mix the 1 cup of corn oil, jalapeño, lemon juice, and oregano together and marinate the catfish filets in this mixture overnight. To make the sauce, sauté the tomatoes, diced white onion, chile ancho, and chile pasilla in a heavy pot over moderately high heat until just tender. Add the chicken broth, red wine vinegar, sugar, achiote paste, and pickling spice; then bring to a boil. Boil until volume has reduced by ⅓, and let cool to room temperature. Carefully puree the mixture in a blender and pass through a strainer using a rubber spatula. Reserve the strained sauce. Season to taste, and set aside at room temperature. Heat the remaining 2 tablespoons of corn oil, and fry the catfish filets for 60 seconds on each side. Lightly brush the tortillas with a small amount of the corn oil, to make the tortillas more pliable. Place a catfish filet in each tortilla, and roll the tortilla around the catfish. With the loose end of the tortilla on the bottom, place in a casserole-type dish. Spoon a small amount of the red chile sauce over each tortilla and bake in a 350° oven for 6 to 7 minutes. Remove the tortillas from the oven and lay two in a crisscross pattern on each plate. Spoon the remaining sauce over the tortillas. Toss the chiffonade of green cabbage, julienne of white onion, cilantro sprigs, and lime juice together. Place this cabbage mixture on the tortillas where they cross over each other. Sprinkle the crumbled queso fresco over the plates and serve.

1	CUP + 2 TABLESPOONS CORN OIL
¼	CUP COARSELY CHOPPED JALAPEÑO
2	TABLESPOONS FRESH LEMON JUICE
2	TABLESPOONS COARSELY CHOPPED MEXICAN OREGANO
8	(3-OUNCE) CATFISH FILETS
½	CUP COARSELY CHOPPED TOMATO
1	TABLESPOON DICED WHITE ONION
1	TEASPOON TOASTED, SEEDED, AND MINCED CHILE ANCHO
1	TEASPOON TOASTED, SEEDED, AND MINCED CHILE PASILLA
½	CUP CHICKEN BROTH
1	TABLESPOON RED WINE VINEGAR
1	TEASPOON SUGAR
1	TEASPOON ACHIOTE PASTE (AVAILABLE IN THE MEXICAN FOODS SECTION)
1	TEASPOON PICKLING SPICE, TIED IN CHEESECLOTH
	KOSHER SALT AND CRACKED BLACK PEPPER TO TASTE
8	(6-INCH) WHITE CORN TORTILLAS
1	CUP FINE CHIFFONADE* OF GREEN CABBAGE
½	CUP VERY FINE JULIENNE OF WHITE ONION
½	CUP CILANTRO SPRIGS
3	TABLESPOONS FRESH LIME JUICE
½	CUP CRUMBLED QUESO FRESCO (WHITE COW'S MILK FARMER'S CHEESE)

A chiffonade is a very fine julienne cut of a leaf vegetable.

Grilled Flat Bread with Rock Shrimp

and Salsa of Papaya, Avocado, and Red Onion

serves 4

To make the flat bread, mix the flour, nonfat dry milk, baking powder, and salt together. Slowly add the lard and water, kneading the dough until it forms a ball. Cover the dough and let it rest for 1 hour. Cut the dough into four pieces and roll each out on a lightly floured surface, making four discs that are 6 inches in diameter and ⅛ inch thick. Set aside, with wax paper separating the pieces of flat bread, in the refrigerator. To make the salsa, mix the papaya, avocado, red onion, red bell pepper, cilantro, and lime juice together. Chill in the refrigerator. Over moderately high heat, sauté the rock shrimp in the corn oil with the white onion, roasted poblano chile, tomato, garlic, and lime zest for 2 to 3 minutes. Season to taste and add the grated pepper Jack cheese. Grill the flat bread for 45 seconds on one side and 10 to 15 seconds on the other side. Spoon the rock shrimp mixture onto the flat bread and fold it over. Cut each sandwich in half and place on a plate. Top with the papaya salsa and serve.

1	CUP ALL PURPOSE FLOUR
¼	CUP NONFAT DRY MILK
⅛	TEASPOON BAKING POWDER
½	TEASPOON KOSHER SALT
2	TABLESPOONS LARD (VEGETABLE SHORTENING MAY BE SUBSTITUTED)
½	CUP WATER
	FLOUR (FOR ROLLING OUT DOUGH)
½	CUP DICED PAPAYA
½	CUP DICED AVOCADO
2	TABLESPOONS FINELY DICED RED ONION
2	TABLESPOONS FINELY DICED RED BELL PEPPER
2	TABLESPOONS CHOPPED CILANTRO
2	TABLESPOONS FRESH LIME JUICE
1 ½	CUPS CLEANED AND UNCOOKED ROCK SHRIMP
1	TABLESPOON CORN OIL
¼	CUP FINELY DICED WHITE ONION
¼	CUP ROASTED, PEELED, SEEDED, AND CHOPPED POBLANO CHILE
¼	CUP FINELY DICED TOMATO
1	TABLESPOON MINCED GARLIC
2	TABLESPOONS MINCED LIME ZEST
	KOSHER SALT AND CRACKED BLACK PEPPER TO TASTE
½	CUP GRATED PEPPER JACK CHEESE

Cracker-Crusted Pork Loin Sandwich
with Chipotle Mayonnaise

serves 4

½	TEASPOON PUREED CHIPOTLE CHILES IN ADOBO SAUCE
½	CUP MAYONNAISE
½	CUP ALL PURPOSE FLOUR
1	TEASPOON BLACK PEPPER
	SALT TO TASTE
½	CUP WATER
4	EGGS
¼	CUP CORN OIL (FOR FRYING)
4	(4-OUNCE) PORK LOIN CUTLETS, POUNDED FLAT
1	CUP RITZ CRACKER CRUMBS
4	SLICES SWISS CHEESE
8	SLICES SOURDOUGH BREAD
8	SLICES GRILLED YELLOW ONION
8	SWEET PICKLE SLICES, CUT LENGTHWISE ("STACKERS")

Mix the chipotle chile puree with the mayonnaise and set aside. Season the flour with the salt and pepper. Mix the water and the eggs together. Preheat the corn oil to 365° in a heavy skillet for frying the pork cutlet. Dust the flattened pork loin with seasoned flour, and then dredge in the egg wash. Let the excess egg wash drip off the cutlets. Coat the pork cutlets with the Ritz cracker crumbs, pressing the crumbs firmly into the cutlets. Pan fry the pork cutlets over high heat for 2 minutes on each side. Lay a slice of Swiss cheese on each warm cutlet, allowing the cheese to melt. Place cutlets on paper towels to absorb any excess oil. Toast the sourdough bread and spread the chipotle mayonnaise on one side of each slice of bread. Lay each pork cutlet on a slice of toast, and then top with the grilled onions and sweet pickle slices. Place a second piece of toast on the top of each sandwich and secure with two sandwich picks. Slice on the diagonal and serve.

Flank Steak Fajitas
on Homemade Tortillas

serves 4

½ CUP DARK BEER

¼ CUP SOY SAUCE

¼ CUP Worcestershire SAUCE

3 TABLESPOONS FRESH LIME JUICE

2 TABLESPOONS CHOPPED JALAPEÑO

2 TABLESPOONS CHOPPED GARLIC

2 TABLESPOONS CHOPPED CILANTRO

1 POUND FLANK STEAK

4 CUPS ALL PURPOSE FLOUR

2 TEASPOONS KOSHER SALT

6 TABLESPOONS LARD
(VEGETABLE SHORTENING MAY BE SUBSTITUTED)

1 CUP WATER

2 TABLESPOONS CORN OIL

½ CUP JULIENNE OF POBLANO CHILE

1 CUP JULIENNE OF YELLOW ONION

1 TABLESPOON MINCED GARLIC

KOSHER SALT AND
CRACKED BLACK PEPPER TO TASTE

Mix the dark beer, soy sauce, Worcestershire sauce, lime juice, jalapeño, chopped garlic, and cilantro together. Cover the flank steak with the mixture, and marinate the flank steak for 3 to 4 hours in the refrigerator. To make the tortillas, combine the flour, 2 teaspoons of salt, and lard; then mix together thoroughly. Slowly add the water to finish the dough. Knead the dough for 5 minutes into a firm, smooth ball. Allow the dough to rest for 15 minutes at room temperature. Cut the ball of dough into twelve golf-ball-size pieces, and then press each ball of dough between two pieces of wax paper in a tortilla press. (Tortilla presses are available at most cooking supply stores. However, you can roll the dough out with a rolling pin also.) Cook the tortillas in a moderately hot cast-iron griddle or cast-iron skillet until they are lightly charred. Remove from the griddle and cover with a cloth to keep warm. Grill the flank steak to a little above medium. Heat the corn oil in a heavy skillet over high heat and sauté the poblano chile, onion, and minced garlic until tender. Season the poblano-onion mixture to taste. Slice the flank steak thinly on the bias. Place the sliced flank steak in the tortillas and spoon the sautéed poblano-onion mixture over the steak. Roll each tortilla around the steak and onion mixture, placing the loose end of the tortilla on the bottom, and serve.

SMALL COURSES

Steamed Artichoke with Smoked Trout Remoulade

serves 4

Boil the trimmed artichokes in salted water for 30 minutes and simmer for another 30 minutes. To prepare the remoulade, mix the mayonnaise, chopped trout, ketchup, whole-grain mustard, carrot, red onion, chives, jalapeño, parsley, and Tabasco sauce together. Set aside in the refrigerator. Remove each artichoke from the water and drain it by holding it upside down with tongs. Place in the center of a plate and open the

4	LARGE TRIMMED ARTICHOKES
	WATER (FOR BOILING ARTICHOKES)
	KOSHER SALT (FOR WATER)
¾	CUP MAYONNAISE
½	CUP CHOPPED SMOKED TROUT
2	TABLESPOONS KETCHUP
2	TABLESPOONS WHOLE-GRAIN MUSTARD
2	TABLESPOONS VERY FINELY DICED CARROT
2	TABLESPOONS VERY FINELY DICED RED ONION
2	TABLESPOONS VERY FINELY CHOPPED CHIVES
1	TABLESPOON VERY FINELY DICED JALAPEÑO
1	TABLESPOON CHOPPED PARSLEY
1	TEASPOON TABASCO SAUCE
4	GREEN ONIONS (FOR GARNISH)
4	BABY CARROTS (FOR GARNISH)

center of the artichoke to remove as much of the choke as possible. Spoon the remoulade into the center of the artichoke, garnish with baby carrots and green onions, and serve.

Crabmeat Skillet Cake
with Greens and Iceberg Lettuce

serves 4

1	EGG
½	TEASPOON KOSHER SALT
4	CUPS ALL PURPOSE FLOUR
½	CUP MILK
½	CUP CHILLED UNSALTED BUTTER, CUT IN CUBES
	FLOUR (FOR ROLLING OUT DOUGH)
1	TABLESPOON VEGETABLE SHORTENING
	FLOUR (FOR SKILLET)
¾	CUP GRATED PEPPER JACK CHEESE
1	CUP SAUTÉED DICED WHITE ONION
1	CUP SAUTÉED DICED POBLANO CHILE
2	TABLESPOONS SAUTÉED MINCED GARLIC
1½	CUPS LUMP CRABMEAT, CLEANED OF ANY SHELL
1	CUP HEAVY CREAM
1	EGG YOLK
½	TEASPOON NUTMEG
	KOSHER SALT AND CRACKED BLACK PEPPER TO TASTE
¼	CUP MAYONNAISE
¼	CUP BUTTERMILK
¼	CUP ROASTED, PEELED, AND PUREED POBLANO CHILE
1	TABLESPOON MINCED GARLIC
1	TABLESPOON FINELY DICED WHITE ONION
1	TABLESPOON GRANULATED GARLIC
3	CUPS WASHED ICEBERG LETTUCE
3	CUPS WASHED MUSTARD GREENS
¼	CUP (1-INCH) CHIVE SECTIONS

Preheat the oven to 350°. To make the dough for the skillet cake, mix the whole egg, ½ teaspoon salt, flour, and milk together. Cut in the butter cubes until the dough is pliable and just breaking apart. Knead the dough until all lumps are smoothed out. Cover the dough with a cloth and allow the dough to rest for 1 hour. On a lightly floured surface, roll out a disc of dough that is 14 inches in diameter and ¼ inch thick. Grease a medium-size cast-iron skillet with the vegetable shortening, applied with a paper towel. Lightly flour the inside of the lubricated cast-iron skillet and carefully lay the dough inside the skillet. Carefully fit the dough into the edges of the skillet. Evenly distribute the grated cheese, sautéed onion, sautéed poblano, and sautéed garlic on the dough around the bottom and up the sides of the skillet. Sprinkle the crabmeat on top of the cheese and vegetables. Mix the heavy cream, egg yolk, and nutmeg together and season to taste. Spoon the custard slowly over the filling in the skillet. Bake in a 350° oven for 40 to 45 minutes (you will know it is done when you can pierce the center of the cake with a paring knife and, upon withdrawing the knife, you find no custard sticking to it). Allow to cool for 30 minutes. Mix the mayonnaise, buttermilk, poblano puree, minced garlic, finely diced white onion, and granulated garlic together, and then season to taste with salt and pepper. Set dressing aside to cool in the refrigerator. Toss the iceberg lettuce, mustard greens, and chive sections in the dressing. Place a small mound of the salad on the left side of each plate. Slice the skillet cake into quarters and place a wedge of skillet cake on the right side of each plate. Serve.

Cast Iron-Cooked Foie Gras
with Grilled Pineapple and
Red Lentil "Chowchow"

serves 4

½   CUP SEASONED RICE VINEGAR

½   CUP COOKED RED LENTILS

½   CUP GRILLED AND DICED PINEAPPLE

2   TABLESPOONS FINELY DICED RED ONION

2   TABLESPOONS FINELY CHOPPED CHIVES

2   TABLESPOONS FINELY CHOPPED JALAPEÑO

    KOSHER SALT AND
    CRACKED BLACK PEPPER TO TASTE

2   CUPS BALSAMIC VINEGAR

4   (3-OUNCE) FOIE GRAS SLICES
    (CHICKEN LIVERS CAN BE SUBSTITUTED)

4   CUPS SMALL ARUGULA LEAVES

Bring the seasoned rice vinegar to a boil and then turn the heat off. Add the red lentils, pineapple, red onion, chives, and jalapeño; then season to taste. Set the "chowchow" aside in a cool place. Bring the balsamic vinegar to a boil, and then lower the heat and reduce in volume until you have a syrup consistency. Set aside in a warm place. Season the foie gras with salt and pepper, and then fry in a heavy cast-iron skillet until brown. Turn the foie gras over and sear for about 20 seconds. Toss the arugula with ¾ of the red lentil "chowchow" and set in a mound in the center of four plates. For each serving, place a seared foie gras slice on top of the dressed arugula. Drizzle the balsamic vinegar syrup over the foie gras and arugula. Place a small mound of the "chowchow" on the center of the foie gras, and serve.

Warm Goat Cheese on a Beefsteak Tomato
with Verbena-Black Bean Sauce

serves 4

1   CUP WATER, RESERVED FROM COOKING THE BLACK BEANS

¼   CUP BALSAMIC VINEGAR

½   CUP EXTRA-VIRGIN OLIVE OIL

3   TABLESPOONS CHOPPED VERBENA (BASIL CAN BE SUBSTITUTED)

2   TABLESPOONS FRESH LEMON JUICE

1   TABLESPOON MINCED GARLIC

1   TEASPOON TOASTED, SEEDED, AND MINCED CHILE ARBOL

    KOSHER SALT AND CRACKED BLACK PEPPER TO TASTE

4   (2½-OUNCE) SLICES OF GOAT CHEESE

2   TABLESPOONS YELLOW CORNMEAL

4   (¾-INCH-THICK) SLICES OF BEEFSTEAK TOMATO

¼   CUP COOKED BLACK BEANS (SEE COOKING DRIED BEANS, PAGE XX)

1   TABLESPOON CHOPPED CHIVES

4   VERBENA SPRIGS

Bring the black bean water to a boil and cook until the water has reduced to the consistency of syrup (about 10 minutes). Set aside in a warm place. Mix the balsamic vinegar, half of the olive oil, chopped verbena, fresh lemon juice, garlic, and chile arbol together and season to taste. Set aside at room temperature. Dip the goat cheese slices into the other ¼ cup of olive oil and then dust with the yellow cornmeal. Season the tomato slices with salt and pepper, and then warm them over moderate heat in a nonstick skillet for about 90 seconds on each side. Place one tomato slice in the center of each plate. Lightly brown the goat cheese in a nonstick skillet over moderate heat and place on top of the tomato. Spoon the black beans over the warm goat cheese. Spoon the verbena dressing around each plate, and then streak with the black bean syrup. Finish each plate with a small verbena sprig, and serve.

Peppered Goat-Cheese Ravioli
with Mild Green Chile Sauce and Pumpkin Seeds

serves 4

2	EGGS
½	TEASPOON KOSHER SALT
½	CUP ROASTED, PEELED, SEEDED, AND PUREED RED BELL PEPPER
3	CUPS ALL PURPOSE FLOUR
½	CUP SOFTENED GOAT CHEESE
1	TABLESPOON CREAM CHEESE
1	EGG YOLK
1	TEASPOON VERY FINELY DICED RED BELL PEPPER
1	TEASPOON VERY FINELY CHOPPED GREEN ONION
	KOSHER SALT AND CRACKED BLACK PEPPER TO TASTE
¼	CUP WARM WATER
1	TABLESPOON FINELY CHOPPED SHALLOT
1	TABLESPOON MINCED GARLIC
1	TABLESPOON EXTRA-VIRGIN OLIVE OIL
½	CUP WHITE WINE
2	CUPS HEAVY CREAM
¼	CUP ROASTED, PEELED, SEEDED, AND PUREED ANAHEIM CHILE
¼	CUP TOASTED AND CHOPPED PUMPKIN SEEDS
	WATER (FOR COOKING RAVIOLI)
	KOSHER SALT (FOR WATER)
¼	CUP CRUMBLED QUESO FRESCO (WHITE COW'S MILK FARMER'S CHEESE)
¼	CUP TOASTED WHOLE PUMPKIN SEEDS (FOR GARNISH)

To prepare the ravioli, start with the dough. Mix 1 egg, ½ teaspoon of salt, and red bell pepper puree together in a food processor. Slowly add the flour to the food processor until the mixture does not stick to the sides of the bowl. Remove the dough from the food processor and knead with your hands until the texture is firm and smooth. Allow to rest for ½ hour at room temperature. Mix the goat cheese, cream cheese, egg yolk, diced red bell pepper, and green onion together, and then season to taste. Set aside in the refrigerator. Using a tabletop hand-crank pasta machine, roll the pasta dough into three very thin sheets. Then cut the pasta sheets into thirty-two 2½-inch rounds. Place 1 teaspoon of the goat cheese filling in the center of half of the pasta rounds. Mix the other egg with ¼ cup of warm water and brush this egg mixture around the edges of the filled pasta rounds. Carefully place the other half of the rounds on top of the filled rounds and crimp the edges by pressing lightly with a fork. Set the raviolis aside in the refrigerator. To make the sauce, sauté the chopped shallots and garlic in the olive oil over moderately high heat until tender. Deglaze the pan (release all the food sticking to the inside of the pan) with the white wine and boil until volume has reduced by ¾. Add the heavy cream, the anaheim chile puree, and the chopped pumpkin seeds; then reduce in volume by ½. Set aside in a warm place. Cook the raviolis in boiling salted water for 6 to 7 minutes. Drain the water until the raviolis are thoroughly dry, and then add the sauce. For each serving, spoon the sauced ravioli into a shallow pasta bowl or onto a small plate, top with the crumbled queso fresco and the toasted whole pumpkin seeds, and serve.

Grilled Lamb Skirt Steak
with Pinto Bean Ravioli and
Poblano Cream Sauce

serves 4

Combine the achiote paste, soy sauce, lime juice, Worcestershire sauce, garlic, 1 teaspoon of chopped cilantro, and jalapeño; then marinate the lamb skirt steak in this mixture for 3 hours in the refrigerator. To make the sauce, bring the cream and poblano chile puree to a boil. Reduce the heat to a simmer and cook until volume has reduced by ⅓. Add the 2 tablespoons of chopped cilantro, season to taste, and set aside in a warm place. Boil the raviolis in salted water for 6 to 7 minutes. Drain the water until the raviolis are thoroughly dry, and then add the sauce. Grill the lamb skirt steaks for 3 minutes on one side and 90 seconds on the other side. Slice the lamb thinly on an angle. For each serving, spoon four raviolis into a shallow pasta bowl or onto a small plate, and then lay the thinly sliced skirt steak like ribbons on the center of the pasta. Top the steak with cheese, toasted pumpkin seeds, and a cilantro sprig and serve.

1	TABLESPOON ACHIOTE PASTE (AVAILABLE IN THE MEXICAN FOODS SECTION)
1	TABLESPOON SOY SAUCE
1	TABLESPOON FRESH LIME JUICE
1	TABLESPOON WORCESTERSHIRE SAUCE
1	TEASPOON MINCED GARLIC
1	TEASPOON CHOPPED CILANTRO
1	TEASPOON CHOPPED JALAPEÑO
4	(4-OUNCE) PIECES OF LAMB SKIRT STEAK (FLANK STEAK CAN BE SUBSTITUTED)
2	CUPS HEAVY CREAM
¼	CUP ROASTED, PEELED, SEEDED, AND PUREED POBLANO CHILE
2	TABLESPOONS CHOPPED CILANTRO
	KOSHER SALT AND CRACKED BLACK PEPPER TO TASTE
16	PINTO BEAN RAVIOLIS, UNCOOKED (SEE PAGE 229)
	WATER (FOR BOILING RAVIOLIS)
	KOSHER SALT (FOR WATER)
½	CUP SMALL PIECES OF SHAVED, DRIED MONTEREY JACK CHEESE (AVAILABLE FROM GOURMET CHEESE SOURCES; YOU CAN ALSO SUBSTITUTE PARMESAN CHEESE)
¼	CUP TOASTED, WHOLE PUMPKIN SEEDS
4	CILANTRO SPRIGS

Lump Crab Cake
with Local Citrus and Organic Greens

serves 4

2	EGG WHITES
1	EGG YOLK
12	OUNCES CLEANED LUMP CRABMEAT
½	TEASPOON FINELY MINCED GARLIC
1	TABLESPOON FINELY DICED YELLOW ONION
½	TABLESPOON FINELY DICED POBLANO CHILE
¼	CUP TOASTED BREADCRUMBS*
½	CUP EXTRA-VIRGIN OLIVE OIL
½	CUP CHOPPED CHIVES
2	TABLESPOONS CORN OIL
1	CUP RUBY RED GRAPEFRUIT SECTIONS
1	CUP ORANGE SECTIONS
1	CUP (1-INCH) CHIVE SECTIONS
1	CUP BABY ORGANIC GREENS (MESCLUN)

To prepare the crab cakes, whip the egg whites to a stiff peak in a chilled stainless-steel bowl. Fold in the egg yolk and set aside in the refrigerator. In a different bowl, mix the crabmeat, garlic, onion, poblano, and breadcrumbs together. Fold in the eggs and form into four small cakes. Set aside in the refrigerator. Puree the olive oil and chopped chives until thoroughly blended. Drain the puree through a very fine strainer. You will use the green chive oil in this recipe, but you may also want to save the puree for later use in a stock or a sauce. Brown the crab cakes in corn oil in a nonstick pan over moderately high heat. Toss the grapefruit, orange, chive sections, and baby organic greens together. Mound the citrus salad in the center of four plates. Top with the crab cakes, and then drizzle the chive oil around the perimeter of the plates and serve.

Toast the bread and allow it to dry out. Grind the toast in a food processor or spice grinder.

"Dallas" Mozzarella
with Pickled Onions and Avocado

serves 4

½	CUP SEASONED RICE VINEGAR
¼	CUP RED WINE VINEGAR
2	TABLESPOONS PICKLING SPICE, TIED IN CHEESECLOTH
2	TABLESPOONS GRANULATED SUGAR
1½	CUPS JULIENNE OF WHITE ONION
1	TABLESPOON DRY MUSTARD
¼	CUP EXTRA-VIRGIN OLIVE OIL
¼	CUP DICED TOMATOES
¼	CUP CILANTRO LEAVES
1	AVOCADO
8	(1½-OUNCE) SLICES OF FRESH MOZZARELLA*
2	TABLESPOONS FERMENTED BLACK BEANS (FROM AN ASIAN FOOD STORE)
¼	CUP BALSAMIC VINEGAR
4	CILANTRO SPRIGS

To pickle the white onion julienne, bring the seasoned rice vinegar, red wine vinegar, pickling spice, and sugar to a boil. Turn off the heat and cool the mixture to room temperature. Add the white onion and chill for at least 1 hour. Mix the dry mustard and the olive oil together. Let it sit for at least 1 hour, and then strain. Set aside at room temperature. Drain the pickled onions and toss them with the diced tomato and cilantro leaves. Then, place a mound of the pickled onion mixture in the upper left quarter of four plates. Cut the avocado into quarters, and then slice each quarter lengthwise into three equal-size pieces. For each serving, lean a slice of the avocado (the stem end) against the pickled onions, and then alternate slices of the mozzarella and avocado in a fan pattern. Add the fermented black beans and the balsamic vinegar to the mustard oil to complete the vinaigrette. Spoon the vinaigrette over the avocado and cheese. Finish each plate with a cilantro sprig placed at the top of the avocado-mozzarella "fan," and then serve.

Paula Lambert's Dallas Mozzarella Company makes some great cheeses. I think you will enjoy this source for excellent cheeses. Please call (214) 741-4072.

Portabello Mushroom in a Cornmeal Crepe

with Sweet Onions and Avocado Relish

serves 4

4	PORTABELLO MUSHROOMS
2	TABLESPOONS OLIVE OIL
	KOSHER SALT AND CRACKED BLACK PEPPER TO TASTE
¼	CUP SOY SAUCE
¼	CUP WORCESTERSHIRE SAUCE
¼	CUP + 2 TABLESPOONS FRESH LIME JUICE
1	TABLESPOON + 1 TEASPOON CHOPPED GARLIC
1	TABLESPOON CHOPPED SERRANO CHILE
½	CUP YELLOW CORNMEAL
¾	CUP ALL PURPOSE FLOUR
1	EGG
¾	CUP MILK
1	TABLESPOON CORN OIL
	FOOD RELEASE SPRAY
¾	CUP DICED AVOCADO
2	TABLESPOONS DICED WHITE ONION
1	TEASPOON SEEDED AND FINELY DICED SERRANO CHILE
2	TABLESPOONS CHOPPED CILANTRO
1	CUP JULIENNE OF YELLOW ONION
½	CUP JULIENNE OF POBLANO CHILE
4	CHARRED SERRANO CHILES
4	LARGE CILANTRO SPRIGS

Brush the portabello mushrooms with the olive oil, and season to taste; then grill for 4 minutes on the top side and 3 minutes on the gill side. Marinate the grilled mushrooms in the soy sauce, Worcestershire sauce, ¼ cup of lime juice, 1 tablespoon of garlic, and chopped serrano chile for ½ hour. To make the crepes, mix the cornmeal and flour together. Add the egg, milk, and corn oil, and then mix until the batter is smooth. Allow the batter to rest for ½ hour in the refrigerator. Cook eight 8-inch-diameter crepes over moderately high heat in a nonstick skillet oiled with food release spray until each crepe is golden brown on both sides. Set them aside at room temperature, with wax paper separating the crepes. Mix together the avocado, remaining 2 tablespoons of lime juice, diced onion, remaining 1 teaspoon of garlic, finely diced serrano chile, and chopped cilantro. Season to taste with salt and pepper and set the relish aside in a cool place. Cut the marinated mushroom into strips that are ¼ inch thick. In a heavy skillet over high heat, sauté the mushroom strips with the julienne of yellow onion and the julienne of poblano chile until the chiles are barely tender. Season the mushroom mixture to taste. Lay the crepes on a flat surface, spoon the sautéed mushroom mixture evenly down the center of each crepe, and roll the crepes around the mixture. For each serving, lay one crepe on a plate, with the loose end of the crepe on the bottom. Lay a second crepe across the first one, making an inverted V. Spoon some avocado relish where the two crepes intersect, top with a charred serrano chile and a cilantro sprig, and then serve.

Grilled Quail, Foie Gras, and Endives

serves 4

½	CUP + 3 TABLESPOONS EXTRA-VIRGIN OLIVE OIL
½	HEAD RADICCHIO, CUT IN QUARTERS
	KOSHER SALT AND CRACKED BLACK PEPPER TO TASTE
2	SEMIBONELESS QUAIL, SPLIT IN HALF LENGTHWISE
4	(1½-OUNCE) SLICES OF FOIE GRAS
¼	CUP CIDER VINEGAR
1	TABLESPOON MINCED GARLIC
1	TABLESPOON FINELY DICED TOMATO
1	TABLESPOON CHOPPED PARSLEY
1	TABLESPOON CHOPPED CHIVES
24	CURLY ENDIVE LEAVES
12	BELGIAN ENDIVE LEAVES

Drizzle 1 tablespoon of the olive oil over the radicchio and season to taste. Grill the radicchio over a moderately hot fire for 30 seconds on each side. Allow to cool to room temperature. Brush the quail with 2 tablespoons of olive oil, and season to taste with salt and pepper. Grill the quail for 5 minutes on one side and 3 minutes on the other side. Season the foie gras with salt and pepper, and quickly brown in a very hot skillet until brown; then turn it over and sear for another 20 seconds. Mix the ½ cup of olive oil, cider vinegar, minced garlic, diced tomato, parsley, and chives together. Season to taste and set aside at room temperature. For each serving, lay six curly endive leaves on a plate. Lay three Belgian endive leaves around on the curly endive and center a grilled radicchio wedge on the curly endive and Belgian endive. Lay a piece of grilled quail on the radicchio wedge and top the quail with a slice of seared foie gras. Drizzle the vinaigrette over the quail, foie gras, and endives; then serve.

Barbecued Quail Baked in Cornmeal Custard
with Green Pea Guacamole

serves 4

4	CUPS ALL PURPOSE FLOUR
1	TEASPOON KOSHER SALT
3	EGGS
½	CUP MILK
½	POUND CHILLED UNSALTED BUTTER, CUT IN CUBES
1	TABLESPOON VEGETABLE SHORTENING
	FLOUR (FOR DUSTING DOUGH)
1	CUP BLANCHED* AND PUREED FRESH PEAS (FROZEN CAN BE SUBSTITUTED)
1	TABLESPOON FINELY DICED RED ONION
2	TABLESPOONS FINELY DICED JALAPEÑO
1	TABLESPOON CHOPPED CILANTRO
1	TABLESPOON FRESH LIME JUICE
	KOSHER SALT AND CRACKED BLACK PEPPER TO TASTE
2	CUPS STRAINED CORN PUREE
2	CUPS HEAVY CREAM
2	EGG YOLKS
1	TABLESPOON CORN OIL
2	CUPS COARSELY CHOPPED, BARBECUED BONELESS QUAIL (IT MAY BE ROASTED OR GRILLED, AND CHICKEN CAN BE SUBSTITUTED; SEE STANDARD PREPARATIONS CHAPTER)
1	CUP DICED YELLOW ONION
1	TABLESPOON MINCED GARLIC
1½	CUPS GRATED PEPPER JACK CHEESE

To make the crust for the corn custard, mix the flour and 1 teaspoon of salt together. Add 1 egg, milk, and butter. Knead the dough until firm and smooth, and then set aside covered with a cloth in a cool place. Allow the dough to rest for ½ hour. Roll out to ¼ inch in thickness and about 14 inches in diameter. Grease an 8-inch fluted tart pan (with a removable bottom) with vegetable shortening on a paper towel. Lightly dust the dough with a little flour. Carefully lay the dough in the tart pan, making sure to get into the corners without tearing the dough. Trim off the dough above the edge of the pan. Mix the green pea puree, red onion, 1 tablespoon of jalapeño, chopped cilantro, and lime juice together. Season to taste and set aside in a cool place. Whisk the strained corn puree, cream, egg

yolks, and remaining 2 eggs together. Season the custard to taste with salt and pepper and set aside in the refrigerator. In a heavy skillet with corn oil over moderately high heat, sauté the quail meat, yellow onion, garlic, and remaining 1 tablespoon of jalapeño until the vegetables are tender. Allow this mixture to cool to room temperature. Evenly distribute the grated cheese on the dough in the bottom of the pan, and then spoon the quail mixture on top of the cheese. Fill with the corn custard and bake in a 325° oven for 50 to 55 minutes. Check to see if it is finished with a clean paring knife; it is done when a knife inserted into the center of the baked custard can be removed with no custard clinging to the knife. Allow the baked corn custard to cool for 30 minutes. Slice the baked custard into four wedges, place on four small plates, and spoon the green pea guacamole on top of the wedges; serve.

*To blanch, boil in salted water for 1 to 2 minutes. Then ice to stop the cooking process.

Smoked Salmon Cheesecake
with Watercress Salad

serves 8

Preheat the oven to 350°. To make the crust, combine the cracker crumbs and the melted butter. Using 2 tablespoons of vegetable shortening on a paper towel, grease a 9½-inch spring release pan. Press the cracker crumb mixture with your fingers so that it completely covers the bottom and sides of the pan. Bake the crust, in the center of the oven, for 5 minutes. Allow the crust to cool to room temperature on a rack. To make the filling of the cheesecake, mix the cornstarch and the cream cheese until smooth and creamy. Add the eggs and beat well. Slowly add the heavy cream, chopped

2	CUPS RITZ CRACKER CRUMBS
6	TABLESPOONS MELTED UNSALTED BUTTER
2	TABLESPOONS VEGETABLE SHORTENING
2	TABLESPOONS CORNSTARCH
1	POUND CREAM CHEESE
2	EGGS
¾	CUP HEAVY CREAM
2	TABLESPOONS CHOPPED CHIVES
1	CUP COARSELY CHOPPED SMOKED SALMON
¼	CUP CHAMPAGNE VINEGAR
2	TABLESPOONS EXTRA-VIRGIN OLIVE OIL
1	TABLESPOON FINELY CHOPPED SHALLOT
2	TABLESPOONS CHOPPED DILL
	KOSHER SALT AND CRACKED BLACK PEPPER TO TASTE
4	CUPS WATERCRESS SPRIGS
6	OUNCES THINLY SLICED SMOKED SALMON
2	TABLESPOONS TOPPIKO CAVIAR (RED FLYING FISH ROE)

chives, and chopped smoked salmon to the batter. Mix the batter thoroughly. Carefully spoon the filling into the crust. Bake at 350° in the center of the oven for approximately 50 minutes, or until a paring knife comes out clean after being inserted into the center of the cheesecake. You can loosely cover the cake with oiled wax paper if it appears to be browning too quickly. Cool to room temperature and refrigerate overnight. Mix the champagne vinegar, extra-virgin olive oil, finely chopped shallots, and chopped dill together. Season to taste and set aside at room temperature. Slice the cheesecake into eighths and place one slice off-center on the left side of each plate. For each serving, place a small mound of the watercress next to the cheesecake, and spoon the vinaigrette over the salad. Place a slice of smoked salmon on top of the cheesecake. Top with a dollop of the caviar and serve.

Smoked Salmon on Buttermilk Corn Griddle Cakes
with Corn Milk Mascarpone

serves 4

To make the griddle cakes, sift the flour, cornmeal, baking powder, and salt into a large bowl. In a small bowl, whisk the eggs and buttermilk together. Add the buttermilk mixture to the dry ingredients and fold in the melted butter. Refrigerate the batter for 1 hour. To make the corn milk mascarpone, puree the corn kernels with the corn stock and pass through a food mill (see note about using food mill on Rock Shrimp Gazpacho recipe, page 84). Fold the sweet corn puree and the chopped chives into the mascarpone cheese, and then refrigerate for at least ½ hour.

¾	CUP ALL PURPOSE FLOUR
½	CUP YELLOW CORNMEAL
1	TABLESPOON BAKING POWDER
1	TEASPOON KOSHER SALT
2	EGGS
¾	CUP BUTTERMILK
2	TABLESPOONS MELTED BUTTER
2	CUPS SWEET CORN KERNELS
½	CUP CORN STOCK (MADE FROM BOILING SHEARED CORNCOBS IN WATER FOR 30 TO 45 MINUTES)
½	CUP FINELY CHOPPED CHIVES
1	CUP MASCARPONE CHEESE
¼	CUP CORN OIL
12	OUNCES THINLY SLICED SMOKED SALMON
20	WHOLE CHIVES

Heat a griddle or a heavy skillet over moderate heat, and grease with the corn oil. Spoon 2 tablespoons of the batter on the griddle and cook until golden brown; then turn over and brown the other side. Repeat with remaining batter, making eight griddle cakes. For each serving, overlap two of the cakes on a plate, and spoon the corn milk mascarpone over the overlapping area. Lay the thinly sliced smoked salmon in a ribbonlike manner on the corn milk mascarpone. Finish the plate with five whole chives, and serve.

Shrimp Cocktail with Bacon Horseradish Sauce
and Sweet Onion and Corn Slaw

serves 4

½	CUP KETCHUP
¼	CUP DICED, RENDERED* HICKORY-SMOKED BACON
½	CUP SEASONED RICE VINEGAR
2	TABLESPOONS FRESH LIME JUICE
2	TABLESPOONS PREPARED HORSERADISH
2	TABLESPOONS FINELY DICED WHITE ONION
1	TABLESPOON FINELY DICED JALAPEÑO
½	CUP MAYONNAISE
½	CUP JULIENNE OF EARLY JERSEY CABBAGE (GREEN OR SAVOY CABBAGE CAN BE SUBSTITUTED)
½	CUP FINE JULIENNE OF WHITE ONION
½	CUP SWEET CORN KERNELS
½	CUP CILANTRO LEAVES
	KOSHER SALT AND CRACKED BLACK PEPPER TO TASTE
12	PEELED, DEVEINED, BOILED, AND CHILLED JUMBO SHRIMP
4	CILANTRO SPRIGS

To prepare the sauce, mix the ketchup, rendered bacon, ¼ cup of seasoned rice vinegar, fresh lime juice, horseradish, diced onion, and jalapeño together. Set aside in the refrigerator. Mix the mayonnaise and the other ¼ cup of the seasoned rice vinegar together. Add the cabbage, julienne of white onion, sweet corn kernels, and cilantro leaves; then season to taste. Set aside in the refrigerator. For each serving, spoon some bacon horseradish sauce into a small dish and hang three shrimp on the rim of the dish. Place this dish off-center on the left side of the plate, and spoon the sweet onion and corn slaw on the right side of the plate. Top the slaw with a cilantro sprig and serve.

To render means to cook the fat until it becomes crisp or to melt the fat.

137

Grilled Shrimp and Pickled Cabbage
with Red Chile-Whiskey Sauce

serves 4

Marinate the shrimp in ¼ cup of corn oil, lime juice, and 1 teaspoon of garlic for 1½ hours. Heat 1 teaspoon of corn oil in a heavy pan over moderately high heat, and then sauté the minced New Mexico chiles and the teaspoon of garlic. Deglaze the pan (release all the food sticking to the inside of the pan) with the whiskey and add the chicken broth, brown sugar, corn syrup, and balsamic vinegar. Boil until the mixture has reduced in volume by ⅓ and allow it to cool to room temperature. Carefully puree in a blender and strain. Bring the rice vinegar to a boil with the pickling spice and then

12	PEELED AND DEVEINED JUMBO SHRIMP
¼	CUP + 1 TEASPOON CORN OIL
¼	CUP FRESH LIME JUICE
2	TEASPOONS MINCED GARLIC
¼	CUP TOASTED, SEEDED, AND MINCED DRIED NEW MEXICO CHILES
¼	CUP WHISKEY
1	CUP CHICKEN BROTH
1	TABLESPOON BROWN SUGAR
1	TABLESPOON DARK CORN SYRUP
1	TABLESPOON BALSAMIC VINEGAR
½	CUP SEASONED RICE VINEGAR
1	TABLESPOON PICKLING SPICE, TIED IN CHEESECLOTH
1	CUP CHIFFONADE* OF GREEN CABBAGE
½	CUP VERY FINE JULIENNE OF RED ONION
¼	CUP COARSELY CHOPPED CILANTRO LEAVES
	KOSHER SALT AND CRACKED BLACK PEPPER TO TASTE
½	CUP CRUMBLED QUESO FRESCO (WHITE COW'S MILK FARMER'S CHEESE)
4	LARGE CILANTRO SPRIGS

turn off the heat. Allow it to cool to room temperature. Add the cabbage and red onion, and let sit for ½ hour; then drain. Add the cilantro leaves and season to taste. Set aside in a cool place. Drain the marinade from the shrimp and grill them over high heat for 1½ minutes on each side, but be careful to not overcook them. Sauce the center of each plate and place a mound of the pickled cabbage in the center of the sauce. Arrange the grilled shrimp around the outside of the cabbage and sprinkle the crumbled queso fresco over the dish. Top each serving with a cilantro sprig and serve.

*A chiffonade is a very fine julienne of a leaf vegetable.

Spinach Enchiladas
with Red Bell Pepper Sauce

serves 4

¾	CUP ALL PURPOSE FLOUR
½	CUP YELLOW CORNMEAL
1	EGG
¾	CUP MILK
3	TABLESPOONS CORN OIL
	FOOD RELEASE SPRAY
1	CUP COARSELY CHOPPED RED BELL PEPPER
1	TABLESPOON DICED CELERY
1	TABLESPOON DICED CARROT
1	TABLESPOON DICED YELLOW ONION
1	TABLESPOON DICED TOMATO
¾	CUP WATER
¾	CUP APPLE JUICE
	KOSHER SALT AND CRACKED BLACK PEPPER TO TASTE
½	CUP SWEET CORN KERNELS
1	TABLESPOON FINELY DICED RED ONION
1	TABLESPOON FINELY DICED POBLANO CHILE
1	TABLESPOON FRESH LIME JUICE
1	TEASPOON CHOPPED CILANTRO
1	TEASPOON MINCED GARLIC
12	CUPS WASHED AND STEMMED SPINACH LEAVES
1	CUP JULIENNE OF WHITE ONION
2	TABLESPOONS MINCED GARLIC

To make the crepes, mix the flour and cornmeal together. Add the egg, milk, and 1 tablespoon of corn oil; then mix until the batter is smooth. Allow the batter to rest for 30 minutes in the refrigerator. Cook eight 8-inch-diameter crepes over moderate heat in a nonstick skillet oiled with food release spray until each crepe is

golden brown on both sides (approximately 90 seconds per side). Set aside at room temperature, with wax paper separating the crepes. To prepare the sauce, combine the red bell pepper, celery, carrot, yellow onion, tomato, water, and apple juice and bring to a boil. Reduce the heat and simmer for 12 minutes. Allow mixture to cool to room temperature, and then carefully puree and pass the sauce through a strainer. Season to taste and set aside at room temperature. Mix the corn kernels, red onion, poblano chile, fresh lime juice, cilantro, and 1 teaspoon of garlic together and season to taste with salt and pepper. Set aside in a cool place. Heat 2 tablespoons of corn oil in a hot, heavy skillet over moderately high heat, and sauté the spinach leaves, julienne of white onion, and 2 tablespoons of garlic until the spinach is just wilted. Season to taste with salt and pepper, and drain. Lay the crepes on a flat surface and evenly distribute the drained, sautéed spinach down the center of each crepe. Roll each crepe around the spinach and place the loose end of the crepe on the bottom. For each serving, spoon some sauce in a small pool in the center of a plate. Lay two spinach-filled crepes for each serving next to each other on the sauce. Spoon the corn salsa across the crepes and serve.

Spiced Turkey Confit
and Cracked Corn Stuffing with Dried Figs and Country Ham

serves 4

Heat the butter in a heavy pan over moderately high heat and sauté the onion until it is tender. Add the grits and chicken broth. Bring the chicken broth to a boil; then decrease the heat to a simmer and cook for 10 minutes, stirring continuously. Fold in the grated cheese, cream, chopped sage, country ham, and dried figs. Season to taste and set aside in a warm place. In a heavy skillet, heat the fat from the confit over moderately high heat and sauté the

1	TABLESPOON MELTED BUTTER
¼	CUP DICED YELLOW ONION
1	CUP UNCOOKED YELLOW SOUTHERN-STYLE GRITS
2½	CUPS CHICKEN BROTH
½	CUP GRATED, DRIED MONTEREY JACK CHEESE (AVAILABLE IN FINE CHEESE STORES; PARMESAN CHEESE CAN BE SUBSTITUTED)
¾	CUP HEAVY CREAM
2	TABLESPOONS CHOPPED FRESH SAGE
¼	CUP JULIENNE OF COUNTRY HAM
½	CUP CHOPPED DRIED FIGS
	KOSHER SALT AND CRACKED BLACK PEPPER TO TASTE
1	TABLESPOON FAT, FROM THE CONFIT*
1	TEASPOON FINELY DICED JALAPEÑO
1	TEASPOON MINCED GARLIC
2	CUPS TURKEY CONFIT*
½	CUP SHAVED, DRIED MONTEREY JACK CHEESE
4	FRESH SAGE SPRIGS

jalapeño and garlic until tender. Add the turkey confit and season to taste with salt and pepper. For each serving, spoon a mound of grits into a crock or bowl. Spoon the turkey confit over the top of the grits and try to keep as much of the confit in the center as possible. Garnish the dish by placing the shaved cheese on the top of the confit. Place a sage sprig on the side of the confit and serve.

Confit (cone-fee) was an old French cooking technique that provided a way to cook poor cuts of meat and to preserve the cooked meat in the fat. The technique was never popular in the United States, but it offers some rich flavors. For this recipe, you will use the meat from two specially cooked turkey legs: In a heavy pot over moderate heat, simmer the turkey legs in chicken fat and olive oil that is flavored with black peppercorns, garlic, bay leaves, kosher salt, and chile arbol until the meat begins to come off the bone (approximately 2 hours). Carefully remove the legs from the fat, and then pull the meat off the bone and partially shred the meat. Cover the meat with the fat and reserve it in the refrigerator for future use (up to one week).

Barbecued Wild Boar Empanadas
with Spiced Mint Honey

serves 4

2½ CUPS ALL PURPOSE FLOUR

¾ CUP NONFAT DRY MILK

1 TABLESPOON BAKING POWDER

½ TEASPOON GRANULATED ONION

½ TEASPOON GRANULATED GARLIC

½ TABLESPOON DARK CHILE POWDER

1 TEASPOON KOSHER SALT

1 TABLESPOON LARD

1¼ CUPS WARM WATER

FLOUR (FOR ROLLING OUT DOUGH)

1½ CUPS WELL-SEASONED, SLOW-COOKED, SMOKE-ROASTED, AND THEN SHREDDED WILD BOAR BUTT (PORK BUTT PREPARED THE SAME WAY CAN BE SUBSTITUTED; SEE STANDARD PREPARATIONS CHAPTER FOR TIPS ON SMOKE ROASTING)

4 CUPS + 1 TABLESPOON CORN OIL (FOR FRYING)

2 TABLESPOONS FINELY DICED WHITE ONION

2 TABLESPOONS ROASTED, PEELED, SEEDED, AND DICED POBLANO CHILE

2 TABLESPOONS TOASTED PINE NUTS

¼ CUP BARBECUE SAUCE (SEE PAGE 59)

KOSHER SALT AND CRACKED BLACK PEPPER TO TASTE

4 TEASPOONS GOAT CHEESE

1 EGG

1 TABLESPOON FINELY CHOPPED MINT

1 TABLESPOON ADOBO SAUCE

¾ CUP HONEY

To make the dough for the empanadas, combine the flour, nonfat dry milk, baking powder, granulated onion, granulated garlic, chile powder, and 1 teaspoon of salt together in a mixing bowl. Slowly add the lard and 1 cup of warm water to the dry ingredients until the mixture forms into one large ball of dough. Let the dough rest for ½ hour. Roll the dough out on a lightly floured flat surface to ⅛ inch in thickness, and then cut into twelve 3-inch rounds. Set aside in a cool place, with wax paper separating the dough rounds. To prepare the filling, chop or grind the barbecued wild boar meat. In a heavy skillet, heat 1 tablespoon of corn oil over moderately high heat and sauté the diced onion and poblano chile until tender. Add the pine nuts, wild boar meat, and Barbecue Sauce; then season to taste. Allow to cool to room temperature. Lay the rounds of dough on a flat surface and place 1 teaspoon of the wild boar filling and ⅓ teaspoon of the goat cheese in the center of each dough round. Mix the ¼ cup of warm water with the egg, and softly brush this egg wash around the edges of the dough. Fold each dough round in half, over the filling, and gently crimp the edges with the tines of a fork. Preheat the 4 cups of corn oil to 350° in a heavy pot. Add the chopped mint and adobo sauce to the honey. When the oil is hot, submerge the empanadas in the oil and fry until they are golden brown and floating in the oil. Place three empanadas overlapping on each plate, drizzle the honey over the top, and serve.

Barbecued Chicken in a Blue Corn Crepe

with Spiced Pickled Onions

serves 4

¾   CUP ALL PURPOSE FLOUR

½   CUP BLUE CORNMEAL

1   EGG

¾   CUP MILK

1   TABLESPOON CORN OIL

    FOOD RELEASE SPRAY

½   CUP SEASONED RICE VINEGAR

2   TABLESPOONS PICKLING SPICE, TIED IN CHEESECLOTH

1   TABLESPOON FINELY DICED JALAPEÑO

½   CUP JULIENNE OF RED ONION

1   CUP JULIENNE OF WHITE ONION

¼   CUP BIAS-CUT GREEN ONION

1   TABLESPOON CORN OIL

½   CUP COARSELY CHOPPED TOMATO

1   TABLESPOON MINCED GARLIC

¼   CUP MALT VINEGAR

2   TABLESPOONS SOY SAUCE

1   TABLESPOON TOASTED, SEEDED, AND MINCED CHILE PASILLA

¼   CUP MOLASSES

2   CUPS SLOW-COOKED, SMOKE-ROASTED, AND SHREDDED CHICKEN MEAT (SEE STANDARD PREPARATIONS CHAPTER FOR TIPS ON SMOKE ROASTING)

    KOSHER SALT AND CRACKED BLACK PEPPER TO TASTE

To make the crepes, mix the flour and blue cornmeal together. Add the egg, milk, and 1 tablespoon of corn oil, and then mix until the batter is smooth. Allow the batter to rest for 30 minutes in the refrigerator. Over moderate heat, cook eight 8-inch-diameter crepes in a nonstick skillet oiled with food release spray until each crepe is golden brown on both sides (approximately 90 seconds per side). Set aside at room temperature with wax paper separating the crepes. Bring the seasoned rice vinegar, pickling spice, and jalapeño to a boil. Remove from the heat and allow to cool to room temperature. Add ½ cup of red onion julienne and ½ cup of white onion julienne to the vinegar mixture. Let the onions pickle, covered in the refrigerator, for at least an hour. Drain the pickling brine from the onion julienne and add the green onion. Mix the onions together well

and set aside in a cool place. To prepare the chicken, heat 1 tablespoon of corn oil in a heavy skillet over high heat. Sauté the other ½ cup of white onion julienne, the chopped tomato, and the garlic until tender. Add the malt vinegar, soy sauce, chile pasilla, and molasses; then mix thoroughly. Add the chicken meat, season to taste, and simmer for 5 minutes. Strain the sauce from the chicken and reserve it. Lay the crepes on a flat surface, spoon the chicken mixture evenly down the center of each crepe, and roll the crepes around the chicken mixture. For each serving, lay a filled crepe on a plate, with the loose end on the bottom. Lay a second crepe next to the first. Spoon the sauce, reserved from cooking the chicken, over the crepes. Place a small mound of the pickled onions on the center of the crepes and serve.

MAIN COURSES

Skillet-Seared Ahi Tuna
with Smoked Ham Hock and
Three-Bean Salad

serves 4

½	CUP + 2 TABLESPOONS EXTRA-VIRGIN OLIVE OIL
¼	CUP FRESH LEMON JUICE
1	TABLESPOON COARSELY CHOPPED OREGANO LEAVES
1	TEASPOON MINCED GARLIC
1	CUP COOKED HARICOT VERT (SMALL FRENCH GREEN BEANS; REGULAR GREEN BEANS CAN BE SUBSTITUTED)
1	CUP COOKED YELLOW WAX BEANS
½	CUP COOKED WHITE BEANS
½	CUP JULIENNE OF SMOKED HAM HOCK MEAT*
½	CUP JULIENNE OF RED ONION
	KOSHER SALT AND CRACKED BLACK PEPPER TO TASTE
4	(8-OUNCE) AHI TUNA STEAKS (SWORDFISH CAN BE SUBSTITUTED)
2	TABLESPOONS LEMON ZEST
4	SPRIGS OF FRESH OREGANO

To make the vinaigrette, mix the ½ cup of extra-virgin olive oil, fresh lemon juice, chopped oregano, and garlic together. Set the dressing aside at room temperature. For the salad, mix the haricot vert, yellow wax beans, white beans, ham hock meat, and red onion together. Season to taste and set aside in a cool place. Heat a heavy or cast-iron skillet until very hot. Season the tuna steaks on both sides with salt and pepper, and then drizzle the 2 tablespoons of olive oil over them, on both sides. Sear** the tuna in the hot skillet for 90 seconds on each side. If you desire the tuna cooked more, increase the cooking time. For each serving, place a mound of the bean salad off-center in the upper left quarter of a plate. Lean a cooked tuna steak against the bean salad, and spoon the vinaigrette over the tuna and the salad. Place a small pile of the lemon zest on top (at the peak) of the tuna. Lay a fresh oregano sprig next to the lemon zest and serve.

*See the Standard Preparations chapter for some thoughts about smoking foods.

**Searing is cooking something on a very hot surface very quickly to seal the surface of the food and achieve some crispness.

Pan-Roasted Dorado
with a Smoked Tomato Vinaigrette

serves 4

1	TABLESPOON COARSELY CHOPPED GARLIC CLOVE
1	TABLESPOON COARSELY CHOPPED SERRANO CHILE
2	TABLESPOONS COARSELY CHOPPED WHITE ONION
1	CUP PEELED AND THEN SMOKED PLUM TOMATOES*
¼	CUP + 3 TABLESPOONS EXTRA-VIRGIN OLIVE OIL
¼	CUP LEMON JUICE
¼	CUP WHITE WINE VINEGAR
	KOSHER SALT AND CRACKED BLACK PEPPER TO TASTE
2	CUPS THICK-CUT RED ONION RINGS
½	CUP BALSAMIC VINEGAR
1	TABLESPOON UNSALTED BUTTER
1	CUP JULIENNE OF ZUCCHINI
1	CUP JULIENNE OF YELLOW SQUASH
1	CUP JULIENNE OF CARROT
1	CUP JULIENNE OF LEEK
1	CUP CORN KERNELS
¼	CUP COARSELY CHOPPED YELLOW ONION
1	TABLESPOON MINCED GARLIC
8	(3-OUNCE) BONELESS PIECES OF DORADO (THE SPANISH NAME FOR MAHI MAHI, THE DOLPHIN FISH [NOT THE MAMMAL])
1	LIME, CUT IN QUARTERS

Heat a heavy or cast-iron skillet until it's very hot. Char** the coarsely chopped garlic, serrano chiles, white onion, and smoked tomatoes. Puree the charred vegetables with the ¼ cup of olive oil, lemon juice, and the white wine vinegar. Season to taste and set aside in a cool place. Place the red onion rings in a shallow baking dish and cover with the balsamic vinegar. Cover with foil and

bake for 10 minutes in a 400° oven. Remove from the oven and set aside in a warm place. ⊕ In a hot skillet with 1 tablespoon of olive oil and 1 tablespoon of butter, sauté the zucchini, yellow squash, carrot, leek, corn, yellow onion, and minced garlic until just tender. Season the vegetables to taste with salt and pepper, and set aside in a warm place. ⊕ Heat the remaining 2 tablespoons of olive oil in a heavy nonstick skillet over moderately high heat. Season the mahi mahi with salt and pepper. Sear (see note on Skilled-Seared Ahi Tuna, page 148) the filets on the interior side*** until they are a light shade of golden brown. Turn the filets over in the skillet and put the skillet in a 400° oven. Roast for 8 to 9 minutes and then squeeze the lime wedges over the mahi mahi filets. ⊕ For each serving, create a nest of the sautéed vegetables in the center of a plate. Lay two mahi mahi filets so they are overlapping each other on top of the vegetables. Spoon the smoked tomato vinaigrette around the perimeter of the plate, top the fish with the balsamic onion rings, and serve.

*See the Standard Preparations chapter for some thoughts about smoking foods.

**Charring is a blackening of the surface of the food by open flame or a very hot skillet.

***The interior side of the fish filet is the side that is against the spine of the fish. Cooking the fish on this side is especially important when there is skin on the filet because the skin will contract and curl the filet.

Pan-Roasted Black Grouper in Gumbo
with Rock Shrimp Remoulade

serves 4

½	CUP ALL PURPOSE FLOUR
½	CUP CLARIFIED BUTTER (SEE PAGE 43)
4	TABLESPOONS OLIVE OIL
½	CUP DICED RED BELL PEPPERS
½	CUP DICED GREEN BELL PEPPERS
½	CUP DICED POBLANO CHILE
½	CUP DICED YELLOW ONION
4	TABLESPOONS MINCED GARLIC
½	CUP TOMATO PASTE
6	CUPS CRAWFISH STOCK (SEE PAGE 42)
	KOSHER SALT AND CRACKED BLACK PEPPER TO TASTE
⅓	CUP MAYONNAISE
⅓	CUP KETCHUP
⅓	CUP CLEANED AND COOKED ROCK SHRIMP
2	TABLESPOONS FRESH LEMON JUICE
1	TABLESPOON VERY FINELY DICED CARROT
1	TABLESPOON VERY FINELY DICED RED ONION
1	TABLESPOON VERY FINELY DICED CHIVES
1	TABLESPOON VERY FINELY DICED PARSLEY
1	TEASPOON TABASCO SAUCE (OPTIONAL; AMOUNT IS DISCRETIONARY)
4	(7-OUNCE) BLACK GROUPER FILETS (SEA BASS OR SNAPPER CAN BE SUBSTITUTED)
2	CUPS SMALL WEDGES OF NEW POTATOES
½	CUP (¾-INCH-LONG) BIAS-CUT GREEN ONIONS
¼	CUP COARSELY CHOPPED CELERY LEAVES

To make gumbo, you must begin with the roux (a thickener). In a hot, heavy pan without oil, cook the flour over moderate heat until it becomes dark. You must stir the flour continuously so that it doesn't burn and become bitter. Add the clarified butter and cook, stirring until the roux becomes dark brown. It is not a quick process (allow 1 to 1½ hours), but the deeper the color, the richer the flavor. Set aside in a warm place. In a hot, heavy pan with 1 tablespoon of olive oil, sauté the red bell pepper, green bell pepper, poblano chile, yellow onion, and garlic until just tender. Add the tomato paste and Crawfish Stock, and then cook until volume has reduced by ⅓. Whisk in the roux a little at a time while the soup is hot, until it thickens to your desired consistency. Season to taste and keep the gumbo in a warm place. To make the remoulade, mix the mayonnaise, ketchup, rock shrimp, lemon juice, carrot, red onion, chives, parsley, and Tabasco sauce together. In yet another hot, heavy skillet, heat the remaining 3 tablespoons of olive oil. Season the grouper filets with salt and pepper, and then sear the interior side* of the filets to a light golden brown. (For information about searing, see the Skillet-Seared Ahi Tuna recipe on page 148.) Add the wedges of new potatoes and the green onions, and then turn the fish over and season the vegetables with salt and pepper. Put the pan in a 400° oven and roast the grouper, potatoes, and green onions for 10 minutes. Remove from the oven. For each serving, spoon the roasted new potatoes and green onions into a mound in the center of a shallow, wide-rimmed soup bowl. Place a grouper filet on top of the potatoes and green onions, and then ladle the gumbo around the potatoes. Sprinkle the celery leaves over the gumbo and spoon the remoulade onto the grouper; then serve.

*The interior side of the fish filet is the side that is against the spine of the fish. Cooking the fish on this side is especially important when there is skin on the filet because the skin will contract and curl the filet.

Pan-Roasted Lobster
with Apple-Cured Bacon, Celery Leaves, and Lime

serves 4

To prepare the vinaigrette, whisk together the lemon juice, corn oil, chives, vinegar, Dijon mustard, garlic, and whole-grain mustard in a chilled stainless-steel bowl. Season to taste and set aside in a cool place. Render the bacon in a heavy skillet over moderately high heat until it is just becoming crisp. Add the new potatoes, red onion, and celery, then cook until the potatoes are tender all the way through. Deglaze the pan (release the food sticking to the inside of the pan) with lime juice and add the corn kernels, green onion, and celery leaves. Season to taste with salt and pepper, and set aside

2	TABLESPOONS FRESH LEMON JUICE
¼	CUP CORN OIL
1	TABLESPOON FINELY CHOPPED CHIVES
1	TABLESPOON WHITE WINE VINEGAR
1	TABLESPOON DIJON MUSTARD
1	TEASPOON MINCED GARLIC
1	TABLESPOON WHOLE-GRAIN MUSTARD
	KOSHER SALT AND CRACKED BLACK PEPPER TO TASTE
½	CUP DICED APPLE-CURED BACON (HICKORY-SMOKED CAN BE SUBSTITUTED*)
2	CUPS SMALL WEDGES OF RAW, UNPEELED NEW POTATOES
½	CUP DICED RED ONION
½	CUP DICED CELERY
¼	CUP FRESH LIME JUICE
½	CUP SWEET CORN KERNELS
¼	CUP BIAS-CUT GREEN ONION
½	CUP COARSELY CHOPPED CELERY LEAVES
2	TABLESPOONS EXTRA-VIRGIN OLIVE OIL
4	(1-POUND) SPLIT LOBSTER TAILS
1	TABLESPOON TOASTED MUSTARD SEEDS

in a warm place. Heat the olive oil in a heavy skillet over high heat. Season the split lobster tails with salt and pepper, and then sear the cut side in the hot olive oil. (For information about searing, see the Skillet-Seared Ahi Tuna recipe on page 148.) Turn the tails over and roast in a 400° oven for 4 minutes. Remove from the oven and keep warm. For each serving, spoon the potato-bacon mixture onto the center of a plate. Loosen the meat from a split lobster tail, and crisscross the two halves. Place the lobster tails on the salad and drizzle the mustard vinaigrette over each of the four plates. Sprinkle the mustard seeds all over and serve.

See the Standard Preparations chapter for some thoughts about smoking foods.

Crisp Rainbow Trout on "Cowboy Couscous"
with Carrot Juice-Lemon Dressing

serves 4

To prepare the dressing, whisk the carrot juice, lemon juice, 2 tablespoons of olive oil, and mayonnaise together. Season to taste and set aside in a cool place. In a heavy pot, bring the water and the grits to a boil. Quickly, but carefully, drain the hot water from the grits and rinse in cold water to stop the cooking process. Do not soak the cooked grits in water. This leaves the grits partially cooked yet still crunchy, like couscous. Mix the grits with the 2 remaining tablespoons of olive oil, carrot, red onion, red bell pepper, cilantro, and chives. Season to taste with salt and pepper, and set aside at room temperature. Heat the peanut oil in a heavy skillet over moderately high heat. Mix the chopped parsley, dark chile powder,

½	CUP CARROT JUICE
¼	CUP LEMON JUICE
4	TABLESPOONS EXTRA-VIRGIN OLIVE OIL
2	TABLESPOONS MAYONNAISE
	KOSHER SALT AND CRACKED BLACK PEPPER TO TASTE
4	CUPS WATER
	COLD WATER (FOR RINSING GRITS)
1½	CUPS SOUTHERN-STYLE YELLOW GRITS, UNCOOKED
2	TABLESPOONS VERY FINELY DICED CARROT
2	TABLESPOONS VERY FINELY DICED RED ONION
2	TABLESPOONS VERY FINELY DICED RED BELL PEPPER
2	TABLESPOONS CHOPPED CILANTRO
2	TABLESPOONS FINELY CHOPPED CHIVES
¼	CUP PEANUT OIL
2	TABLESPOONS CHOPPED PARSLEY
1	TABLESPOON DARK CHILE POWDER
1	TEASPOON KOSHER SALT
1	CUP BLUE CORNMEAL
8	(3-OUNCE) BONELESS RAINBOW TROUT FILETS, WITH SKIN

and ½ teaspoon of salt into the blue cornmeal; then dust the trout filets with this mixture. Fry the trout in the hot oil for 2 minutes, with the interior side* down first; then turn over and fry for 90 seconds. Remove from the oil and carefully place on a couple of paper towels to absorb any excess oil. For each serving, spoon a mound of the "couscous" onto the center of the plate and crisscross two trout filets on top. Spoon the dressing around the perimeter of the plate and serve.

The interior side of the fish filet is the side that is against the spine of the fish (the skin is on one side; the spine is on the other). Cooking the fish on this side is especially important when there is skin on the filet because the skin will contract and curl the filet.

Filet of Salmon Cooked Campfire-Style
with Pears, Cucumber, and Pickled Beets

serves 4

To prepare the vinaigrette, puree the seasoned rice vinegar, 2 tablespoons of lemon juice, adobo sauce, chipotle chile in adobo sauce, chopped cilantro, shallots, and garlic in a blender. Decrease the blender speed and slowly add the corn oil until the dressing is smooth. Set aside in a cool place. Mix the soy sauce, honey, brown sugar, ¼ cup of lemon juice, and crushed red chile together; then marinate the salmon filets for 4 hours in this sauce. Smoke roast the salmon in a stove-top smoker (available from Williams-Sonoma cookware stores nationwide; call (800) 541-1262) over hickory wood shavings for 4 minutes on moderately high heat and 9 minutes on moderate heat. (See the Standard Preparations chapter for some thoughts about smoke roasting.) You can certainly use an outdoor grill for the salmon as an alternative. Toss the shaved carrot, cucumbers, pears, beets, radish sprouts, and watercress in the remaining 2 tablespoons of lemon juice. For each serving, make a mound of the salad in the center of a plate and set a salmon filet on the mound. Spoon the vinaigrette around the perimeter of the plate. Top the salmon filet with a cilantro sprig and serve.

¼	CUP SEASONED RICE VINEGAR
¼	CUP + 4 TABLESPOONS FRESH LEMON JUICE
1	TABLESPOON ADOBO SAUCE
1	TEASPOON PUREED CHIPOTLE CHILE IN ADOBO SAUCE
1	TABLESPOON CHOPPED CILANTRO LEAVES
1	TEASPOON CHOPPED SHALLOT
1	TEASPOON MINCED GARLIC
½	CUP CORN OIL
¼	CUP SOY SAUCE
¼	CUP HONEY
¼	CUP BROWN SUGAR
1	TABLESPOON CRUSHED RED CHILES
4	(7-OUNCE) BONELESS SALMON FILETS
¾	CUP SHAVED CARROT
¾	CUP HALVED (LENGTHWISE), SEEDED, AND SLICED CUCUMBER
¾	CUP QUARTERED, CORED, AND SLICED (LENGTHWISE) PEARS
¾	CUP JULIENNE OF PICKLED BEETS
¾	CUP RADISH SPROUTS
1	CUP WATERCRESS SPRIGS
4	CILANTRO SPRIGS

Steamed and Seared Scallops

with Cilantro Leaves, Dandelion Greens, and Ginger

serves 4

Toss the cilantro leaves, leek, ginger, and dandelion greens together in the lemon juice. Cover and chill in the refrigerator. Steam the scallops in a steamer over high heat with boiling water until they are just cooked, approximately 2½ minutes. For each serving, place five small mounds (one for each scallop) of the dandelion green salad around the bottom of a shallow bowl. You can also place the mounds in five individual little bowls on a large plate.

1	CUP CILANTRO LEAVES
1	CUP FINE JULIENNE OF LEEK
¼	CUP VERY FINE JULIENNE OF GINGER
1	CUP YOUNG (SMALL) DANDELION GREENS (AVAILABLE IN HEALTH FOOD STORES)
¼	CUP FRESH LEMON JUICE
20	JUMBO SCALLOPS
¼	CUP COOKED BLACK BEANS
1	TABLESPOON TAMARIND PASTE (LOOK IN THE ETHNIC FOODS SECTION OF YOUR GROCERY STORE)
¼	CUP SOY SAUCE
2	TABLESPOONS SESAME OIL
¼	CUP PEANUT OIL
2	TABLESPOONS LEMON ZEST

Top each mound with the cooked black beans. Mix the tamarind paste, soy sauce, and sesame oil together. In a heavy pan, heat the peanut oil over high heat until it is almost smoking. Spoon the soy sauce and tamarind mixture over the little mounds of salad. Using a very hot griddle or heavy skillet (not the pan with the peanut oil), sear* the scallops on one side. Place each seared scallop on a mound of salad, with the seared side up. Add lemon zest on the top of each scallop. Very carefully spoon the smoking hot peanut oil over the scallops and serve.

Searing is cooking something on a very hot surface very quickly to seal the surface of the food and achieve some crispness.

Grilled Shrimp with Chipotle-Creamed Leeks
on a Golden Cornmeal Cake

serves 4

Marinate the shrimp in ½ cup of corn oil, lime juice, and 1 tablespoon of cracked black pepper for 1 hour. To make the cornmeal cakes, bring the water to a boil and dissolve the 2 tablespoons of salt and the sugar in it. Add the cornmeal and simmer for 8 minutes; then stir in the grated cheese, diced tomato, and green onion. Grease a small baking sheet pan with the vegetable shortening, and spread the cornmeal mixture into the pan until it's approximately 1 inch thick. Refrigerate for 1 hour, and then cut into four rounds that are 3 inches in diameter. Set aside in the refrigerator. For the sauce, sauté the julienne of leek and the garlic in a heavy skillet over mod-

16	PEELED AND DEVEINED JUMBO SHRIMP
½	CUP + 2 TABLESPOONS CORN OIL
¼	CUP FRESH LIME JUICE
1	TABLESPOON CRACKED BLACK PEPPER
1½	CUPS WATER
2	TABLESPOONS KOSHER SALT
½	CUP SUGAR
1	CUP YELLOW CORNMEAL
¼	CUP GRATED DRIED JACK CHEESE (AVAILABLE IN GOURMET CHEESE SHOPS; PARMESAN CHEESE CAN BE SUBSTITUTED)
¼	CUP FINELY DICED TOMATO
¼	CUP BIAS-CUT GREEN ONION
2	TABLESPOONS VEGETABLE SHORTENING
4	CUPS JULIENNE OF LEEK WHITES
2	TABLESPOONS MINCED GARLIC
1½	CUPS HEAVY CREAM
1	TABLESPOON PUREED CHIPOTLE CHILE IN ADOBO SAUCE
	KOSHER SALT AND CRACKED BLACK PEPPER TO TASTE

erately high heat with 1 tablespoon of corn oil until they are just tender. Add the cream and the chipotle chile puree, and then cook until the mixture has reduced in volume by ⅓. Season to taste and set aside in a warm place. Brown the cornmeal cakes on a hot nonstick griddle, or skillet, with the remaining 1 tablespoon of corn oil, and place a cake in the center of each plate. Grill or broil the shrimp for 2½ minutes on each side. Spoon the creamed leeks over the cornmeal cakes. For each serving, interlock two of the shrimp and place these shrimp on top of the cake. Arrange the remaining shrimp around the cake and serve.

Spit-Roasted Chicken Marinated in Lemon and Garlic

with Warm Potato Salad

serves 4

2   (2½-POUND) CHICKENS, INNARDS REMOVED

1½ CUPS EXTRA-VIRGIN OLIVE OIL

½   CUP FRESH LEMON JUICE

1   THINLY SLICED LEMON

½   CUP COARSELY CHOPPED GARLIC

2   TABLESPOONS CRUSHED RED CHILES

½   CUP CHICKEN BROTH

¼   CUP SEASONED RICE VINEGAR

2   TABLESPOONS SUGAR

1   TABLESPOON TOASTED CELERY SEEDS

1   TABLESPOON TOASTED CUMIN SEED

1   TABLESPOON TOASTED MUSTARD SEEDS

2   TABLESPOONS CORNSTARCH

1   TABLESPOON WATER

1   CUP LARGE-CUT DICED AND BOILED RUSSET POTATO

1   CUP PEELED, DICED, AND ROASTED SWEET POTATO (OR YAM)

1   CUP SMALL WEDGE-CUT AND BOILED NEW POTATOES

1   CUP (1-INCH-LONG) BIAS-CUT AND BLANCHED* GREEN ONION

KOSHER SALT AND CRACKED BLACK PEPPER TO TASTE

 Marinate the chicken (if you are going to roast the chicken in the oven, you can split the chicken lengthwise along the spine) in the olive oil, lemon juice, sliced lemon, garlic, and crushed red chiles for at least 6 hours. Tie the legs together under the chicken and trim the first joint of the wing off (no need to do this if you're roasting the chicken in the oven); then slide onto the rotisserie spike. Charbroil the skewered chickens on the rotisserie for 2½ hours over moderately high heat (or roast for 1 hour and 45 minutes in a 375° oven). Break the chicken down by cutting out the backbone and then separating the breast from the thigh and the leg. Remove the thighbone by twisting it firmly and pulling. You should end up with four pieces per chicken: two breasts and two leg/thigh pieces Set aside in a warm place.  To make the warm potato salad, bring the chicken broth, rice vinegar, sugar, celery seed, cumin seed, and mustard seed to a boil; cook until it has reduced in volume by ⅓. Mix the cornstarch with the water. Use this mixture as necessary to thicken the potato salad dressing. Toss the cooked potatoes and green onions in the dressing; then season to taste. Set aside in a warm place.  For each serving, place a mound of the warm potato salad in the center of the plate. Interlock the breast and the thigh with the leg, and then place the chicken on top of the salad and serve.

To blanch, boil in salted water until just tender and barely cooked. Then drain, and chill with ice water to stop the cooking process. Drain and refrigerate.

Roasted Half Chicken
with Cornbread and Chorizo Stuffing

serves 4

To make the stuffing, sauté the carrot, celery, yellow onion, poblano chile, garlic, and chorizo in the corn oil in a heavy pan over high heat until the vegetables are tender and the chorizo is fully cooked. Add the apple juice and chicken broth, and then bring to a boil until volume has reduced by ⅓. Cool to room temperature. Add the cornbread, biscuits, cilantro, and green onions and mix thoroughly. Spoon the stuffing into a 9-inch nonstick pan and bake in a 375° oven for 35 minutes. Set aside in a warm place. Cut the first joint off each wing, and then season each half chicken with salt and pepper. Mix the

2	TABLESPOONS DICED CARROT
2	TABLESPOONS DICED CELERY
2	TABLESPOONS DICED YELLOW ONION
1	TABLESPOON DICED POBLANO CHILE
1	TABLESPOON CHOPPED GARLIC
½	CUP COOKED AND DRAINED CHORIZO (A SPICY MEXICAN PORK SAUSAGE)
2	TABLESPOONS CORN OIL
¾	CUP APPLE JUICE
¾	CUP CHICKEN BROTH
1½	CUPS CRUMBLED CORNBREAD
1½	CUPS CRUMBLED BUTTERMILK BISCUITS
2	TABLESPOONS CHOPPED CILANTRO
2	TABLESPOONS CHOPPED GREEN ONIONS
2	(2½-POUND) CHICKENS, CUT IN HALF
	KOSHER SALT AND CRACKED BLACK PEPPER TO TASTE
2	TABLESPOONS HONEY
1	TABLESPOON RED WINE VINEGAR
¼	CUP MILD NEW MEXICO RED CHILE PUREE
3	TABLESPOONS MELTED BUTTER
2	CUPS CLEANED AND BLANCHED* GREEN BEANS

honey, red wine vinegar, red chile puree, and 1 tablespoon of the melted butter together. Roast the chicken in a 400° oven for 10 minutes, brushing the honey mixture on the chicken repeatedly during the cooking. Reduce the temperature to 325° and continue roasting and basting for 20 more minutes. Reserve the remaining honey glaze. Separate the breast from the thigh and the leg; then remove the thighbone by twisting it firmly and pulling. You should end up with four pieces per chicken: two breasts and two leg/thigh pieces. Set aside in a warm place. Sauté the green beans over moderately high heat in the remaining 2 tablespoons of melted butter until the beans are tender, and then season to taste with salt and pepper. For each serving, spoon a mound of the cornbread and chorizo stuffing onto the center of a plate. Place the green beans so they are cascading down from the stuffing toward the right front quarter of the plate. Fit a chicken breast and a leg/thigh piece together and place on top of the stuffing and green beans. Brush the honey glaze over the chicken and serve.

To blanch, boil in salted water until just tender and barely cooked. Then drain, and chill with ice water to stop the cooking process. Drain and refrigerate.

Roasted Breast of Chicken
with Jicama Hash Browns

serves 4

4   (8-OUNCE) CHICKEN BREASTS WITH
    FIRST TWO WING JOINTS REMOVED

¼   CUP FRESH ORANGE JUICE

¼   CUP BROWN SUGAR

¼   CUP SOY SAUCE

½   CUP CORN OIL

2   TABLESPOONS FRESH LIME JUICE

2   TABLESPOONS CHOPPED FRESH MINT

1   TABLESPOON FINELY CHOPPED GINGER

1   TABLESPOON CHILE-GARLIC PASTE
    (AVAILABLE IN ORIENTAL MARKETS)

2   TABLESPOONS CHOPPED GARLIC

4   CUPS GRATED JICAMA (AVAILABLE IN SPECIALTY
    GROCERY STORES; POTATO CAN BE SUBSTITUTED)

1½ CUPS FINE JULIENNE OF WHITE ONION

½   CUP FINE JULIENNE OF POBLANO CHILE

    KOSHER SALT AND CRACKED BLACK PEPPER TO TASTE

¼   CUP SOUR CREAM, DILUTED WITH
    1 TABLESPOON OF WATER

4   TABLESPOONS RED BELL PEPPER KETCHUP
    (SEE PAGE 52)

Marinate the chicken breasts in the orange juice, brown sugar, soy sauce, ¼ cup of corn oil, lime juice, mint, ginger, chile-garlic paste, and 1 tablespoon of chopped garlic for 4 hours. Toss the grated jicama (HICK-a-muh) with the remaining 1 tablespoon of chopped garlic, white onion, and poblano chile. Then season to taste. From the jicama mixture, make patties that are 5 inches in diameter and ½ inch thick. Heat the remaining ¼ cup of corn oil in a heavy, nonstick skillet over moderately high heat and cook the jicama hash brown patties until they are a dark golden brown. Set the patties aside in a warm place. Sear* the chicken breasts in a heavy skillet; then turn the breasts over and roast in a 375° oven for 12 minutes. For each serving, carefully place the jicama hash browns on a plate and place a chicken breast on top of them. Using a squirt bottle, drizzle the diluted sour cream over the hash browns and chicken. Place a dollop of the Red Bell Pepper Ketchup on the chicken breast and serve.

Searing is cooking something on a very hot surface very quickly to seal the surface of food and achieve some crispness.

Sugar- and Chile-Cured Duck Breast and Roasted Duck Leg

with Green Chile Macaroni

serves 4

2	WHOLE DUCKLINGS, 4 POUNDS EACH
½	CUP GRANULATED SUGAR
¼	CUP DARK CHILE POWDER
¼	CUP KOSHER SALT
2	TABLESPOONS CRACKED BLACK PEPPER
1	TABLESPOON CLARIFIED BUTTER (SEE PAGE 43)
1	CUP + ½ CUP SWEET CORN KERNELS
2	TABLESPOONS CHOPPED SHALLOTS
½	CUP WHITE WINE
¼	CUP COLD UNSALTED BUTTER, CUT IN CUBES
3	TABLESPOONS RED BELL PEPPER KETCHUP (SEE PAGE 52)
	KOSHER SALT AND CRACKED BLACK PEPPER TO TASTE
1	TABLESPOON CORN OIL
¼	CUP DICED RED BELL PEPPER
¼	CUP DICED RED ONION
1	TABLESPOON MINCED GARLIC
2	CUPS COOKED MACARONI
½	CUP ROASTED, PEELED, SEEDED, AND PUREED POBLANO CHILE
½	CUP GRATED PEPPER JACK CHEESE
½	CUP HEAVY CREAM

Break each of the ducklings down by carefully removing a boneless breast and then removing the thigh and leg, together in one piece, from the carcass. Mix the sugar, chile powder, ¼ cup of salt, and 2 tablespoons of pepper together. Cut any excess fat and sinewy tissue off the breasts, and then rub the breasts in the sugar and chile dry cure. Let the breasts cure for at least 2 hours and no more than 4 hours. "French" the leg bones by making a circular cut 1½ inches down each leg bone and scraping the skin and other tissue from the bone. Season the thigh/leg pieces, and then roast in a 400° oven for 5 minutes; reduce the heat to 325° and roast for 25 more minutes. Remove from the oven and allow to cool to room temperature. Cut the thighs and legs apart, and then pull the meat off the thigh. Set the thigh meat and the roasted legs aside in a warm place. To make the sauce, heat the clarified butter in a heavy pan over high heat, and sauté 1 cup of corn kernels and the shallots for 2 minutes. Add the white wine and cook until the wine has reduced in volume by ½. Allow the mixture to cool to room temperature, and then puree in a blender, slowly adding the butter cubes. Do not overblend! Stir in the Red Bell Pepper Ketchup and strain the sauce. Season to taste and set aside in a warm place. For the macaroni, heat the corn oil in a heavy pan over moderately high heat, and then sauté the red bell pepper, red onion, garlic, duck thigh meat, and remaining ½ cup of corn kernels until just tender. Add the macaroni, poblano puree, cheese, and heavy cream. Stir the macaroni frequently until all the ingredients are combined thoroughly. Season to taste with salt and pepper, and set aside in a warm place. Brush off the excess dry cure from the breasts and grill for 90 seconds on the skin side first; then turn them over and grill for 3 minutes. With the skin side up, roast in a 400° oven for 4 minutes. For each serving, spoon the macaroni into a small skillet or dish, and brown under the broiler. Place it on the left side of a plate. Spoon the sauce in a pool on the right side of the plate. Cut the breasts in half on an angle and place both halves on the sauce, with a roasted leg separating the breast halves. Serve.

Pomegranate-Grilled Pork Sirloin
with Apples, Hominy, and Green Chile

serves 4

1	CUP POMEGRANATE MOLASSES (AVAILABLE FROM MIDDLE EASTERN FOOD MARKETS)
¼	CUP PUREED CHIPOTLE CHILES IN ADOBO SAUCE
¼	CUP HONEY
4	(8-OUNCE) PORK SIRLOIN STEAKS
½	GALLON CHICKEN BROTH
1	CUP COARSELY DICED SMOKED HAM HOCK MEAT
½	CUP TOASTED, SEEDED, AND CHOPPED NEW MEXICO GREEN CHILES
¼	CUP TOASTED, SEEDED, AND CHOPPED CHILE ANCHO
1	TABLESPOON CORN OIL
1	CUP JULIENNE OF RED ONION
½	CUP COOKED PINTO BEANS
1	CUP COOKED YELLOW HOMINY
1	CUP QUARTERED, CORED, AND SLICED THICK RED DELICIOUS APPLE
2	CUPS BRUSSELS SPROUT LEAVES (PEEL THE OUTER LEAVES OFF)
2	TABLESPOONS MINCED GARLIC
	KOSHER SALT AND CRACKED BLACK PEPPER TO TASTE

Mix the pomegranate molasses, pureed chipotle chiles in adobo sauce, and honey together. Reserving ¼ cup of the marinade, marinate the pork sirloins in this mixture for at least 4 hours (and no longer than 6 hours) in the refrigerator. In a heavy pan, bring the chicken broth, smoked ham hock meat, and the chiles to a boil; then cook until volume has reduced by ¾. Strain the sauce and set aside in a warm place. Brush the marinade off the pork sirloins. Grill the sirloins over moderately high heat for about 2 minutes, and then turn them over and grill for 2 more minutes. Turn the pork sirloins over again and lay the steaks perpendicular to the previous grill marks to create cross marks on the surface of the steaks; then repeat the procedure on the other side of the steaks. Finish in a 375° oven for 2 minutes on each side; then brush with the reserved ¼ cup of the marinade. In a heavy skillet, heat the corn oil over moderately high heat and sauté the red onion, pinto beans, hominy, apples, Brussels sprout leaves, and garlic; then season to taste. For each serving, place a mound of the apple and hominy mixture in the center of a plate. Set a pork sirloin steak on the mixture. Drizzle the sauce around the perimeter of the plate and serve.

167

Grilled Pork Tenderloin
with Smoked Tomato Grits and Asparagus

serves 4

In a heavy pan, bring 2 cups of chicken broth, the espresso, and the chile ancho to a boil. Cook until mixture has reduced in volume by ¾, season to taste, strain, and set aside in a warm place. To make the grits, bring 1 cup of chicken broth to a boil, add the grits, and reduce the heat. Add the garlic, white onion, and sage. Allow the mixture to simmer for 10 minutes over low heat. Stir in the milk and smoked tomato puree; then season to taste with salt and pepper. Season the pork tenderloins with salt and pepper; grill for 2 minutes on one side and then 2 minutes on the other side. Repeat the procedure, turning the tenderloins perpendicular to the first grill marks to achieve cross marks. Set aside at room temperature. In a heavy skillet, heat the corn oil over moderately high heat and sauté the red onion, asparagus spears, and apricots until just tender. Finish with the bok choy leaves, and season to taste with salt and pepper. For each serving, spoon the vegetables onto a plate so they spread from the center toward the left bottom quarter of the plate. Scoop the grits into a high mound in the center of the plate. Slice a tenderloin into five pieces and shingle the slices around the right front of the grits. Drizzle the sauce in thin ribbons over the pork tenderloin, and serve.

3½	CUPS CHICKEN BROTH
½	CUP ESPRESSO
¼	CUP TOASTED, SEEDED, AND CHOPPED CHILE ANCHO
	KOSHER SALT AND CRACKED BLACK PEPPER TO TASTE
1	CUP WHITE SOUTHERN-STYLE GRITS, UNCOOKED
1	TABLESPOON MINCED GARLIC
½	CUP FINELY DICED WHITE ONIONS
¼	CUP CHOPPED FRESH SAGE
½	CUP MILK
½	CUP SMOKED TOMATO PUREE*
4	(6-OUNCE) PORK TENDERLOINS
1	TABLESPOON CORN OIL
½	CUP JULIENNE OF RED ONION
20	PEELED ASPARAGUS SPEARS
½	CUP FRESH, COARSELY CHOPPED APRICOTS
2	CUPS BOK CHOY LEAVES (SPINACH LEAVES CAN BE SUBSTITUTED)

See the Standard Preparations chapter for some thoughts about smoking foods.

Grilled Pork Tenderloin and Braised Back Ribs

with Blue Cheese Bread Pudding

serves 4

½   GALLON CHICKEN STOCK (SEE PAGE 39)

1   QUART DR PEPPER SODA

1   CUP ROASTED AND COARSELY CUT WHITE ONION

1   CUP TOASTED, SEEDED, AND COARSELY CUT CHILE ANCHO

¼   CUP CHOPPED GARLIC

¼   CUP DARK CHILE POWDER

½   CUP BARBECUE SAUCE (SEE PAGE 59)

2   (1½-POUND) RACKS OF BABY BACK PORK RIBS

     KOSHER SALT AND CRACKED BLACK PEPPER TO TASTE

     FOOD RELEASE SPRAY

20   SLICES OF STALE FRENCH BREAD

½   CUP CRUMBLED MAYTAG FARMS BLUE CHEESE*

¾   CUP HEAVY CREAM

1   EGG YOLK

2   EGGS

¼   CUP DICED HICKORY-SMOKED BACON

¼   CUP FINELY DICED YELLOW ONION

¼   CUP FINELY DICED CARROT

1   TABLESPOON MINCED GARLIC

2   CUPS CHICKEN BROTH

½   CUP ROASTED, PEELED, SEEDED, AND PUREED POBLANO CHILE

4   (4½-OUNCE) PORK TENDERLOINS

¼   CUP PLUM JELLY

2   TABLESPOONS DIJON MUSTARD

2   TABLESPOONS SEASONED RICE VINEGAR

1   TABLESPOON TABASCO SAUCE

1   TABLESPOON PREPARED HORSERADISH

Bring the Chicken Stock, Dr Pepper, white onion, chile ancho, chopped garlic, chile powder, and Barbecue Sauce to a boil in a heavy pot over high heat. Lower to moderately high heat and simmer strongly. Cut the baby back rib racks into three-bone racks and rub with salt and pepper; then cook them in the braising liquid over moderately high heat for 1 hour. Reduce the heat and simmer lightly for another hour. Remove the ribs from the braising liquid. Strain the braising liquid and boil until it has reduced enough in volume so it has the consistency of a good, thick barbecue sauce. Brush the ribs with the sauce and roast in a 300° oven for 20 minutes. Set aside in a warm place. Preheat your oven to 350°. To make the blue-cheese bread pudding, spray the inside of four baking cups of a nonstick muffin tin. Starting with the slices of stale French bread, place alternating layers of the French bread and the crumbled blue cheese in the four baking cups, filling them to the top. Whip the cream, egg yolk, and whole eggs together, and then season with salt and pepper. Very carefully and slowly, pour the custard into the cups, over the bread and blue cheese, until the cups are full. Allow a couple of minutes for the custard to soak into the bread before repeating the procedure. Bake for 35 minutes. Remove from the oven and allow to cool to room temperature. Do not unmold from the muffin tin until the bread pudding has cooled. To prepare the sauce, render the bacon (cook until the fat is beginning to crisp) in a heavy pan over moderately high heat, and then sauté the yellow onion, carrot, and minced garlic until just tender. Add the chicken broth and the poblano chile puree, and then bring to a boil. Cook until volume has reduced by ⅓ and then season to taste with salt and pepper. Set aside in a warm place. Season the pork tenderloins with salt and pepper. Grill for 2 minutes on each side. Repeat the grilling procedure, turning the tenderloin perpendicular to the first grill marks to achieve cross marks. For each serving, spoon the green chile sauce in a pool in the center of a plate and set one blue-cheese bread pudding in the center of the sauce. Rest two of the three-bone racks of baby back ribs against the left rear and left side of the bread pudding. Mix the plum jelly, Dijon mustard, rice vinegar, Tabasco sauce, and horseradish together and reserve a couple of tablespoons of this mixture. Glaze the pork tenderloin with the plum jelly mixture. For each serving, slice a pork tenderloin in half, cutting it at a 30° angle. Stand one of the two tenderloin halves in the left front and lay the other half down on the right side of the bread pudding. Drizzle a small amount of the plum glaze over the tenderloin and serve.

Maytag Farms, in Newton, Iowa, produces one the finest blue cheeses in the United States. For more information, call (515) 792-1133.

Pork Tenderloin with a Poblano and Yam Gratin

served with Maple Syrup-Balsamic Sauce

serves 4

4	(8-OUNCE) PORK TENDERLOINS
2	CUPS DARK BEER
½	CUP SOY SAUCE
2	TABLESPOONS DICED JALAPEÑO
2	TABLESPOONS CHOPPED CILANTRO
2	TABLESPOONS FRESH LIME JUICE
2	TABLESPOONS BROWN SUGAR
2	CUPS CHICKEN BROTH
½	CUP MAPLE SYRUP
¼	CUP BALSAMIC VINEGAR
¼	CUP TOMATO KETCHUP
2	CUPS ROASTED, PEELED, AND SLICED YAMS (OR SWEET POTATOES)
½	CUP COOKED, PEELED, AND PUREED YAMS
½	CUP THINLY SLICED YELLOW ONION
½	CUP GRATED DRIED MONTEREY JACK CHEESE (AVAILABLE IN GOURMET CHEESE SHOPS)
¼	CUP VERY FINE JULIENNE OF POBLANO CHILE
1	EGG YOLK
2	WHOLE EGGS
1½	CUPS HEAVY CREAM
2	TABLESPOONS VEGETABLE SHORTENING
1½	CUPS BIAS-CUT SUGAR SNAP PEAS
2	TABLESPOONS UNSALTED BUTTER
	KOSHER SALT AND CRACKED BLACK PEPPER TO TASTE

 Marinate the pork tenderloin in the dark beer, soy sauce, jalapeño, cilantro, lime juice, and brown sugar for at least 2 hours and no more than 4 hours.  To make the sauce, bring the chicken broth to a boil and cook until volume has reduced by ½. Add the maple syrup, balsamic vinegar, and tomato ketchup; then bring to a boil and again reduce in volume by ½. Set aside in a warm place.  Mix the sliced yams, pureed yams, sliced onion, cheese, and julienne of poblano chile in a bowl. In another bowl, whisk the egg yolk, whole eggs, and cream together. Pour the custard over the yam mixture and mix. Grease a 9-inch nonstick baking pan using the vegetable shortening and a paper towel; then spoon the yam mixture into the pan. Bake in a 350° oven for 45 minutes and allow to cool to room temperature before cutting into four 3-inch-diameter circles. Place in a nonstick pan.  Grill the tenderloins for 2 minutes on each side. Repeat the procedure, turning the tenderloins perpendicular to the first grill marks to achieve cross marks. Reheat the yam gratin and, using a spatula, place one circle of yam gratin in the center of each plate. Spoon the sauce around the gratin. Slice each tenderloin into five slices and shingle the sliced tenderloin around the gratin. Sauté the bias-cut sugar snap peas in the butter over moderate heat until they are just tender. Season to taste and place on top of the gratin and serve.

Grilled Colorado Lamb Loin and Green Corn Sauce
with White Bean Puree

serves 4

2	TABLESPOONS EXTRA-VIRGIN OLIVE OIL
¾	CUP SWEET CORN KERNELS
¼	CUP + 1 TABLESPOON DICED YELLOW ONION
2	CUPS CHICKEN BROTH
¼	CUP ROASTED, PEELED, SEEDED, AND PUREED POBLANO CHILE
2	TABLESPOONS CHOPPED FRESH CILANTRO
¼	CUP HEAVY CREAM
	KOSHER SALT AND CRACKED BLACK PEPPER TO TASTE
¼	CUP DICED SALT PORK
1	TABLESPOON FINELY DICED CARROT
1	TABLESPOON FINELY DICED CELERY
2	TABLESPOONS MINCED GARLIC
1½	CUPS COOKED WHITE BEANS
2	TABLESPOONS CHOPPED FRESH MINT MARIGOLD (TARRAGON MAY BE SUBSTITUTED)
4	(6-OUNCE) LAMB LOIN FILETS
¼	CUP SLICED SHIITAKE MUSHROOMS
¼	CUP QUARTERED BUTTON MUSHROOMS
½	CUP ASPARAGUS TIPS

To prepare the sauce, heat 1 tablespoon of the olive oil in a heavy pan over high heat. Sauté ½ cup of the corn kernels and ¼ cup of yellow onion until tender. Add 1 cup of the chicken broth and boil until volume has reduced by ½. Add the poblano puree and chopped cilantro and then simmer for 5 minutes. Allow the sauce to cool to room temperature, and then puree in a blender and pass through a food mill (see note about food mill on Rock Shrimp Gazpacho recipe, page 84). Finish the sauce with the cream and the ¼ cup of corn kernels. Season to taste and set aside in a warm place. ⒭ To make the white bean puree, render the salt pork (cook until the fat begins to crisp) in a heavy pan over moderately high heat. Add the carrot, 1 tablespoon of yellow onion, celery, and 1 tablespoon of garlic; then sauté until tender. Add the cooked white beans and the other cup of chicken broth; then boil until the broth has almost evaporated. Puree the mixture, add the mint marigold, and season to taste with salt and pepper. Set aside in a warm place. ⒭ Season the lamb filets with salt and pepper and then grill them for 90 seconds on each side. Repeat the grilling procedure, turning the filets perpendicular to the first grill marks to achieve cross marks. Finish in a 400° oven for 4 minutes, and then set aside and allow to cool to room temperature. ⒭ Over moderately high heat, sauté the mushrooms, remaining 1 tablespoon of garlic, and asparagus tips in the remaining 1 tablespoon of olive oil, and then season to taste with salt and pepper. For each serving, spoon the white bean puree off-center toward the upper right quarter of the plate. Ladle the sauce in a pool off-center in the lower left quarter of the plate. Place the sautéed mushrooms and asparagus so they are cascading down from the mound of white bean puree toward the right front quarter of the plate. Slice a lamb loin filet into four slices and shingle them (arrange in a fanlike shape) against the white bean puree from the left rear to the front center of the plate and serve.

Balsamic-Glazed Rack of Lamb and Plum Ketchup
with Chile-Cheese Baked Potato

serves 4

1	CUP MALT VINEGAR (MAY NEED ADDITIONAL ½ CUP IF PLUMS ARE HARD)
1	CUP GRANULATED SUGAR (MAY NEED ADDITIONAL ½ CUP IF PLUMS ARE HARD)
2	TABLESPOONS DRY MUSTARD
¼	TEASPOON GROUND NUTMEG
1	TABLESPOON GROUND CINNAMON
¼	TEASPOON GROUND CLOVE
¼	TEASPOON CAYENNE PEPPER
2	CUPS COARSELY CUT FRESH PLUMS
	KOSHER SALT AND CRACKED BLACK PEPPER TO TASTE
4	LARGE RUSSET POTATOES, WASHED AND PATTED DRY
1	CUP AMY'S QUESO (SEE PAGE 19)
1	CUP SWEET CORN KERNELS
1	CUP BIAS-CUT GREEN ONIONS
½	CUP BALSAMIC VINEGAR
½	CUP RED TABLE WINE
¼	CUP SOY SAUCE
¼	CUP CONCORD GRAPE JELLY
2	TABLESPOONS DIJON MUSTARD
1	TABLESPOON MINCED GARLIC
4	(14-OUNCE) RACKS OF LAMB
2	TABLESPOONS EXTRA-VIRGIN OLIVE OIL
2	TABLESPOONS TOASTED MUSTARD SEEDS

Make the plum ketchup first. In a nonreactive*, heavy pan, bring the malt vinegar, sugar, dry mustard, nutmeg, cinnamon, clove, and cayenne pepper to a boil. Add the plums, decrease the heat, and simmer for 1 hour. (If the plums are hard, cook for an additional ½ hour and add another ½ cup of malt vinegar and another ½ cup of sugar.) Allow the mixture to cool to room temperature, and then pass it through a food mill (see the Rock Shrimp Gazpacho recipe, page 84, for information about food mills). Stir, season to taste, and chill in the refrigerator for at least 1 hour. Preheat your oven to 375° and bake the potatoes for 1 hour and 15 minutes. Allow the potatoes to cool slightly, and then lay the potatoes down flat and cut off the top ⅓ of each potato horizontally. Carefully scoop out the potato meat from the top and bottom, leaving the skins intact, and place the potato meat in a bowl. Combine the potato meat with Amy's Queso, corn kernels, and green onion. Return the potato mixture to the hollowed-out potato bottoms, and bake in a 400° oven for 10 minutes. Set aside in a warm place. To make the glaze for the lamb racks, bring the balsamic vinegar, red wine, soy sauce, grape jelly, Dijon mustard, and minced garlic to a boil in a heavy, nonreactive* pan. Cook until volume has reduced by ⅔ and set aside at room temperature. Preheat your oven to 400°. Season the lamb racks with salt and pepper. Heat the olive oil in a heavy skillet until very hot and sear** off the lamb racks on all the fleshy surfaces (sear the red meat areas). Then place the skillet with the lamb in the oven for 8 to 9 minutes to cook the lamb to a little below medium-rare. Brush the balsamic glaze on the racks during the last 3 minutes of the cooking time. Slice each lamb rack into three chops. For each serving, place a chile-cheese baked potato across the upper left quarter of a plate. Rest three lamb chops against the potato, and then spoon a dollop of the plum ketchup on the lamb chops. Sprinkle the toasted mustard seeds over the plate and serve.

*A nonreactive pan is made of a metal that won't be stained or pitted. Try using cast iron, ceramic-lined pots, or black anodized steel.

**Searing is cooking something on a very hot surface very quickly to seal the surface of the food and achieve some crispness.

Chile- and Sugar-Cured Black Buck Antelope
with a Rich Sauce of Local Mushrooms and Dried Chiles

serves 4

8	(4-OUNCE) BLACK BUCK ANTELOPE CHOPS (ANY VENISON CHOP OR LAMB CHOP MAY BE SUBSTITUTED)
½	CUP GRANULATED SUGAR
½	CUP DARK CHILE POWDER
¼	CUP KOSHER SALT
2	TABLESPOONS + 1 TEASPOON CORN OIL
2	TABLESPOONS TOASTED, SEEDED, AND MINCED CHILE ANCHO
2	TABLESPOONS TOASTED, SEEDED, AND MINCED CHILE PASILLA
2	TABLESPOONS TOASTED, SEEDED, AND MINCED CHILE GUAJILLO
4	CUPS CHICKEN BROTH
1	CUP VEAL DEMI-GLACE (SEE PAGE 41)
½	CUP COARSELY CHOPPED WHITE CORN TORTILLAS
1	TABLESPOON MOLASSES
½	CUP QUARTERED BUTTON MUSHROOMS
½	CUP SLICED CHANTERELLE MUSHROOMS (OYSTER MUSHROOMS MAY BE SUBSTITUTED)
2	TEASPOONS MINCED GARLIC
1	CUP COOKED, PEELED, AND DICED BUTTERNUT SQUASH*
½	CUP BLANCHED GREEN BEANS**
½	CUP BLANCHED YELLOW WAX BEANS**
½	CUP (½-INCH) BIAS-CUT PIECES OF GREEN ONION
½	CUP COOKED BLACK BEANS
	KOSHER SALT AND CRACKED BLACK PEPPER TO TASTE

To cure the antelope, mix the granulated sugar, dark chile powder, and ¼ cup of salt together, and then rub into the meat. Set aside in the refrigerator for at least 1 hour and no more than 2 hours. Heat 1 teaspoon of the corn oil in a heavy pan over high heat. Sauté the chile ancho, chile pasilla, and chile guajillo until tender. Add the chicken broth, Veal Demi-Glace, white corn tortillas, and molasses; then bring to a boil and continue boiling until volume has reduced by ¾. Strain the sauce through a fine strainer. In a separate skillet, heat 1 tablespoon of corn oil and sauté the button mushrooms, chanterelle mushrooms, and 1 teaspoon of garlic until just tender. Pour the strained sauce in with the mushrooms and simmer for 5 minutes. Set aside in a warm place. Remove any dry cure from the meat of the antelope, and then grill over moderately high heat for 2 minutes on each side. Repeat the grilling procedure, turning the chops perpendicular to the first grill marks to achieve cross marks and this time grilling for only 90 seconds on each side. Heat the remaining 1 tablespoon of corn oil in a heavy skillet over moderately high heat, and then sauté the butternut squash, green beans, yellow wax beans, green onions, black beans, and remaining 1 teaspoon of garlic until just tender. Season to taste. For each serving, spoon a mound of the squash mixture off-center toward the upper right quarter of the plate. Spoon the sauce in a pool in the lower left quarter of the plate. Place two chops so that the bones are resting against the mound of vegetables, and serve.

*To cook the squash, split it, season it, and then bake it in a 375° oven for 45 minutes.

**To blanch, boil in salted water until just tender and barely cooked. Then drain, and chill with ice water to stop the cooking process. Drain and refrigerate.

Skillet-Seared Venison Medallions and Mashed Potatoes
with Cola Soda and Chile Sauce

serves 4

In a heavy pan, bring the cola, Veal Demi-Glace, tomato, yellow onion, and garlic to a boil. Reduce the heat, and then simmer until the volume has reduced by ⅔. Allow the sauce to cool to room temperature and then puree. Set aside in a warm place. Boil the potatoes in 4 cups of water salted with 1 tablespoon of kosher salt until tender. Drain the water off and roast the potatoes in a 350° oven for 15 minutes. Put the potatoes in a mixer (not a blender or a food processor) and add the butter, milk, sour cream, and chopped cilantro. Thoroughly mix until the mixture is smooth. Season to taste and set aside in a warm place. Heat 2 tablespoons

1	CUP COLA SODA (COCA-COLA, PEPSI, DR PEPPER, ETC.)
1	CUP VEAL DEMI-GLACE (SEE PAGE 41)
½	CUP COARSELY CHOPPED TOMATO
1	TABLESPOON MINCED CHILE ARBOL
½	CUP DICED YELLOW ONION
1	TABLESPOON MINCED GARLIC
2½	CUPS PEELED AND QUARTERED RUSSET POTATOES
4	CUPS WATER
1	TABLESPOON KOSHER SALT
¾	CUP UNSALTED BUTTER
¼	CUP MILK
2	TABLESPOONS SOUR CREAM
1	TABLESPOON CHOPPED CILANTRO
	KOSHER SALT AND CRACKED BLACK PEPPER TO TASTE
3	TABLESPOONS CORN OIL
8	(3½-OUNCE) VENISON MEDALLIONS (BEEF MEDALLIONS MAY BE SUBSTITUTED)
1	CUP BIAS-CUT SUGAR SNAP PEAS
½	CUP JULIENNE OF RED ONION
½	CUP SWEET CORN KERNELS

of the corn oil in a heavy skillet over high heat. Season the venison medallions with salt and pepper, and then sear* for 2 minutes on each side. Heat the remaining 1 tablespoon of corn oil in a heavy skillet over high heat, and then sauté the sugar snap peas, red onion, and corn kernels until just tender. Season to taste with salt and pepper. For each serving, place a mound of mashed potatoes off-center toward the top of a plate. Spoon the vegetables over the potatoes so that the vegetables are cascading down toward the left side of the plate. Lean a venison medallion against the potatoes, facing the front of the plate, and then spoon the sauce over the medallion and serve.

Searing is cooking something on a very hot surface very quickly to seal the surface of the food and achieve some crispness.

Grilled Veal Flank Steak and Portabello Mushroom
with Sun-Dried Tomato Hash

serves 4

4	(6-OUNCE) VEAL FLANK STEAKS (BEEF FLANK STEAKS MAY BE SUBSTITUTED)
1 ¼	CUPS + 4 TABLESPOONS EXTRA-VIRGIN OLIVE OIL
½	CUP SOY SAUCE
6	TABLESPOONS MINCED GARLIC
3	CUPS CHICKEN BROTH
1	CUP VEAL DEMI-GLACE (SEE PAGE 41)
½	CUP DICED SMOKED HAM HOCK
½	CUP COARSELY CHOPPED DRIED NEW MEXICO GREEN CHILES
	KOSHER SALT AND CRACKED BLACK PEPPER TO TASTE
¾	CUP DICED LEEKS
¾	CUP DICED YELLOW ONION
1	CUP COARSELY CHOPPED SUN-DRIED TOMATOES
½	CUP CHOPPED CALAMATA OLIVES
3	CUPS LARGE-DICED (½ INCH) AND COOKED NEW POTATOES (BOIL UNTIL TENDER)
4	LARGE PORTABELLO MUSHROOMS, STEMS AND GILLS REMOVED
½	CUP BALSAMIC VINEGAR

Marinate the veal flank steaks in 1 cup of olive oil, soy sauce, and 2 tablespoons of minced garlic for 2 hours and no longer than 3 hours. To make the sauce, bring the chicken broth, Veal Demi-Glace, smoked ham hock, and dried New Mexico green chiles to a boil. Reduce the heat, and then simmer until volume has reduced to 1 cup; strain. Season to taste and set aside in a warm place.

To make the tomato hash, heat 2 tablespoons of olive oil in a heavy pan over moderately high heat. Sauté the leeks, yellow onion, sun-dried tomato, olives, and 2 tablespoons of garlic until tender. Add the potatoes and continue cooking for 3 to 4 minutes until the potatoes start to break down. Season to taste with salt and pepper, mix together thoroughly, and form into four patties, 4 inches in diameter. Set aside in a cool place. Brush the portabello mushrooms with ¼ cup of olive oil, balsamic vinegar, and 2 tablespoons of garlic (reserve some of this mixture); grill for 90 seconds on each side. Repeat the grilling procedure, turning the mushrooms perpendicular to the first grill marks to achieve cross marks. Set aside in a warm place and brush with the balsamic vinegar and olive oil mixture. Remove the veal flank steak from the marinade and grill for 90 seconds on each side. Repeat the procedure, turning the flank steak perpendicular to the first grill marks to achieve cross marks. Heat the remaining 2 tablespoons of olive oil over moderately high heat and sear* the sun-dried tomato hash patties in a nonstick skillet. For each serving, place a grilled portabello mushroom upside down in the center of a plate and lay a hash patty on the mushroom. Slice a veal flank steak very thinly on the bias and place the slices ribbonlike on the hash. Spoon the sauce around the perimeter of the plate and serve.

*Searing is cooking something on a very hot surface very quickly to seal the surface of the food and achieve some crispness.

West Texas Barbecued Flank Steak

with Green Chile Mashed Potatoes and Sweet Corn Salsa

serves 4

4	TABLESPOONS DARK CHILE POWDER
2	TABLESPOONS KOSHER SALT
2	TABLESPOONS GRANULATED GARLIC
2	TABLESPOONS GRANULATED ONION
2	TABLESPOONS BROWN SUGAR
2	TABLESPOONS CRACKED BLACK PEPPER
1	TABLESPOON TOASTED AND GROUND CUMIN SEEDS
1	TEASPOON CAYENNE PEPPER
2	(1-POUND) BEEF FLANK STEAKS
2½	CUPS PEELED AND QUARTERED RUSSET POTATOES
4	CUPS WATER
1	TABLESPOON KOSHER SALT (FOR BOILING THE POTATOES)
½	CUP UNSALTED BUTTER
¼	CUP MILK
2	TABLESPOONS SOUR CREAM
½	CUP ROASTED, PEELED, SEEDED, AND PUREED POBLANO CHILE
	KOSHER SALT AND CRACKED BLACK PEPPER TO TASTE
¾	CUP ROASTED SWEET CORN KERNELS
2	TABLESPOONS FINELY DICED RED ONION
2	TABLESPOONS FINELY DICED RED BELL PEPPER
1	TABLESPOON FINELY DICED JALAPEÑO
2	TABLESPOONS CHOPPED CILANTRO
2	TABLESPOONS FRESH LIME JUICE

To cure the flank steak, mix the dark chile powder, 2 tablespoons of kosher salt, granulated garlic, granulated onion, brown sugar, cracked black pepper, toasted cumin, and cayenne pepper together, and rub into the flank steak. Let the flank steak sit for 2 hours in the refrigerator. In a wood-burning grill, build a small fire with hickory wood on the side of the grill (you want to cook the meat on the opposite side of the grill from the fire). Smoke roast the flank steak for 1½ hours. (See the Standard Preparations chapter for some thoughts about smoke roasting.) Set aside in a warm place. To make the mashed potatoes, boil the potatoes in lightly salted water until tender. Drain the water and roast the potatoes in a 350° oven for 15 minutes. Put the potatoes in a mixer (not a blender or food processor) and add the butter, milk, sour cream, and roasted poblano puree. Mix until the potatoes are smooth. Season to taste and set aside in a warm place. For the corn salsa, mix the corn kernels, red onion, red bell pepper, jalapeño, cilantro, and lime juice together. Season to taste with salt and pepper, and set aside in a cool place. For each serving, spoon the green chile mashed potatoes onto the center of a plate. Slice the flank steak on the bias, ¼ inch thick. Lay the slices across the mashed potatoes, top with the salsa, and serve.

Pan-Roasted Beef Filet in Coffee and Molasses Shellac
with Chipotle-Bacon-Cheese Grits

serves 4

To make the grits, bring the chicken broth to a boil and add the grits. Decrease the heat and simmer for 10 minutes over low heat, stirring frequently. Stir in the milk, grated cheddar cheese, cooked bacon, and pureed chipotle chile. Season to taste and set aside in a warm place.

To prepare the shellac for use in this recipe, add the double espresso and the molasses to the Glace de Viande. Stir the ingredients together and set the shellac aside in a warm place.

1	CUP CHICKEN BROTH
1	CUP YELLOW SOUTHERN-STYLE GRITS, UNCOOKED
½	CUP MILK
½	CUP GRATED CHEDDAR CHEESE
½	CUP DICED AND COOKED HICKORY-SMOKED BACON
1	TABLESPOON PUREED CHIPOTLE CHILES IN ADOBO SAUCE
	KOSHER SALT AND CRACKED BLACK PEPPER TO TASTE
2	TABLESPOONS DOUBLE ESPRESSO
2	TABLESPOONS MOLASSES
¾	CUP GLACE DE VIANDE (SEE PAGE 41)
4	(8-OUNCE) CENTER-CUT BEEF TENDERLOIN FILETS
2	TABLESPOONS CORN OIL
1	CUP JULIENNE OF WHITE ONION
1	TABLESPOON MINCED GARLIC
6	CUPS CLEANED SPINACH LEAVES
2	TABLESPOONS WHOLE UNSALTED BUTTER

Season the beef filets with salt and pepper. Then sear* them in hot corn oil in a heavy skillet for 3 minutes over moderately high heat. Turn the filets over and sear for 2 more minutes, and then place the skillet with the filets in a 400° oven for 7 minutes. Remove from the oven, brush with half the shellac, and allow to cool to room temperature. In a hot, heavy skillet sauté the white onion, garlic, and spinach leaves in the butter until the spinach is just wilted; then season to taste with salt and pepper. For each serving, spoon a mound of the grits onto the center of a plate and top with the sautéed spinach. Cut each beef filet from the top to the bottom at an angle. Place half a filet, with the cut side facing the front of the plate, on the spinach leaves and grits. Place the other half of the filet on the plate so that it's also facing the front of the plate, leaning against the grits and the other half of the filet. Drizzle the shellac around the perimeter of the plate and serve.

Searing is cooking something on a very hot surface very quickly to seal the surface of the food and achieve some crispness.

Grilled Tenderloin of Beef Filet
with Fricassee of Crawfish Tails and Bone Marrow

serves 4

To prepare the sauce, heat the clarified butter in a wide, heavy pot. Add the crawfish shells and cook for 4 to 5 minutes over high heat. Add the carrot, celery, onion, 2 tablespoons of garlic, and parsley and sauté until the vegetables are just sticking to the pot. Deglaze** the pot with the brandy and burn the alcohol off. Boil until the brandy has reduced in volume by ½. Add the white wine and reduce it in volume by ½, and then add the water. Bring the water to a boil and reduce in volume by ¾. Whisk the tomato paste into the mixture and strain. Continue reducing the stock until the volume is 1 cup. Season to taste and place in a warm place. Season the beef filets with salt and pepper, and grill for 3 minutes on one side and 2 minutes on the other side. Repeat the grilling procedure, turning the steaks perpendicular to the first grill marks to achieve cross marks. Set the steaks aside to rest and allow the juices to settle. In a hot, heavy skillet, heat the unsalted butter over moderately high heat and sauté the potato balls, haricot vert, crawfish tail meat, and the remaining 1 tablespoon of garlic until just tender. Season to taste with salt and pepper, and add the beef marrow to the vegetables immediately before serving. For each serving, spoon the sauce in a pool in the center of a plate and place a beef filet on the sauce. Spoon the sautéed vegetables with the beef marrow and crawfish tail meat around the beef filet, and then serve.

2	TABLESPOONS CLARIFIED BUTTER (SEE PAGE 43)
4	CUPS CRAWFISH SHELLS (SHRIMP, LOBSTER, OR CRAB SHELLS WILL WORK)
½	CUP COARSELY CHOPPED CARROT
½	CUP COARSELY CHOPPED CELERY
½	CUP COARSELY CHOPPED YELLOW ONION
3	TABLESPOONS MINCED GARLIC
¼	CUP COARSELY CHOPPED PARSLEY
½	CUP BRANDY
1	CUP FULL-BODIED WHITE WINE
8	CUPS WATER
¼	CUP TOMATO PASTE
	KOSHER SALT AND CRACKED BLACK PEPPER TO TASTE
4	(8-OUNCE) CENTER-CUT BEEF TENDERLOIN FILETS
2	TABLESPOONS UNSALTED BUTTER
¾	CUP SMALL, RAW POTATO BALLS (USE A SMALL MELON BALL SCOOP)
¾	CUP BLANCHED* HARICOT VERT, OR SMALL GREEN BEANS
1½	CUPS CRAWFISH TAIL MEAT (ROCK SHRIMP MAY BE SUBSTITUTED)
1	CUP PIECES OF BEEF MARROW (ASK YOUR BUTCHER FOR THESE)

*To blanch, boil in salted water until just tender and barely cooked. Then drain, and chill with ice water to stop the cooking process. Drain and refrigerate.

**To deglaze means to use a liquid to release all the food sticking to the inside of the pan.

Grilled Sirloin Steak and Sweet Potato Fries
with "Buzzard Breath" Barbecue Sauce

serves 4

To make the barbecue sauce, bring the Veal Stock, tomato paste, Dr Pepper, malt vinegar, Dijon mustard, molasses, and chipotle chiles in adobo sauce to a boil in a heavy pan. Cook until volume has reduced by ½, and then reduce the heat and simmer for 10 minutes. Season to taste and set aside in a warm place. To prepare the pepper relish, bring the rice vinegar and pickling spice to a boil. Allow the mixture to come to room temperature and remove the pickling spice. In a separate bowl, combine the red onion, red bell pepper, yellow bell pepper, poblano, carrot, and cilantro; then pour the rice vinegar over the relish. Set aside in a cool place. Heat the peanut oil

1	CUP VEAL STOCK (SEE PAGE 40)
¼	CUP TOMATO PASTE
¼	CUP DR PEPPER SODA
¼	CUP MALT VINEGAR
2	TABLESPOONS DIJON MUSTARD
2	TABLESPOONS MOLASSES
2	TABLESPOONS PUREED CHIPOTLE CHILES IN ADOBO SAUCE
	KOSHER SALT AND CRACKED BLACK PEPPER TO TASTE
¼	CUP SEASONED RICE VINEGAR
2	TABLESPOONS PICKLING SPICE, TIED IN A CHEESECLOTH
2	TABLESPOONS FINELY DICED RED ONION
2	TABLESPOONS FINELY DICED RED BELL PEPPER
2	TABLESPOONS FINELY DICED YELLOW BELL PEPPER
1	TABLESPOON FINELY DICED POBLANO CHILE
1	TABLESPOON FINELY DICED CARROT
1	TABLESPOON CHOPPED CILANTRO
4	CUPS PEANUT OIL (FOR FRYING)
4	CUPS LENGTHWISE-CUT WEDGES OF MEDIUM-SIZED SWEET POTATO (OR YAM)
4	(12-OUNCE) SIRLOIN STRIP STEAKS

in a heavy pot to 350°. Fry the sweet potato wedges until they are crisp and light brown, approximately 4½ minutes. (It is best to fry these potatoes in small batches.) Place on paper towels to absorb any excess oil, and then season to taste with salt and pepper. Season the steaks with salt and pepper, and then grill for 2½ minutes on each side. Repeat the grilling procedure, this time turning each steak perpendicular to the first grill marks to achieve cross marks and only cooking for 2 minutes on each side. Allow the steaks to rest at room temperature to settle the juices. Save the juice from the steaks and pour it into the barbecue sauce. For each serving, spoon the barbecue sauce into a pool in the center of a plate. Set some sweet potato fries in the upper right quarter of the plate and rest a steak against the fries (the steak should be in the pool of barbecue sauce). Spoon the pepper relish over the steak and serve.

Barbecue Beef Short Ribs
with Red Chile Pinto Beans and Mustard Greens

serves 4

¼	CUP + 2 TABLESPOONS CORN OIL
8	(4-OUNCE) THICK-CUT BEEF SHORT RIBS
	KOSHER SALT AND CRACKED BLACK PEPPER TO TASTE
8	CUPS CHICKEN BROTH
4	CUPS DR PEPPER SODA
1	CUP ROASTED AND COARSELY CHOPPED WHITE ONION
1	CUP TOASTED, SEEDED, AND COARSELY CHOPPED CHILE ANCHO
½	CUP BARBECUE SAUCE (SEE PAGE 59)
¼	CUP + 2 TABLESPOONS CHOPPED GARLIC
¼	CUP DARK CHILE POWDER
½	CUP DICED YELLOW ONION
¼	CUP CHOPPED, SMOKED HAM HOCK MEAT
1	CUP COOKED PINTO BEANS (SEE PAGE 45 FOR SOME THOUGHTS ABOUT COOKING DRY BEANS)
¼	CUP TOASTED, SEEDED, AND PUREED CHILE ANCHO
2	TABLESPOONS BROWN SUGAR
1	CUP JULIENNE OF WHITE ONION
4	CUPS CLEANED MUSTARD GREENS, WITHOUT STEMS
¼	CUP MALT VINEGAR

Heat ¼ cup of corn oil in a heavy roasting pan over high heat. Season the beef short ribs with salt and pepper, and then sear* the meaty parts of the ribs until they are a rich dark brown. Add the chicken broth, Dr Pepper, roasted white onion, chopped chile ancho, Barbecue Sauce, ¼ cup of garlic, and dark chile powder to

the roasting pan and bring to a boil. Boil the ribs for 45 minutes, and then decrease the heat and simmer the ribs for another hour. Remove the ribs from the braising liquid and strain the liquid. Bring the braising liquid to a boil and cook until it has reduced in volume by ¾; then season to taste with salt and pepper. Brush this sauce on the ribs (reserve some sauce to serve with meal) and roast them in a 250° wood-fired grill (or oven) for 45 minutes. (See Standard Preparations chapter for tips on cooking this way.) Set aside in a warm place.  Heat 1 tablespoon of corn oil in a heavy pot over moderately high heat, and then sauté the yellow onion, 1 tablespoon of garlic, and smoked ham hock until just tender. Add the cooked pinto beans, pureed chile ancho, and brown sugar. Simmer for 20 minutes and season to taste with salt and pepper. Spoon the beans into four individual crocks and set aside in a warm place. Heat the remaining 1 tablespoon of corn oil in a heavy pan over moderately high heat, and then sauté the julienne of white onion, remaining 1 tablespoon of garlic, and mustard greens until the greens are just wilted. Add the malt vinegar and season to taste with salt and pepper. For each serving, place a bed of the cooked mustard greens in the center of a plate and crisscross two ribs on top of the greens. Serve with a crock of red chile pinto beans and the reserved sauce on the side.

Searing is cooking something on a very hot surface very quickly to seal the surface of the food and achieve some crispness.

Grilled Rib Eye Steak and Blueberry Barbecue Sauce

with Roasted-Garlic Mashed Potatoes

serves 4

To make the sauce, bring the blueberries, rice vinegar, tomato ketchup, yellow onion, brown sugar, Dijon mustard, and jalapeño to a boil in a heavy pot. Boil for 5 minutes, and then decrease the heat and simmer for 10 minutes, stirring frequently. Allow the sauce to cool to room temperature and then puree in a blender. Strain the sauce and whisk in 2 tablespoons of unsalted butter. Season to taste with salt and pepper, and set aside in a warm place. To prepare the mashed potatoes, boil the potatoes in 4 cups of water salted with 1 tablespoon of kosher salt until tender. Drain the water from the potatoes and roast them in a 350° oven for 15 minutes. Put the potatoes in a mixer (not a blender or food processor) and add the remaining ¾ cup of unsalted butter, milk, sour cream, and roasted garlic. Mix until the mashed potatoes are smooth. Season to taste with salt and pepper, and set aside in a warm place.

1	CUP FRESH BLUEBERRIES
2	TABLESPOONS SEASONED RICE VINEGAR
2	TABLESPOONS TOMATO KETCHUP
2	TABLESPOONS FINELY DICED YELLOW ONION
1	TABLESPOON BROWN SUGAR
1	TABLESPOON DIJON MUSTARD
1	TEASPOON FINELY DICED JALAPEÑO
¾	CUP + 2 TABLESPOONS UNSALTED BUTTER
	KOSHER SALT AND CRACKED BLACK PEPPER TO TASTE
2½	CUPS PEELED AND QUARTERED RUSSET POTATOES
4	CUPS WATER
1	TABLESPOON KOSHER SALT
¼	CUP MILK
2	TABLESPOONS SOUR CREAM
¼	CUP ROASTED AND CHOPPED GARLIC
4	(12-OUNCE) RIB EYE STEAKS
1	CUP FAVA BEANS
	(BIAS-CUT SUGAR SNAP PEAS CAN BE SUBSTITUTED)
1	CUP CORN KERNELS
1	CUP FINE JULIENNE OF RED ONION
1	TABLESPOON CLARIFIED BUTTER (SEE PAGE 43)

Season the steaks with the salt and cracked black pepper, and then grill for 3 minutes on each side. Repeat the grilling procedure, this time turning the steaks perpendicular to the first grill marks to achieve cross marks and grilling each side for only 2 minutes. Allow to rest at room temperature. Sauté the fava beans, corn kernels, and julienne of red onion in the clarified butter in a heavy skillet over moderately high heat. Season to taste with salt and pepper, and set aside in a warm place. For each serving, place a mound of mashed potatoes in the upper right quarter of the plate and spoon a pool of the blueberry sauce in the center of the plate. Lean a steak against the mashed potatoes and in the sauce. Spoon the sautéed vegetables in front of the steak and serve.

Cowboy-Cut Rib Eye Steak
with Buttered Hominy and Red-Eye Gravy

serves 4

In a heavy pot, bring the Veal Stock, smoked ham hock meat, espresso, maple syrup, 1 teaspoon of garlic, and chile ancho to a boil. Cook until it has reduced in volume by ¾ and then strain. Season to taste and set the gravy aside in a warm place. Heat 1 tablespoon of clarified butter in a heavy skillet over moderately high heat. Sauté the hominy, shiitake mushrooms, button mushrooms, and red onion until just tender. Set aside. Season the

3	CUPS VEAL STOCK (SEE PAGE 40)
1	CUP DICED, SMOKED HAM HOCK MEAT*
½	CUP ESPRESSO
2	TABLESPOONS MAPLE SYRUP
2	TABLESPOONS + 1 TEASPOON CHOPPED GARLIC
2	TABLESPOONS TOASTED, SEEDED, AND MINCED CHILE ANCHO
	KOSHER SALT AND CRACKED BLACK PEPPER TO TASTE
¼	CUP + 1 TABLESPOON CLARIFIED BUTTER (SEE PAGE 43)
2	CUPS COOKED YELLOW HOMINY
½	CUP SLICED SHIITAKE MUSHROOMS
½	CUP QUARTERED BUTTON MUSHROOMS
½	CUP JULIENNE OF RED ONION
4	(18-OUNCE) RIB EYE STEAKS
1	CUP BRUSSELS SPROUT LEAVES

rib eye steak with salt and pepper. Heat the ¼ cup of clarified butter in a heavy skillet over high heat and sear** one side of the steak for 3 minutes and the other side of the steak for 2 minutes; then roast in a 400° oven for 7 minutes. Allow the steaks to rest at room temperature so the juices will settle. Add the Brussels sprout leaves and remaining 2 tablespoons of garlic to the hominy and mushrooms immediately before serving. Season to taste with salt and pepper. For each serving, spoon the hominy mixture into a large, shallow soup bowl. Place a steak on top of the hominy. Present the gravy on the side and serve with the steak.

*See the Standard Preparations chapter for some thoughts about smoking foods.

**Searing is cooking something on a very hot surface very quickly to seal the food and achieve some crispness.

CAST-IRON COOKING

CAST-IRON COOKING EXISTED LONG BEFORE THE FIRST PIONEERS ventured into the frontier now known as the American West. Because cast-iron pots and skillets were dependable, they could endure the hardships of a cross-country trip in a rigid wagon. As the settlers traveled across America, these cooking utensils became some of the most valuable items on their journey. Good cooks, past and present, have come to appreciate cast-iron pots and pans as an integral part of their cookware. As you will learn, the Dutch oven is one of the more versatile cooking utensils available. Cast-iron skillets are versatile also—remember *Throw Momma from the Train?* Cast iron distributes heat evenly because of its density and weight, and then retains heat much better than most alloys. Overall, a cast-iron skillet and a Dutch oven will be worthwhile additions to your cooking equipment collection.

To season cast iron, heat it slowly until it becomes quite warm; then wipe it out until the inside surface is clean and dry. Pour a small amount of vegetable oil in the pan and lightly coat the inside of the pan with the oil, using a paper towel. Should the pan become rusty or dirty in the future, simply repeat the procedure. A skillet can be placed directly over a fire, but it is important when using a Dutch oven to have two separate fires: one for the oven to cook on and the other to provide new embers for the cooking fire so its temperature remains constant. A small shovel is valuable for moving the coals from one fire to the other and for helping extinguish the fire.

Although wood-burning cooking fires infuse aromatic scents into the foods during grilling, charcoal briquettes are better for cast iron because they provide a more concentrated heat than natural coals. I have not found a consistently accurate formula to determine the amount of charcoal to use, but I will offer a couple of general guidelines for you when using your Dutch oven:

- If you are stewing or deep frying, use ⅔ of the coals under the oven and ⅓ on top. If you are baking, use ⅓ of the coals underneath the oven and ⅔ on top.
- You will not need as many coals on a hot day as you will on a cold day. You will need more coals on a windy day than on a still day, and you will need more coals at higher altitudes.

Here are several more cast-iron tips for you:

- Make sure you have some heavy oven mitts, preferably leather, for handling the hot cookware.
- Keep your skillet or Dutch oven as level as possible by placing rocks or bricks under the sides of the pan.
- Keep enough height between the fire and the pan for the air to circulate so the fire doesn't smother itself.
- If you do not want to carry both a skillet and a Dutch oven with you when you are outdoors, simply turn the lid of the Dutch oven over, making sure to keep it level, and use it as a skillet.
- To clean your cast iron, do not use a metal scrubber or steel wool; use a plastic scrubber. This will prevent you from removing the patina and seasoning from your pan.

You now have a good start on cooking outdoors next to the Roaring Fork River or wherever you can appreciate the great outdoors. Good luck!

Bean Casserole

makes 1 gallon

2	CUPS DRY RED KIDNEY BEANS
2	CUPS DRY PINTO BEANS
2	CUPS DRY BLACK BEANS
	WATER (FOR SOAKING BEANS)
2	CUPS DICED YELLOW ONION
1	CUP DICED POBLANO CHILE
2	TABLESPOONS TOASTED AND MINCED CHILE ARBOL
2	TABLESPOONS CHOPPED GARLIC
2	TABLESPOONS CORN OIL
1	LARGE SMOKED HAM HOCK, APPROXIMATELY 10 OUNCES
1	GALLON CHICKEN BROTH
1	CUP BARBECUE SAUCE (SEE PAGE 59)
¼	CUP TOMATO PASTE
	KOSHER SALT AND CRACKED BLACK PEPPER TO TASTE
1	CUP RITZ CRACKER CRUMBS
1	CUP GRATED CHEDDAR CHEESE

Soak the beans overnight. Over a fire, in a hot cast-iron pot or Dutch oven, sauté the onions, chiles, and garlic in the corn oil until they are just tender. Add the beans and the remaining ingredients except the cracker crumbs, cheddar cheese, salt, and pepper, and bring to a boil. Move the pot to the side of the fire to reduce the heat to a simmer and cook until the beans are tender, approximately 1½ hours. Season to taste. Mix the cracker crumbs and the cheddar cheese together. For each serving, ladle 6 ounces of the cooked beans into a bowl or crock, and then top with the cheese-cracker mixture. Lightly brown the top if possible and serve.

Roaring Fork's Pork Ribs

serves 4

4	(2-POUND) ST. LOUIS-STYLE (RIB BONES ARE 4 TO 5 INCHES LONG) RACKS OF PORK RIBS*, CUT IN 4-BONE SECTIONS
	KOSHER SALT AND CRACKED BLACK PEPPER TO TASTE
½	GALLON CHICKEN STOCK (SEE PAGE 39)
½	GALLON DR PEPPER SODA
1	CUP DICED ONION
½	CUP DARK CHILE POWDER
¼	CUP CHOPPED GARLIC
¼	CUP FINELY CHOPPED CHIPOTLE CHILES IN ADOBO SAUCE

Season the ribs with salt and pepper. Over a fire, in a hot cast-iron pot or Dutch oven, brown the ribs. Add the remaining ingredients and bring to a boil. Allow to boil for 15 minutes, and then move the pot to the side of the fire to reduce the heat and simmer for 1½ hours. Remove the ribs from the liquid and finish in a smoker for 2 hours (using hickory wood) if possible (see the Standard Preparations chapter for some thoughts and procedures regarding smoking food). If a smoker is not available, finish the ribs in your oven at 275° for 2 hours. Continue to simmer until the cooking liquid has reduced in volume to 1 quart. You may strain the sauce, but it is not necessary. Brush the ribs with some of the sauce during the last 15 minutes of their cooking time and serve.

*This recipe will also work for beef short ribs.

Green Chile Pork

serves 4

2	TABLESPOONS CORN OIL
2	POUNDS COARSELY CUT BONELESS COUNTRY-STYLE PORK RIBS
	KOSHER SALT AND CRACKED BLACK PEPPER TO TASTE
2	CUPS DICED YELLOW ONION
¼	CUP MINCED JALAPEÑO CHILE
1	CUP SEEDED, STEMMED, AND MINCED DRIED NEW MEXICO GREEN CHILES
¼	CUP MINCED GARLIC
2	CUPS ROASTED, PEELED, AND PUREED POBLANO CHILE
1	CUP GRATED PEPPER JACK CHEESE
24	(6-INCH) FLOUR TORTILLAS
¼	POUND BUTTER

Over a fire, in a cast-iron pot or Dutch oven, heat the corn oil. Season the pork with salt and pepper. When the oil is hot, add the pork, onions, jalapeño, New Mexico dried chiles, and garlic. Cook over the fire until the pork is tender, approximately 1½ hours. Add the poblano chile puree and simmer for 45 minutes to 1 hour. Season to taste with salt and pepper. Serve the green chile pork from a kettle or crock, topped with the grated cheese. Lightly brown the cheese if possible. Grill the tortillas and brush with the butter. Spoon the green chile pork into the tortillas and roll them up.

Western Beef Hash
with Fried Eggs and Tomatillo Sauce

serves 4

1	CUP QUARTERED TOMATILLOS
½	CUP COARSELY CUT WHITE ONION
1	COARSELY CUT ANAHEIM (OR GREEN) CHILE
½	CUP CHICKEN BROTH
1	TEASPOON COARSELY CUT GARLIC
	KOSHER SALT AND CRACKED BLACK PEPPER TO TASTE
¼	CUP CORN OIL
1	CUP DICED YELLOW ONION
2	TABLESPOONS FINELY DICED SERRANO CHILE
2	TABLESPOONS MINCED GARLIC
2	CUPS SMOKE-ROASTED* AND SHREDDED BEEF BRISKET
1	CUP COOKED AND DICED POTATO (TO COOK, BOIL UNTIL TENDER)
8	LARGE EGGS

Over a fire, in a cast-iron skillet or an inverted Dutch oven lid, lightly blacken the tomatillos, white onion, and anaheim chile. Add the chicken broth and coarsely cut garlic, and then puree the mixture and season to taste. Set aside in a warm place. Using 1 tablespoon of the corn oil in a cast-iron skillet over the fire, sauté the yellow onion, serrano chile, and minced garlic until tender. Mix the shredded beef, potatoes, and sautéed vegetables together in a bowl and season to taste with salt and pepper. Form into four patties. Using 2 tablespoons of the corn oil in a hot cast-iron skillet or an inverted Dutch oven lid, sauté the patties until they are crisp on the outside. Set aside in a warm place. Using the remaining corn oil, fry the eggs in the skillet or an inverted Dutch oven lid. For each serving, place a hash patty on a plate and spoon the tomatillo sauce over the patty. Set two fried eggs on top of the beef hash, and serve.

See Standard Preparations chapter for some thoughts about smoke roasting.

"One-Armed" Rib Eye Steak
with Black Bean and Smoked Onion Sofrito

serves 4

2 CUPS (¼-INCH-THICK) JULIENNE OF YELLOW ONION

1 CUP DICED RAW BACON

1 CUP BIAS-CUT GREEN ONION

1 CUP PEELED, SEEDED, AND COARSELY CUT TOMATO

1 CUP WASHED, COOKED, AND DRAINED BLACK BEANS
  (FOR OUTDOOR COOKING, USE CANNED BEANS,
  NOT DRY BEANS)

½ CUP COARSELY CUT GARLIC CLOVES

½ CUP ROASTED, PEELED, AND SEEDED JULIENNE
  POBLANO CHILE

½ CUP CHOPPED CILANTRO

4 TABLESPOONS UNSALTED BUTTER

  KOSHER SALT AND
  CRACKED BLACK PEPPER TO TASTE

4 (18-OUNCE) BONE-IN RIB EYE STEAKS

2 TABLESPOONS TRUFFLE OIL*
  (OPTIONAL BUT REALLY GOOD!)

1 CUP CRUMBLED QUESO FRESCO
  (WHITE COW'S MILK FARMER'S CHEESE)

Smoke roast the yellow onion over hickory in a small smoker or a Weber grill until the onion becomes translucent. (See the Standard Preparations chapter for some thoughts about smoke roasting.) Sauté the bacon, in a cast-iron skillet over a fire, with the green onion, tomato, black beans, garlic, roasted poblanos, smoked yellow onions, and cilantro for 5 minutes. Finish the sofrito with the butter and season to taste. Heat a cast-iron skillet or an inverted Dutch oven lid over the fire until very, very hot. Salt and pepper the steaks thoroughly but not excessively, and cook them on the cast iron to the desired degree of doneness. Immediately before removing the steaks from the skillet, drizzle the truffle oil on top of them. Place each of the steaks on a plate. Spoon the sofrito over the top of the steaks (where the bone leaves the steak) and sprinkle the queso over the top.

Truffle oil is available at Williams-Sonoma cooking supply stores. Contact Williams-Sonoma at (800) 541-1262 for further assistance.

Southwestern Turkey Casserole

serves 4

½	CUP UNSALTED BUTTER
4	CUPS RAW TURKEY BREAST, COARSELY CUT INTO CHUNKS
½	CUP DICED YELLOW ONION
¼	CUP DICED CARROT
¼	CUP DICED CELERY
1	CUP PEELED, DICED, AND BLANCHED* RUSSET POTATO
½	CUP CORN KERNELS
3	TABLESPOONS MINCED GARLIC
¼	CUP ROASTED, PEELED, SEEDED, AND CHOPPED POBLANO CHILE
2	CUPS CHICKEN BROTH
¼	CUP ALL PURPOSE FLOUR
2	TABLESPOONS TOASTED CUMIN SEEDS
½	CUP CHOPPED CILANTRO
	KOSHER SALT AND CRACKED BLACK PEPPER TO TASTE

In a heavy cast-iron pot or Dutch oven over a fire, heat half the butter and then sauté the turkey, onion, carrot, and celery. Cook the vegetables until they are just tender. Add the potatoes, corn, garlic, and roasted poblano chile. Sauté briefly, and then add the chicken broth. In a different cast-iron skillet over a fire, heat the other half of the butter until melted and mix in the flour, stirring constantly until they are thoroughly combined, making a roux (a thickener). Add the roux to the casserole to thicken it to your desired consistency. Flavor the casserole with the toasted cumin seeds and the cilantro, and then adjust the seasoning with the salt and pepper. Serve hot. Biscuits make a great accompaniment for this casserole.

To blanch, boil in salted water until tender. Then drain and cool.

Braised Duckling in Mole Poblano

serves 4

2	TABLESPOONS SESAME OIL
2	(4-POUND) DUCKS, CLEANED AND CUT INTO QUARTERS
	KOSHER SALT AND CRACKED BLACK PEPPER TO TASTE
1	CUP DICED YELLOW ONION
1	TABLESPOON SESAME SEEDS
½	CUP SEEDED AND MINCED CHILE PASILLA
½	CUP SEEDED AND MINCED CHILE ANCHO
½	CUP ROASTED, PEELED, AND SEEDED POBLANO CHILE
1	GALLON CHICKEN BROTH
½	CUP GRATED BITTERSWEET CHOCOLATE
½	CUP DICED PINEAPPLE
½	CUP WHITE BREAD, TORN INTO SMALL PIECES
½	CUP CRUSHED, RIPE PLANTAINS (BANANA MAY BE SUBSTITUTED)
3	TABLESPOONS MINCED GARLIC
3	TABLESPOONS CREAMY PEANUT BUTTER
3	TABLESPOONS GRANULATED SUGAR
1	SPLIT VANILLA BEAN (YOU CAN SUBSTITUTE 1 TEASPOON OF VANILLA EXTRACT)

In a heavy cast-iron pot or Dutch oven, heat the sesame oil over a fire. Rub the pieces of duck with the salt and pepper, and then brown them in the hot sesame oil until they have a rich, brown color. Remove the pieces of duck and set aside in a warm place. Sauté the onion, sesame seeds, chile pasilla, chile ancho, and poblano chile in the same pot until the chiles are tender. Add the chicken broth, chocolate, pineapple, bread, crushed plantain, garlic, peanut butter, and sugar. Scrape the seeds from the vanilla bean into the mixture. Bring the mixture to a boil and then decrease the heat to a simmer by moving the pot to the side of the fire. Let the sauce simmer for 30 minutes. Remove from the heat, and puree the mole—do not seal the blender airtight while pureeing a hot liquid—and then return it to the pot. Put the pieces of duck in the mole and simmer for 1½ hours. Remove the duck from the mole and serve with the sauce on the side.

Fried Turkey in the Style of East Texas
with Cornbread Chorizo Dressing

serves a whole bunch

The turkey needs two to three days to cure, so we will discuss this step first. Mix the ½ cup of kosher salt, ½ cup of cracked black pepper, granulated garlic, and cayenne pepper together. Rub the turkey with this mixture both inside and outside. Repeat this procedure several times over the two- to three-day curing period.

When the turkey is finished curing, in a very large cast-iron pot*, heat the peanut oil, reserving several tablespoons, to approximately 360° (cooking thermometers are available at most cooking supply stores). Very carefully lower the turkey into the pot, head first. This prevents air pockets from building up in the body cavity and causing hot oil to splash out. Fry the turkey, completely submerged in the oil, for 35 to 40 minutes. Use a heavy bale hook or a couple of very heavy forks to remove the turkey from the pot, being very careful to allow the hot oil to drain out of the body cavity. Let the turkey rest for 5 minutes so the juices can settle before carving. Meanwhile, to make the stuffing, heat 2 tablespoons of the reserved peanut oil in a heavy cast-iron pot or Dutch oven over a hot fire, and sauté the carrot, diced yellow onion, poblano chile, celery, and minced garlic until just tender. Add the chorizo,

½	CUP KOSHER SALT
½	CUP CRACKED BLACK PEPPER
½	CUP GRANULATED GARLIC
¼	CUP CAYENNE PEPPER
1	(20- TO 22-POUND) WHOLE TURKEY
5	GALLONS PEANUT OIL
¼	CUP DICED CARROT
¼	CUP DICED YELLOW ONION
¼	CUP DICED POBLANO CHILE
¼	CUP DICED CELERY
2	TABLESPOONS MINCED GARLIC
1	CUP COOKED AND DRAINED CHORIZO (PORK SAUSAGE CAN BE SUBSTITUTED)
1	CUP APPLE JUICE
1	CUP CHICKEN BROTH
2	CUPS CRUMBLED CORNBREAD
2	CUPS CRUMBLED BISCUITS
¼	CUP CHOPPED GREEN ONION
2	TABLESPOONS CHOPPED CILANTRO

apple juice, and chicken broth, and cook until volume has reduced by ½. Cool this mixture to room temperature and then mix in the cornbread, biscuits, green onion, and cilantro. Wipe out your pan and thoroughly coat with the remaining bit of peanut oil; add the dressing and bake (covered) in moderately high heat for 30 to 40 minutes. (Refer to the beginning of this chapter for specifics about baking in cast iron.) Carve the turkey and serve with the cornbread chorizo dressing.

Turkey fryers are available and can be more easily obtained than a large cast-iron pot, but cast iron conducts the heat much better.

205

Pan-Fried Canyon Trout
with a Salad of Spring Melons and Green Onions

serves 4

Heat the raspberry vinegar in a skillet over a moderately hot spot of the fire and dissolve the sugar in the vinegar. Cook until the vinegar-sugar mixture has reduced in volume by ¼. Cool the vinegar mixture (as much as possible in the great outdoors), and add the watermelon, cantaloupe, honeydew, green onion, and chives to the raspberry vinegar. Set the salad aside. Season the cornmeal with the salt

½	CUP RASPBERRY VINEGAR
¼	CUP SUGAR
2	CUPS DICED WATERMELON
2	CUPS CANTALOUPE BALLS
2	CUPS DICED HONEYDEW MELON
1	CUP FINE BIAS-CUT GREEN ONION
½	CUP (1-INCH) CHIVE SECTIONS
2	TABLESPOONS FINE BIAS-CUT GARLIC CHIVES (IF AVAILABLE)
1	CUP YELLOW CORNMEAL
	KOSHER SALT AND CRACKED BLACK PEPPER TO TASTE
4	BONELESS, WHOLE RAINBOW TROUT FILETS (APPROXIMATELY 6 OUNCES EACH)
¼	CUP VEGETABLE SHORTENING
4	LIME WEDGES
20	WHOLE CHIVES (OR BABY WILD ONIONS IF POSSIBLE)

and pepper. Dust the trout filets with the seasoned cornmeal. Heat the shortening in a cast-iron skillet over a hot spot of the fire until the fat is hot but not smoking.

Carefully place the dusted trout filets, with the skin side up, in the hot oil. Cook for approximately 90 seconds to 2 minutes, and then turn over and cook for approximately 1 minute. Gently absorb any surface oil by carefully dabbing it off with a paper towel. For each serving, place a mound of the melon salad in the center of a plate, and then lay a trout filet across the salad. Squeeze a lime wedge over the trout, and then top the trout filet with five whole chives.

Pan de Campo
with Plum Tomatoes, Cilantro Pesto, and Goat Cheese

serves 4

½	CUP VEGETABLE SHORTENING
2	CUPS ALL PURPOSE FLOUR
2	TEASPOONS BAKING POWDER
2	TEASPOONS KOSHER SALT
1	TEASPOON SUGAR
½	CUP MILK
3	SMALL PLUM TOMATOES, SLICED LENGTHWISE
6	OUNCES GOAT CHEESE
1	CUP CILANTRO LEAVES
2	TABLESPOONS TOASTED PINE NUTS
2	TABLESPOONS ROASTED GARLIC CLOVES
2	TABLESPOONS ROASTED AND PEELED POBLANO CHILE
¼	CUP OLIVE OIL
	KOSHER SALT AND CRACKED BLACK PEPPER TO TASTE

To make the pan de campo, coat the inside of your Dutch oven with a small amount of the shortening. Thoroughly mix together the flour, baking powder, 2 teaspoons of salt, sugar, and milk, but do not knead the dough too much because it will become tough. Roll the dough into a disc that's about ½ inch thick. (The pan de campo will be crispier if you roll the dough out thinner than this.) Place the rolled-out dough into the Dutch oven and perforate the dough with a few punctures from a fork. Bake* for approximately 12 minutes, and then turn the bread over** and place the sliced tomatoes and goat cheese evenly around on the bread. Bake for approximately 6 minutes. In a blender, puree the cilantro, pine nuts, roasted garlic, roasted poblano, and olive oil. Drizzle this pesto over the top of the pan de campo. Slice the pan de campo into four equal pieces and serve.

This recipe requires the baking distribution of the coals for your Dutch oven, which was discussed in the introduction to this chapter: Place ⅓ of the coals under the oven and ⅔ on top of the oven.

**You must lift the lid of the oven (and temporarily remove the coals) when you turn the bread over; then replace the lid, along with the coals.*

Farm Biscuits

makes about 20

VEGETABLE SHORTENING (FOR COATING THE PAN)

3 CUPS ALL PURPOSE FLOUR

1 CUP MILK

6 TABLESPOONS VEGETABLE OIL

6 TEASPOONS BAKING POWDER

1 TEASPOON SALT

Coat the inside of your Dutch oven with a small amount of vegetable shortening and preheat the Dutch oven to approximately 350° over a moderately hot spot of the fire. You can determine the approximate temperature of the oven by looking at the bottom of it: At 350°, there should be no visible gray streaks. In a bowl, mix the remaining ingredients together. Roll out the dough to 1 inch in thickness, and cut biscuits that are 1½ inches in diameter. Put the biscuits into the oven right next to each other, and cover. Place ⅓ of the hot coals underneath the Dutch oven and ⅔ of the hot coals on top of the oven. Bake for 15 to 20 minutes and serve.

Vegetables & Starches

Arepas with Braised Greens and Tomato Jam

serves 4

3	CUPS WATER
1½	CUPS YELLOW CORNMEAL
1	CUP GRANULATED SUGAR
2	TABLESPOONS KOSHER SALT
2	TABLESPOONS VEGETABLE SHORTENING
¾	CUP SEEDED AND CHOPPED TOMATO
2	TABLESPOONS PECTIN
1	TABLESPOON FINELY DICED JALAPEÑO
1	TABLESPOON CORN OIL
2	TABLESPOONS EXTRA-VIRGIN OLIVE OIL
1	CUP FINE JULIENNE OF WHITE ONION
4	CUPS CLEANED SPINACH LEAVES
2	CUPS RHUBARB CHARD (A CHARD IS A TYPE OF GREEN LEAF FOR COOKING)
	KOSHER SALT AND CRACKED BLACK PEPPER TO TASTE

Bring the water to a boil and add the cornmeal, ½ cup of sugar, and 2 tablespoons of salt. Reduce the heat and simmer for 8 minutes. Grease a small sheet pan with the shortening and spread the cooked cornmeal mixture evenly over the pan. Allow the mixture to chill in the refrigerator for at least 1 hour, and then cut into eight 3-inch round discs. These are the arepas. Keep in a cool place. In a heavy pan, simmer the tomatoes and dissolve the other ½ cup of sugar in the tomatoes. Add the pectin and jalapeño, then chill in the refrigerator for at least 1 hour. Crisp the outsides of the arepas to a light, golden brown in a nonstick skillet with corn oil over moderately high heat. Heat the olive oil in a heavy skillet over moderately high heat and sauté the white onion, spinach, and chard until just wilted; then season to taste. For each serving, place two of the arepas overlapping each other in the center of a plate. Spoon the sautéed greens over the arepas, top with the tomato jam, and serve.

Basmati Rice Cake and Grilled Asparagus
with Lemon, Parsley, and Olive Oil

serves 4

Preheat an oven to 450° and roast the mushroom caps until they are dried, approximately 12 to 15 minutes. Chop coarsely and set aside. Bring the water and rice to a boil; stir the rice and lower the heat to a simmer. Cover the pot and cook for 25 minutes or until the water is gone. Mix in the grated cheese and dried shiitake mushroom caps; then season to taste. Spread the rice mixture evenly on half of a sheet pan

20   LARGE, FLAT SHIITAKE MUSHROOMS CAPS, STEMS REMOVED

2¼   CUPS WATER

1½   CUPS BASMATI RICE, UNCOOKED

1   CUP GRATED, DRIED MONTEREY JACK CHEESE (AVAILABLE IN GOURMET CHEESE SHOPS; PARMESAN CHEESE CAN BE SUBSTITUTED)

KOSHER SALT AND CRACKED BLACK PEPPER TO TASTE

1   TABLESPOON CORN OIL

24   (5-INCH-LONG) PEELED ASPARAGUS SPEARS

¼   CUP EXTRA-VIRGIN OLIVE OIL

¼   CUP FRESH LEMON JUICE

2   TABLESPOONS FINELY CHOPPED PARSLEY

½   CUP FINE JULIENNE OF RADISH

and chill in the refrigerator for at least 1 hour. Cut into four rectangles (approximately 4 inches by 2½ inches), and then cut each of those strips diagonally, making eight long triangles. Set aside. Heat the corn oil in a nonstick skillet over moderate heat and carefully crisp the outsides of the rice cakes so that they don't break and are golden brown, approximately 90 seconds on each side. Grill the asparagus (or use your electric broiler) very quickly, being careful not to burn it. Combine the olive oil, lemon juice, and parsley. For each serving, place two rice cakes overlapping each other and lay six grilled asparagus spears across the top of them. Spoon the lemon juice, parsley, and olive oil mixture over the asparagus. Top the asparagus with the radish julienne and serve.

Black Bean and Goat Cheese Soufflé
with Chipotle-Lime Cream

serves 4

In a small bowl, combine the sour cream, chipotle puree, and lime juice thoroughly and refrigerate. In another bowl, mix the diced green tomato, red onion, and chile arbol together. Season to taste and refrigerate. In a heavy pan, bring the heavy cream to a boil and cook until it has reduced in volume by ½. Combine with the mashed black beans and mix thoroughly. Allow the black bean mixture to cool to room temperature. Add the egg yolks, granulated onion, granulated garlic, poblano, red bell pepper, butter, and flour; then mix thoroughly. Preheat the oven to 375°. In a chilled stainless-steel bowl, whip the egg whites with the sugar and cream of tartar until they hold firm peaks. Carefully fold the egg whites and black bean mixture together so the egg whites don't break down. Coat the inside of four 4-ounce ramekins with the food release spray and spoon the soufflé mixture into the ramekins until they are ¾ full. Place 1 teaspoon of the goat cheese into the middle of each soufflé (just place it on top of the soufflé mixture). Bake for 12 minutes, and then remove from the oven. Spoon the chipotle-lime cream over the soufflés, and then top with the green tomato relish. Serve each soufflé in its ramekin on top of a folded napkin, set on a plate.

¼	CUP SOUR CREAM
¼	TEASPOON PUREED CHIPOTLE CHILES IN ADOBO SAUCE
2	TABLESPOONS FRESH LIME JUICE
¼	CUP FINELY DICED GREEN TOMATO
1	TABLESPOON FINELY DICED RED ONION
½	TEASPOON MINCED CHILE ARBOL
	KOSHER SALT AND CRACKED BLACK PEPPER TO TASTE
1¼	CUPS HEAVY CREAM
¾	CUP COOKED BLACK BEANS, MASHED
2	EGG YOLKS
½	TEASPOON GRANULATED ONION
½	TEASPOON GRANULATED GARLIC
1	TABLESPOON FINELY DICED POBLANO CHILE
1	TABLESPOON FINELY DICED RED BELL PEPPER
3	TEASPOONS SOFTENED UNSALTED BUTTER
2	TABLESPOONS ALL PURPOSE FLOUR
6	EGG WHITES
½	TEASPOON GRANULATED SUGAR
½	TEASPOON CREAM OF TARTAR
	NONSTICK FOOD RELEASE SPRAY
4	TEASPOONS GOAT CHEESE

Blue Cheese Bread Pudding
with Green Chile Stew

serves 4

½   CUP DICED UNCOOKED HICKORY-SMOKED BACON
     (THIS MAY BE OMITTED FOR A VEGETARIAN DISH;
     BUT ADD 1 TABLESPOON OF CORN OIL IN ITS PLACE)

¼   CUP FINELY DICED CARROT

1   TABLESPOON MINCED GARLIC

¼   CUP FINELY DICED WHITE ONION

1   CUP ROASTED, PEELED, AND PUREED POBLANO CHILE

1   CUP CHICKEN BROTH

     KOSHER SALT AND CRACKED BLACK PEPPER TO TASTE

1   TEASPOON CORN OIL

¼   CUP JULIENNE OF WHITE ONION

¼   CUP TOASTED PUMPKIN SEEDS
     (AVAILABLE IN THE MEXICAN FOODS SECTION)

1   TABLESPOON HONEY

     NONSTICK FOOD RELEASE SPRAY

20   TO 24 (¼-INCH-THICK) SLICES OF STALE
     FRENCH BREAD

1   CUP CRUMBLED MAYTAG FARMS BLUE CHEESE*

2   EGG YOLKS

2   WHOLE EGGS

2   CUPS HEAVY CREAM

¼   TEASPOON GROUND NUTMEG

¼   TEASPOON CAYENNE PEPPER

Render (cook until the fat is beginning to crisp) the bacon or heat the tablespoon of corn oil in a heavy skillet over moderately high heat, and then add the carrot, garlic, and diced white onion and sauté until tender. Add the poblano chile puree and chicken broth and then simmer over moderate heat until volume has reduced by ⅓. Season to taste and set aside this green chile stew in a warm place.

Heat 1 teaspoon of corn oil in a heavy skillet over moderately high heat and sauté the julienne of white onion until tender. Add the toasted pumpkin seeds and honey to the sautéed onion. Mix thoroughly and set aside at room temperature. ⓡ Preheat the oven to 350°. Coat the inside of four 4-ounce ramekins with a healthy amount of the food release spray. In the ramekins, layer the slices of stale French bread with the crumbled blue cheese, starting with the bread. Fill to the top of the ramekins, compressing the bread and cheese as you fill the ramekins. In a bowl, combine the egg yolks, whole eggs, heavy cream, nutmeg, and cayenne, and season to taste with salt and pepper. Very slowly pour the custard into the ramekins, allowing the dried bread time to absorb the custard; continue adding custard until each ramekin is almost full. Bake for 30 minutes. Remove from the oven and allow to come to room temperature. ⓡ For each serving, ladle some green chile stew into a shallow, wide-rimmed soup bowl. Unmold one bread pudding and place it in the center of the bowl. Spoon the pumpkin seed and onion compote over the top of the bread pudding, and serve.

*Maytag Farms, in Newton, Iowa, produces one the finest blue cheeses in the United States. For more information, call (515) 792-1133.

Roasted Corn and Truffle Tamale

serves 4

16 TO 20 DRIED CORNHUSKS

WARM WATER (FOR SOAKING CORNHUSKS)

2 CUPS MASA HARINA
(CORN FLOUR AVAILABLE IN THE MEXICAN FOODS SECTION)

¼ CUP LARD (MARGARINE OR BUTTER CAN BE SUBSTITUTED)

¼ CUP TRUFFLE OIL*

¾ CUP WATER

½ CUP SWEET CORN KERNELS

½ CUP ROASTED AND DICED ASPARAGUS SPEARS

¼ CUP DRIED MUSHROOMS

2 TABLESPOONS TOASTED, SEEDED, AND MINCED CHILE ANCHO

2 TABLESPOONS MINCED BLACK TRUFFLE PEELINGS
(OPTIONAL BUT REALLY GOOD!)

1 TABLESPOON MINCED GARLIC

KOSHER SALT AND CRACKED BLACK PEPPER TO TASTE

2 TABLESPOONS CORN OIL

1 CUP JULIENNE OF RED ONION

½ CUP HALVED CHERRY TOMATOES

½ CUP HALVED YELLOW TEARDROP TOMATOES

¼ CUP VERY FINE JULIENNE OF SEEDED JALAPEÑO

1 CUP BRUSSELS SPROUT LEAVES
(PEEL OFF THE OUTER LEAVES AND USE THEM)

2 TABLESPOONS JULIENNE OF BLACK TRUFFLE (OPTIONAL)

Soak the dried cornhusks in warm water to make pliable. Slowly and thoroughly mix the masa with the lard, truffle oil, and ¾ cup of water. Add the corn kernels, diced asparagus, dried mushrooms, chile ancho, minced black truffle peelings, and garlic to the masa mixture and season to taste. Divide the masa mixture into sixteen pieces and mold each piece into a cylindrical shape; then flatten each slightly with the palm of your hand. Wrap each of the sixteen pieces of molded masa mixture in a cornhusk (use only eight cornhusks for this) and lay the unsecured flaps of each cornhusk on the bottom of a perforated pan (an insert for a steamer). Place the insert on top of the bottom pan of boiling water and steam the tamales for 45 minutes. ☝ Heat the 2 tablespoons of corn oil in a heavy skillet.

Sauté the red onion, cherry tomatoes, yellow teardrop tomatoes, jalapeño julienne, Brussels sprout leaves, and black truffle julienne until the Brussels sprout leaves are bright green. Season to taste with salt and pepper. ☝ Open eight of the remaining, unused cornhusks and, with a thin strip from each of the husks, tie each of these unused husks about ¾ inch from the top, leaving the remainder of the husk open. Measure 8 inches from the top of the husks and cut off the bottoms so all the tied husks are the same length. These manicured cornhusks will be used for serving the tamales. Remove the tamales from the husks they were steamed in and lay them on the open, manicured husks. Spoon the vegetable mix onto the center of four plates in a mound, lean the tamales against it, and serve.

*You can buy truffle oil from Williams-Sonoma cooking supply stores. Call (800) 541-1262 for further assistance.

Oven-Dried Shiitake Mushrooms
with Ancho Chile Mayonnaise and Red Pepper Relish

serves 4

16	SHIITAKE MUSHROOM CAPS, WITH STEMS REMOVED
¾	CUP + 2 TABLESPOONS OLIVE OIL
	KOSHER SALT AND CRACKED BLACK PEPPER TO TASTE
3	EGG YOLKS
1	TABLESPOON MINCED GARLIC
1	TABLESPOON TOASTED, SEEDED, AND MINCED ANCHO CHILE
2	TEASPOONS FRESH LIME JUICE
1	TEASPOON ACHIOTE PASTE (AVAILABLE IN THE MEXICAN FOODS SECTION)
½	TEASPOON TABASCO SAUCE
1	TABLESPOON CHOPPED CILANTRO
½	CUP ROASTED, PEELED, AND DICED RED BELL PEPPER
2	TABLESPOONS FINELY DICED WHITE ONION
16	VERY SMALL CILANTRO SPRIGS

Preheat the oven to 400°. Toss the shiitake mushroom caps in mixture of 2 tablespoons of olive oil, salt, and pepper. Place mushroom caps on a nonstick cookie sheet pan and bake until the mushrooms are crispy, approximately 10 to 12 minutes. Remove from the oven and set aside in a warm place. To make the mayonnaise, in a blender combine the egg yolks, garlic, ancho chile, 1 teaspoon of lime juice, achiote paste, and Tabasco sauce. With the blender running on a low speed, slowly add the remaining ¾ cup of olive oil to thicken the mayonnaise. Stir in the chopped cilantro, season to taste with salt and pepper, and set aside in a cool place. Mix together the diced red bell pepper, white onion, and the remaining 1 teaspoon of lime juice; then season to taste with salt and pepper. Place the mushroom caps on each plate at three, six, nine, and twelve o'clock, and then spoon the mayonnaise onto the caps. Top with the red bell pepper relish and the cilantro sprigs and serve.

Wild Mushroom Ravioli
with Green Onion Sauce and Toasted Pumpkin Seeds

serves 4

¼	CUP ROASTED, PEELED, AND PUREED YELLOW BELL PEPPER
2	EGGS
½	TEASPOON KOSHER SALT
3	CUPS ALL PURPOSE FLOUR
	FLOUR (FOR ROLLING OUT DOUGH)
2	TABLESPOONS OLIVE OIL
1	CUP SLICED SHIITAKE MUSHROOMS
1	CUP SLICED BUTTON MUSHROOMS
1	TABLESPOON + 1 TEASPOON MINCED GARLIC
	KOSHER SALT AND CRACKED BLACK PEPPER TO TASTE
¼	CUP GRATED, DRIED MONTEREY JACK CHEESE
1	TABLESPOON FINELY DICED SHALLOT
½	CUP FINELY CHOPPED GREEN ONION
2	TABLESPOONS ROASTED, PEELED, AND PUREED POBLANO CHILE
2	CUPS CHICKEN BROTH
½	CUP COARSELY CUT SPINACH LEAVES
¼	CUP WARM WATER
	WATER (FOR COOKING RAVIOLI)
	KOSHER SALT (FOR WATER)
½	CUP SHAVED, DRIED MONTEREY JACK CHEESE
½	CUP TOASTED PUMPKIN SEEDS
4	CILANTRO SPRIGS

To prepare the ravioli, first make the pasta. In a food processor, mix the yellow pepper puree, 1 egg, and ½ teaspoon of salt together. Slowly add the flour until the mixture begins breaking into pecan-size pieces. Remove from the food processor and knead by hand until the dough comes together in a ball. Cut the dough into four equal pieces. On a lightly floured, flat surface, roll the dough out into four sheets (approximately 4 inches by 16 inches), with a pasta roller or a rolling pin. You might need to dust the pasta dough with a little extra flour as you roll it out to keep it from sticking to the roller(s). Cover the pasta dough with a napkin. Heat 1 tablespoon of olive oil in a heavy skillet over moderately high heat, and then sauté the mushrooms and 1 teaspoon of garlic until tender. Season to taste. Place in a food processor and "pulse" into a coarsely chopped mixture. Add the grated cheese to thicken the mixture, and then chill in the refrigerator for at least 1 hour. Heat the other tablespoon of olive oil in a heavy pan over moderately high heat and sauté the remaining 1 tablespoon of garlic, shallot, and green onion until tender. Add the poblano puree and the chicken broth, and then bring to a boil. Reduce the heat and simmer until volume has reduced by ½. Add the spinach and puree in a blender. Season to taste and keep warm. Cut the four pasta sheets into forty-eight 2-inch squares (each sheet will make twelve squares). Mix the remaining egg with ¼ cup of warm water for an egg wash. Place a tea-spoonful of the mushroom mixture in the center of a pasta square and brush the egg wash around the edges of the pasta. Fit another pasta square on top of the one with the filling and press softly, moving around the edges from the center out. Crimp the edges of the ravioli gently, using the tines of a fork. Repeat with remaining pasta squares and filling. Cook the ravioli in lightly salted, boiling water for 2 minutes; then reduce the heat and simmer for 3 minutes. Drain the ravioli and place them in four shallow, wide-rimmed soup bowls. Spoon the green onion sauce over the ravioli. Garnish with a small cluster of the shaved cheese. Sprinkle the toasted pumpkin seeds over the ravioli. Finish each serving with a cilantro sprig in the center of the ravioli, and serve.

Pumpkin and Corn "Risotto"
with Huitlacoche

serves 4

2	TABLESPOONS CLARIFIED BUTTER (SEE PAGE 43)
1	CUP SWEET CORN KERNELS
½	CUP DICED YELLOW ONION
1	TABLESPOON MINCED GARLIC
1	TABLESPOON TOASTED, SEEDED, AND MINCED CHILE ARBOL
¾	CUP PEELED, ROASTED, AND DICED PUMPKIN (BUTTERNUT SQUASH CAN BE SUBSTITUTED)
¾	CUP PEELED, DICED, AND BLANCHED* RUSSET POTATOES
1	CUP HEAVY CREAM
½	CUP GRATED, DRIED MONTEREY JACK CHEESE (AVAILABLE FROM GOURMET CHEESE STORES; PARMESAN CHEESE CAN BE SUBSTITUTED)
¼	CUP HUITLACOCHE (CORN FUNGUS AVAILABLE AT MEXICAN SPECIALTY STORES; YOU CAN SUBSTITUTE DRIED WILD MUSHROOMS)
	KOSHER SALT AND CRACKED BLACK PEPPER TO TASTE
¼	CUP FINELY BIAS-CUT GREEN ONION
½	CUP SHAVED, DRIED MONTEREY JACK CHEESE

Heat the clarified butter in a heavy pan over moderately high heat and sauté the corn, yellow onion, garlic, and chile arbol until tender. Add the pumpkin and potatoes and lightly brown them. Add the cream and grated cheese, and then simmer for 3 minutes. Add the huitlacoche to the pumpkin-potato mixture and warm. Season to taste and finish the dish by stirring in the green onions. Spoon the "risotto" into four shallow, wide-rimmed soup bowls, top with the shaved cheese, and serve.

To blanch, cook until just tender in boiling, salted water. Then drain and submerge in ice water until chilled. Drain and refrigerate.

Pan-Fried "Dallas" Mozzarella Cheese
with Black Bean Cake and Tomatillo Salsa

serves 4

4	(2-OUNCE) SLICES OF FRESH MOZZARELLA CHEESE*
¼	CUP EXTRA-VIRGIN OLIVE OIL
¼	CUP YELLOW CORNMEAL
¼	CUP FINELY DICED WHITE ONION
1	TABLESPOON FINELY DICED, SEEDED JALAPEÑO
1	TABLESPOON MINCED GARLIC
2	TABLESPOONS CHOPPED CILANTRO
1½	CUPS COOKED BLACK BEANS
¼	CUP + 2 TABLESPOONS ALL PURPOSE FLOUR
1	TEASPOON BAKING POWDER
	KOSHER SALT AND CRACKED BLACK PEPPER TO TASTE
1	CUP COARSELY CUT TOMATO
1	TABLESPOON COARSELY CUT GARLIC
1	TABLESPOON BALSAMIC VINEGAR
½	TEASPOON CHIPOTLE CHILES IN ADOBO SAUCE
½	CUP FINELY DICED TOMATILLO
2	TABLESPOONS FINELY DICED RED ONION
1	TEASPOON MINCED CHILE ARBOL
2	TABLESPOONS FRESH LIME JUICE
	FLOUR (FOR DUSTING CAKES)
4	CILANTRO SPRIGS

Dip the fresh mozzarella slices in the olive oil and dredge in the yellow cornmeal. Cover and chill in refrigerator. Reserve 3 tablespoons of the leftover olive oil. In a heavy skillet, heat 1 tablespoon of the reserved olive oil over moderately high heat, and sauté the white onion, jalapeños, and minced garlic until tender. Add 1 tablespoon of cilantro and the cooked black beans; then mash with a fork or potato masher until all the lumps are gone from all the ingredients. Add the flour and baking powder, and then season to taste. Form four patties that are each 4 inches in diameter and 1 inch thick, and set aside in a cool place. To make the sauce, heat a cast-iron skillet until very hot, and char** the tomatoes and coarsely cut garlic. Puree the tomatoes and garlic in a blender with the balsamic vinegar, chipotle chiles, and 1 tablespoon of the reserved olive oil. Season to taste with salt and pepper and set aside at room temperature. To prepare the salsa, combine the tomatillo, red onion, chile arbol, lime juice, and remaining 1 tablespoon of cilantro. Season to taste with salt and pepper, and set aside in the refrigerator. Lightly dust the black bean cakes with flour. Heat the remaining tablespoon of the reserved olive oil in a nonstick skillet over moderate heat, and then brown the black bean cakes and the cornmeal-dusted mozzarella. For each serving, spoon some of the tomato-garlic sauce in a pool in the center of a plate. Place a black bean cake in the center of the sauce, and place a warm mozzarella slice on top of the bean cake. Place a dollop of the tomatillo salsa on the mozzarella and a cilantro sprig on the salsa; then serve.

*My good friend Paula Lambert of Dallas, Texas, makes some of the best mozzarella (and a lot of other cheeses) anywhere. For more information, call (214) 741-4072.

**To char, in a very hot skillet, cook the tomatoes until they have a light black coating (approximately 5 minutes).

Roasted Onion Empanadas

serves 4

To make the Indian grill bread, mix the flour, nonfat dry milk, baking powder, and ½ teaspoon of salt together. Slowly add the lard and the ½ cup of water, kneading until the dough forms into a ball. Cover the dough and allow it to rest for 1 hour. Roll the dough out on a lightly floured surface to a thickness of ⅛ inch, and cut it into eight discs, 3 inches in diameter each. Set discs aside in the refrigerator, with wax paper in between the pieces. Make sure the onions and garlic are well drained. Combine

1	CUP ALL PURPOSE FLOUR
¼	CUP NONFAT DRY MILK
⅛	TEASPOON BAKING POWDER
½	TEASPOON KOSHER SALT
2	TABLESPOONS LARD (VEGETABLE SHORTENING CAN BE SUBSTITUTED)
½	CUP + ¼ CUP WATER
	FLOUR (FOR ROLLING OUT DOUGH)
½	CUP ROASTED AND CHOPPED YELLOW ONION
1	TEASPOON ROASTED AND CHOPPED GARLIC
1	TEASPOON CHOPPED CILANTRO
2	TABLESPOONS GRATED HOT PEPPER JACK CHEESE
	KOSHER SALT AND CRACKED BLACK PEPPER TO TASTE
2	EGGS
2	TABLESPOONS HONEY
1	TEASPOON MINCED CHIPOTLE CHILE IN ADOBO SAUCE
4	CUPS CORN OIL (FOR FRYING)
4	CILANTRO SPRIGS

the onion, garlic, cilantro, and cheese, and then season to taste. Mix the eggs with the remaining ¼ cup of warm water. Lay the Indian grill bread discs on a flat surface and place 1 teaspoon of the filling just off-center on one of the discs; gently brush the egg wash around the edges of the disc, and then fold it over in half. Crimp the edges with a fork. Set aside in the refrigerator. Repeat with remaining discs. Mix the honey and chipotle chile together. Set aside at room temperature. Heat the corn oil for frying the empanadas to 350° in a heavy, deep pot over moderately high heat. Fry the empanadas until they float on the surface and become golden brown. For each serving, overlap two of the empanadas on a plate and drizzle the chipotle honey over them. Garnish with a cilantro sprig and serve.

Green Chile Macaroni

serves 4

Heat the corn oil in a heavy pan over high heat and sauté the diced poblano chile, red bell pepper, red onion, and garlic until just tender. Add the corn kernels and sauté quickly. Add the macaroni, poblano puree, cream, and pepper Jack cheese. Stir until all the ingredients are thoroughly mixed. Season to taste and serve.

1 TABLESPOON CORN OIL
¼ CUP DICED POBLANO CHILE
¼ CUP DICED RED BELL PEPPER
¼ CUP DICED RED ONION
1 TABLESPOON MINCED GARLIC
½ CUP SWEET CORN KERNELS
2 CUPS COOKED ELBOW MACARONI
½ CUP ROASTED, PEELED, AND PUREED POBLANO CHILE
¾ CUP HEAVY CREAM
½ CUP GRATED HOT PEPPER JACK CHEESE
KOSHER SALT AND CRACKED BLACK PEPPER TO TASTE

Roasted Garlic Mashed Potatoes

serves 4

WATER (FOR BOILING)
KOSHER SALT (FOR WATER)
2½ CUPS PEELED RUSSET POTATOES, CUT IN EIGHTHS
UNSALTED BUTTER (FOR PAN)
½ CUP MILK
½ CUP UNSALTED BUTTER
¼ CUP ROASTED AND CHOPPED GARLIC
¼ CUP FINELY BIAS-CUT GREEN ONION
2 TABLESPOONS COARSELY DICED GREEN CABBAGE
KOSHER SALT AND CRACKED BLACK PEPPER TO TASTE

Preheat your oven to 350°. Bring lightly salted water to a boil and cook the potatoes until they are tender (about 10 to 15 minutes). Drain the potatoes well, place them on a buttered sheet pan, and roast them in the oven at 400° for 8 to 10 minutes so they will dry. Put the potatoes in a mixing bowl and mash with a paddle on a low speed. Add the milk, ½ cup butter, and roasted garlic. Mix thoroughly until all the milk and butter are absorbed. Fold the green onion and cabbage into the potatoes. Season to taste and serve hot.

Green Bean Casserole

serves 4

Preheat your oven to 350°. Render (cook until the fat is beginning to crisp) the bacon in a heavy pan over moderately high heat and sauté the green beans until they are just tender. Add the pecans and crisp onions; then season to taste. Grease a heavy roasting pan with the butter and put the green bean mix-ture in it. Sprinkle the crumbled cornbread over the top and bake for 15 minutes. Remove from the oven and allow to cool slightly before serving.

½	CUP DICED HICKORY-SMOKED BACON
2	CUPS PICKED, BLANCHED* GREEN BEANS
½	CUP ROASTED PECANS
1	CUP CRISP FRIED ONIONS
	KOSHER SALT AND CRACKED BLACK PEPPER TO TASTE
2	TABLESPOONS CLARIFIED BUTTER (SEE PAGE 43)
1	CUP CRUMBLED CORNBREAD

To blanch, cook until just tender in boiling, salted water. Then drain and submerge in ice water until chilled. Drain and refrigerate.

Sautéed Spinach

serves 4

3	TABLESPOONS CLARIFIED BUTTER (SEE PAGE 43)
1½	CUPS JULIENNE OF YELLOW ONION
2	TABLESPOONS MINCED GARLIC
6	CUPS CLEANED, STEMMED SPINACH LEAVES
	KOSHER SALT AND CRACKED BLACK PEPPER TO TASTE

Heat the butter in a heavy skillet over high heat and sauté the onions until tender. Add the garlic and spinach, and then sauté until the spinach is just wilt-ed. Season to taste and serve.

Pinto Bean Ravioli

serves 4

Mix the red pepper puree, 2 eggs, and the ½ teaspoon of salt together in a food processor. Slowly add the flour to the mixture until the dough begins breaking into pecan-size pieces; then remove it from the food processor. Knead by hand until the dough comes together in a ball. Cut the dough into four equal portions and, on a lightly floured, flat surface, roll out into four ⅛-inch-thick sheets with a pasta roller or a rolling pin. Cover the dough with a napkin. Heat 1 teaspoon of olive oil in a heavy skillet over moderate heat and sauté the jalapeño and garlic until tender; then add the cooked pinto beans. Mash with a fork, or a potato masher, until all the lumps are gone. Season to taste and add the grated cheese. Cut the four pasta sheets into a total of forty-eight 2-inch squares (twelve squares per sheet). Mix 2 egg yolks with the warm water to make an egg wash. Place 1 teaspoon of the pinto bean mixture in the center of a pasta square and brush the egg wash around the edges. Fit another pasta square on top of the one with the filling and press down softly around the edges from the center out; then crimp the edges by applying slight pressure with the tines of a fork. Repeat with remaining pasta squares and filling. Cook the ravioli in lightly salted, boiling water for 2 minutes. Then reduce the heat and simmer for 3 minutes. Drain the ravioli and place them in four shallow, wide-rimmed soup bowls. Drizzle 1 tablespoon of olive oil over each of the four servings of ravioli. Top with the shaved cheese and toasted pumpkinseeds; then serve.

¼	CUP ROASTED, PEELED, AND PUREED RED BELL PEPPER
2	EGGS
½	TEASPOON KOSHER SALT
3	CUPS ALL PURPOSE FLOUR
	FLOUR (FOR ROLLING OUT DOUGH)
4	TABLESPOONS + 1 TEASPOON EXTRA-VIRGIN OLIVE OIL
1	TABLESPOON FINELY DICED JALAPEÑO
1	TEASPOON MINCED GARLIC
1½	CUPS COOKED PINTO BEANS
	KOSHER SALT AND CRACKED BLACK PEPPER TO TASTE
½	CUP GRATED, DRIED MONTEREY JACK CHEESE (AVAILABLE FROM GOURMET CHEESE SHOPS; PARMESAN CHEESE CAN BE SUBSTITUTED)
2	EGG YOLKS
¼	CUP WARM WATER
	WATER (FOR BOILING RAVIOLI)
	KOSHER SALT (FOR WATER)
1	CUP SHAVED, DRIED MONTEREY JACK CHEESE
½	CUP TOASTED PUMPKIN SEEDS (AVAILABLE IN THE MEXICAN FOOD SECTION)

BREADS & DESSERTS

Jalapeño Spoonbread

serves 4

2	TABLESPOONS CLARIFIED BUTTER (SEE PAGE 43)
2	TABLESPOONS ROASTED, SEEDED, AND DICED POBLANO CHILE
2	TABLESPOONS SEEDED AND DICED JALAPEÑO
1	TABLESPOON MINCED GARLIC
4	TABLESPOONS CHOPPED GREEN ONION
1¼	CUPS WATER
¾	CUP YELLOW CORNMEAL
	KOSHER SALT AND CRACKED BLACK PEPPER TO TASTE
1	CUP BUTTERMILK
6	EGGS
¼	CUP GRATED CHEDDAR CHEESE
4	TABLESPOONS MOLASSES

Preheat your oven to 350°. Heat 1 tablespoon of the clarified butter in a heavy pan over moderately high heat and sauté the roasted poblano, jalapeño, garlic, and green onion until just tender. Pour the water over the vegetables and bring to a boil. Add the cornmeal and stir continuously until the mixture is smooth, being sure to keep the mixture from sticking to the bottom and burning. Season to taste.

Add the buttermilk, eggs, cheese, and the remaining 1 tablespoon of the clarified butter to the heavy pan, and combine the ingredients thoroughly. Keeping mixture in the pan, bake in the preheated 350° oven for 20 minutes. Remove from the oven and allow to cool for 3 to 4 minutes before scooping out with a spoon or ice cream scoop. Divide the spoonbread between four plates, drizzle the molasses over the spoonbread, and serve.

Rustic Baked Biscuits
with Roasted Chiles and Corn

yields 2 dozen

½	CUP SOFTENED UNSALTED BUTTER
2	TABLESPOONS GRANULATED SUGAR
½	TEASPOON KOSHER SALT
2	EGGS
3	CUPS CAKE FLOUR
2	TABLESPOONS BAKING POWDER
1	TABLESPOON CHOPPED CILANTRO
½	CUP WHOLE MILK
1	CUP SWEET CORN KERNELS
½	CUP ROASTED, PEELED, AND DICED POBLANO CHILE
1½	CUPS GRATED CHEDDAR CHEESE
	FLOUR (FOR ROLLING OUT DOUGH)
2	TABLESPOONS VEGETABLE SHORTENING (BUTTER CAN BE SUBSTITUTED)

Mix the butter, sugar, and ½ teaspoon of salt together in a mixing bowl. Add the eggs and 1½ cups of flour, and continue mixing until smooth. Add the remainder of the flour, the baking powder, and the cilantro, and mix into the dough. Add the milk, corn, roasted poblano, and cheddar cheese to the dough, and mix until the ingredients are combined. Preheat your oven to 375°. Roll the dough out on a flat, lightly floured surface to ½ inch in thickness, and then cut the dough into 2-inch-diameter biscuits. Grease a sheet pan with the shortening and place the uncooked biscuits on the sheet pan; bake for 13 to 14 minutes. Allow the biscuits to cool for 2 to 3 minutes, and then serve.

Milk Bread
with Marigold Mint and Onions

yields 2 dozen

3	CUPS HIGH-GLUTEN BREAD FLOUR
3	CUPS ALL PURPOSE FLOUR
½	CUP GRANULATED SUGAR
2	TABLESPOONS KOSHER SALT
2	TABLESPOONS INSTANT YEAST
2	CUPS WHOLE MILK, AT ROOM TEMPERATURE
½	CUP UNSALTED BUTTER, AT ROOM TEMPERATURE
2	EGGS, AT ROOM TEMPERATURE
1	CUP DICED WHITE ONION
½	CUP CHOPPED MARIGOLD MINT (TARRAGON CAN BE SUBSTITUTED)
	FOOD RELEASE SPRAY
2	EGG YOLKS
¼	CUP WARM WATER
2	TABLESPOONS SOFTENED UNSALTED BUTTER

Preheat your oven to 375°. Mix the flours, sugar, and salt together. In a separate bowl, mix the yeast and milk together. Add the ½ cup unsalted butter, eggs, and milk mixture to the flour. Mix well until the dough is smooth, and then add the diced onion and the chopped marigold mint. Allow the dough to rest for 10 minutes. Coat the inside of a nonstick muffin tin with the food release spray. Cut the dough into twenty-four 1-ounce pieces and roll into balls (approximately the size of golf balls). Place two of the dough balls into each muffin cup and allow to proof, or double in size. Mix two egg yolks with the ¼ cup of warm water, and very lightly brush this egg wash over the rolls. Bake in the oven until golden brown on top, about 12 minutes. Remove from the oven and brush the 2 tablespoons of softened butter on the rolls. Allow them to cool for a couple of minutes before removing from the mold and serving.

Southwestern Green Chile Cornbread

yields 2 dozen

1	CUP SOFTENED UNSALTED BUTTER
¾	CUP GRANULATED SUGAR
4	EGGS
½	CUP ROASTED, PEELED, AND DICED POBLANO CHILE
1½	CUPS SWEET CORN KERNELS
½	CUP GRATED CHEDDAR CHEESE
½	CUP GRATED MONTEREY JACK CHEESE
1	CUP ALL PURPOSE FLOUR
1	CUP YELLOW CORNMEAL
2	TABLESPOONS BAKING POWDER
½	CUP SUN-DRIED CHERRIES (RAISINS CAN BE SUBSTITUTED)
1	TEASPOON KOSHER SALT
2	TABLESPOONS VEGETABLE SHORTENING

Preheat your oven to 375°. Mix the butter and sugar together. Slowly add the eggs one at a time to the butter mixture. Add the remaining ingredients, except the vegetable shortening, and mix thoroughly. Grease a 9-inch square pan, or a cast-iron cornbread-stick mold, with the shortening and pour the batter into the pan. Bake for 45 minutes, or until golden brown. Allow to cool for a couple of minutes before cutting into squares, or unmolding, and serving.

235

Blue Cheese Lavosh Cracker

makes 4 sheets

2	CUPS WHOLE WHEAT FLOUR
5	CUPS ALL PURPOSE FLOUR
1	TABLESPOON + 1 TEASPOON KOSHER SALT
1	TEASPOON INSTANT YEAST
1½	CUPS WARM WATER
1	TEASPOON OLIVE OIL
	FLOUR (FOR ROLLING OUT DOUGH)
	FOOD RELEASE SPRAY
4	CUPS CRUMBLED MAYTAG FARMS BLUE CHEESE*
3	CUPS GRATED PARMESAN CHEESE

Preheat your oven to 350°. Mix 2 cups of wheat flour and 4 cups of all purpose flour with the 1 tablespoon of salt. In a separate bowl, mix the yeast with the water, and then add this yeast mixture and the olive oil to the flour. Mix the dough for 3 to 4 minutes until it is firm, and then cut into four equal-size pieces. Let the dough rest for 15 minutes. Roll each of the four pieces of dough out separately on a flat, lightly floured surface until each piece is the size of a sheet pan. Coat four sheet pans with the food release spray and stretch each piece of dough to completely cover one pan; then lay the dough on the pan. Perforate the dough with a fork and allow it to rest for another 3 minutes. Combine the crumbled blue cheese with the remaining 1 cup of all purpose flour and mix thoroughly until the flour is absorbed. Add the Parmesan cheese and salt, and then mix thoroughly. Sprinkle the cheese mixture over the four sheets of dough and bake for 7 to 8 minutes, until the crust is crisp. Allow the crackers to cool for a couple of minutes, and then break into medium-size pieces and serve.

*Maytag Farms, in Newton, Iowa, produces one of the finest blue cheeses in the United States. For more information, call (515) 792-1133.

Indian Flat Bread

serves 4

1   CUP ALL PURPOSE FLOUR

¼   CUP NONFAT DRY MILK

½   TEASPOON BAKING POWDER

¼   TEASPOON KOSHER SALT

1   TABLESPOON LARD
    (VEGETABLE SHORTENING CAN BE SUBSTITUTED)

½   CUP WATER

    FLOUR (FOR ROLLING OUT DOUGH)

Mix all the dry ingredients together, and then add lard and water, and continue to mix slowly until the dough forms a ball. Cover the dough and let rest for 1 hour. On a flat, lightly floured surface roll out dough to ⅛ inch in thickness. Cut into four 6-inch rounds and layer with wax paper separating the dough rounds. Grill the bread for 45 seconds on one side and about 15 seconds on the other side. You may use this flat bread as you would a tortilla.

NOTE: *This bread may also be cooked on a griddle or a cast-iron skillet.*

Chile-Spiked Apples and Blueberries

serves 4

2	TABLESPOONS UNSALTED BUTTER
3	CUPS CORED AND SLICED GOLDEN DELICIOUS APPLES
½	CUP GRANULATED SUGAR
2	TABLESPOONS BROWN SUGAR
½	TEASPOON CAYENNE PEPPER
1	TABLESPOON ALL PURPOSE FLOUR
1	CUP FRESH BLUEBERRIES, WASHED
4	CUPS CORN OIL (FOR FRYING)
2	(8-INCH) FLOUR TORTILLAS, IN FINE JULIENNE
2	TABLESPOONS CINNAMON SUGAR
4	(8-INCH) FLOUR TORTILLAS
4	SCOOPS VANILLA ICE CREAM
¼	CUP POWDERED SUGAR

Heat the butter in a heavy skillet over moderate heat and sauté the sliced apples for 90 seconds. Add the granulated sugar, brown sugar, and cayenne pepper and then gently stir in the flour. Allow it to cool for 2 or 3 minutes and then add the blueberries; set aside. Preheat your oven to 350°. Heat the corn oil in a heavy pot over moderately high heat to 360° and then fry the julienne of tortillas in small batches until they are floating on the surface and crisp. Place on paper towels to absorb any excess oil. Sprinkle cinnamon sugar (reserve some) over the fried tortilla strips. For each serving, place a whole tortilla in a crock or individual cast-iron kettle, and bake until the tortilla is crisp, about 4 minutes. Sprinkle remaining cinnamon sugar over the four baked tortillas and leave in the crock or kettle. Then place a scoop of vanilla ice cream in each. Spoon the apple and blueberry mixture over the ice cream, dust the fried tortillas with powdered sugar and place on top of the fruit and ice cream, and serve.

Grilled Fruit Brochette and Chilled Berry Consommé

with Pineapple Sorbet

serves 4

1	CUP COARSELY CUT STRAWBERRIES
1	CUP + 16 RASPBERRIES
1¼	CUPS GRANULATED SUGAR
2¼	CUPS WATER
12	SLICES OF JALAPEÑO
4	LARGE PIECES OF PINEAPPLE
4	LARGE PIECES OF HONEYDEW MELON
4	LARGE PIECES OF PAPAYA
4	LARGE, WASHED STRAWBERRIES
4	SUGARCANE SKEWERS (AVAILABLE IN FINE GROCERY STORES AND GOURMET FOOD STORES)
4	SCOOPS OF PINEAPPLE SORBET (OR YOUR FAVORITE FLAVOR; PREFERABLY STRAWBERRY, RASPBERRY, HONEYDEW, PAPAYA, OR BLUEBERRY)
16	BLUEBERRIES

Combine the coarsely cut strawberries, 1 cup of raspberries, 1 cup of sugar, and 2 cups of water and bring to a boil. Lower the heat and simmer for 4 minutes. Allow the mixture to cool to room temperature and pass through a fine strainer. Set the strained fruit aside in the refrigerator. Bring the ¼ cup of water and the ¼ cup of sugar to a boil and dissolve the sugar. Lower the heat, add the sliced jalapeño, and simmer for 1 minute. Remove the jalapeños from the simple syrup and allow them to cool to room temperature. Dispose of simple syrup, or save it for later use (e.g., in a spicy sour mix or in lemonade). Arrange the pineapple, honeydew melon, papaya, and large strawberries on the sugarcane skewers, and then grill for 30 seconds on each side. For each serving, place a scoop of sorbet off-center in a shallow, wide-rimmed soup bowl and lay a grilled fruit brochette across the center of the bowl. Ladle some chilled fruit consommé over the skewer and into the bowl. Float three of the candied jalapeño slices and four each of the whole raspberries and blueberries in the bowl, and then serve.

239

Strawberries and Spiced Honey

serves 4

⬡ Combine the honey with the chipotle chile powder and the lemon juice. Allow to sit at room temperature for 30 minutes. ⬡ Spoon the honey into small ramekins, and place each ramekin in the center of a large, shallow, wide-rimmed soup bowl. Arrange crushed ice around the ramekins. Place the strawberries on the ice and serve.

1 CUP WILDFLOWER HONEY (WHATEVER IS NATIVE TO YOUR REGION)

1 TEASPOON CHIPOTLE CHILE POWDER (CAYENNE CAN BE SUBSTITUTED)

1 TEASPOON FRESH LEMON JUICE

CRUSHED ICE

6 CUPS WASHED, RIPE WHOLE STRAWBERRIES

Cranberry and Jalapeño Ice

serves 8

3 CUPS CRANBERRY JUICE

3 CUPS APPLE JUICE CONCENTRATE

2 CUPS CRANBERRIES

½ CUP GRANULATED SUGAR

2 TABLESPOONS LEMON JUICE

¼ CUP FINELY CHOPPED JALAPEÑO

2 TABLESPOONS MINCED ORANGE ZEST

SEASONAL FRUIT (OPTIONAL)

⬡ Bring the cranberry juice, apple juice concentrate, and cranberries to a boil in a heavy pan. Lower the heat and simmer for 6 to 7 minutes, until the berries pop open. Remove from the heat and pass through a strainer, saving the berries and the juice. Puree the berries with 1 cup of the juice, and then pass through the strainer again, discarding the pulp left in the strainer. ⬡ Add the sugar, lemon juice, jalapeño, and orange zest to the juice from the puree, and then cool to room temperature. Pour into a shallow, freezer-proof dish and place in the freezer. Remove from the freezer after 30 minutes and stir with a fork; repeat this procedure every ½ hour until the fruit ice freezes solid (about 4 hours). Scoop into a dish alone or with fresh seasonal fruit, and serve.

A Tart of Peaches, Dried Chiles, and Mint

serves 8

Preheat your oven to 375°. Sift the flour, salt, and baking powder together and, using a food processor, cut in the cubed butter. Add the milk very slowly until the dough becomes smooth and firm. Allow the dough to rest for 30 minutes, and then roll out to ⅛ inch in thickness and 2 inches larger than the diameter of the tart mold. Lightly flour the inside of the tart mold and very carefully lay the dough inside the tart pan so it doesn't tear. Make sure that the

2½	CUPS SIFTED ALL PURPOSE FLOUR
½	TEASPOON KOSHER SALT
½	TEASPOON BAKING POWDER
⅔	CUP COLD, UNSALTED BUTTER, CUT IN CUBES
⅓	CUP COLD MILK
	FLOUR (FOR TART MOLD)
2	TABLESPOONS UNSALTED BUTTER
6	CUPS PEELED, PITTED, AND SLICED PEACHES
1	TEASPOON MINCED CHILE ARBOL
1	TABLESPOON MINCED LEMON ZEST
2	TABLESPOONS CHOPPED FRESH MINT
1	CUP GRANULATED SUGAR
¼	CUP BROWN SUGAR
½	TEASPOON GROUND NUTMEG
1	TABLESPOON CORNSTARCH
8	SMALL SCOOPS OF VANILLA ICE CREAM
8	FRESH MINT SPRIGS

dough fits into the bottom edges of the pan. Heat the 2 tablespoons of butter in a heavy pan over moderate heat and sauté the peaches, chile arbol, lemon zest, and fresh mint until just tender. Add the granulated sugar, brown sugar, nutmeg, and cornstarch to the peaches, and then mix together. Pour into the dough-lined tart mold and bake for 30 minutes. Decrease the heat to 325° and bake for another 30 minutes. Remove from the oven and allow the tart to cool for 10 minutes. For each serving, place a scoop of the ice cream on top of a slice of the tart, garnish with a mint sprig, and serve.

Blackberry Pie

serves 8

2½ CUPS SIFTED ALL PURPOSE FLOUR

½ TEASPOON KOSHER SALT

½ TEASPOON BAKING POWDER

⅔ CUP + 2 TABLESPOONS COLD, UNSALTED BUTTER, CUT IN CUBES

⅓ CUP COLD MILK

FLOUR (FOR PIE PAN)

6 CUPS WASHED BLACKBERRIES (HUCKLEBERRIES CAN BE SUBSTITUTED)

½ TEASPOON GROUND CINNAMON

1 CUP GRANULATED SUGAR

1 TABLESPOON CORNSTARCH

1 CUP SOUR CREAM

Preheat your oven to 350°. Sift the flour, salt, and baking powder together and, using a food processor, mix in the cubed butter. Add the milk very slowly until the dough becomes smooth and firm. Allow the dough to rest for 30 minutes, and then roll out to ⅛ inch in thickness and 2 inches larger than the diameter of the pie pan. Lightly flour the inside of the pie pan and very carefully lay the dough inside the pie pan so it does not tear. Make sure that the dough fits into the bottom of the pan. Toss the blackberries, cinnamon, sugar, and cornstarch together and pour into the unbaked pie shell. Bake for 30 minutes at 350 degrees. Remove the pie from the oven and allow to cool for 10 minutes. For each serving, place a dollop of the sour cream on top of a slice of the pie and serve.

Peach and Huckleberry Cobbler
with Butter Pecan Ice Cream

serves 8

¼ CUP + 2 TABLESPOONS UNSALTED BUTTER

4 CUPS PEELED, PITTED, AND SLICED PEACHES

2 CUPS FRESH HUCKLEBERRIES
(BLACKBERRIES CAN BE SUBSTITUTED)

¾ CUP BROWN SUGAR

1 TABLESPOON MINCED LEMON ZEST

1 TABLESPOON FRESH LEMON JUICE

½ TEASPOON GROUND NUTMEG

½ CUP ALL PURPOSE FLOUR

¼ CUP GRANULATED SUGAR

½ CUP CHOPPED PECANS

1 TABLESPOON GROUND CINNAMON

8 SCOOPS OF BUTTER PECAN ICE CREAM

Preheat your oven to 375°. Grease a square 9-inch glass baking dish with the 2 tablespoons of butter. Toss the peaches and huckleberries together with the brown sugar, lemon zest, lemon juice, and nutmeg. Spoon the fruit mixture into the dish.

Combine the ¼ cup of butter, flour, sugar, chopped pecans, and cinnamon until the mixture becomes mixed and crumbly. Sprinkle the topping mix evenly over the peach and huckleberry filling, and then bake for 30 minutes until the topping is golden brown. Allow it to cool for 5 minutes and spoon onto a plate. Top each serving of cobbler with a scoop of butter pecan ice cream, and serve.

Chile-Spiked Fig Cakes
with Butterscotch and Clove Cream

serves 8

Preheat the oven to 350°. Mix ⅓ cup of granulated sugar, 1 cup of brown sugar, maple syrup, dark corn syrup, and 1 cup of heavy cream together in a heavy pot over high heat. Bring the ingredients to a boil, and then lower the heat and simmer for 5 minutes. Remove from the heat and allow the butterscotch sauce to cool for ½ hour. Using a mixer on low speed, combine the remaining ½ cup of granulated sugar, 1 tablespoon of brown sugar, and the butter in a bowl for 3 minutes. Add the egg, orange zest, and vanilla to the mixing bowl and mix thoroughly. Add the flour and baking powder to the mixing bowl and combine thoroughly. Fold in the buttermilk and allow the batter to rest for 5 minutes. Whip the remaining ½ cup of heavy cream with the clove and powdered sugar until it is firm; then refrigerate. Coat the inside of eight 4-inch ramekins with the food release spray. Spoon 2 tablespoons of the batter into each ramekin. In each ramekin, arrange the four pieces of one fig upright in the batter to resemble roughly the fig's original shape. Sprinkle the remaining brown sugar over the surface of the batter and figs. Bake for 30 minutes until golden brown; remove from the oven. Allow to cool for 10 minutes, and carefully unmold the cakes. Spoon some butterscotch sauce in a pool in the center of each plate and place a fig cake in the center of the sauce. Place a dollop of the clove cream on the top right side of each cake so that it cascades down the side; serve.

½	CUP + ⅓ CUP GRANULATED SUGAR
1⅛	CUPS BROWN SUGAR
¼	CUP MAPLE SYRUP
¼	CUP DARK CORN SYRUP
1½	CUPS HEAVY CREAM
4	TABLESPOONS SOFTENED UNSALTED BUTTER
1	EGG
1	TEASPOON MINCED ORANGE ZEST
1	TEASPOON FRESH VANILLA BEAN SEEDS, SCRAPED FROM INSIDE THE BEAN (½ TEASPOON OF VANILLA EXTRACT CAN BE SUBSTITUTED)
½	CUP ALL PURPOSE FLOUR
½	TEASPOON BAKING POWDER
2	TABLESPOONS BUTTERMILK
1	TEASPOON FRESHLY GROUND CLOVE
1	TABLESPOON POWDERED SUGAR
	FOOD RELEASE SPRAY
8	FRESH, RIPE FIGS, CUT IN QUARTERS

Toffee Chocolate Pecan Pie

serves 8

Preheat the oven to 350°. Sift the flour, salt, and baking powder together and, using a food processor, mix in the cold cubes of butter. Add the milk very slowly until the dough becomes smooth and firm. Allow the dough to rest for 30 minutes. Roll out to ⅛ inch in thickness and 2 inches larger than the diameter of the pie pan. Lightly flour the inside of the pie pan and very carefully lay the dough inside the pie pan so it does not tear. Make sure that the dough fits into the bottom edges of the pan. Cover the bot-

2½	CUPS SIFTED ALL PURPOSE FLOUR
½	TEASPOON KOSHER SALT
½	TEASPOON BAKING POWDER
⅔	CUP COLD, UNSALTED BUTTER, CUT IN CUBES
⅓	CUP COLD MILK
	FLOUR (FOR PIE PAN)
½	CUP COARSELY CHOPPED CHOCOLATE-COVERED TOFFEE BARS
4	EGGS
1	CUP CORN SYRUP
4	TABLESPOONS CLARIFIED BUTTER (SEE PAGE 43)
½	CUP GRANULATED SUGAR
1	TABLESPOON FRESH VANILLA SEEDS SCRAPED FROM INSIDE THE BEAN (1 TEASPOON VANILLA EXTRACT CAN BE SUBSTITUTED)
¾	CUP SEMISWEET CHOCOLATE CHIPS
1	CUP COARSELY CHOPPED PECANS
8	SCOOPS OF VANILLA ICE CREAM

tom of the uncooked crust with the chopped chocolate-covered toffee bars. In a bowl, mix the eggs, corn syrup, clarified butter, sugar, and vanilla together. Add the chocolate chips and pecans to the mixture and pour into the pie shell. Bake for 50 minutes. Remove from the oven and allow the pie to cool for 15 minutes. Cut into wedges, top each with a scoop of vanilla ice cream, and serve.

Chocolate "Mole" Empanadas
with Fruit Salsa

serves 4

To prepare the sauce, simmer the coarsely cut mango, granulated sugar, and vanilla together for 15 minutes, and then pass through a strainer. Set sauce aside at room temperature. To make the filling for the empanadas, melt the semisweet chocolate and allow it to cool for 2 minutes. Fold in the cream cheese, brown sugar, cinnamon, and chile powder; then place in the refrigerator to chill for 1 hour. Lay the Indian Flat Bread on a level surface and place a tablespoon of the filling just off-center on each piece of the

½	CUP PEELED AND COARSELY CUT PIECES OF MANGO
2	TABLESPOONS GRANULATED SUGAR
1	TEASPOON FRESH VANILLA SEEDS SCRAPED FROM THE BEAN (½ TEASPOON VANILLA EXTRACT CAN BE SUBSTITUTED)
½	CUP SEMISWEET CHOCOLATE CHIPS
1	CUP CREAM CHEESE
2	TABLESPOONS BROWN SUGAR
½	TEASPOON GROUND CINNAMON
½	TEASPOON DARK CHILE POWDER
8	(6-INCH-DIAMETER) PIECES OF INDIAN FLAT BREAD, UNCOOKED (SEE PAGE 237)
1	EGG
¼	CUP WARM WATER
2	TABLESPOONS JULIENNE OF STRAWBERRY
2	TABLESPOONS BLUEBERRIES
2	TABLESPOONS DICED MANGO
1	TABLESPOON RASPBERRY VINEGAR
1	TABLESPOON CHOPPED MINT
4	CUPS CORN OIL (FOR FRYING)
¼	CUP POWDERED SUGAR
4	MINT SPRIGS

bread. Mix the egg and the ¼ cup of warm water and brush gently around the perimeter of the flat bread. Fold the flat bread in half over the filling and press together around the edges. Crimp the edges by applying gentle pressure with a fork around the open edges of the empanada. Set aside in the refrigerator for 1 hour. Combine the julienne of strawberry, blueberries, diced mango, raspberry vinegar, and chopped mint together. Set aside in a cool place. Bring the corn oil to 350° in a heavy pot over moderately high heat. Carefully fry the empanadas until they are golden brown and floating on the surface. Carefully remove from the hot oil and place on a paper towel to absorb any excess oil. For each serving, spoon a pool of the mango sauce in the center of a plate and overlap two empanadas in the center of the sauce. Dust the plate with powdered sugar. Spoon the fruit salsa into the vortex of the empanadas, garnish with a mint sprig, and serve.

Grilled Pound Cake
with Vanilla Syrup and
Blueberry "Chowchow"

serves 4

(R) Bring ½ cup of sugar, water, and 2 tablespoons of vanilla to a boil in a heavy pan, and then lower the heat and simmer for 2 minutes. Set aside at room temperature. (R) Preheat your oven to 300°. Grease a nonstick loaf pan with the softened butter. Mix the remaining 1 cup of sugar and the butter cubes together until the mixture is creamy. Add orange zest and the remaining 2 tablespoons of vanilla and mix well. Add the egg yolks one at a time and mix thoroughly. Combine the flour, baking powder, and salt together in a separate bowl, and then slowly add to the butter and sugar mixture. Whip the egg whites in a cold, stainless-steel bowl until they have firm peaks, and then fold ⅓ of them into the butter and sugar mixture. Slowly fold in the remaining egg whites. Pour into the loaf pan and bake for 55 minutes or until a paring knife inserted into the middle of the cake comes out clean. Allow the cake to cool for 15 minutes. (R) Combine the halved blueberries, chives, strawberries, mint, and seasoned rice vinegar, and then set aside at room temperature. (R) Slice the pound cake into 1-inch-thick slices; then toast the slices on the grill or under your electric broiler. For each serving, place a slice of grilled pound cake in the center of the plate and spoon the blueberry "chowchow" across it. Spoon the vanilla syrup around the perimeter of the plate and serve.

1½ CUPS GRANULATED SUGAR

¾ CUP WATER

4 TABLESPOONS FRESH VANILLA SEEDS SCRAPED FROM THE BEAN (2 TEASPOONS OF VANILLA EXTRACT CAN BE SUBSTITUTED)

2 TABLESPOONS SOFTENED BUTTER

1 CUP COLD, UNSALTED BUTTER, CUT IN CUBES

2 TABLESPOONS MINCED ORANGE ZEST

6 EGGS, SEPARATED

1½ CUPS ALL PURPOSE FLOUR

1 TEASPOON BAKING POWDER

1 TEASPOON KOSHER SALT

1½ CUPS FRESH, HALVED BLUEBERRIES

2 TABLESPOONS FINELY DICED CHIVES

2 TABLESPOONS FINELY DICED STRAWBERRIES

2 TABLESPOONS FINELY DICED MINT

2 TABLESPOONS SEASONED RICE VINEGAR

249

Chocolate Bread Pudding
with Candied Pecans and Whiskey Sauce

serves 4

Heat butter in a double boiler over simmering water. Combine ⅓ cup of sugar and 1 egg; then stir into the melted butter. Add the hot water slowly and stir until the mixture thickens, approximately 6 to 7 minutes. Remove from the heat and slowly add the ¼ cup heavy cream and the whiskey. Set aside at room temperature. In a heavy pan, heat the coarsely chopped pecans and ½ cup of granulated sugar until the sugar is caramelized and is coating the pecans. Pour this mixture on a nonstick sheet pan. Cool to room temperature and break into small clusters. Preheat the oven to 350°.

4	TABLESPOONS UNSALTED BUTTER
1 ⅓	CUPS GRANULATED SUGAR
1	EGG
½	TABLESPOON HOT WATER
¼	CUP HEAVY CREAM
¼	CUP WHISKEY
1	CUP COARSELY CHOPPED PECANS
	FOOD RELEASE SPRAY
24	TO 32 STALE THINLY SLICED PIECES OF BREAD (OR STALE SLICES OF POUND CAKE)
1	CUP SEMISWEET CHOCOLATE CHIPS
2	EGG YOLKS
2	EGGS
2	CUPS + 1 CUP HEAVY CREAM
¼	TEASPOON NUTMEG
½	TEASPOON GROUND CINNAMON
¼	CUP POWDERED SUGAR
2	TABLESPOONS FINELY CHOPPED FRESH MINT

With food release spray, coat the inside of four muffin cups in a nonstick muffin pan. Then alternate layers of the stale sliced bread with the candied pecans and the chocolate chips until the muffin cups are almost full. Mix the egg yolks, whole eggs, 2 cups of heavy cream, nutmeg, cinnamon, and the remaining ½ cup of sugar together and very slowly pour the custard into the muffin cups. You must allow the bread to absorb the custard completely (wait 30 seconds or so each time you add more custard). Bake for 30 minutes and then remove from the oven and allow the bread puddings to cool. Whip the remaining 1 cup of heavy cream with the powdered sugar until firm and fold in the chopped fresh mint. Chill in the refrigerator. Carefully remove the bread puddings from the molds and place in the center of the serving plates. Spoon the whiskey sauce over the puddings and top with the minted cream; then serve.

Vanilla Cream Custard
with Raspberries and Pecans

serves 4

1	CUP COARSELY CHOPPED PECANS
1½	CUPS GRANULATED SUGAR
5	EGG YOLKS
2	CUPS HEAVY CREAM
2	TABLESPOONS FRESH VANILLA SEEDS SCRAPED FROM A SPLIT BEAN (1 TABLESPOON OF VANILLA EXTRACT CAN BE SUBSTITUTED)
1½	CUPS FRESH RASPBERRIES
4	MINT SPRIGS

In a heavy pan, heat the chopped pecans and ½ cup of sugar over moderately high heat until the sugar caramelizes and sticks to the pecans. Remove from the heat and allow to cool to room temperature on a nonstick sheet pan; then break into small clusters. Preheat your oven to 325°. Whisk the egg yolks and ½ cup of sugar until "ribbons" of custard fall to the bowl as you lift the whip. Bring the cream and vanilla seeds to a boil. Remove from the heat, and pour over the egg yolks. Whisk the mixture until creamy, and then pass it through a strainer. Put the raspberries in four shallow baking dishes (ramekins), and pour the custard over the raspberries. Bake for 35 minutes; then remove from the heat and allow to cool to room temperature for ½ hour. Refrigerate the creme brulee for at least 1 hour. Cover the top of the creme brulee evenly with remaining ½ cup of sugar and crisp the sugar with a small butane blowtorch (available at any hardware store). Place each ramekin in the center of a plate and sprinkle the candied pecans around the custard dish. Garnish each with a mint sprig and serve.

White Bean Cake
with Milk Chocolate Sauce and Strawberries

serves 8

2½	CUPS ALL PURPOSE FLOUR
3	TEASPOONS BAKING POWDER
1	TEASPOON BAKING SODA
½	TEASPOON + ¼ TEASPOON GROUND NUTMEG
½	TEASPOON + ¼ TEASPOON GROUND MACE
1	CUP + 2 TABLESPOONS GRANULATED SUGAR
½	CUP COLD, UNSALTED BUTTER, CUT IN CUBES
¾	CUP CORN OIL
3	EGGS
⅓	CUP COLD MILK
1½	CUPS COOKED AND PUREED WHITE BEANS
1	TABLESPOON + 1 TEASPOON MINCED LEMON ZEST
1	TABLESPOON FRESH LEMON JUICE
2	TABLESPOONS SOFTENED UNSALTED BUTTER
1½	POUNDS POWDERED SUGAR
1	CUP HEAVY CREAM
1½	CUPS MILK CHOCOLATE CHIPS
1	TABLESPOON FRESH VANILLA SEEDS SCRAPED FROM THE BEAN (1 TEASPOON OF VANILLA EXTRACT CAN BE SUBSTITUTED)
2	CUPS FRESH, QUARTERED STRAWBERRIES

Preheat the oven to 350°. Sift the flour, baking powder, baking soda, ½ teaspoon of nutmeg, and ½ teaspoon of mace together in a mixing bowl. In a different bowl, mix 1 cup of sugar and the cubed butter together until the mixture is soft; then slowly add the corn oil. Add the eggs to the sugar and butter mixture, and mix thoroughly. Add the dry ingredients and mix them in thoroughly. Slowly add the milk, and when it is incorporated, add ½ cup of white bean puree, 1 teaspoon of lemon zest, and lemon juice. Mix together thoroughly. Grease a 10-inch nonstick cake pan with the softened butter. Pour the batter into the pan and bake for 35 minutes. Remove from the oven and allow to cool for 15 minutes. To make the frosting, in a mixer with a paddle, mix 1 cup of white bean puree with 1 tablespoon of lemon zest, the powdered sugar, and ¼ teaspoon each of nutmeg and mace, until the consistency is soft and creamy. Split the cake horizontally in the middle and spread ⅓ of the frosting on the top side of the bottom half; then place the top half of the cake on the frosting. Gently spread the remaining frosting over the top of the cake and allow the frosting to harden before cutting. Bring the heavy cream almost to a boil and remove from the heat. Stir in the chocolate chips and the vanilla and whisk until smooth. Allow to cool to room temperature; then chill in the refrigerator. Sprinkle the remaining 2 tablespoons of sugar over the strawberries and let sit in the refrigerator for ½ hour. For each serving, spoon a pool of the chocolate sauce in the center of each plate and place a wedge of the cake just off-center toward the upper left quarter of the plate. Spoon the strawberries over the rear third of the cake and serve.

INDEX

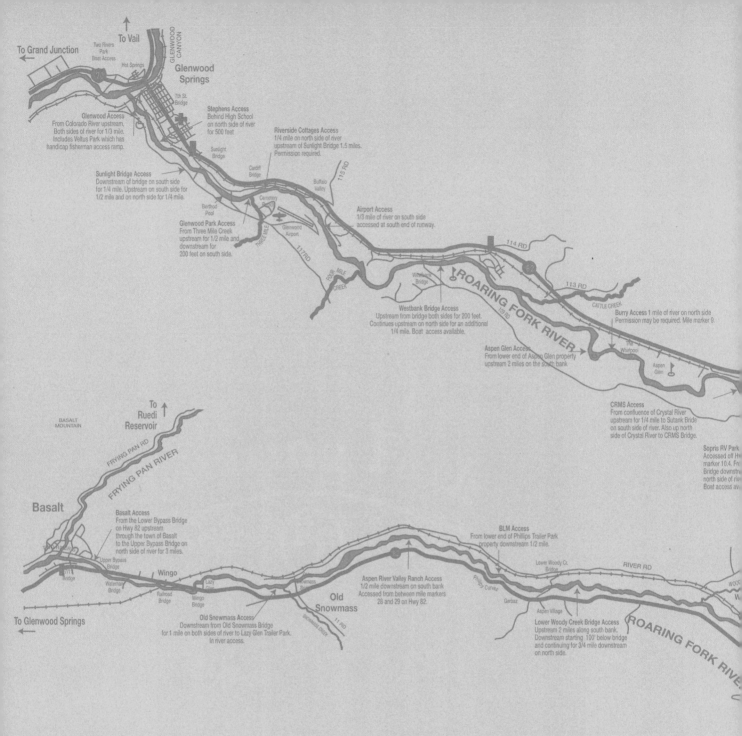

To Grand Junction ←

To Vail ↑

GLENWOOD CANYON

Two Rivers Park Boat Access

Hot Springs

Glenwood Springs

7th St. Bridge

Glenwood Access
From Colorado River upstream. Both sides of river for 1/3 mile. Includes Veltus Park which has handicap fisherman access ramp.

Stephens Access
Behind High School on north side of river for 500 feet.

Riverside Cottages Access
1/4 mile on north side of river upstream of Sunlight Bridge 1.5 miles. Permission required.

Sunlight Bridge

Cardiff Bridge

115 RD

Buffalo Valley

Sunlight Bridge Access
Downstream of bridge on south side for 1/4 mile. Upstream on south side for 1/2 mile and on north side for 1/4 mile.

Cemetery Bend

Berthod Pool

Airport Access
1/3 mile of river on south side accessed at south end of runway.

Glenwood Park Access
From Three Mile Creek upstream for 1/2 mile and downstream for 200 feet on south side.

THREE MILE

Glenwood Airport

117 RD

FOUR MILE CREEK

Westbank Bridge

107 RD

ROARING FORK RIVER

114 RD

113 RD

CATTLE CREEK

Westbank Bridge Access
Upstream from bridge both sides for 200 feet. Continues upstream on north side for an additional 1/4 mile. Boat access available.

Burry Access 1 mile of river on north side Permission may be required. Mile marker 9.

The Whirlpool

Aspen Glen Access
From lower end of Aspen Glen property upstream 2 miles on the south bank

Aspen Glen

CRMS Access
From confluence of Crystal River upstream for 1/4 mile to Sutank Bride on south side of river. Also up north side of Crystal River to CRMS Bridge.

BASALT MOUNTAIN

To Ruedi Reservoir ↑

FRYING PAN RD

FRYING PAN RIVER

Basalt

Basalt Access
From the Lower Bypass Bridge on Hwy 82 upstream through the town of Basalt to the Upper Bypass Bridge on north side of river for 3 miles.

Upper Bypass Bridge

Bridge

Wingo

Waterway Bridge

Railroad Bridge

Wingo Bridge

Lazy Glen

SNOWMASS CREEK

Snowmass

Old Snowmass

11 RD

Sopris RV Park
Accessed off Hw marker 10.4. Fro Bridge downstream north side of rive Boat access av

BLM Access
From lower end of Phillips Trailer Park property downstream 1/2 mile.

Lower Woody Ct. Bridge

RIVER RD

WOOD W

Aspen River Valley Ranch Access
1/2 mile downstream on south bank Accessed from between mile markers 28 and 29 on Hwy 82.

PINBER Curves

Garbaz

Aspen Village

ROARING FORK RIVER

To Glenwood Springs ←

Old Snowmass Access
Downstream from Old Snowmass Bridge for 1 mile on both sides of river to Lazy Glen Trailer Park. In river access.

Lower Woody Creek Bridge Access
Upstream 2 miles along south bank. Downstream starting 100' below bridge and continuing for 3/4 mile downstream on north side.

Map provided by Tim Heng, Rivers Publishing, and redrawn by Johnny Guzman.